Selected Lectures from the 7th International Congress on Mathematical Education

Choix de conférences du 7ᵉ Congrès international sur l'enseignement des mathématiques

Canadian Cataloguing in Publication Data

International Congress on Mathematical Education (7th : 1992 : Université Laval)

Selected lectures from the 7th International Congress on Mathematical Education : Québec, 17-23 August 1992 = Choix de conférences du 7ᵉ Congrès international sur l'enseignement des mathématiques : Québec, 17-23 août 1992

Includes bibliographical references.
Texts in English and French.
Held at Université Laval.
ISBN 2-7637-7370-2

1. Mathematics – Study and teaching – Congresses. 2. Mathematics – Congresses. I. Robitaille, David F. II. Wheeler, David H. III. Kieran, Carolyn. IV. Title. V. Title : Choix de conférences du 7ᵉ Congrès international sur l'enseignement des mathématiques. VI. Title : Selected lectures from the Seventh International Congress on Mathematical Education. VII. Title : Choix de conférences du septième Congrès international sur l'enseignement des mathématiques.

QA11.A1I572 1992   510'.7   C94-940508-6E

Données de catalogage avant publication (Canada)

Congrès international sur l'enseignement des mathématiques (7ᵉ : 1992 : Université Laval)

Selected lectures from the 7th International Congress on Mathematical Education : Québec, 17-23 August 1992 = Choix de conférences du 7ᵉ Congrès international sur l'enseignement des mathématiques : Québec, 17-23 août 1992

Comprend des réf. bibliogr.
Textes en anglais et en français.
Tenu à l'Université Laval.
ISBN 2-7637-7370-2

1. Mathématiques – Étude et enseignement – Congrès. 2. Mathématiques – Congrès. I. Robitaille, David F. II. Wheeler, David H. III. Kieran, Carolyn. IV. Titre. V. Titre : Choix de conférences du 7ᵉ Congrès international sur l'enseignement des mathématiques. VI. Titre : Selected lectures from the Seventh International Congress on Mathematical Education. VII. Titre : Choix de conférences du septième Congrès international sur l'enseignement des mathématiques.

QA11.A1I572 1992   510'.7   C94-940508-6F

Selected Lectures from the 7th International Congress on Mathematical Education

Choix de conférences du 7ᵉ Congrès international sur l'enseignement des mathématiques

QUÉBEC
17-23
August / *août*
1992

Edited by/
sous la direction de

David F. Robitaille
David H. Wheeler
Carolyn Kieran

LES PRESSES DE L'UNIVERSITÉ LAVAL
Sainte-Foy, 1994

Cover illustration / *Illustration de la couverture*
  « Sous les parasols, Vieux-Québec », pastel, 1992
  Collection de la Faculté des sciences de l'éducation, Université Laval
  Lucienne Zegray
  Canadian artist / *Artiste canadienne*

Cover design / *Conception de la couverture*
  Norman Dupuis

Layout / *Mise en page*
  Éditions l'Ardoise, Québec

Les Presses de l'Université Laval
  Cité universitaire
  Sainte-Foy (Québec)
  Canada G1K 7P4

CONTENTS

TABLE DES MATIÈRES

PREFACE

Every International Congress on Mathematics Education (ICME) is structured around a "scientific program," but mathematics education is not a science of the same character as mathematics or most of the other sciences. The definition of our field is fuzzier, it overlaps a number of other domains, and its achievements are less likely to achieve consensus. Furthermore, mathematics education is an applied science and its practices vary considerably with the social, economic, and cultural environments in which it takes place. An international meeting on mathematics education must therefore provide opportunities not only for the dissemination of what is currently known about the major problems, advances, and trends in the field worldwide, but also for interaction, and possibly confrontation, among participants whose views of the purposes and methods of mathematics education are radically different.

The sequence of quadrennial ICME's has increasingly emphasized the intrinsic importance for mathematics educators of face-to-face debate and discussion. The ICME programs have increasingly incorporated these activities within the scientific sessions, not leaving them to the corridors and cafeterias. For example, the programs for the more recent congresses have included a substantial number of working groups whose mandate requires the leaders to encourage and facilitate the exchange of views among participants.

Past ICME programs, other than the first, have tended to downplay the role of the traditional lecture. This is perhaps not surprising since the inefficacy of the traditional lecture as a teaching method is one of the few items of education lore that has almost acquired the status of a consensual truth. The program for ICME–6, in 1988, offered only four plenary lectures during the week; and, although a large number of smaller presentations, or mini-lectures, took place within the groups, the feedback from that Congress suggested that the marginalization of the lecture had gone too far. The International Program Committee for ICME–7, therefore, decided to schedule about 40 lectures in one-hour slots in addition to the plenary lectures and the mini-lecture presentations to groups. Invitations were issued—some specifying the lecture topic, others leaving the topic open—to a selection of the best theoreticians, researchers, and practitioners in the field around the world. Forty-two lectures were eventually included in the ICME–7 program.

Twenty-seven of those lectures are represented in this volume. In a few cases the speaker did not want the lecture published here; in a few others, the editors decided that the treatment of the topic was not suitable for this publication. The papers that remain sample the very best work in the field of mathematics education today.

The sample is, however, heavily biased. The lectures were only one component in the ICME–7 program. It is clear that they do not by themselves cover the field of mathematics education, nor do they combine to give a complete picture of the ICME–7 program as a whole. Readers should consult the *ICME–7 Proceedings* to obtain a more comprehensive view of the overall state of mathematics education internationally. There they will see that the lecture topics complement the topics treated in the other program strands: the plenary lectures, the Working Groups, the Topic Groups, the reports of ongoing work by the official Study Groups of the International Commission on Mathematical Instruction (ICMI), the reports of the ICMI Studies, the miniconference on calculators and computers, and so on. Here, however, in detail, are the records of some fine talks, well worth the time of any mathematics educator to read and reflect upon.

The editors acknowledge the contribution of a number of people to the preparation of this volume. Considerable gratitude is owed the authors of the selected papers who met their deadlines and patiently negotiated the cuts and other modifications we asked them to make. The main work of keyboarding the final texts, preparing the artwork, and copy editing the papers was carried out at the University of British Columbia under the direction of Stuart Donn and with the assistance of Sue Bryant, Cynthia Nicol, Sandra Crespo, Sandra Robinson, and Susan Dawson. The complete text was formatted and converted to camera-ready form by Thérèse Gadbois, Éditions l'Ardoise, Québec. Claude Gaulin and Bernard Hodgson supervised the final stages of the preparation of this volume and coordinated them with the production of the *ICME–7 Proceedings*. Jacques Chouinard and Suzanne Allaire saw the publication through its final production stages by Les Presses de l'Université Laval. We thank all of the above most warmly.

David F. Robitaille
David H. Wheeler
Carolyn Kieran

December 1993

x

PRÉFACE

Chaque Congrès international sur l'enseignement des mathématiques (ICME) se construit autour d'un « programme scientifique » — quoique la didactique des mathématiques ne soit pas une science de même nature que les mathématiques ou la plupart des autres sciences. Sa définition est plus floue, elle chevauche plusieurs autres domaines et ses résultats font moins facilement consensus. De plus, la didactique des mathématiques est une science appliquée et sa pratique varie considérablement selon le milieu social, économique et culturel où elle s'applique. Une rencontre internationale sur l'enseignement des mathématiques doit donc fournir l'occasion non seulement de faire connaître la situation actuelle dans le monde concernant les problèmes, les progrès et les tendances dans ce domaine, mais également de susciter des échanges, voire des confrontations, entre des participants et participantes ayant une vision radicalement différente des buts et des méthodes de l'éducation mathématique.

Les congrès ICME ont lieu tous les quatre ans. D'une fois à l'autre, on a accordé une importance sans cesse croissante aux discussions et aux débats face à face. On a fait une place de plus en plus grande à de telles activités dans le programme scientifique — au lieu de les laisser survenir spontanément dans les corridors et les cafétérias. C'est ainsi que le programme des derniers congrès ICME comprenait un nombre important de groupes de travail dont les responsables avaient pour tâche d'encourager et de faciliter les échanges de points de vue entre participants et participantes.

Aux congrès ICME précédents, sauf au premier, on a eu tendance à ne mettre qu'un petit nombre de grandes conférences au programme. Cela n'est peut-être pas étonnant, compte tenu que l'inefficacité de la conférence traditionnelle comme mode d'enseignement fait pratiquement consensus depuis longtemps en éducation. Ainsi, durant toute la semaine du congrès ICME-6 en 1988, seulement quatre conférences plénières avaient été prévues ; malgré la présentation d'un grand nombre d'exposés plus courts dans les groupes, les commentaires reçus à propos du congrès ont souligné que la place des grandes conférences était devenue trop marginale. C'est pourquoi le Comité international du programme d'ICME–7 a décidé de mettre à l'horaire une quarantaine de conférences d'une heure — en plus des conférences plénières et des exposés faits dans les groupes. Certains des meilleurs théoriciens, chercheurs et praticiens du domaine dans le monde furent incités à parler, les uns sur un sujet déterminé, les autres sur un thème de leur choix. Finalement, quarante-deux conférences d'une heure furent présentées.

Les textes de vingt-sept de ces conférences sont reproduits dans ce volume. Quelques conférenciers ont préféré ne pas publier leur texte ici. Par ailleurs, les rédacteurs ont dû omettre certaines conférences parce que le traitement du sujet ne convenait pas à cette publication. Les textes présentés ici constituent une sélection des meilleurs travaux dans le domaine de l'éducation mathématique aujourd'hui.

Ces conférences, qui constituaient l'un des volets du programme d'ICME–7, ne sauraient toutefois prétendre couvrir tout le champ de l'éducation mathématique, pas plus d'ailleurs qu'elles ne peuvent donner une image complète du contenu scientifique du programme. Le volume des *Actes d'ICME–7* fournit une vision plus globale de la situation mathématique au plan international. On y constatera que les thèmes traités dans les conférences sont complémentaires des sujets abordés ailleurs dans le programme : conférences plénières, groupes de travail, groupes thématiques, Groupes d'étude officiels de la Commission internationale de l'enseignement mathématique (CIEM), Études de la CIEM, mini-congrès sur les calculatrices et les ordinateurs, etc. Dans le présent volume, on trouvera les textes de conférences remarquables, dont la lecture devrait intéresser tous ceux qui œuvrent en éducation mathématique et leur fournir matière à réflexion.

L'équipe de rédaction désire souligner la contribution de nombreuses personnes. Nous sommes très reconnaissants envers les auteurs des textes choisis d'avoir respecté les échéances que nous avions fixées et d'avoir accepté les coupures et autres modifications que nous leur avions demandées. La saisie des versions finales des articles, le graphisme et la correction des textes ont été réalisés principalement à l'Université de la Colombie-Britannique, sous la direction de Stuart Donn et avec l'aide de Sue Bryant, Cynthia Nicol, Sandra Crespo, Sandra Robinson et Susan Dawson. La mise en page du texte et le montage final ont été effectués par Thérèse Gadbois, des Éditions l'Ardoise, à Québec. Claude Gaulin et Bernard Hodgson ont supervisé les dernières étapes de la production de ce volume et en ont assuré la coordination avec celle des *Actes d'ICME–7*. Jacques Chouinard et Suzanne Allaire se sont chargés de l'étape finale de publication par Les Presses de l'Université Laval. Nous remercions toutes ces personnes très chaleureusement.

David F. Robitaille
David H. Wheeler
Décembre 1993   Carolyn Kieran

CONTRIBUTION DE L'APPRENTISSAGE DE LA GÉOMÉTRIE À LA FORMATION SCIENTIFIQUE

Gérard Audibert

Université des sciences et techniques du Languedoc, France

Le texte qui suit a pour but de répondre à la question suivante : La géométrie est-elle actuellement essentielle à la formation scientifique des élèves ayant entre 11 et 18 ans?

Il est constitué de quatre paragraphes analysant quatre aspects de la géométrie :

- la géométrie, discipline de service ;

- la géométrie, discipline proche des activités spontanées des élèves ;

- la géométrie et la formation scientifique ;

- la géométrie et le dessin.

LA GÉOMÉTRIE DISCIPLINE DE SERVICE

Mesures

Dans ses *Éléments de géométrie* Alexis Claude Clairaut (1741) écrit : « la mesure des terrains m'a paru ce qu'il y avait de plus propre à faire naître les premières propositions de géométrie ». Il ajoute dans la quatrième partie de son traité que la mesure des solides a été sans doute un des premiers objets qui ait pu fixer l'attention des géomètres. Jacques Hadamard (1901) dans ses leçons de géométrie élémentaire n'hésite pas à consacrer un chapitre entier aux « notions sur la topographie ». Ces deux illustres mathématiciens n'ont donc pas peur de faire jouer à la géométrie un rôle de discipline de service.

Géographie

Si nous examinons les notions nécessaires à une initiation à la géographie nous trouvons : triangulation, latitude, longitude, parallèles, méridiens, projecteur, nivellement, échelle, courbe de niveau, coupe, pente, etc. Nous

1

y trouvons beaucoup de concepts introduits en géométrie. Cette dernière joue donc un rôle de discipline de service pour la géographie.

Examinons encore trois autres secteurs d'activités professionnelles ou scientifiques : la cristallographie, le bureau d'études, la robotique.

Cristallographie

En cristallographie les 32 groupes ponctuels de symétrie cristallographique jouent un rôle privilégié. Chacun de ces groupes est la réunion d'un nombre fini de rotations et de symétries-rotations, les axes de rotation et les plans de symétrie passant tous par un même point ; une symétrie-rotation est le produit d'une rotation autour d'une droite D et d'une symétrie orthogonale par rapport à un plan P, D et P étant orthogonaux entre eux. Considérons par exemple le groupe des douze rotations conservant globalement le tétraèdre régulier, groupe dont le symbole international Hermann-Mauguin est 23. Il peut être illustré par la figure 1 représentant en perspective cavalière un tétraèdre régulier, un axe de rotation de 180° et un axe de rotation de 120° ou 240°. Comme nous avons 3 axes de rotation de 180° et 4 axes de rotation de 120° ou 240° conservant globalement le tétraèdre régulier, le groupe 23 est donc constitué par 12 (3 + 8 + 1) rotations dont les axes passent par le centre de gravité G du tétraèdre régulier. Des notions géométriques nécessaires à la cristallographie apparaissent à propos de ces groupes ponctuels de symétrie cristallographiques. Les polyèdres, la géométrie de l'espace et la structure euclidienne sont particulièrement indispensables.

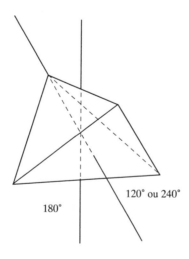

180°

120° ou 240°

Figure 1

Bureau d'études

Si nous examinons des activités de traçage en bureau d'études nous y trouvons les principales constructions géométriques, les perspectives, le tracé des intersections courantes de surface. Il est indéniable que la géométrie est au service de ce bureau d'études, on peut même dire que ces activités de traçage ne sont que de la géométrie. Si nous devons par exemple obtenir le tracé de l'intersection d'une sphère et d'un cylindre tel qu'il est représenté en perspective cavalière sur la figure 2, il nous faut utiliser la sphère, le cylindre, les équations paramétriques de courbes gauches, la perspective cavalière. D'une manière plus générale nous voyons que la géométrie est au service du bureau d'études.

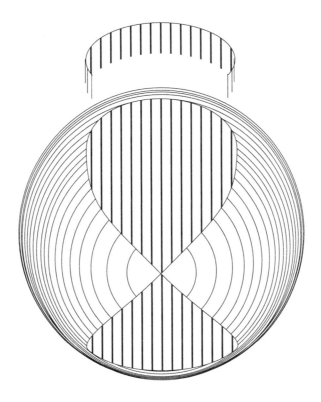

Figure 2

Robotique

Examinons le robot ACMA S 18 utilisé en métallurgie du soudage. Il est représenté par la figure 3. Les six articulations de ce robot font que certaines parties du robot pivotent autour d'autres parties ou encore que certaines parties ont un mouvement de rotation autour d'autres parties. Si on représente ces liaisons on obtient la figure 4 où six cylindres et leurs axes A, B, C, D, E, F schématisent ces liaisons.

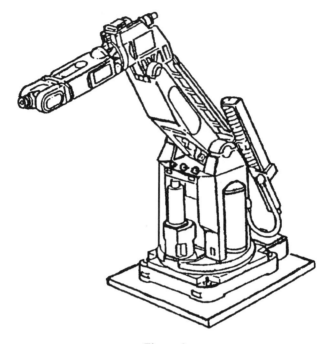

Figure 3

Plusieurs repères sont aussi nécessaires pour analyser la situation : un repère fixe lié au socle du robot OXYZ, un repère O'X'Y'Z' lié au porte outil, des repères O"X'Y'Z' ou O"X"Y"Z" liés à l'outil. Nous avons représenté ces repères orthonormés sur la figure 4. Les notions géométriques nécessaires à l'étude des robots sont donc les rotations, les translations, les mouvements de rotation et de translation et aussi les changements de repères orthonormés. Nous avons là des notions de géométrie au service de la robotique.

Pour la mesure des terrains et des solides, la géographie, la cristallographie, le bureau d'études et la robotique, la géométrie est une discipline de service. Nous pourrions multiplier les exemples et constater de plus que la géométrie de l'espace et la structure euclidienne sont des outils particulièrement privilégiés.

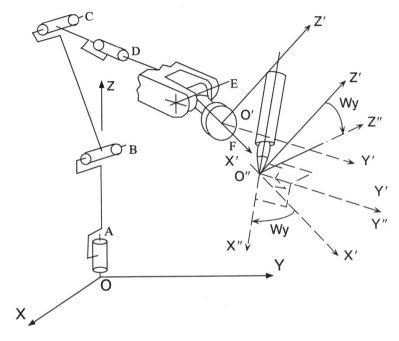

Figure 4

LA GÉOMÉTRIE, DISCIPLINE PROCHE DES ÉLÈVES

Observons des élèves ayant une douzaine d'années cherchant en classe le problème suivant :

Le périmètre d'un triangle est de 12 cm ; sachant que la mesure d'un côté est toujours un nombre entier, dessinez le triangle. Existe-t-il plusieurs solutions ?

Nous faisons quelques constatations. Tout d'abord les élèves ont une grande activité matérielle ; ils dessinent de nombreux triangles, mesurent, échangent leurs dessins. D'autre part ils utilisent des démarches de pensée variées : font des essais, rectifient des erreurs, vérifient, voient des contradictions, fournissent des explications, cherchent des contre-exemples. Et enfin abordent des relations et des concepts ; ils réfléchissent notamment à la notion d'approximation, prennent contact avec l'inégalité triangulaire et avec la plus courte distance entre deux points.

Plus généralement la géométrie est propice à des activités spontanées des élèves à condition de valoriser trois aspects essentiels de la géométrie : l'activité matérielle, la recherche de problèmes, les démarches de pensée. Examinons séparément ces trois aspects.

Activité matérielle

La géométrie est à la base de nombreuses activités matérielles, notamment des activités d'atelier (atelier de menuiserie) ou de terrain ; on peut par exemple tracer au sol une piscine rectangulaire de 5 m sur 10 m. Mais aussi des constructions de maquettes, notamment les constructions des cinq polyèdres réguliers. On peut demander par exemple aux élèves de tracer le patron d'un dodécaèdre régulier ; il doit alors obtenir deux patrons semblables à celui représenté par la figure 5. On lui demande alors de construire le dodécaèdre. On peut lui demander aussi de fabriquer la maquette du ballon de football représenté par la figure 6 (d'après Luca Pacioli, 1509). Mais l'activité matérielle la plus importante en géométrie pour des élèves ayant entre 11 et 18 ans consiste à dessiner des objets et en premier lieu des polyèdres, comme par exemple celui représenté par la figure 7. Là encore nous retrouvons essentiellement la géométrie euclidienne de l'espace à trois dimensions.

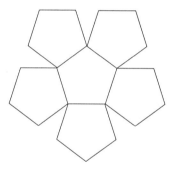

Figure 5

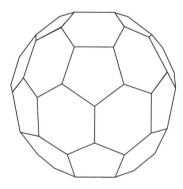

Figure 6

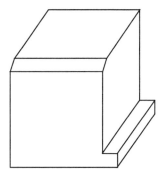

Figure 7

Résolution de problème

La résolution de problème reste une activité prioritaire dans l'enseignement de la géométrie. Certains problèmes sont restés présents durant plusieurs siècles : celui de la trisection de l'angle (partager un angle donné en trois parties égales), celui de la duplication du cube (construire un cube de volume double de celui d'un cube donné) ou celui de la démonstration du postulat des parallèles. Des livres sont conçus comme des recueils de problèmes de géométrie : celui de Lame (1818), celui de Ritt (1847) ou ceux de Yaglom (1962, 1968, 1973). Certains problèmes plus scolaires que nous venons de citer sont souvent proposés. Il en est ainsi du problème :

Circonscrire à un quadrilatère donné un autre quadrilatère semblable à une figure donnée

que l'on trouve dans Lame (1818) et qui est aussi longuement développé dans Yaglom (1968).

Mais si les problèmes énoncés précédemment ne sont pas proches de nos élèves, nous disposons par ailleurs d'une grande variété de problèmes de géométrie qui eux intéresseront vivement nos élèves. Donnons-en quelques exemples :

Découpe un disque de 15 cm de rayon. Trace un angle de 120° comme le montre la figure 8. Enlève le morceau du disque qui se trouve dans cet angle. Fabrique avec le reste un chapeau de clown ayant la forme d'un cône. Quelle est la hauteur de ce cône ? Quel est le rayon du cercle de base de ce cône ?

ABC est un triangle fixe. MNPQ est un rectangle variable. Les points M et N sont sur le côté BC du triangle, le point P sur le côté AC, Q sur le côté AB. Déterminer l'ensemble des positions possibles pour le centre du rectangle variable MNPQ.

Peut-on couper un cube de telle sorte que cette section soit un pentagone ?

Peut-on couper un tétraèdre régulier de telle sorte que cette section soit un triangle rectangle isocèle ?

Une salle de classe a pour dimension 7 m de long, 5 m de large et 3 m de haut. Un fil est tendu verticalement du plafond au sol. Une balle de revolver traverse la salle. Elle part d'un des coins du plafond et aboutit à la base d'un mur en son milieu. La balle se déplace en ligne droite à partir de ce coin et coupe le fil à 1,5 m au-dessus du sol. À quelle distance de chaque mur le fil était-il placé ?

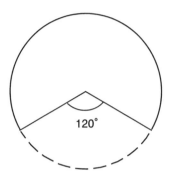

Figure 8

Toutefois, pour que face à un problème l'élève soit intéressé, curieux et actif, encore faut-il apporter un grand soin aux énoncés. Les énoncés doivent utiliser un symbolisme rudimentaire, un vocabulaire simple (celui du dictionnaire familial suffit amplement la plupart du temps) et être courts. Ils seront alors vite compris et bien exploités par les élèves. Malheureusement un grand nombre d'énoncés de nos livres scolaires, surtout ceux qui exigent explicitement des démonstrations, ne sont pas adaptés à nos élèves. Ces derniers ont l'impression qu'on leur demande de jongler avec des subtilités linguistiques ou des manies de professeurs.

Démarches de pensée

Les élèves lorsqu'ils pratiquent avec cœur la géométrie utilisent les démarches de pensée les plus riches et les plus fondamentales parmi celles qui sont nécessaires à la formation de l'esprit scientifique. On peut trouver dans la thèse de Chevalier (1984) et dans Audibert (1982) une étude détaillée de démarches de pensée géométriques. Nous avons pu observer de très près la richesse de ces démarches chez de jeunes élèves.

On pourra examiner par exemple le travail de Kar, une élève de 11 ans et 7 mois, présenté de la page 569 à 577 dans Audibert (1982). Cette élève cherchait le problème suivant :

On donne deux cercles et un rectangle, quel est le plus grand nombre possible de points d'intersection ?

Donnons en deux phrases ce qui nous semble essentiel dans les démarches suivies par les élèves. Les contradictions y jouent un grand rôle ; qu'elles prennent la forme de contradictions observées ou de contradictions logiques (Audibert, 1982). L'empirisme et les démarches expérimentales y tiennent une place importante (Audibert, 1983) ainsi que les vérifications, les contre-exemples et les tâtonnements (Chevalier, 1984, 1988).

GÉOMÉTRIE ET FORMATION SCIENTIFIQUE

La géométrie est proche des activités spontanées des élèves par les réalisations matérielles qu'elle suscite, par la résolution des problèmes qu'elle propose, par les démarches de pensée qu'elle nécessite.

De plus la géométrie avec sa matérialité, ses résolutions de problèmes et ses démarches de pensée développe des aptitudes indispensables dans les activités scientifiques et techniques. Mais l'apprentissage de la géométrie introduit d'autres processus contribuant à la formation scientifique des élèves. Nous allons en examiner quelques-uns dans la suite de ce paragraphe.

Dans l'enseignement traditionnel de la géométrie une place importante est donnée à la démonstration. Mais la forme scolaire donnée à la démonstration a estompé la richesse et la variété des processus intellectuels qui doivent accompagner l'enseignement de la géométrie. Ces processus se reconnaissent à travers les mots clefs suivants : symbolisme, formalisme, abstraction, structures, raisonnement, propriétés, démonstrations, images mentales, concepts. La pratique de ces processus est indispensable aux sciences et aux techniques ; la géométrie en est une bonne initiation.

Donnons quelques exemples d'activités géométriques et montrons l'émergence au cours de ces activités du raisonnement, des images mentales, du formalisme ou des concepts.

Exhaustivité

Le raisonnement prend des aspects multiples, mais une de ses formes semble très adaptée à la géométrie qui s'adresse aux élèves. C'est l'analyse exhaustive de tous cas que présente une situation.

On peut par exemple décrire les douze premiers polygones réguliers ; ou bien chercher toutes les positions relatives de deux cercles d'un même plan ; ou bien étant donné deux triangles ABC et A'B'C', chercher parmi les six relations $\angle A = \angle A', \angle B = \angle B', \angle C = \angle C', AB = A'B', BC = B'C', AC = A'C'$ toutes les familles de relations qui entraînent l'égalité des deux triangles ; ou encore chercher toutes les classes de triangles obtenues en prenant trois sommets d'un cube, deux triangles égaux étant dans la même classe ; ou encore tous les patrons d'un cube ; ou bien toutes les sortes de sections d'un cube ou d'un tétraèdre régulier. On peut réaliser aussi d'autres inventaires exhaustifs plus difficiles : classer toutes les courbes planes du second degré (les coniques), classer toutes les isométries du plan ou de l'espace ; classer toutes les surfaces du second degré (quadriques) ; classer toutes les matrices réelles d'ordre 2 ou 3 ; faire l'inventaire des polyèdres réguliers ; faire l'inventaire des groupes finis d'isométries.

Image mentale

La géométrie inculque des images mentales qui sont nécessaires en sciences et techniques. Elle montre aussi comment s'élaborent et s'utilisent les images mentales, ce qui par la suite permet au professionnel en activité de créer les images mentales qui lui sont indispensables.

La formation des images mentales s'obtient grâce à l'observation et à la réalisation d'objets (rare) et de dessins (moins rare) que nous proposons à nos élèves ; ces images vont cristalliser les concepts et les relations, et leur donner ainsi l'efficacité nécessaire. Donnons deux exemples d'images mentales. La trigonométrie repose essentiellement sur une image mentale : le cercle trigonométrique qui est représenté par la figure 9. Tant que l'élève n'est pas capable de réfléchir en ayant bien amené cette image dans sa tête, il faut l'obliger à dessiner ce cercle et à compléter son dessin pour organiser et justifier ses raisonnements.

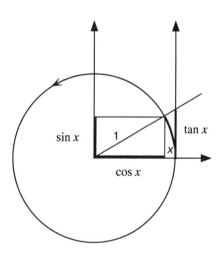

Figure 9

En dessin technique les vues (AFNOR, 1978) nécessitent une image mentale permettant de coordonner l'objet, les projections et le dessin lui-même. Cette image mentale peut s'élaborer à partir de maquettes et de multiples dessins, mais nous proposons avec la figure 10 un dessin de synthèse représentant en perspective cavalière l'objet, ses six projections sur les six faces intérieures d'un cube contenant l'objet, et ce cube presque totalement développé, faisant apparaître ainsi les six vues de l'objet. C'est cette figure 10 que nous proposons comme dessin essentiel à la formation de l'image mentale accompagnant l'usage des vues en dessin technique.

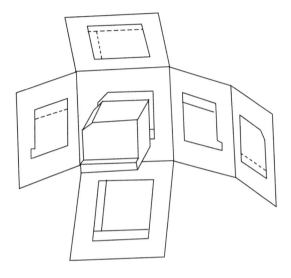

Figure 10

Déplacements et matrices

Les déplacements dans l'espace se réduisent à des rotations ou à des translations. Ils peuvent se ramener à du calcul matriciel plus facile à pratiquer. Mais comment passer de ces déplacements géométriques à ce calcul formel ? Pour comprendre ce passage, examinons tout d'abord les déplacements plans et illustrons la situation au moyen de la figure 11.

Considérons un plan P et un repère orthonorme $A\vec{i}\,\vec{j}$ dans ce plan. Un déplacement de ce plan est le produit d'une translation définie par le vecteur $\vec{AB} = a\vec{i} + b\vec{j}$ suivie d'une rotation r de centre B, d'angle t telle que $r(\vec{i}) = \vec{u}$ et $r(\vec{j}) = \vec{v}$. Plaçons le plan P dans l'espace à trois dimensions et considérons le point C n'appartenant pas à P et $\vec{CA} = k$. $C\vec{i}\,\vec{j}\,\vec{k}$ est un repère de l'espace. Alors la matrice de passage de la base $\vec{i}\,\vec{j}\,\vec{k}$ à la base $\vec{u}\,\vec{v}\,\vec{w}$, ou $\vec{w} = \vec{CB}$, est

$$S = \begin{bmatrix} \cos t & -\sin t & a \\ \sin t & \cos t & b \\ 0 & 0 & 1 \end{bmatrix}$$

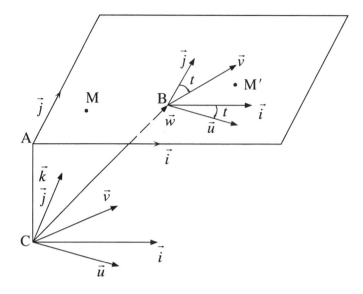

Figure 11

Un point M du plan P se déplace en M'. Si x et y sont les coordonnées de M' dans le repère B$\vec{u}\,\vec{v}$, quelles sont ses coordonnées dans le repère A$\vec{i}\,\vec{j}$? Les coordonnées de M' dans le repère C$\vec{u}\,\vec{v}\,\vec{w}$ sont x, y et 1. Dans le repère C$\vec{i}\,\vec{j}\,\vec{k}$ elles sont donc données par la matrice colonne

$$S\begin{bmatrix} x \\ y \\ 1 \end{bmatrix} = \begin{bmatrix} \cos t & -\sin t & a \\ \sin t & \cos t & b \\ 0 & 0 & 1 \end{bmatrix} \bullet \begin{bmatrix} x \\ y \\ 1 \end{bmatrix} = \begin{bmatrix} x\cos t - y\sin t + a \\ x\sin t + y\cos t + b \\ 1 \end{bmatrix}$$

Les coordonnées de M' dans A$\vec{i}\,\vec{j}$ sont donc

$$x\cos t - y\sin t + a$$
$$y\sin t + y\cos t + b$$

Nous avons ramené les déplacements à une matrice S réelle d'ordre 3. On montrerait si on voulait continuer cette analyse que des compositions de déplacements dans le plan se réduisent à du calcul matriciel. De même un déplacement de l'espace peut se ramener à du calcul portant sur des matrices d'ordre 4 de la forme

$$\begin{bmatrix} a_1 & a_2 & a_3 & a \\ b_1 & b_2 & b_3 & b \\ c_1 & c_2 & c_3 & c \\ 0 & 0 & 0 & 1 \end{bmatrix} \quad \text{où} \quad \begin{bmatrix} a_1 & a_2 & a_3 \\ b_1 & b_2 & b_3 \\ c_1 & c_2 & c_3 \end{bmatrix} \quad \text{est une matrice orthogonale}$$

Si bien que pas à pas nous passons de la géométrie plane à la géométrie de l'espace puis au calcul matriciel. Cette démarche qui consiste à passer d'une situation assez tangible (déplacement dans le plan) à une autre plus formelle (le calcul matriciel) est assez générale en sciences. La géométrie qui fait pratiquer cette démarche a donc un rôle formateur vis-à-vis des sciences et des techniques.

Concepts

L'accès aux concepts peut être considéré depuis la géométrie d'Euclide comme l'essence même de la géométrie. Nous ne nous étendrons donc pas sur la manière de passer des polygones réguliers aux concepts de rotation ou de groupe, ou de l'équilibre d'une poutre aux torseurs, ou de l'angle droit au produit scalaire, ou de l'orientation de l'espace aux déterminants, etc.

GÉOMÉTRIE ET DESSIN

Le dessin ou plus généralement les graphismes jouent un rôle important dans les sciences ; et de la représentation graphique à la représentation symbolique il n'y a quelquefois qu'un pas. Le dessin est aussi une des clefs de l'activité géométrique ; il n'y a pas de géométrie sans dessin ; et il n'y a pas de dessin sans géométrie. Ainsi le dessin géométrique va contribuer de façon importante à la formation scientifique. Dans la revue *Repère* n° 4 éditée par l'IREM en France nous avons eu l'occasion d'ébaucher un inventaire des rôles joués par le dessin en géométrie. Nous allons ici insister sur certains rôles propices à la formation scientifique.

Matérialité

Utiliser correctement les instruments de dessin nécessite un apprentissage de la part de l'élève. Tracer des parallèles, des perpendiculaires, mesurer des angles est difficile à 11 ans. Mais c'est le prix à payer pour accéder à la précision, à la minutie, à la rigueur. La connaissance des différentes représentations de l'espace, des vues, des perspectives fait partie de la culture scientifique minimum. Les règles de représentations de la perspective cavalière peuvent être introduites dès 11 ans (Audibert, 1990) ; les vues du dessin technique (AFNOR, 1978) étudiées vers 15 ou 16 ans. Cette pratique du dessin géométrique mettant en relation l'activité manuelle et la réflexion conceptuelle est peut-être l'activité la plus formatrice dans la voie qui mène aux sciences et aux techniques.

Résolution de problème

Le dessin va permettre de commencer tout de suite à chercher le problème : « avant de faire quoi que ce soit, je décide de faire un dessin pour y voir plus clair », dit Marc. La réalisation ou l'observation du dessin va donner des idées. Mais aussi, certaines idées auront besoin d'être synthétisées au moyen d'un petit dessin à main levée. Puis les dessins vont permettre la démarche expérimentale, les vérifications ; ils vont fournir des contre-exemples. Ensuite ils vont susciter l'organisation du raisonnement. Enfin ils vont permettre de clarifier, d'agrémenter l'exposé de la solution.

Calcul

Dans notre enseignement de la géométrie, le calcul numérique puis le calcul algébrique ont pris trop de place par rapport au dessin. L'interaction entre le calcul et le dessin est extrêmement fructueuse et doit être cultivée.

Donnons un exemple : la figure 12 représente un cube ABCDEFGH et AG un axe de rotation d'ordre 3, ainsi que les trois pyramides ABCGF, ACDHG et AEFGH qui réunies donnent le cube. Chacune de ces pyramides de sommet A et de base carrée a un volume égal au $\frac{1}{3}$ du volume du cube ; d'où le coefficient $\frac{1}{3}$ intervenant dans le volume d'une pyramide. Le dessin, illustrant la réalité spatiale, doit donner du sens à la formule indiquant que le volume de la pyramide est égal au tiers de la base multiplié par la hauteur.

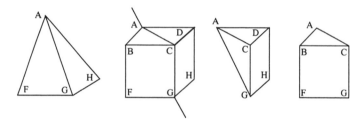

Figure 12

Les rotations et les symétries ne peuvent pas se réduire à des matrices. Les applications linéaires mêmes ne seront vraiment comprises que si on voit bien une base se déformer, ou plus concrètement encore comme sur la figure 13, si le repère de départ O $\overrightarrow{OA}$ $\overrightarrow{OB}$ $\overrightarrow{OC}$ à partir duquel nous avons dessiné un parallélépipède se déforme pour donner à l'arrivée un repère O $\overrightarrow{OA'}$ $\overrightarrow{OB'}$ $\overrightarrow{OC'}$ à partir duquel nous avons dessiné un autre parallélépipède.

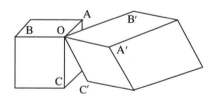

Figure 13

Les équations et les fonctions ne prennent pleinement leur sens qu'avec le tracé des courbes et des surfaces correspondantes. Les fonctions sin x, cos x, tan x, x^2, e^x, ln x, $\sqrt{x}$, $\frac{1}{x}$ sont inséparables de leurs représentations graphiques.

Configuration et image mentale

Parmi toutes les figures utilisées en géométrie un certain nombre d'entre elles que nous appelons configurations ont un statut un peu particulier. Une configuration ou dessin fondamental est un dessin qui illustre un concept ou une propriété importante, qui respecte de fortes contraintes d'équilibre et qui est socialement reconnu.

La figure 14 représentant un hexagone régulier, son cercle circonscrit et le centre de ce cercle, est une configuration. La figure 15 en est une autre, elle représente un cylindre ; la figure 16 est une configuration associée au théorème de Thalès.

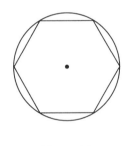

Figure 14

Figure 15   Figure 16

Les concepts importants ont besoin d'être associés à des configurations. C'est ainsi que nous avons des configurations pour la répartition de masse, pour la perpendiculaire commune à deux droites, pour l'exponentielle, pour l'hyperboloïde à une nappe dont le galbe si rectiligne donne tout son sens au concept de surface réglée (cf. figures 17, 18, 19, 20).

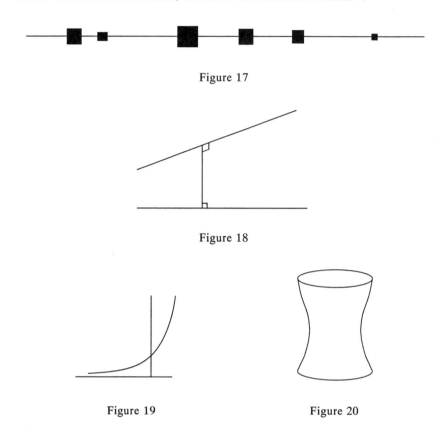

Figure 17

Figure 18

Figure 19   Figure 20

Pour que les concepts et les propriétés atteignent toute leur efficacité, non seulement ils doivent être illustrés par une ou plusieurs configurations, mais encore cette configuration doit très vite laisser la place à une image mentale. Il y a image mentale s'il y a référence à un objet, un dessin ou une configuration en l'absence de cet objet, ce dessin ou cette configuration.

Par exemple si $y = f(x)$ est une fonction réelle définie sur $\mathbf{R}$, continue et paire et si nous connaissons la moyenne de cette fonction sur l'intervalle $(0,10)$, soit $\frac{1}{10}\int_0^{10} f(x)\,dx$, on peut se demander quelle est sa moyenne sur $(-10, +10)$. Une image mentale du concept de moyenne donne immédiatement la réponse à cette question.

Il nous semble que la notion d'image mentale, sa formation, son usage ne sont pas suffisamment pris en compte dans l'enseignement de la géométrie et plus généralement des mathématiques.

CONCLUSION

Le texte qui précède avait pour but de développer des arguments justifiant l'affirmation suivante : la géométrie est actuellement essentielle à la formation scientifique des élèves ayant entre 11 et 18 ans. Nous ne connaissons pas d'autre discipline dont le rôle dans la formation scientifique d'élèves de cet âge soit aussi efficace.

RÉFÉRENCES

AFNOR (1978). *Dessins techniques. Principes généraux. Principes de représentations.* N.F EO4520 Septembre 1978, édité par l'Association française de normalisation (AFNOR).

Audibert, G. (1982). *Démarches de pensée et concepts utilisés par les élèves de l'enseignement secondaire en géométrie euclidienne plane* (vol. 1-2). (Nouvelle édition: 1984) Paris: APMEP.

Audibert, G. (1989). Empirisme et géométrie de l'espace chez l'élève ayant entre 11 et 18 ans. *Annales de didactique et de sciences cognitives.* IREM de Strasbourg, 65-86.

Audibert, G. (1990). *La perspective cavalière.* Paris: APMEP n° 75.

Chevalier, A. (1984). *Le problème QAT: Symétrie, vérification, algorithme de construction, la pratique de l'élève.* Montpellier: IREM, Université des sciences et des techniques du Languedoc.

Chevalier, A. (1988). *Procédures de construction de triangles.* Montpellier: IREM, Université des sciences et des techniques du Languedoc.

Clairaut, A.C. (1741). *Éléments de géométrie* (vol. 1-2). Paris: Gauthier-Villars (édition de 1920).

Hadamard, J. (1901). *Leçons de géométrie élémentaire,* tome 2. Paris: Armand Colin (8e éd., 1949).

Lame, G. (1818). *Examen des différentes méthodes employées pour résoudre les problèmes de géométrie.* Paris: Me Vve Courcier Imprimeur libraire (édition Hermann 1903).

Ritt, M. (1847). *Problème de géométrie et de trigonométrie.* Paris: Hachette.

Pacioli, Luca (1509). *Divine proportion.* Librairie du compagnonnage (édition de 1980).

Yaglom, I.M. (1962). *Geometric transformations I* (trans. by A. Shields). New York: Random House.

Yaglom, I.M. (1968). *Geometric transformations II* (trans. by A. Shields). New York: Random House.

Yaglom, I.M. (1973). *Geometric transformations III* (trans. by A. Shields). New York: Random House.

DIAGNOSTIC TEACHING

Alan Bell

University of Nottingham, England

The Diagnostic Teaching Project began in about 1980 at a time when national and international surveys of mathematics attainment were arousing considerable surprise and concern, both on account of apparently low levels of achievement and relatively small yearly gains. This contrasted sharply with the perceptions of the teacher in the classroom who saw herself as teaching, day by day, a considerable amount of material which the pupils apparently learned, at least to some degree, and retained, at least for a short time. Thus the aim of our research on *Diagnostic teaching* has been to develop a way of teaching which contributes clearly to long term learning and which promotes transfer. The key aspects of this method are the identification and exposure of pupils' misconceptions and their resolution through "conflict-discussion". Conceptual diagnostic tests also play a part both in helping pupils to become aware of their misconceptions and enabling the teacher to observe progress.

The teaching materials for a particular topic aim to begin with a rich situation containing various items of information and with an invitation to consider what further information can be found out from what is given. Following this initial exploration, there is a focus on a few particular questions that contain important conceptual obstacles. The questions are deliberately posed in such a way as to allow misconceptions to come to the surface, if they exist, and thus to create a conflict which can be discussed and resolved. The third phase of the teaching cycle consists of exercises with built-in feedback of correctness. The new awareness reached during the conflict-discussion is thus put into practice in a situation in which pupils know immediately if they have made an error, and can reconsider their response.

BACKGROUND

We ourselves were just completing a commission for the Cockcroft Committee of Inquiry to conduct a review of existing research on mathematics teaching and to make it available to the profession (Bell et al., 1983). Most of the key principles adopted and tested in the Project derived from this review and analysis of research on teaching. In particular, there was the recognition that pupils develop their own methods for dealing with tasks, often ignoring the standard methods they have been taught (Jones, 1975; McIntosh, 1978), which led to the principle of beginning with the presentation of the tasks which were the target of the teaching, observing pupils approaches, and providing teaching which enabled them to develop from this starting point towards complete and correct methods; similarly, it was believed that these should be meaningful whole tasks rather than parts of a procedure which could only be understood later (Gold, 1978). The notion of cognitive conflict derived from Genevan training studies (Inhelder, Sinclair, & Bovet, 1974) and the importance of feedback of correctness from Gelman's (1969) conservation training studies. The value of intensity of experience was highlighted by a Gagné type training study by Trembath and White (1979) in which learning with a stronger mastery criterion took 25% more time but produced 50% more learning.

THE PROJECT

The key features of the diagnostic teaching methodology are:

- initial presentation of the target tasks, which are those which pupils should be able to tackle by the end of the teaching sequence;
- choice of tasks to cover the key concepts and likely misconceptions;
- choice of sufficiently hard critical tasks to provide cognitive conflict;
- provision of some form of feedback of correctness;
- intensive discussion aimed at resolving the conflict and forming a newly integrated knowledge structure;
- making the key principles explicit, in general terms, in the course of this discussion;
- further problems, with feedback, to consolidate the insights gained;
- flexibility of task, to ensure an appropriate level of challenge for students having varying initial levels of understanding of the concept;
- returning to the same conceptual points on further occasions, including using different contexts, until it is clear that the understanding is permanent and transferable.

A fuller discussion of the theoretical and experimental psychological background to the theory appears in Bell (1993a); and experimental tests of the importance of cognitive conflict, of the intensity of discussion, and the method as a whole appear in Swan (1983a, b), Bell et al. (1985), and Bell (1992, 1993b). Here I wish to emphasize the implications of the work for the treatment of the various curriculum areas which have been studied, describing the findings with regard to pupils' concepts and misconceptions, the tasks developed, and the ways of developing them into interesting and effective lessons. The topics treated are geometric reflections, decimals, additive structures with directed numbers and rates.

GEOMETRIC REFLECTIONS

The objectives here were the construction and recognition of the reflections of figures in single axes. Typical misconceptions led to results which looked like the confusion of reflections with half turns or with translations (Figure 1). Less common ones were that a horizontal or vertical figure became horizontal or vertical, and that the reflected figure could be similar to the original figure, if not congruent (Figure 1, Nos. 5, 6). Figure 1 shows a typical Marking Homework conflict task.

The following worksheet was given to Edward Green for homework. Mark the work, correcting all the mistakes. In your books, explain where Edward is going wrong.

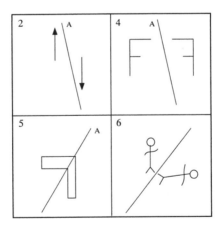

Figure 1

A teaching experiment with 11 and 12 year olds, in which the control class used a well known series of individualized booklets, showed the marked superiority for retention which has been the characteristic of all our experiments with the diagnostic teaching method. The two graphs in Figure 2 show the scores of each pupil in pre, post and (two month) delayed tests.

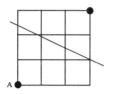 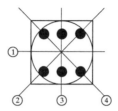

Figure 2

THE NUMBER CURRICULUM

The curriculum in number includes pure and applied aspects, with the applied situations normally coming first. Thus children's first experiences of number can be identified as the recognition of a similarity and an ordering among sets of, say, one, two, three milk bottles on the doorstep, and the association of these with the learnt sequence of words one, two, three, four, ... The concepts "more" and "less" come readily into use, corresponding, in the practical situation, to sets of bottles which match, one for one, leaving extra bottles over, or bottles missing; while in the number sequence they correspond to words which appear later or earlier in the learnt sequence. Addition follows, again with situational and number sequence aspects; addition facts emerge both from putting sets together and counting, and from counting along within the number sequence. This parallel development of the recognition of numerical and operational structure within practical situations, and of operations as properties of the number system, continues at each stage. Fractions first come into play to describe relative quantities—half a glass of drink, or three quarters of the cake. Only much later is an independent existence as numbers attributed to them. The same is true of fraction operations—comparison, addition, multiplication. Similarly, directed numbers are believed to have been used first to designate excesses or deficits, from a standard weight, of sacks of grain. And in all these cases the number or the operation may play several roles. Natural numbers may count sets of objects, or identify positions in an ordering; comparison and take-away situations both correspond to subtraction, and to counting back (or up) in the number sequence.

Traditional teaching has assumed that what needs to be taught are the methods of computing in the pure number systems; and that applications present no conceptual difficulty, but may make the computation practice more interesting—indeed, may demonstrate its relevance to practical situations. But as the sets of possible problem structures in each conceptual field have been analyzed and their difficulty levels studied, it has become clear that wide variations in difficulty among problem types exist, and that the problems in textbooks usually cover only a few of the easier types. Hence, in order to enable pupils to operate freely and with understanding in these fields, teaching needs to be directed at the whole range of problem structures. This teaching should probably aim to make the pupils aware of the different structures, and their interrelationships, and of how the more difficult ones may be dealt with. This will be discussed further in relation to each of the problem fields.

DECIMALS

The teaching experiment in this field focused on the comparison of a conflict with a positive-only approach. Typical tasks were the following:

1. Write down the next three terms in this sequence: 0.3, 0.6, 0.9, ... (Adding on 0.3's)

2. Read this scale:

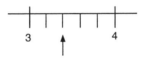

3. Which decimal has the largest value: 5.248, 5.4, or 5.63?

For the *conflict* group these were first presented as shown, to allow the errors to be made, then pupils were asked to do the same task on the number line and, sometimes, also on the calculator. For the *positive-only* teaching, the same tasks were used, but with the number line first, thus forewarning the pupils and avoiding conflict.

The results are shown below.

Results mean %					
	Pre	Post	Del	Gain Pre-del	
Conflict N = 22	44	78	80	+36*	* difference between groups significant
Positive-only N = 25	52	75	76	+24*	p = 0.012

The conflict group covered less material than the positive-only group, because of the time taken up by the discussions. So these results are particularly important, since they conflict strongly with common teaching assumptions that discussing wrong approaches confuses students and should be avoided—and that time cannot be afforded for intensive discussions of particular points. For further details, see Swan (1983a, b, c).

ADDITIVE STRUCTURES WITH DIRECTED NUMBERS

The work in this field began with a series of interviews studying pupils' performance in combining directed numbers by addition and subtraction. (About 80% of the sample were successful at addition, 40% with subtraction.)

Addition was in general performed meaningfully, with reference to the number line or to ideas of "quantities less than zero". (e.g. $^-5 + {}^-9$ was seen as the addition of two quantities of the same kind.) For subtraction, most pupils had no such conceptualization, but worked from rules such as "subtract is go to the left" or "two minuses make a plus". These rules were subject to extensive degeneration; for example, $^-9 - {}^-2 = 11$ because "minusing two negatives equals a positive," and $7 - {}^-2 = 5$ because "negative is to the left," and "subtract is go to the left". The expression $5 - 12 + 8 - 3$ tended to be seen as two pairs of numbers subtracted, e.g. $(5 - 12) + (8 - 3)$ and the correctness of rearrangements judged by whether these pairs remained intact (or reversed). An application to bank balances presented difficulty in overcoming the reversals of the time order, for example, when a change and final state were given and the initial state was to be found.

The diagnostic conclusion from the interview study was that the conceptual foundations for directed numbers and their operations were too thin. More experience was needed with situations from which directed numbers derived their meaning, and in which operations of both addition and subtraction were possible. This meant, essentially, Money and Temperature. But a further set of situations appeared to be of interest—Pop Charts and League Tables, in which positions are denoted by ordinal numbers, and moves are directional. (The system therefore works in a similar way to the negative part of the number scale.) Interviews and tests in this field revealed the following misconceptions:

1 Count the start and finish

"Norwich has gone up 6 places from 9th position. Where are they now?"

Answer: 4th

This is not particularly related to directionality, but has occurred quite extensively in some groups. The pupils do not realize the importance of counting off from the start or finish numbers when finding a difference.

2 Up is increase

"Norwich has gone up 6 places from 9th position. Where are they now?"

Answer: 15th

The normal direction of increasing numbers, from 9 up 6 to 15 dominates.

3 More means add

"Liverpool scored 6 more goals this month than they did last month. They scored 13 goals this month. How many did they score last month?"

Answer: 19 goals

The difficulty of relating the time-order with the order of number of goals leads to a breakdown, and the word "more" dominates.

4 Difference means subtract

"A traveller went from Dakar, where the temperature was 31°, to Reykjavik, where it was −3°. How much did the temperature fall?"

Answer: 28°

31 down to −3 is 31, subtract 3, i.e. 28; a minus sign has to be "used" and the size of the answer does not cause conflict with expectation.

5 Position and move confused

"The afternoon temperature was 8°, but then fell 6° by nightfall. What was the temperature at nightfall?"

Answer: 6°

Linguistically, the confusion is between falling by 6° and falling to 6°. The "position" interpretation tends to be dominant.

6 Sign denotes region

"The temperature changed from −6° to −2°. How much was the change and was it a rise or a fall?"

Answer: rise of −4°

The degrees below zero are thought of as negative degrees even when they are moves. Similarly, a journey from a point 6 miles north of a given town to 2 miles north of the same town may be described as a journey 4 miles north, since it is "in the north".

Similar misconceptions occur in temperature, money, and journey contexts, but differ somewhat in their degree of incidence and their character. Most of them occur also in dealing with ranking structures, such as Pop Charts or League Tables, where the ordering is like that of the negative number scale.

"Up is increase," "more means add" and "difference means subtract" occur because the correct interpretation of the problem requires some reversal of thought from its "normal" direction, which is a cognitive strain. The misconceptions have been expressed here in the form of the implicit beliefs held by the pupils. It seems necessary to do this in order to enable us to feel the reasonableness of the misconception from the pupil's point of view; we need to do this to have sufficient imaginative identification with the pupil's viewpoint to be able to set up a situation which will convincingly show him/her what is the correct view. This is the importance, and the difficulty, of the diagnostic step from recognizing an *error*—a wrong answer—to explaining it by identification of the *misconception* that is the pupil belief which governs it.

Two further examples of tasks will be given to show how an attractive situation may be developed according to the principles noted above.

On this world weather map (See Figure 3) the initial task is of course to fill the gaps. This involves answering questions of all three types, in which the unknown may be the final state, the change, or the initial state. Corrective feedback is provided in that the whole network should link together, and there are certain points at which the same answer should be reached from two different directions (i.e., for D and E, G and H, M and N, P and Q). Following this, there should be a discussion on what kinds of different question do we have here, leading to the identification of the three types mentioned, and considering also the question "In what ways do these operations relate to addition and subtraction?" The outcome should be the recognition that the first kind of task, the forward task, is a kind of addition, although it does not always involve adding numerical parts of the directed numbers involved. The second type, change unknown, is a type of subtraction, though again not necessarily involving subtraction of the numerical parts; and the third type of question might be regarded as a subtraction in that it is the removal of a previously added quantity but, at the same time, it could be regarded as adding on the opposite change to that indicated. In the first two cases, the question of when numerical parts are to be added and when subtracted, and how the resulting sign is to be determined are also issues to be considered. This is not with the intention of extracting and then memorizing these as rules, but rather to *become aware* of them since they are significant aspects of the way in which the system works—that is they are additional insights.

The next activity might well consist of the pupils making up, in groups, another such map with a similar set of questions built in. This will shed further light on the relationships within the system, and the questions suggested above for discussion may come into play again. Indeed, some of the above discussion might in fact be reserved for this point. We may note here the way in which the diagnostic teaching principles are exemplified. We are focusing strongly on the key concepts in the field, providing feedback of correctness, ensuring through the development of further questions and

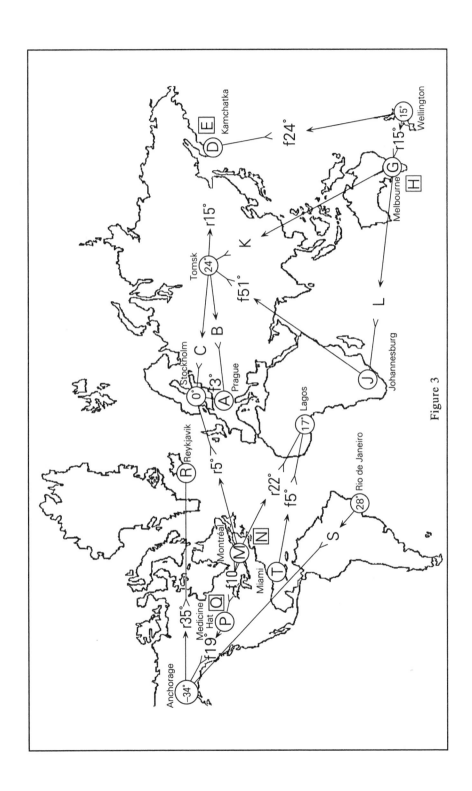

Figure 3

the request to make up the pupils' own, that sufficiently hard challenges will be presented. There is intensive discussion, the making explicit of the contained principles and repetition with a change of view point.

A revisiting of similar principles, but now in a fresh context can be illustrated by the task below, Top Twenty. (See Figure 4.) This can be developed in a very similar way, beginning by filling the gaps, and asking for two ways of checking (e.g. by getting the two-week change from the separate changes and, then alternatively, getting it from the positions at the beginning and the end).

In making up a similar one of their own, pupils can be asked such questions as "How many gaps can you have in one line?", "Can they be anywhere?" Questions about whether this is a form of addition or subtraction and in what way arise as before.

RATES

This field concerned multiplicative problems involving price, speed, currency exchange and other rates, with decimal numbers; our work focused on the choice of the correct operation. The teaching experiment is described in Bell (1992), and analyses of the pupils' conceptual structures are in Bell and Onslow (1987) and Bell et al. (1989). The main *numerical* misconceptions in this field, perhaps now well known, are that multiplying makes bigger and division makes smaller, and division must be of a large number by a smaller. Division by a number less than one (e.g. $8 \div 0.5$) tends to be rejected and effectively replaced by multiplication (in this case, taking half). The strong awareness of pupils of the size implications of the operations is worthy of note, as well as their failure to observe the changes in them when decimals and fractions less than one are involved. These size relations may have been the subject of comment by the teacher in the primary school, or they may simply have been abstracted by the pupils from their number experience. Equally important, and less obvious, is the increase in difficulty of *recognizing the operation* in a problem when the numbers involved change from small whole numbers to large numbers, or to decimal numbers (such as 3.7, which can typically reduce facility in a test item from 90% to 60%).

Some further work on enlargement and mixture problems considered problems of the following type:

A picture of a painting in a book on art is 1 cm high and 9 cm long. If the actual painting is 9.7 cm high, how long is it?

A bridge across a big river is 0.6 miles long. On a map this measures 14.7 mm. What is the scale of the map, in millimeters to one mile?

NAME OF RECORD	Position Jan 14th			Position Jan 21st			Position Jan 28th	
Pipes of Peace	(	)		1st	Down 1		(	)
Relax	(	)	Up 4	2nd	Up1		(	)
What Is Love?	(	A)	Down 1	3rd			(	)
That's Living All Right	(	)	Up 14	4th	Up1		(	B)
A Rockin" Good Way	(	)	Up 8	5th			(	)
Bird of Paradise	(	)	Up 13	6th	Down 1		(	)
Marguerita Time	(	)		7th	Down 8		(	)
Tell Her About It	(	C)	Down 4	8th			(	)
Running With The Night	(	)		9th	Down 7		(	D)
Islands In The Stream	(	)	Down 2	10th			(	)
Nobody Told Me	(	)		11th	Up 5		(	)
Hold Me Now	(	)	Down 3	12th			(	)
Wonderland	(	)		13th	Up 5		(	)
Love of The Common People	(	)		14th	Down 14		(	)
Love Is A Wonderful Colour	(	E)	Up 13	15th			(	)
Wishful Thinking	(	)	Up 20	16th	Up 7		(	)
King of Pain	(	)		17th	Down 4		(	)
Thriller	(	)	Down 6	18th			(	)
Straight Ahead	(	)	Down 4	19th			(	)
Here Comes the Rain	(	)		20th	Up 9		(	)

Figure 4

As well as the points noted above, we observed preferences for multiplying or dividing by an integer, these preferences applying both to the numbers as written and as they appear when decimal points are ignored. The numbers in a given problem may be such that these preferences lead to a reversal of the correct order if the decimal point is ignored (as in $8 \div 0.77$) or whether or not the decimal point is taken into account (as in $0.39 \div 0.89$).

There is also a preference for an exact division where possible, with or without ignoring the decimal points (e.g. 0.24 ÷ 48 may be reversed).

Also some pupils have a weak grasp of the numerator and denominator roles of the two quantities in a rate, which leads to an error consisting of a reversal of the quantities in the rate, for example, treating miles per hour as if it were hours per mile.

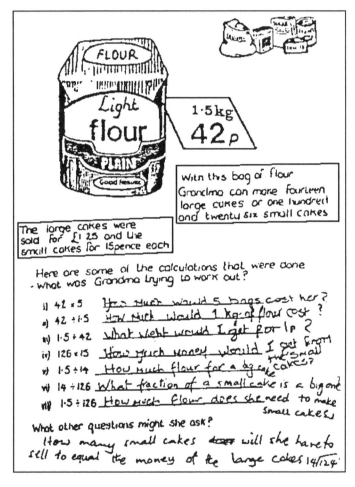

Figure 5

It was also shown that in proportion-type problems with one factor equal to 1, covering change of size (map-scale and enlargement) and mixture problems, some with the same units of measure and some with different units in the two compared situations, there was a preference for working *within* each measure (which implies *across* the two situations). But in same-unit (enlargement) problems the preference was to work with the two quantities within each object (see examples above). There was also evidence of the relative ease of making estimates of ratio comparisons compared with estimates of the results of multiplication (Bell et al., 1989).

Differences in difficulty level such as these are indications of factors affecting the perceptions of problem structure. It follows that the curriculum provision should certainly include examples of each different type. It is also plausible that pupils would be helped in understanding the problem field if they were made aware of these factors and their effect; that is, the recognition of what kinds of problem exist in the area, and what methods are appropriate for each. We have not so far experimented with the explicit teaching of problem structures but our observations suggest that it is feasible.

Examples of teaching material in this field are published elsewhere (Bell, 1992, 1993a). Here we include a single example. (See Figure 5.)

Most texts still ignore the results of this research. In a typical unit on division with decimal numbers there is first instruction about how to divide, then some practice, and finally some "problems". But there is rarely any demand to choose the operation—almost all the problems are divisions. Few, if any, divisions of smaller by bigger numbers are included; there is no focus on potential misconceptions, still less any arousal of conflict.

However, a few recent texts have begun to make use of these ideas and results. (See Figure 6.)

This example focuses well on a key concept and likely misconception; but it is "positive only", not aimed at provoking conflict or intensive discussion.

CONCLUSIONS

I wish, in this final section, to offer some general reflections, based on the experience of the Diagnostic Teaching Project, on current teaching practices and on which aspects most need changing.

The greatest need is to provide *time for reflection, review, diagnosis and response.* Often time is more or less rigidly allocated to specific text book units or syllabus items. Teaching is directed to mastery of the designated new method or idea, and errors or slowness arising from imperfect mastery of previous work are either ignored or dealt with briefly and superficially. These are the aspects of practice which have led to the persistence of the widespread and serious misconceptions which have been exposed by the research. Treating errors *seriously and constructively,* as indicating conceptual points which may need substantial attention, could offer great improvements.

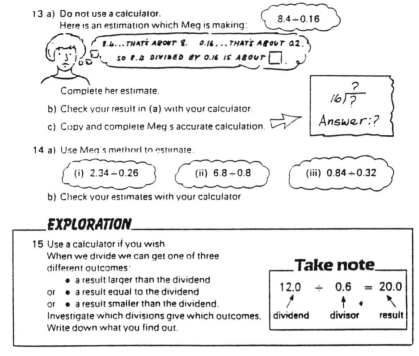

(National Mathematics Project, 1987)

Figure 6

Also indicated is a move away from the separate *independent teaching of each specific point* within a topic towards the offering of *minimal but powerful instructional inputs*, which are then *stretched* in discussion with the pupils to exploit all their implications.

For example, a new method, once learnt, could be explored to see to what range of problems it applies, and in what circumstances it breaks down. Similarly, the regular practice of asking pupils to make up questions of their own, to raise awareness of the characteristics of the types of problem being dealt with and to extend the ideas to further types of problem can be very beneficial.

There is also a need for more *differentiated methods of teaching*. Many classes experience a single mode of teaching almost exclusively, whether it be exposition and exercises, discussion or investigation. There needs to be more conscious deployment of these and other distinct teaching strategies aimed at different objectives—strategy acquisition, conceptual understanding or fluency. The assumption that the development of fluency in, for example, knowledge of multiplication facts, will take place sufficiently in the course of other mathematical activity has left some pupils with intolerable handicaps. (Making pupils as well as teachers more sharply aware of the different objectives of mathematical learning and the appropriate learning methods is a major aim of our current project which has followed on from that on diagnostic teaching.)

REFERENCES

Bell, A.W. (1993a). Principles for the design of teaching. *Educational Studies in Mathematics, 24*(1), 5-34.

Bell, A.W. (1993b). Some experiments in diagnostic teaching. *Educational Studies in Mathematics, 24*(1), 115-137.

Bell, A. (1992). Problem solving, mathematical activity and learning. In J. P. Ponte (Ed.), *Mathematical problem solving and information processing: Research in contexts of practice.* Berlin: Springer.

Bell, A., Greer, B., Grimison, L., & Mangan, C. (1989). Children's performance on multiplicative word problems: Element of a descriptive theory. *Journal for Research in Mathematics Education, 20*(5), 434-449.

Bell, A., & Onslow, B. (1987). Multiplicative structures. Development of the understanding of rates/intensive quantities. In J.C. Bergeron, N. Herscovics & C. Kieran (Eds.), *Proceedings of the Eleventh Conference of the International Group for the Psychology of Mathematics Education* (Vol. 2, pp. 275-281).

Bell. A., Swan, M., Onslow, B., Pratt, K., & Purdy, D. (1985). *Diagnostic teaching: teaching for long term learning.* Report of an ESRC Project. Nottingham: Shell Centre for Mathematical Education.

Bell, A., Costello, J., & Küchemann, D. (1983). *A review of research in math-ematical education, Part A: Research on learning and teaching.* London: NFER-Nelson.

Gelman, R. (1969). Conversation acquisition: A problem of learning to attend to relevant attributes. *Journal of Experimental Child Psychology, 7*(2), 167-187.

Gold, A.P. (1978). *Cumulative learning versus cognitive development.* Unpublished doctoral dissertation, University of California, Berkeley.

Inhelder, B., Sinclair, H., & Bovet, J. (1974). *Learning and the development of cognition.* London: Routledge.

Jones, D.A. (1975). Don't just mark the answer – have a look at the method. *Mathematics in School,* May, 29-31.

McIntosh, A. (1978). Some subtractions: What do you think you are doing? *Mathematics Teaching, 83,* 17-19.

National Mathematics Project (1987). London: Longmans.

Swan, M.B. (1983a). *Teaching decimal place value: a comparative study.* Nottingham: Shell Centre for Mathematical Education.

Swan, M.B. (1983b). Teaching decimal place value: a comparative study of conflict and positive-only approaches. In R. Hershkowitz (Ed.), *Proceedings of the Seventh Conference of the International Group for the Psychology of Mathematics Education* (pp. 211-216.

Swan, M.B. (1983c) *The meaning and use of decimals: diagnostic test and teaching material.* Nottingham: Shell Centre for Mathematical Education.

Trembath, R.J., & White, R.T. (1979). Mastery achievement of intellectual skills, *Journal of Experimental Education, 47*, 247-252.

READING, WRITING AND MATHEMATICS: RETHINKING THE "BASICS" AND THEIR RELATIONSHIP

Raffaella Borasi and Marjorie Siegel

University of Rochester, Rochester, United States

This paper argues that conceptualizing knowledge, teaching and learning as the construction of meaning through a process of inquiry, rather than in terms of transmission, can help us rethink the nature of reading, writing and mathematics—the so-called "basics"—and suggest new ways to integrate reading and writing in mathematics instruction that take advantage of significant shifts that have occurred in the fields of mathematics education and language education in the last twenty years.

A TRANSMISSION VIEW OF THE BASICS

Much of traditional instruction, especially in mathematics, has been informed by the following set of assumptions:

- that *knowledge* is a body of established facts and techniques, which results from the accumulation of isolated results, and can thus be broken down and passed along by experts to novices (logical positivistic view of knowledge);

- that *learning* is the acquisition of isolated bits of information and skills, achieved mainly by listening, watching, memorizing, and practising (behaviorist view of learning);

- that *teaching* is the direct transmission of knowledge from teachers and textbooks to students (direct instruction view of teaching).

Within this transmission model, mathematics is seen as a body of context- and value-free facts and techniques that are hierarchically organized (Bishop, 1988; NCTM, 1989; NRC, 1989). Similarly, reading is reduced to a set of skills that can be mechanically applied to a text so as to extract the information contained in the material, with reading instruction focusing mainly on ways to "decode" the text so that the reader can "receive" the author's meaning (Rosenblatt, 1978; Harste, Woodward, & Burke, 1984). Writing, in turn, is treated as a matter of transcribing previously formed ideas onto paper so as to communicate to an audience (Connolly, 1989).

These views have limited the use of reading and writing in mathematics classes inasmuch as reading and writing are seen as obstacles that may interfere with learning. Indeed, reviews of the literature on reading mathematics (O'Mara, 1981; Pinne, 1983; Nolan, 1984; Siegel, Borasi, & Smith, 1989) confirm that most educational researchers have concentrated on two dimensions of reading mathematics regarded as major obstacles to learning from mathematical texts: (1) learning the specialized language of mathematics, and (2) the comprehension of word-problems, with special attention paid to the way in which the syntactic and semantic organization of word-problems may affect students' interpretation and solution of the task. Writing mathematics, on the other hand, has received little attention in a transmission model since the emphasis is on "receiving" information (i.e., reading) and writing in school is done primarily to display what has been learned so that it can be evaluated by the teacher (Pimm, 1987; Connolly, 1989).

INQUIRY AS A FRAMEWORK FOR RETHINKING THE BASICS

The commonsense views about knowledge, teaching, and learning that constitute the transmission model have been challenged by scholars working within such diverse intellectual traditions as philosophy, psychology, sociology, anthropology and, of course, mathematics education.

First of all, the transmission assumption that absolute knowledge is attainable has been criticized on philosophical grounds by semioticians such as Peirce (Skagestad, 1981; Siegel & Carey, 1989) and radical constructivists (Cobb, Wood, & Yackel, 1990; Confrey, 1990; von Glasersfeld, 1991). This assumption has also been challenged by historical (Kuhn, 1970; Lakatos, 1976; Kline, 1980) as well as sociological and anthropological studies of how scientific knowledge is actually developed (Latour & Woolgar, 1979; Knorr-Cetina, 1981, 1983). Together, these scholars propose that knowledge is generated by a continuous process of inquiry motivated by uncertainty and doubt, and sanctioned by social negotiations occurring within a community of inquirers. Thus, all knowledge, including mathematics, is viewed as constructed out of the context in which it is produced, and hence fallible.

Studies on children's learning informed by Piaget's (1970) model of cognitive development, cognitive science (Gardner, 1985), and Vygotsky's (1962, 1978) socio-cultural theory of learning, on the other hand, have offered potent critiques of the behavioristic view of learning embedded in the transmission model. With respect to the learning of mathematics specifically, several researchers have shown that the learner must actively construct a personal understanding of concepts and techniques if meaningful learning is to take place. (See, for example, Ginsburg, 1983, 1989; and Steffe, von Glaserfeld, Richards, & Cobb, 1983.)

Finally, the idea that knowledge and learning are acts of construction situated in a community of practice implies that instruction can no longer be defined as the efficient transmission of information from teacher to student. Rather, teachers will have to take on the more challenging job of supporting students' inquiries in their classrooms. This will involve creating a rich environment that invites students to engage in inquiry as well as a new set of social norms and values to support the inquiry process—such as an appreciation of the students' need to take initiative and responsibility for their own learning rather than expect the teacher to "teach" them, seeing learning as a collaborative rather than an individualistic practice, and regarding uncertainty and confusion as an integral part of the construction of knowledge that should be exploited as a positive force.

Woven throughout all these critiques of the transmission model is a new portrait of inquiry as a social, constructed, and contingent process of knowing that suggests a powerful new model for teaching and curriculum. Such a model is compatible with the recent calls for reform in school mathematics put forth by influential professional organizations in the U.S. (NCTM, 1989, 1991; NRC, 1989, 1990, 1991) as well as the work of mathematics education researchers associated with radical constructivism and/ or a "humanistic" view of mathematics education (Brown, 1982; Davis, Maher, & Noddings, 1990; Lampert, 1990; Ernest, 1991; von Glasersfeld, 1991; Borasi, 1992).

The views of knowledge, learning, and language assumed by the inquiry model have also influenced the field of language education and led to the development of new theories of reading and writing that emphasize the process of generating and reflecting on meaning in the context of a discourse community. Writing has come to be seen as an act of meaning construction in which writers work out what they mean in the process of writing rather than in advance. This shift has inspired the "process approach" to writing instruction, which involves transforming classrooms into writing workshops where students can brainstorm ideas, write drafts, participate in peer response groups, revise and edit their texts. These kinds of writing experiences have also found a place within content area classes (including mathematics) as a result of the "Writing to Learn" movement (Connolly & Vilardi, 1989). Similarly, reading is now conceptualized as a meaning-making process involving the negotiation of reader, text, and context (e.g., Rosenblatt, 1978; Carey, Harste, & Smith, 1981; Goodman, 1984; Siegel, 1984). As in the new theories of writing, language is not seen as a fixed code for transmitting the message from author to reader but an open potential out of which the reader generates a textual interpretation unique to the context in which it is produced. Hence, the idea of a single correct meaning for a given text has been replaced by the expectation that readers' interpretations will vary. The instructional implications of these theories can be seen in classrooms where "whole language" is practiced. (See Harste, Woodward, & Burke, 1984; Goodman, 1986; Harste, Short, & Burke, 1988; and Edelsky, Altwerger, & Flores, 1991, for an introduction to the theory, research, and practice of whole language.)

A mathematics classroom based on the inquiry model outlined in this section will look quite different from those with which we are most familiar, as will the use of reading and writing. In the section that follows, we will report in depth on a specific classroom experience so as to ground our discussion of the integration of reading, writing and mathematics in an inquiry classroom.

IMAGES OF READING, WRITING AND MATHEMATICAL ACTIVITIES IN AN INQUIRY CLASSROOM

The classroom experience we have chosen to report is a three-week unit on "Taking a Census" developed in a U.S. middle school mathematics classroom. This experience was part of the "Reading to Learn Mathematics for Critical Thinking" research project (hereafter abbreviated as RLM), an interdisciplinary attempt to develop, document, and analyze instructional experiences that synthesized reading and mathematics in collaboration with classroom teachers. (See Borasi & Siegel, 1988, in preparation, for a detailed description of this project.)

The impetus for the unit (which was an independent effort, planned and carried out solely by the classroom teacher, Lisa Grasso) was the 1990 U.S. Census. Lisa was ready to begin a unit on statistics with her class just around the time the census was going to be taken and the media was full of information about this event. Lisa saw this as an opportunity for her students to engage in genuine mathematical inquiry while at the same time learning the rudiments of statistics in a meaningful context. With these goals in mind, she suggested that, while the U.S. Census was being taken, the members of the class could themselves design and take a census of their school.

A crucial dimension of this experience was that the students had full responsibility for taking the school census, including choosing and formulating the questions to be asked, tabulating and analyzing the responses, and communicating the most significant results to the rest of the school. The first phase of the unit thus consisted of designing a questionnaire to be completed by all the students in the school. To inspire the students with an example, Lisa shared some reading material about the U.S. Census—including brief essays about the history of the U.S. Census, tables and other diagrams reporting some interesting results from past censuses, and examples of census forms. Lisa also invited the students to bring to class newspaper articles dealing with this current event. Over 30 such articles were contributed and were read and discussed in the first five minutes of every class.

In the meantime, Lisa asked each student to write down ten questions that s/he would be interested in asking her/his schoolmates. These questions were collected and duplicated and, working in pairs, the students were asked to categorize them. The categories that were generated were written on the board, and specific questions listed under each category, taking care to eliminate similar questions. In the class discussion that followed, consensus was reached as to which ten questions should be included in the school census questionnaire. The students then collaborated on re-writing each of these questions and their answers, looking once again at the U.S. Census forms to see how questions were phrased and answers structured in questionnaires of this kind.

The school census forms were distributed and completed by all the students in the school, during the morning homeroom period on the day after U.S. Census Day, 1990. Out of 557 students enrolled in the school, 491 responded to the questionnaire. To involve each student directly in the analysis of this data, Lisa assigned each student a packet of completed census forms from a given homeroom. Each student thus became the "enumerator" for that homeroom, responsible for tabulating the responses of students in that homeroom, sharing those results with the rest of the class so that school-wide statistics could be created, and ultimately reporting the results back to the students in that homeroom.

The tabulation of the school census questionnaire was carried out in class, both for logistical and pedagogical reasons. To this point, the students had not had any formal instruction in statistics. This had been a conscious decision on the part of the teacher; she hoped that in the process of trying to make sense of the data, the students themselves would develop a need for statistical concepts and techniques that could then be introduced in a meaningful and contextualized way. This, indeed, is what happened.

For example, responses to the question "How many people live in your household?" (1, 2, ... 10) were not easy to tabulate, due to the range of possible answers, and thus led to the introduction of the notions of frequency and histograms by the teacher. The concepts of mean, median and mode, also useful to summarize responses to this type of items, were instead introduced through the in-class reading of a chapter from *How to lie with statistics* (Huff, 1954). Unlike traditional textbooks, this text presents the concepts of mean, median and mode in a discursive way, weaving together technical explanations with significant examples from everyday life. To facilitate the comprehension of this technical text and help students make connections with their initial problem, Lisa asked the students to read the text silently a paragraph at a time, stopping each time to share their comments and questions with the rest of the class.

The analysis of the data also raised more general questions about statistics and the potential shortcomings of data collected through questionnaires. For example, newspaper articles on the problem of "counting the homeless" as part of the national census raised the question of how representative their school census data were, considering that a number of students in the school had not completed the questionnaire. This concern was addressed through the reading of yet another excerpt from *How to lie with statistics,* which dealt with the problem of sampling.

Another important aspect of the unit was the awareness that, in the end, each student was responsible for reporting back to the students in their assigned homeroom. To provide some support for this culminating activity, Lisa required each enumerator to prepare a poster summarizing what s/he thought were the most interesting results of the census taken in his/her homeroom, and then to use that poster as a guide for an oral presentation. Lisa herself prepared a poster summarizing the results of the school-wide census, and discussed it with the class. While the teacher's poster provided a demonstration of how to construct a poster, each student was left to decide the questions to focus on in his/her poster, what statistics to use so as to report specific results effectively, what modes of representation to employ (summary statements, tables, graphs, etc.), as well as how to organize the information to be both understandable and attractive. The variety of posters students produced showed how they took advantage of the open-ended nature of this task, as well as their understanding of the statistical techniques they had learned and the information generated by the school census.

IMPLICATIONS FOR INTEGRATING READING AND WRITING IN MATHEMATICS INSTRUCTION

The experience described above provides evidence of how mathematics instruction as a whole is transformed in an inquiry classroom. It also illustrates some key characteristics of such a classroom, such as: the fundamental role played by sustained inquiry around a topic of interest to the students; the students' involvment in defining the directions of such inquiry; the supportive and instrumental (rather than dominant) role played by the learning of specific mathematical content and techniques; the collaborative nature of the students' activity; the motivating role played by errors and inconsistencies. Reading and writing can play a number of complementary roles in this kind of instructional context. This section explores three issues in more depth: (a) the kinds of reading and writing activities mathematics students can productively engage in; (b) the roles of these activities in a specific mathematical inquiry; and (c) the ways these activities can help to establish a learning environment supportive of inquiry.

For this analysis, we will draw mainly on the existing literature on "writing to learn mathematics" (e.g., Connolly & Vilardi, 1989; Countryman, 1992; Gere, 1985) as well as on the findings of the previously mentioned RLM project. The Census Unit described in the previous section will often be used to illustrate our points.

What kinds of reading and writing activities could support mathematics instruction when approached in a spirit of inquiry?

Possible texts

The variety of texts used in the Census Unit may have been surprising, especially when compared with the limited range of texts traditionally employed in school mathematics. Mathematics students can indeed benefit from reading and/or writing essays, newspaper articles, stories, reports, tables, graphs, questionnaires, journal entries, and even lists of ideas and/or questions generated in class discussions—just to name a few. (See Borasi & Brown, 1985; Borasi & Siegel, 1990; and Rose, 1989, for further suggestions.) Moreover, these texts may deal with a great variety of content, including technical mathematics, real-life applications of mathematics, issues in the history and philosophy of the discipline, aspects of classroom dynamics and instruction, feelings and experiences about mathematics, and even topics that have little to do with mathematics directly (as in the case of several of the articles about the U.S. Census read by Lisa's students).

Significant dimensions of writing

It was not only what the students read or wrote, but also how they did so, that differentiates the Census Unit from traditional mathematics instruction. The writing was never done just for the teacher nor just for evaluation purposes; rather, students always had a very specific purpose and audience, which determined the content, format, and style of their written product. One sees, for example, how the construction of specific questions for the school census questionnaire was informed by the students' desire to collect certain information in a form suitable for statistical analysis. In an inquiry classroom, writing is not only purposeful but generative in that it helps the author further organize and enhance his/her thinking. Hence, revising one's written work is seen as both necessary and valuable, since it provides a means to reflect on and refine one's thinking. Similarly, sharing one's writing

41

with others is encouraged since it can provide valuable feedback as well as contribute a different perspective. Unless the author is at the stage of "publishing" his/her work, this feedback and the subsequent revisions it may inspire should focus on the content rather than surface features of the text.

Significant dimensions of reading

The ways students used reading in the Census Unit may also seem quite unusual. Except for the readings from *How to lie with statistics,* the students did not read primarily to "learn the content" of the text. Students also read specific texts so as to have a model for their own product (as in the case of the U.S. Census forms); to find possible connections with their specific project (as with most of the reading material about the U.S. Census); to extract relevant data (as they did when they read their schoolmates' responses to their questionnaire); or to revise their product (as when editing questions for the school census questionnaire and their posters). These multiple purposes shift the focus of reading from "recovering the author's message" to generative meaning-making. The text then becomes a "springboard" for generating ideas, formulating questions, making connections, identifying limitations of one's work, as well as gathering relevant information.

In order to support this process, reading can no longer be done by individual students in isolation, nor reduced to "decoding" the text. Rather, as they read, students should be encouraged to construct and share with others their interpretations, hypotheses, and connections. Various "transactional reading strategies", offering concrete ways for students to interact, have been developed by reading researchers (e.g., Harste, Short, & Burke, 1988; Siegel, 1984) and adapted in our RLM experiences in the context of mathematics instruction (Borasi & Siegel, 1990, in preparation). The way Lisa's students read the excerpts from *How to lie with statistics*—i.e., in class, stopping at intervals to talk to each other about what they have read, raising questions about specific points in the text and making connections to the inquiry in progress—provides an example of this kind of strategy.

What roles can reading and writing play within the process of inquiry itself?

As suggested by the Census Unit as well as other RLM experiences, reading and writing can play some important and differentiated roles at various points in the process of inquiry. In what follows, we have tried to identify and briefly discuss some of these roles:

- As the students begin their inquiry, they can increase their understanding of the domain being explored through appropriate readings (a role played by the various materials on the U.S. Census read by Lisa's students); writing about their initial understanding of the domain also helps make explicit what each student already knows and identifies issues and questions that can make the reading more productive with respect to the inquiry to be undertaken.

- Formulating specific questions to guide inquiry can be supported by a generative reading of the previously mentioned texts, by looking at examples of existing questions and problems, and by examining and expanding upon the initial efforts of individual students to articulate their questions in writing.

- Brainstorming about ways to explore the question(s) thus identified can be aided by some preliminary writing in which each student articulates his/her own ideas; creating a written record of the ideas generated during the discussion is also helpful.

- Mathematical concepts and techniques, as well as other information necessary to conduct the inquiry, can be learned with the support of appropriate "reading and writing to learn activities" (e.g. Borasi & Siegel, 1990; Rose, 1989)—as Lisa's students did when they learned the concepts of mean, median and mode.

- Whenever the inquiry involves the collection and analysis of data, reading and writing are employed in specialized ways in order to extract such data, make sense of it, and report its elaboration (as illustrated in the Census Unit when the students tabulated and analysed the responses to their school census).

- Preliminary results can be better organized, reflected upon, and shared with peers when they are put in writing; successive revisions of this writing can contribute to the students' elaboration of these findings.

- As the inquiry proceeds, it is important to encourage students to reflect on the process as well as the product of their activity; in addition to class discussions, journal writing can be a valuable vehicle to promote such reflections and provide a natural outlet through which students can voice their concerns.

- Writing becomes especially important when students decide to communicate the results of their inquiry to outside audiences; in this case, the main goal becomes organizing one's results in a clear and convincing way, though it is likely that this process will also further clarify the author's thinking (as certainly happened when

43

Lisa's students prepared their posters); editing is important at this stage and requires a specialized reading of one's own text, aimed at finalizing the clarity and coherence of the argument and refining the language and style.

• Finally, the generative reading of the students' final products and/ or other texts connected with the topic investigated can provide new ideas and help set directions for future inquiry.

How can reading and writing contribute to the creation of a learning environment that supports student inquiry in the mathematics classroom?

As argued earlier, inviting students to engage in mathematical inquiry is not just another instructional strategy to be added on to current classroom practices; rather, teachers will need to create a learning environment where students can come to value the new assumptions and social norms associated with making inquiry. This process will require explicit attention especially in the first weeks of the course, though reflections and explicit discussions about the new approach should continue as the students engage in inquiry. Whether at the beginning of the year, or throughout the process, reading and writing activities can contribute in complementary ways.

Supporting the articulation and discussion of students' beliefs

Years of traditional mathematics instruction have led most students to develop beliefs about mathematics, learning, and teaching that reflect a transmission worldview (Schoenfeld, 1989; Borasi, 1990); hence, students may be inclined to reject inquiry as a legitimate way of learning mathematics, especially if their beliefs are not explicitly addressed. Writing can provide a valuable way to help students articulate and discuss their beliefs with others. Writing assignments, such as journals, autobiographical essays, letters, asking students to report their feelings and experiences about mathematics (Borasi & Rose, 1989; Buerk, 1981; Tobias, 1989) can provide a valuable starting point since they reveal some of the students implicit beliefs and expectations about school mathematics. Making explicit students' conceptions of mathematics as a discipline, however, may require more structured tasks—such as questionnaires addressing specific issues regarding the nature of mathematics, or writing and sharing metaphors that capture one's image of mathematics (Buerk, 1981). The power of these activities can be further enhanced when they are combined with the generative reading of texts that highlight "humanistic" aspects of mathematics usually neglected in school—such as its historical development, or applications that show the role played by context and culture as well as connections with everyday life.

Supporting the explicit discussion of social norms

The new social norms implicit in an inquiry model of instruction cannot be simply imposed by the teacher, but rather need to be negotiated with the whole class. For many students, however, this kind of discussion may at first feel strange and intimidating since their input on these issues has never been invited in school. Writing down feelings and opinions prior to sharing them publicly can encourage students to participate more actively in these discussions. Recording the results of these discussions on newsprint, so that they are available for future reference, also helps validate the students' voice.

Implicitly establishing new patterns of classroom discourse

There are also more indirect, and yet even more powerful, ways in which reading and writing practices can contribute to the development of social norms compatible with an inquiry model in the mathematics classroom. Whenever students write and share that writing not only with the teacher but also with peers, new channels of communication are automatically opened, thus breaking the traditional pattern of classroom discourse in which communication is channeled through, and therefore controlled, by the teacher (Cazden, 1986; Mehan, 1979). Students' voices can also be heard and valued more when reading is approached as a social and generative activity, where students are encouraged to bring to bear their own experiences, background knowledge, and interests, to the task and their intepretations of the text are considered as important as the original message that the author may have intended to communicate.

CONCLUSION

Throughout this paper we have argued that language and communication have a central role in the production of knowledge when inquiry is understood as socially constructed. Indeed, our classroom research has shown that reading and writing often become such an integral part of student inquiry that it is hard to imagine one could conduct meaningful mathematical inquiry without them. Consequently, reading and writing may appear more transparent and thus invisible in a mathematics classroom grounded in an inquiry model, while at the same time assuming a much more fundamental role in the learning of mathematics.

NOTE

The research reported in this paper was made possible in part by a grant from the U.S. National Science Foundation (award # MDR–8850548); the opinions reported here, however, are solely the authors'.

REFERENCES

Bishop, A. (1988). *Mathematical encul-turation*. Dordrecht, The Netherlands: Kluwer Academic Publishers.

Borasi, R. (1990). The invisible hand operating in mathematics instruction: Students' conceptions and expecta-tions. In T.J. Cooney & C.R. Hirsch (Eds.), *Teaching and learning math-ematics in the 1990s*. 1990 Yearbook of the National Council of Teachers of Mathematics (pp. 174-182). Reston, VA: National Council of Teachers of Mathematics.

Borasi, R. (1992). *Learning mathemat-ics through inquiry*. Portsmouth, NH: Heinemann.

Borasi, R., & Brown, S.I. (1985). A "novel" approach to texts. *For the Learning of Mathematics, 5*(1), 21-23.

Borasi, R., & Rose, B.J. (1989). Journal writing and mathematics instruction. *Educational Studies in Mathematics, 20*(4), 347-365.

Borasi, R., & Siegel, M. (1988). *Read-ing to learn mathematics for critical thinking*. Grant proposal sent to the National Science Foundation. (Award # MDR–8850548).

Borasi, R., & Siegel, M. (1990). Read-ing to learn mathematics: New questions, new connections, new chal-lenges. *For the Learning of Mathe-matics, 10*(3), 9-16.

Borasi, R., & Siegel, M. (in preparation). *Reading to learn mathematics for crit-ical thinking*. Final report to the National Science Foundation. (Award # MDR–8850548).

Brown, S.I. (1982). On humanistic alter-natives in the practice of teacher education. *Journal of Research and Development in Education, 15*(4), 1-12.

Brown, S.I., & Cooney, T.J. (1988). Stalking the dualism between theory and practice. In *Second Conference on Systematic Cooperation between Theory and Practice in Mathematics Education, Part I:* Report, ed. P.F.L. Verstappen (pp. 21-40. Lochem, The Netherlands: National Institute for Curriculum Development.

Buerk, D. (1981). *Changing the concep-tion of mathematical knowledge in intellectually able, math-avoidant women*. Unpublished doctoral disser-tation, State University of New York at Buffalo.

Carey, R., Harste, J., & Smith, S. (1981). Contextual constraints and discourse processes: A replication study. *Read-ing Research Quarterly, 16*(2), 382-410.

Cazden, C. (1986). Classroom discourse. In M. Wittrock (Ed.), *Handbook of research on Teaching* (3rd ed.) (pp. 432-463). New York: Macmillan.

Cobb, P., Wood, T., & Yackel, E. (1990). Classrooms as learning environments for teachers and researchers. In R.B. Davis, C.A. Maher & N. Noddings (Eds.), *Constructivist views on the teaching and learning of mathematics* (pp. 125-146). Reston, VA: National Council of Teachers of Mathematics.

Confrey, J. (1990). What constructivism implies for teaching. In R.B. Davis, C.A. Maher & N. Noddings (Eds.), *Constructivist views on the teaching and learning of mathematics* (pp. 107-122). Reston, VA: National Council of Teachers of Mathematics.

Connolly, P. (1989). Writing and the ecology of learning. In P. Connolly & T. Vilardi (Eds.), *Writing to learn mathematics and science* (pp. 1-14). New York: Teachers College Press.

Connolly, P., & Vilardi, T. (Eds.) (1989). *Writing to learn mathematics and science.* New York: Teachers College Press.

Countryman, J. (1992). *Writing to learn mathematics.* Portsmouth, NH: Heinemann.

Davis, R.B., Maher, C.A., & Noddings, N. (Eds.) (1990). *Constructivist views on the teaching and learning of mathematics.* Reston, VA: National Council of Teachers of Mathematics.

Edelsky, C., Altwerger, B., & Flores, B. (1991). *Whole language: What's the difference?* Portsmouth, NH: Heinemann.

Ernest, P. (1991). *The philosophy of mathematics education.* New York: Falmer.

Gardner, H. (1985). *The mind's new science.* New York: Basic Books.

Gere, A.R. (Ed.) (1985). *Roots in the sawdust: Writing to learn across the disciplines.* Urbana, IL: National Council of Teachers of English.

Ginsburg, H.P. (1983). *The development of mathematical thinking.* New York: Academic Press.

Ginsburg, H.P. (1989). *Children's arithmetic* (2nd ed.). Austin, TX: Pro-Ed.

Goodman, K. (1984). Unity in reading. In A. Purves & O. Niles (Eds.), *Becoming readers in a complex society* (pp. 79-114) (83rd Yearbook of the National Society for the Study of Education). Chicago: National Society for the Study of Education.

Goodman, K. (1986). *What's whole in whole language?* Portsmouth, NH: Heinemann.

Harste, J., Woodward, V., & Burke, C. (1984). *Language stories and literacy lessons.* Portsmouth, NH: Heinemann.

Harste, J., Short, K., & Burke, C. (1988). *Creating classrooms for authors.* Portsmouth, NH: Heinemann.

Huff, D. (1954). *How to lie with statistics.* New York: Norton.

Kline, M. (1980). *Mathematics: The loss of certainty.* New York: Oxford University Press.

Knorr-Cetina, K. (1981). *The manufacture of knowledge.* Oxford: Pergamon Press.

Knorr-Cetina, K. (1983). The ethnographic study of scientific work: towards a constructivist interpretation of science. In K. Knorr-Cetina & M. Mulkay (Eds.), *Science observed* (pp. 115-140). London: Sage Publications.

Kuhn, T. (1970). *The structure of scientific revolutions.* Chicago, IL: The University of Chicago Press.

Lakatos, I. (1976). *Proofs and refutations.* Cambridge, UK: Cambridge University Press.

Lampert, M. (1990). When the problem is not the question and the solution is not the answer: Mathematics knowing and teaching. *American Educational Research Journal, 27,* 29-63.

Latour, B., & Woolgar, S. (1979). *Laboratory life.* Princeton, NJ: Princeton University Press.

Mehan, H. (1979). *Learning lessons.* Cambridge, MA: Harvard University Press.

National Council of Teachers of Mathematics (NCTM) (1989). *Curriculum and evaluation standards for school mathematics.* Reston, VA: National Council of Teachers of Mathematics.

National Council of Teachers of Mathematics (NCTM) (1991). *Professional standards for teaching mathematics.* Reston, VA: National Council of Teachers of Mathematics.

National Research Council (NRC) (1989). *Everybody counts: A report to the nation on the future of mathematics education.* Washington: National Academic Press.

47

National Research Council (NRC) (1990). *Reshaping school mathematics: A philosophy and framework for curriculum.* Washington: National Academic Press.

National Research Council (NRC) (1991). *Moving beyond myths: Revitalizing undergraduate mathematics.* Washington: National Academic Press.

Nolan, J. (1984). Reading in the content area of mathematics. In M. Dupuis (Ed.), *Reading in the content areas: Research for teachers* (pp. 28-41). Newark, DE: International Reading Association.

O'Mara, D. (1981). The process of reading mathematics. *Journal of Reading, 25*, 22-30.

Piaget, J. (1970). *Genetic epistemology.* New York: Columbia University Press.

Pimm, D. (1987). *Speaking mathematically: Communication in mathematics classrooms.* London: Routledge.

Pinne, S. (1983). *Teaching reading in the mathematics class.* (ERIC Document Reproduction Service No. ED 228 919).

Rose, B.J. (1989). Writing and mathematics: Theory and practice. In P. Connolly & T. Vilardi (Eds.), *Writing to learn mathematics and science* (pp. 15-30). New York: Teachers College Press.

Rosenblatt, L. (1978). *The reader, the text, the poem.* Carbondale, IL: Southern Illinois University Press.

Schoenfeld, A.H. (1989). Exploration of students' mathematical beliefs and behavior. *Journal for Research in Mathematics Education, 20*(4), 338-355.

Siegel, M. (1984). *Reading as signification.* Unpublished doctoral dissertation, Indiana University, Bloomington.

Siegel, M., Borasi, R., & Smith, C. (1989). A critical review of reading in mathematics instruction: The need for a new synthesis. In S. McCormick & J. Zutell (Eds.), *Cognitive and social perspectives for literacy research and instruction* (pp. 269-277). Thirty-eight Yearbook of the National Reading Conference. Chicago: The National Reading Conference, Inc.

Siegel, M., & Carey, R.F. (1989). *Critical thinking: A semiotic perspective.* Bloomington: (ERIC Document Reproduction Service No. ED 21-22).

Skagestad, P. (1981). *The road of inquiry.* New York: Columbia University Press.

Steffe, L.P., von Glasersfeld, E., Richards, J., & Cobb, P. (1983). *Children's counting types: Philosophy, theory and applications.* New York: Praeger Scientific.

Tobias, S. (1989). Writing to learn science and mathematics. In P. Connolly & T. Vilardi (Eds.), *Writing to learn mathematics and science* (pp. 48-55). New York: Teachers College Press.

von Glasersfeld, E. (Ed.) (1991). *Radical constructivism in mathematics education.* Dordrecht, The Netherlands: Kluwer Academic Publishers.

Vygotsky, L.S. (1962). *Thought and language.* Cambridge, MA: MIT Press.

Vygotsky, L. S. (1978). *Mind in society.* Cambridge MA: Harvard University Press.

TEACHERS USING VIDEOTAPES AS REFERENCE POINTS TO ASSESS THEIR STUDENTS

John L. Clark

Toronto Board of Education, Canada

Teachers in the Toronto Board of Education, Ontario, Canada, are using videotapes as a resource to assess the progress of their students in mathematics and language. The Board comprises 113 elementary and 41 secondary schools with approximately 72 000 regular day-school students, over half of whom speak a language other than English in their homes. The videotapes are part of a curriculum resource known as Benchmarks.

For almost thirty years, up until the development of the Benchmarks, the Board did not have any formal system-wide testing. There were general guidelines for principals and teachers to use in assessing students and reporting to parents. The guidelines stressed daily observation of students as a vital source of information about student progress. Generally, each local school, in cooperation with its community of parents, was responsible for its own assessment and reporting procedures. In May of 1987, however, the Board mandated the development of standards of student achievement in mathematics and language at the end of Grades 3, 6, and 8 (ages 8, 11, and 13) to be used by teachers for assessment and reporting. The resulting standards are known as Benchmarks. The Board intends to develop Benchmarks for its secondary schools.

DEVELOPMENT OF BENCHMARKS

Staff from the Board's Curriculum Department worked with practising teachers to develop assessment tasks. They believed that traditional evaluation schemes were inadequate because they emphasized products of learning over processes, and therefore did not reflect the emphasis in existing curricula of active learning and problem solving. They believed that traditional testing programs did not acknowledge sufficiently the professional knowledge which teachers have about their students, and were skeptical that student achievement can be adequately captured in a number or test score. Also, given the

49

highly multicultural composition of the Board's current student population brought about by recent immigration, they felt that traditional testing programs placed many students at a disadvantage. Thus the committees aimed to develop an alternative approach to assessment which was more attuned to existing priorities for student learning.

The assessment tasks that were developed were based on the official curriculum prescribed by the Ontario Ministry of Education. They covered most of the curriculum in arithmetic, geometry, and measurement, and problem solving was integrated throughout. About one-quarter of the tasks were traditional paper and pencil type questions, but in most tasks, students estimated, measured, formulated and solved problems, gave oral explanations, and worked with a wide variety of manipulative materials.

A ten-percent representative sample (about 350 students) was randomly selected at each of the three grades, 3, 6 and 8. Recently retired teachers were hired and trained to administer the assessment tasks. They interviewed each student on the average for about four hours, videotaping about half of each performance. After the data had been collected, the videotaped performances were scored holistically by teams of teachers, and the paper and pencil work was scored in the usual manner.

The results of the assessment were organized into three Benchmark libraries in mathematics, one for each grade. Each library contains videotapes and printed information; for example, the Grade 6 library contains twelve videotape and fifteen print Benchmarks. The libraries provide a rich resource of information about student learning which teachers of all grades are to use as reference points when assessing their students.

Each video Benchmark consists of printed information about the task as well as the videotape itself. The printed information contains a statement of the objectives of the task, a description of the task, holistic scoring criteria for each of five levels of performance, and the percentage of students attaining each level. On the videotape, a narrator provides a summary of the printed information and, depending on the time taken to perform the task, there are from one to three sample student performances at each of the top three levels. The videotape ends with an unrated student performance that the viewer is invited to rate using the holistic scoring criteria and the performances viewed previously.

A SAMPLE VIDEO BENCHMARK

The videotape entitled *Tell a Story* from the Grade 6 library lasting 12 minutes was demonstrated in the ICME lecture. In this task, students were asked to choose one of three pictures, create a mathematical problem based on the picture, and state the problem orally. The three pictures were of winter Olympic events, six dogs, and a child holding a basin. Following is a transcription of the problems stated orally by students on the video at the top three levels (numbered five, four, and three). Also following, for each level, are the holistic scoring criteria developed by teams of teachers from an analysis of problems given by *all* students in the Grade 6 sample. Student performances rated at levels two and one are not demonstrated on Benchmark videos, but holistic criteria and percentages are, and are provided below for this Benchmark. Finally, the unrated problem for this task is presented below which the viewer (reader) is invited to rate.

Level Five

14% of all students produced level-five problems.

Student A chooses a picture of a child holding a basin and says: *The boy has a bowl. He wanted to find out how long it was around the outside so he measured the diameter and did the diameter times π equals the circumference. What is ... the diameter is 30 cm and π is ... What is the circumference?*

Student B chooses a picture of winter Olympics and says: *Hyman Zerbreggan won 5 medals at the Olympics—3 gold medals, 1 silver medal, and 1 bronze medal. The silver was worth $50, the bronze was worth $20, and the gold was worth $100. How much were the medals worth altogether?*

Holistic scoring criteria

The student tells a multi-step story problem that involves more than one mathematical operation. The story problem is logical, creative, realistically relates to the picture and allows a numerical solution. If units (e.g. dollars) are worked into the story, they are appropriately chosen and used. The student sees the task as a challenge and shows a high level of interest and commitment.

Level Four

29% of all students produced level-four problems.

Student C chooses a picture of six dogs with the caption "Is it 5:00 yet?" and says: *It is 4:15 right now and they want to know if it is 5:00. How long do they have to wait?*

Student D chooses the picture of the winter Olympics and says: *If John had 15 friends and ⅔ of them went to the Olympics, how many friends went to the Olympics?*

Holistic scoring criteria

The student may tell a multi-step story problem with one-digit numbers or a one-step story problem with multi-digit numbers. The student understands the task and relates the story to the picture. Elements of the picture may be used in original ways. The student is interested and committed and requires little coaching.

Level Three

28% of all students produced level-three problems.

Student E chooses the poster of six dogs, acts out the characters, and says: *"Is it 5:00 yet? I think so Randolph. Good, she should be home soon. I am home, puppies—time for supper."* They give out one plate of dog food. *Out of all these six dogs, how would you split the dog food—one plate—for these six doggies?*

Student F chooses the picture of winter Olympics and says: *If there are 22 heads in this picture, and you take away the heads of the athletes, how many heads would be left?*

Holistic scoring criteria

The student tells a one-step story problem which can be solved easily. One-digit numbers are probably used. The student understands the task but may present the information and various elements of the story problem without properly stating a mathematical problem. The student may require some coaching.

Level Two

16% of students produced level-two problems. There are no demonstrations of these on the video.

Holistic scoring criteria

The student tells a very simple story with an attempt to incorporate a mathematical problem, or tells a story problem similar to one modelled by the evaluator. The story may be garbled, units may be confused, and numbers may be incorporated illogically. The student seeks hints and approval from the evaluator. Much coaching is required.

Level One

13% of students produced level-one problems. There are no demonstrations of these on the video.

Holistic scoring criteria

Very limited response or no response at all.

Unrated student

The viewer (reader) is invited to rate the following problem. Student G chooses the picture of the six dogs and says: *There were 150 puppies in the pound and a customer came and bought 126, how many were left?*

IMPLEMENTATION OF THE BENCHMARKS

The plan for implementing Benchmarks in schools is long-term and school-based. Because of the magnitude of what teachers have been asked to do, it is understood that the complete process will take several years. During the introductory years, teachers familiarized themselves with the problem libraries, experimented with the use of Benchmarks in classrooms, and worked towards their integration into daily practices. The implementation model is intended to be collaborative; teachers in each school are expected to work together and share their experiences. To support the implementation process, principals, teachers and consultants were given intensive in-service instruction not only on Benchmarks, but also on strategies for working collaboratively within a school.

There are major differences between Benchmarks and traditional testing programs. First, the Benchmarks are not tests. They provide information about student achievement in the kinds of activities which many teachers now use in their classrooms for teaching purposes. The Benchmarks, therefore, combine teaching with assessment so that as students engage in daily learning activities, teachers can make more informed judgments about the quality of their students' work, using the Benchmarks as reference points.

Second, unlike most traditional testing programs, the teachers and principal of each school are in control of the assessment of their own students and of how information about students will be reported to parents. Teachers are expected to work on developing ways in which Benchmarks will assist them in the assessment of their students. Principals, teachers, and parents are expected to work together to develop procedures for reporting how well children are doing according to the Benchmarks criteria. To support the development of reporting procedures in the local school, a central committee is developing guidelines, and possible models, for report cards and teacher-parent-student interviews.

The approach taken to assessment by the Board has predictably met with difficulties at the implementation stage. One difficulty is teacher resistance to change. Teachers who value an active approach to learning and daily observation of students as an important source of assessment information have welcomed Benchmarks as an affirmation of their beliefs and support for their practices. But, obviously, teachers whose instruction consists mainly of textbook exercises and skill-based tests tend to resist the general philosophy and approach of Benchmarks. These teachers view the program as an additional responsibility, not one which can be integrated with what they are presently doing.

A second difficulty with implementation occurs in schools where teachers have been accustomed to working in isolation, mostly behind closed classroom doors. If there has been no tradition in the school of working collaboratively, discussing children's learning, and attempting to improve teaching and assessment practices, then the program challenges established patterns of communication in the school and the principal's leadership.

A third difficulty results from the fact that all of the videotaped performances are in teacher-student interviews and teachers have classes of many students who often work in groups. It is expected, however, that teachers will make the transition from Benchmark tasks to their classrooms because many teachers already make individual assessments of students who do most of their work in groups. Teachers, especially of younger children, know how to extract information about individual students from whole class situations through careful observation so that they can tell parents about the progress of their children. The fact that teachers are able to do this indicates just what a complex art teaching really is.

Lastly, the overall non-prescriptive and decentralized approach which the Board has taken to assessment through Benchmarks has engendered some criticism from parents and teachers who believe in traditional assessment practices, especially standardized tests, and desire more uniformity across the school system. Assessment practices are controversial; underlying them are strongly-held beliefs about the goals of education, and how and what children should learn in schools.

STRENGTHS OF BENCHMARKS

Although Benchmarks have encountered some difficulties, they have also demonstrated many important strengths compared with traditional forms of assessment. First is the enhancement of teachers' assessment skills. Because traditional forms of assessment are usually developed and administered by people outside classrooms, they have had the effect of "deskilling" teachers. When assessment is done on behalf of teachers, they tend to separate assessment from teaching. With Benchmarks, however, teachers are expected to evaluate and refine their assessment practices and are provided with the resources to do this. For most teachers, the use of holistic scoring to assess student achievement in any subject is new, certainly in mathematics. But teachers have learned that it is a powerful method which can assess simultaneously many elements of students' work: knowledge of mathematical content and problem-solving processes, ability to reason and communicate, and disposition towards mathematics. The advantage of videotaped student performances is that the viewer can actually observe how individual students solve problems and apply their knowledge. Holistic scoring has also been used extensively in the language Benchmarks, and since most elementary school teachers teach both mathematics and language, they are learning a skill which can be used to assess students' oral and written work in mathematics and in language, and in other subjects as well.

There is research (Ministry of Education of Ontario, 1980) which indicates that the method which elementary school teachers use most frequently to evaluate their students is observation; teachers observe their students constantly as they engage in daily classroom activities. Holistic scoring fits perfectly with observation. As teachers watch students performing tasks on videotapes, and discuss holistic scoring criteria with colleagues, they sharpen their observation skills with the result that the judgments that they make of their own students performing similar tasks become more informed and systematic. For example, having viewed and discussed the videotape, *Tell a Story,* when teachers have their own students generate mathematical problems, they are better able to judge the quality of the attempts.

Working with Benchmarks has led teachers to examine other aspects of their assessment practices. One critical aspect which is not very often examined is the records which teachers keep to document a student's progress. In traditional assessment, where tests are the primary source of information, records frequently consist of what some teachers call "mark books" in which there is one line per student with a row of marks which may be averaged or converted to a letter grade. Because of the emphasis in Benchmarks on observation of processes, teachers are revising their record-keeping methods so that they can retain more comprehensive information about each student. Teachers are finding that they need at least a full page per student, and with the emphasis on student writing, they need ways to retain samples of students' written work, so they are also experimenting with the use of folders in mathematics in ways that they have used in connection with the teaching of language and art.

A second strength demonstrated by Benchmarks is that teachers are led to evaluate their own classroom instruction. On the videotapes teachers see exemplary classroom tasks: students estimating the cost of a restaurant bill, measuring and pouring water, and solving problems with a calculator. Teachers may then consider that perhaps they should do more work with estimation, actually have their students pour and measure water, or let their students solve problems with a calculator. In this sense, Benchmarks are not only a resource for assessing student achievement, but also for evaluating teachers' instructional methods. This is the result of Benchmark tasks having been designed so that they reflect as much as possible good classroom activities based on Ministry of Education curriculum guidelines. Benchmarks have operationalized curriculum guidelines so that what is expected of the students is actually demonstrated and made explicit to both teachers and parents. Benchmarks have aligned assessment with learning.

Another situation in which Benchmarks facilitate instructional evaluation is when teachers from different grades work together with videotapes. They will almost certainly discuss a task from the point of view of how the content or the thinking involved in the task might develop from one grade to the next. For example, a Grade 1 teacher watching Grade 3 students estimate and measure lengths might consider what younger children should be learning about the concept of length. Also, in any class, students are at different levels of progress so that a Grade 2 teacher, for example, will likely have students who perform an activity at as high a level as many Grade 3 students. In this way, all teachers are led to think about the implications of a Benchmark for their own curriculum and students.

A third major strength of Benchmarks is the emphasis on teachers working collaboratively. The approach taken by the Board to implementation is school-based where it is the responsibility of the principal to initiate and support teachers working together with Benchmark libraries. Principals have reported that they have observed some teachers in their schools for the first time discussing what they do in their classrooms with colleagues. Collaborative work takes different forms. One of the most effective is "self-reflective cycles"; teachers plan learning activities as a group, experiment with the plan in their classrooms, and then evaluate their shared experiences. Such a cycle of planning, experimenting, and evaluating frequently leads to a new cycle with different Benchmark activities. In this way, teachers engage in authentic ongoing research into their professional practices.

A fourth strength of Benchmarks is that they provide a vehicle for teachers and principals to communicate to parents what schools are doing for their children in mathematics. Parents do not often get good information about the goals of the mathematics curriculum. Schools are showing the videotapes to parents, often getting them to try the same activities the students did. Parents are learning that solving good problems in mathematics using manipulative materials is not just play. Parents observe some students on videotapes doing well and others having difficulty, and they have a better appreciation of how well their own children might do on similar tasks. They realize that children are at different stages in their intellectual development and can be helped to move ahead from any level. Parents understand that teachers can assess their children by observing them in daily classroom activities.

Another benefit of Benchmarks, which is only now emerging, is that better information about children's progress can be reported to parents. Schools have been working with the program for two years now and are just beginning to deal with this most important phase. The primary concern of parents that initiated the Benchmarks experiment was that there were no system-wide standards with which their children's progress could be compared. Teachers were employing their own benchmarks, which in some cases embodied standards that were either too high or too low. Principals and teachers are now exploring how they can report their students' progress using Benchmarks as reference points. What is emerging is the realization that traditional report cards are inadequate to convey the richness of information that teachers are gaining about their students. Schools are exploring more creative ways to use parent interviews: for example, having students not only attend interviews, but also contribute their self-evaluations. Also, when a teacher now reports on the progress of a student, this judgment can be substantiated by a broader base of qualitative and quantitative evidence, and by reference to a set of standards representing achievement across all schools. Teachers use the descriptive language of the holistic scoring criteria to report students' progress both in parent interviews and in writing anecdotal reports.

Finally, Benchmarks facilitate a more equitable form of assessment. Many people in our diverse community are critical of the inequity produced by traditional assessment practices that stress exclusively paper and pencil tests. They believe that many students who have difficulty answering questions on such tests could solve problems in real situations or by using manipulative materials. A strength of Benchmarks is that they have led teachers to use expanded modes of assessment that allow students to show what they know through practical demonstrations and discussion in problem solving situations. The alignment of assessment with teaching and learning has created greater opportunities for students to demonstrate their abilities. As teachers explore the use of holistic scoring and foster more active learning in their classrooms, they are emphasizing in their assessments a broader range of cognitive and affective components, and therefore utilizing a more equitable form of assessment.

CONCLUSION

The approach taken to assessment by the Toronto Board of Education through Benchmarks respects the commitment and professionalism of its teachers and principals. The Board believes that in the long run, this is the way to improve the standard of education which it offers to its community. It believes that educational change is not a matter of paper, but of people. The overall effectiveness of Benchmarks will not be in the problem libraries—they are simply materials in boxes—but in their potential to be used by teachers, principals, parents, and students for the improvement of student learning. The strengths of Benchmarks lie in the integration of student assessment with human dimensions of education; student learning, teacher professional development, collaborative communities, and equitable assessment.

NOTE

Further information can be obtained by writing to: The Benchmark Program, The Toronto Board of Education, 155 College St., Toronto, ON, Canada, M5T 1P6.

REFERENCES

Clark, J. L. (1990). Benchmarks in mathematics. *The Ontario Mathematics Gazette, 29*(2), 17-20.

Clark, J. L. (1991). Benchmarks in mathematics II. *The Ontario Mathematics Gazette, 30*(1), 19-25.

Clark, J. L. (1992). The Toronto Board of Education's Benchmarks in mathematics. *The Arithmetic Teacher: Focus issue. 39*(6), 51-55.

Larter, S. (1991). *Benchmarks: The development of a new approach to student evaluation.* Toronto: Toronto Board of Education.

Ministry of Education of Ontario (1980). *Teacher interaction and observation practices in the evaluation of student achievement.* Toronto: Author.

THE TRANSITION TO
SECONDARY SCHOOL MATHEMATICS

David Clarke

Australian Catholic University, Australia

For most Australian children, schooling consists of 7 years of primary school, followed by 6 years at high school. In the state of Victoria, grade 6 is the last year of primary school, and grade 7 is the first year of secondary school (high school). Grade 6 classes are taught predominantly by a single teacher, while grade 7 classes have many different teachers, who each specialize in the various academic subjects. The transition from primary school to high school has been recognized for some time as a particularly significant point in a student's educational career. This was certainly true for Cathy and Darren: their experience of the transition from primary school to secondary school illustrates the major factors operating at this crucial time.

Cathy and Darren were pupils in different grade 6 classes, in neighboring primary schools. In grade 7, Cathy and Darren began high school as members of the same grade 7 class. When Cathy was in grade 6 she was asked, "How good are you at mathematics?" She replied, "Average." In response to the same question, Darren said that he was "the best" in his class. Both Darren's and Cathy's grade 6 teachers agreed with their students' estimation of their own competence.

After one year in high school, Cathy and Darren were again asked, "How good are you at mathematics?" Cathy replied, "I understand everything," while Darren said, "I'm not smart at maths." The grade 7 mathematics teacher thought that Cathy had "high ability" at mathematics, while Darren's mathematics competence was "very poor." These opinions were shared by Darren and Cathy's grade 7 classmates. By the end of grade 8 everyone, including Cathy and Darren, thought that Darren was poor at mathematics and that Cathy was very talented.

This dramatic change in the perceived mathematical competence of Cathy and Darren might be explained by the relative competence of the two grade 6 classes from which Cathy and Darren had graduated. Indeed, test performances of the two classes suggest that the pupils in Cathy's grade 6 class were far more mathematically able than those in Darren's grade 6 class. As members of the same grade 7 class, perceptions of the mathematical competence of Cathy and Darren could be compared in relation to the same academic environment. However, differences in classroom context do not explain the fact that throughout grades 6, 7 and 8 Darren's and Cathy's scores on a test of "mathematical ability" and on a test of "mathematical knowledge" were effectively identical (See Table 1).

Table 1. Mathematics test scores for Cathy and Darren.

		Grade 6	Grade 7	Grade 8
Ability Test	Cathy	53.5	54	55
	Darren	51	52	54
Knowledge Test	Cathy	32	34	33
	Darren	28	32	33

Given the known errors associated with testing, it is clear that the differences in the relative perceived competence of Cathy and Darren cannot be justified by measurable differences in competence. Further, pupils were not told their scores on either of the tests reported in Table 1. Student perceptions of their own and their classmates' mathematical competence were based upon student participation in class and performance on teacher-designed class tests. It appeared that in grade 7 minor differences in classroom and test performance were exaggerated in the process of typification (See Clarke, 1986) which led to the establishment of a classroom consensus regarding the relative mathematical competence of Cathy and Darren. Table 2 compares the differences in perceived competence with a class ranking compiled from the final three tests undertaken by the pupils in grade 7. Perceived rankings were obtained two months prior to the final testing and illustrate the exaggerated difference in perceived rank already evident, and suggest the typification process which endorsed Cathy's competence and so challenged Darren's academic self-concept with regard to mathematics.

Table 2. Grade 7 class rankings in mathematical competence: Cathy and Darren.

Grade 7	Cathy	Darren
Perceived Rank (self)	10	13
Perceived Rank (class)	4	19
"Actual" Rank (from Ability, Knowledge, and Class Tests – mean rank)	7	12

Central to the change in Darren's perception of his own mathematical competence was the significance attached to the final class Number Skills Test. In this test, pupils scoring less than 80% were assigned to special classes in grade 8 designed to correct perceived mathematical inadequacies. Pupils scoring more than 80% joined more advanced grade 8 algebra classes. On the Number Skills Test, Cathy scored 81% and Darren scored 76%. Although Darren's perceptions of his grade 7 rank were obtained prior to the administration of this Number Skills Test, it appeared from subsequent interview data, that the final test result confirmed for Darren his revised estimate of his own competence.

From the intensive study of Cathy, Darren and eight other pupils (Alison, Andrea, Annette, Bernie, Brian, Cameron, Chris, and Davie) four factors emerged as central to any consideration of student mathematical behavior during the transition from primary to secondary school. The ten pupils studied came from four different primary schools, but all ten pupils commenced high school as members of the same grade 7 mathematics class. For each student studied, the challenge represented by secondary school mathematics can be most usefully described in terms of:

- conceptions of mathematical competence;
- the mathematics classroom as social context;
- the individuality of mathematical behavior; and,
- the experience of transition as discontinuity.

Each of these factors is discussed briefly below.

SECONDARY SCHOOL MATHEMATICS: FOUR FACTORS

Conceptions of mathematical competence

The findings of this study suggest the existence within mathematics classrooms of a consensus conception of competence to which all participants, teacher and pupils, subscribe. This conception of competence is embodied in the construct "good at math", one application of which is in the generation of a hierarchy of competence. Such is the degree of consensus about what behaviors constitute competence that pupils are located in rank order within the resulting hierarchy with a high degree of consistency across all participants. Clarke (1986) reported results from both this study and from related studies, and examined the implications of such a consensus conception of competence for learning and teaching in mathematics classrooms.

In grade 7 Darren was asked, "Would you like people to think you were smart at mathematics?" His reply illustrated the interdependence of ability, self-concept and classroom conceptions of competence.

> Well, I'm not smart at maths. So it doesn't matter. I know most of the stuff, but people don't think I'm smart at it.

Perhaps the most important feature of Darren's reply is his recognition that it is not sufficient to "know your stuff" if your competence does not receive the sanction of class and teacher. The significance of the mathematics classroom as a social context in which such information is exchanged was a recurrent feature of the study.

The mathematics classroom as social context

Classroom learning is an inherently social process and the meanings which participants construct from their mathematical activities and their interaction with teacher and peers are social constructions, the result of their immersion in the social context that is the mathematics classroom, embedded, as it is, in enfolding institutional, societal and cultural dimensions. Clarke (1987b) reported the impact of social factors on the mathematical behavior of the children in this study.

Bernie demonstrated the significance of the mathematics classroom as social context when he attempted to distance himself in class from his less academically-inclined friends. While Bernie succeeded in improving his test performances, the quality of his classroom participation, and the understanding of mathematics displayed in interview tasks, his classmates continued to describe him as a disruptive underachiever. Unlike Darren, Bernie progressively overcame the persistence of a typification based on his behavior at the commencement of high school. Darren, by contrast, acquiesced to a typification process which labelled him as both disruptive and academically unsuccessful. For both pupils the commencement of secondary school mathematics offered a severe challenge to the positive self-concepts with which they left primary school.

For other pupils, such as Cathy and Andrea, acquiescence to the classroom typification involved improved self-esteem and a consequent increase in the quality of their classroom participation. Despite her heightened self-esteem and her feelings of success in overcoming the challenge of secondary school mathematics, Andrea did not display the level of mathematical competence shown by either Darren or Bernie, either in tests or in interviews.

Clarke (1987b) drew some specific conclusions regarding the social dynamics of the mathematics classroom:

- A student's success at mathematics can be constrained by the social demands of the classroom.

- A teacher's conception of effective instruction must acknowledge the need of some pupils for regular personal recognition of their efforts.

- Mathematics instruction serves to communicate social values and beliefs which may colour the pupil's conceptions of the goals of that instruction and contribute to a more or less productive rationale for learning.

- Despite the teacher's pedagogical aspirations, her efforts must be filtered through the perceptions and expectations of individual students, whose interpretations of her motives and requirements may mistakenly reinforce non-productive classroom practices.

- A student wishing to change the nature of his or her classroom practices may have difficulty if social interactions with the peer group are predicated on a persistent typification derived from earlier practice.

- The teacher's capacity to promote academic effort through value-modelling will vary with her status as a "significant other" to each individual student.

It was suggested (Clarke, 1987b) that teacher awareness of the impact of students' social concerns on their mathematics learning might be best maintained through a procedure like the IMPACT program (Clarke, 1987a).

The IMPACT procedure was extensively field-tested in 1984 with 750 grade 7 students in 37 classrooms in 19 schools across Victoria. The procedure consisted of the completion by students, every two weeks, of a brief questionnaire intended to serve both to stimulate student reflection on their mathematics learning and as a mechanism whereby each student could communicate confidentially (but not anonymously) with the teacher concerning the learning of mathematics and the experience of the secondary mathematics classroom. As a result of the 1984 field-testing, the IMPACT instrument was refined and a revised version included in Clarke (1989b). This revised version is reproduced as Figure 1.

Name:

Class:

Teacher:

Date:

- What was the best thing to have happened in Maths in the last two weeks?

- Write down one new problem which you can now do.

- What would you most like more help with?

- How do you feel in Maths classes at the moment? (Circle the words that apply to you).
  a) Interested   b) Relaxed   c) Worried
  d) Successful   e) Confused   f) Clever
  g) Happy   h) Bored   i) Rushed
  j) Write down one word of your own ....

- What is the biggest worry affecting your work in Maths at the moment?

- How could we improve Maths classes?

Figure 1. The IMPACT instrument.

Samples of student responses can be found in Clarke (1987a, 1989b). Student responses to questions such as "What is the greatest worry affecting your work in mathematics at the moment?" were as likely to refer to social context as they were to academic content.

The individuality of mathematical behavior

Anomalous personal constructions and idiosyncratic conceptions were documented for all ten students in this study. All students experienced the same grade 7 mathematics classroom—the same teacher, the same basic activities. The observed individuality of behavior, despite these common environmental features, provides a compelling argument for the significance of the individual's beliefs, values, conceptions, perceptions, goals and perspectives.

Every classroom exchange is a consequence of both cognitive and social factors. The cognitive aspect of student behavior can be described in terms of mini-procedures, and inferences can be drawn concerning specific student constructions, such as the meaning Bernie attributed to his diagrams of fractions. For instance, Bernie consistently employed two mini-procedures to compare fractions. First, the size of the denominator was invoked through the rule: "The larger the denominator, the smaller the fraction." Second, the meaning of a fraction diagram depended on how many it was seen to be "out of." The decision as to how many parts the circle was implicitly sub-divided into was an arbitrary one in which the size of the denominator gave an indication of the approximate magnitude of the number of subdivisions, but did little more than set a lower bound. In practice, this meant that a particular fraction could be represented by one or more distinct circular diagrams. For example, thirty-five thirty-sixths might be represented as either greater than or less than one-half. Interestingly, every diagram was subdivided into quarters. And these quarters remained inviolate. Other fractions were drawn in terms of their perceived size relative to multiples of a quarter.

There is an urgent need for explanatory frameworks which do simultaneous justice to both the cognitive and the social aspects of mathematical behavior. It is necessary to conceptualize "mathematical behavior" as a structured web of behaviors. Figure 2 sets out the structure employed in this study. This structure was successful in *locating*, *integrating* and *explaining* data. Particular student behaviors were successfully located within the descriptive framework. Relationships between behavior samples were rendered more apparent, since the data, which might have been a collection of unconnected observations, interview excerpts and test performances, could be viewed as an array of behavioral elements, whose structure suggested likely links between data sets. Explanations for behavioral changes could then be sought in both the data and the emergent relationships.

65

Cognitive	Mathematical Abilities	Mathematical Understanding	(Mathematical Skills and Procedures)
	• Inclinations • Cognitive strategies	• Replication • Association • Explanation	
	Mathematical Performance • Task completion – achievement – competence	Individual Student Classroom Practices	Practices of the Learning Environment
Affective	Mathematical Self-concept • self-perceptions of ability • attributions • gender • ethnicity	Conceptions of Mathematics • nature of mathematical activity • conceptions of competence • attitudes	(Values and Beliefs)
	Personal		**Environmental**

Figure 2. The structure of student mathematical behavior.

Certain sub-categories of each element (cell) emerged as distinctive. Mathematical Abilities were identified with *inclinations* to specific mathematical behaviors, with *cognitive strategies*, and with the capacity to function *metacognitively*, and Understanding of Mathematics was taken to encompass the successful *replication* of terms and procedures, the degree and diversity of *association* between related mathematical (and non-mathematical) entities by which a concept or procedure acquires meaning, and the quality of *explanation* or demonstration which a student might provide for a concept or procedure. Self-concept would encompass *gender* and *ethnicity*, as well as *self-perceptions of ability*, and *attributions* of success and failure. Mathematical Performance was identified specifically with *task completion*, either as a single demonstration (achievement) or through reliable and consistent success (competence). Conceptions of Mathematics involves student *perceptions of the nature of mathematical activity, conceptions of competence,* and aspects of *attitudes to mathematics.* Figure 2 also incorporates the use of Cognitive and Affective, and Personal and Environmental as meaningful delimiters on the two-dimensional array within which the elements of mathematical behavior are located. The inclusion of both Individual Student Classroom Practices and Practices of the Learning Environment within a student's mathematical behavior represents a recognition that student behaviors (both thoughts and actions) are shaped, constrained, mediated and expressed by those social and mathematical practices sanctioned within the classroom. This point is elaborated below.

It appears common for research in education to focus on one or two isolated aspects of behavior without making any explicit statement regarding the theoretical basis for doing so. Relatively complex behavior conglomerates such as verbal behavior, mathematical behavior, scientific or religious practices, aesthetic appreciation, the behaviors of social transactions, instructional practices, and so on, require that the validity of their independent study be explicitly justified. For more narrowly defined behavior categories, such as reading comprehension, spatial reasoning, faith, aggression, or praise, this obligation becomes a methodological imperative.

If the differences in students' mathematical behaviors are to be explained, such explanations must involve the realization of the essential individuality of the learning process and recognition of the complexity of the web of behaviors being studied. A model of individual behavior must refer to more than just the actions, thoughts and beliefs of a single student, since those actions may only derive their meaning from their contribution to the realisation of the group's goals; the thoughts lose significance if considered in isolation from the thoughts, motives and expectations of others; and the beliefs lose coherence once considered outside the societal context which gave them shape. But the boundaries between individual mathematical behavior, other types of behavior and the behaviors of other individuals must be clear if the structure is to have integrity. The descriptive framework of mathematical behavior employed in this study is an example of a minimal behavior web and of the lowest level of complexity which can justifiably form the focus of legitimate learning research. Further details of this argument can be found in Clarke (1992).

Transition as discontinuity

Discontinuity emerged as a crucial element in a general theory of transition which is detailed in the remainder of this paper. The significance of transition as discontinuity was graphically illustrated in the case studies of Cathy and Darren. (See Clarke, 1985, for more detail.) While both Cathy and Darren were members of the same grade 7 mathematics class, their

67

initiation into secondary mathematics was dramatically different. This difference arose from the personal nature of each student's experience of the discontinuity inherent in the transition to secondary school. What is a challenge and a promise of independence to some students may appear threatening and coercive to others.

> You're not allowed to be a child here.
>
> (Grade 7 girl, mid-year.)

One inference which might be drawn from the use of "discontinuity" as the dominant characteristic of the commencement of secondary school mathematics is that high school and primary school should be perceived by students to be very different. Use of a semantic differential questionnaire enabled the location of these two constructs in a multi-dimensional semantic space, together with other constructs, including the construct "Home." Home was included both as a reference point and because discussions of the transition from primary to secondary school frequently make use of metaphors associated with home. Students are described as leaving the security of primary school where they are known, for the anonymity of high school.

Differences in student perceptions of primary school and high school and the associated and consequent differences in their responses to the environmental change of transition can be seen in greatest detail by contrasting the detailed perceptions of individual students. The semantic differential offered one means of categorizing the perceptions of all ten children. This instrument as much as any other demonstrated the idiosyncratic nature of those student perceptions which influence the choice of behavior models among adults and peers, and enabled comparisons to be made between the environments of high school, primary school and home. For instance, among the ten students central to this research, by December of grade 7 (the conclusion of the first year of secondary schooling in Victoria), three distinct perceptions were evident:

a. Alison and Cameron identified both primary and high school as possessing similar characteristics and as being distinct from home.

b. Brian, Cathy, Chris and Darren perceived primary school and home in very similar terms, distinct from high school.

c. Bernie, Annette, Andrea and Davy associated high school more closely with home.

It is inappropriate to identify a particular perception as being most desirable. Andrea's very close association of home, high school, my friends and myself could certainly indicate a successful adjustment to high school. And Cathy's very similar perceptions of primary school, home and mother could be construed as relating characteristics associated with secure, caring environments. However, Cathy clearly identified the commencement of secondary schooling with independence and a "coming of age", and attached a high level of personal significance to her successful negotiation of the challenge represented by secondary school. It would be inappropriate, therefore, to depict Cathy as longing for the lost security of primary school. It was possible, however, to identify the key elements which characterized the challenge of secondary school and secondary mathematics for each student.

Each of the case studies became a stepping stone to more general statements and ultimately to the development of a general theory of transition. An individual student's experience of the challenge of secondary mathematics can then be seen as a consequence of the individual's response to transition as manifest within each element of the student's mathematical behavior. That is, the phenomenon of transition is played out in each aspect of a student's mathematical behavior. In the remainder of this paper, the elements of this general theory are set out and illustrated through reference to the individual students.

A GENERAL THEORY OF TRANSITION

Any theory of transition must confront those phenomena most frequently associated with the transition experience. The theory proposed here takes its structure from three key aspects of the transition process, each of which is embodied in a single word. These are *Discontinuity, Challenge,* and *Adjustment.* In the following discussion, the significance of each term is outlined and the nature of its contribution to a theory of transition made clear. Figure 3 is a schematic representation of the proposed theory of transition in which each key aspect is located in relation to other contributing or consequent factors. It was the identification of this structure within the case study data which provided the 'grounded key' from which the subsequent theory emerged. While the theory is dealt with in more elaborate detail in Clarke (1989a), the following discussion relates structural elements to specific recommendations.

It is suggested that discontinuity is an inevitable (and defining) characteristic of transition and the commencement of secondary school mathematics, and that the personal discontinuity is experienced by each individual as a challenge to established roles and behaviors. The consequent (and essential) process of adjustment may be realized through either acquiescence by the individual to the expectations and judgements of others, or through a process of self-realization in which individuals accept responsibility for their own learning behavior and assert that responsibility through conscious choice. Institutional and societal pressures encourage acquiescence, with regression a common result. Case study data demonstrated, however, that the transition experience can lead to growth through self-realization, and recommendations are made by which this outcome might be facilitated.

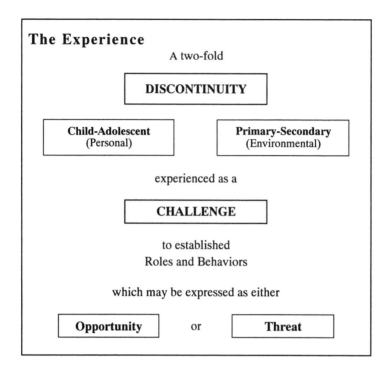

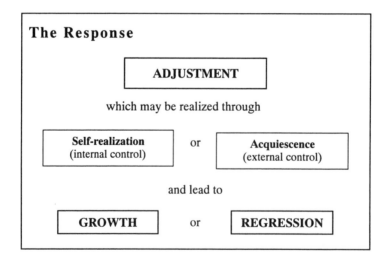

Figure 3. A schematic representation of the theory of transition.

The key elements: Discontinuity, Challenge and Adjustment, which characterize the theory of transition set out in Figure 3, can be related in detail to the experiences of the ten students who provided the focus for this study. Evidence for the process whereby student behavior adjusted in response to the challenge of commencing secondary mathematics could be found in every facet of a student's mathematical behavior (Figure 2). However, while the commencement of secondary mathematics could be characterized as a response to discontinuity with the general structure displayed in Figure 3, the particular adjustments to an individual's mathematical behavior were highly idiosyncratic. It was not just that each student responded differently to a common grade 7 experience. Each student construed the social and academic contexts differently, and the observed changes in student behavior were a consequence of the dynamic between the individual's evolving mathematical behavior and the individual's classroom reality. This study has specific practical implications for teachers responsible for initiating students into secondary mathematics. Discontinuity, Challenge and Adjustment provide a structure for the discussion of these practical implications.

Discontinuity

It is inappropriate and unrealistic to recommend uniformity of primary mathematics curricula as a means to minimize the discontinuity experienced by students during transition.

Any such proposed uniformity ignores the responsibility of schools to devise programs to meet the perceived needs of the community in which the school is embedded. Consideration of cultural, socio-economic and language factors and the documented differences between school policy and the classroom implementation of mathematics programs make it clear that such prescription would be unrealistic. Other factors such as school size, community aspirations, and peer group values, standards, behaviors and proficiency act to ensure that some experience of discontinuity is an *inevitable* component of the transition to secondary school.

Primary and secondary school teachers must become better informed about each others' beliefs and practices, so that each can implement an optimally effective mathematics program, with informed consideration of the others' practices.

The inevitable differences in educational orientation and practice between the generalist and the specialist require specific acknowledgement in the teaching practices of both. The nature of the discontinuity was a function of each individual's educational and personal history, but two aspects of secondary school mathematics could be identified specifically with the experience of transition as discontinuity: language and pace.

Secondary mathematics teachers, by virtue of their specialist expertise, have a far greater fluency in the use of formal mathematical language than their primary counterparts. Teacher explanations of previously met content using unfamiliar and abstract terms, and textbooks which employ exclusively technical language with levels of redundancy much lower than that of normal conversation can serve to render mystical that which was once familiar.

Assessment techniques are required which are sensitive to more than the recall of a fact or the replication of a procedure. If the abstract structures of which secondary mathematics largely consists are to be founded on a meaningful understanding of basic concepts and skills, teachers must monitor student construction of these abstract structures with a greater sensitivity than has previously been the case. This need is receiving increasing recognition (Clarke, 1989b).

Secondary teachers of mathematics must be sensitive to the destructive possibilities of excessive pace of instruction. Equally, more able students reported finding progress too slow. It may be that other classroom structures are required: interactive within-class grouping, for instance (See Yackel, Cobb, Wood, Wheatley, & Merkel, 1990) or that new instructional practices will better enable teachers to cater to the competency-range (See Sullivan & Clarke, 1991a, b).

> The individuality of each student's experience of the mathematics classroom makes it essential that a mechanism be established whereby the teacher can both monitor and respond to the changing needs of each student.

Such a mechanism has been trialled with some success (Clarke, 1987a).

Challenge

The commencement of secondary school unquestionably represents a significant challenge to established behaviors and roles. Several of the study students interpreted this challenge socially and measured the success of their first year of secondary school in social terms. The first year of secondary mathematics presented students with few new academic challenges, though possibly with reminders of earlier defeats. Even though the algebra met during grade 7 amounted to no more than generalized arithmetic, it appeared to provide some students with positive learning experiences. This may have been due to its novelty, the lack of preconceptions as to its difficulty, or the extent to which its relative sophistication represented a mathematical coming of age.

> The commencement of secondary mathematics offers some students the chance to experience success in new areas for which past inadequacies represent no disadvantage.

The challenge offered by secondary mathematics had an impact on all aspects of student mathematical behavior. Whether the challenge was successfully met appeared to depend as much on the social resources available to the student as it did on individual cognitive capabilities. The frequent reference to social concerns in students' accounts of their experience of the secondary mathematics classroom makes it clear that secondary schools must view the social adjustment of beginning students as an essential correlate to their academic progress.

Adjustment

By mid-year 8, all ten study students had indicated their contentment with the high school environment. All had established a role for themselves within the secondary school community. The significance of this achievement was recognized by the study children and represented as such. Not all the children developed roles conducive to academic success. The differences in the nature of each student's adjustment call into question the findings of studies which draw superficial conclusions of the form, "Most students ... quickly adjust ... The majority report that they prefer high school." (Power & Cotterell, 1981). This superficial satisfaction cannot usefully inform the actions of those educators concerned to ensure that a pupil's initial experiences of secondary school maximize the likelihood of that child's continued successful participation in all aspects of secondary schooling.

While social adjustment dominated the children's accounts of the transition to secondary schooling, a study concerned with mathematical behavior must address the question of academic adjustment. Academic adjustment as a goal of the transition process should encompass the development of mathematical and other academic practices, attitudes and beliefs optimally likely to lead to continued academic success in the secondary environment. If "familiarity" was the key to social adjustment, then 'continuity' appeared to have a similar significance in the academic domain. The negative side of the adjustment process involves feelings of social dislocation and academic discontinuity. Both are inevitable components of the transition process, and the minimization of discontinuity has already been discussed. However, the challenge offered by new studies in a new environment can represent a beneficial discontinuity, and the consequent adjustment can be a process of personal growth for the student. Darren and Chris responded in very different ways to the loss of role experienced in year 7, and with very different consequences. While Chris found ways to establish within the new community something of the status he had held in the old, Darren acquiesced to a role, determined for him by the high school community, characterized by a passive approach to learning, a non-academic class profile, and by disruptive classroom behavior. The implications for their continued successful participation in secondary mathematics were very different.

Both social and academic behavior may be enhanced in a classroom environment which requires students to accept greater responsibility for their learning and their social interactions and which offers them strategies by which they might do so.

CONCLUSIONS

The transition from primary school to secondary school has arguably become a major 'status passage'. As the transition from home to school may be seen as co-incident with the transition from infancy to childhood, and the transition from school to work co-incident with the transition from adolescence to adulthood, so the transition from primary to secondary school is co-incident with the transition from childhood to adolescence.

Schools are concerned, among other things, with cultural maintenance; however, the increasing multiculturalism of contemporary communities raises the question of "Whose culture?". This question takes on a very personal dimension once it is recognized that mathematics (as one aspect of culture) is constructed by individuals both independent of formal schooling and coincident with formal schooling. Studies of the development of mathematical knowledge have frequently adopted a product-oriented approach, where the concern was with the identification of competence levels within a population, or a clinical approach, where the concern was with the processes of individual cognition. Neither approach can adequately describe the process of learning mathematics; in particular, because both fail to give practical recognition to the social context in which personal mathematics is constructed and mathematical competence attained and displayed. This social context takes in the school as the purveyor of the commodity "school mathematics"; the home as the embodiment of certain values and beliefs relating to education and the utility of mathematics; community, society and culture as enfolding environments; and the mathematics classroom as the location explicitly identified with the learning of mathematics.

> The same effort which secondary schools expend in developing familiarity as an aid to social adjustment must be exerted in presenting new mathematics content in ways familiar to the student, drawing on instructional techniques and cognitive strategies with which the student is already confident.

This approach would involve changes in the nature of communication in the secondary mathematics classroom, calling for an increase in the opportunity provided for students to express their mathematical understandings and articulate their strategies, and for constructive teacher-student dialogue about learning to be a regular part of the classroom routine.

Andrea's successful negotiation of the passage from childhood to adolescence encouraged an optimistic approach to the academic aspects of transition. Bernie had the courage to give the academic challenge priority over social alliances with evident success. The pathways by which students made their transition to secondary school were many, various, and highly idiosyncratic. It is clear that a theory of transition cannot prescribe an optimal pathway for any individual. However, this discussion has set out those factors which appeared to exert the most significant influence. Where possible, recommendations have been made concerning practices by which the challenge of secondary mathematics might be more likely to result in a student's personal growth.

The transition from primary to secondary mathematics appears to involve separate adjustments within the domain of each element of mathematical behavior, and these may occur at entirely different times. The necessity to employ a model of mathematical behavior which provides a means of relating the environmental and personal with the affective and cognitive is clear. The most significant finding of this study and its most emphatic statement concerning the commencement of secondary school mathematics is that the social and academic adjustments required by transition are inextricably linked and, in many ways, mirror each other. Attempts to facilitate student development must acknowledge this.

REFERENCES

Clarke, D.J. (1985). The impact of secondary schooling and secondary mathematics on student mathematical behaviour. *Educational Studies in Mathematics, 16*(3), 231-251.

Clarke, D.J. (1986). Conceptions of mathematical competence. *Research in Mathematics Education in Australia, 2,* 17-23.

Clarke, D.J. (1987a). The interactive monitoring of children's learning of mathematics. *For the Learning of Mathematics, 7*(1), 2-6.

Clarke, D.J. (1987b). *The social dynamics of the mathematics classroom.* Paper presented to the 10th annual conference of the Mathematics Education Research Group of Australasia, James Cook University of North Queensland, Townsville.

Clarke, D.J. (1989a). *Mathematical behaviour and the transition from primary to secondary school.* Unpublished doctoral thesis, Monash University, Clayton, Victoria, Australia.

Clarke, D.J. (1989b). *Assessment alternatives in mathematics.* Canberra: Curriculum Development Centre.

Clarke, D.J. (1992). *Finding structure in diversity: The study of mathematical behavior.* Paper presented to the 1992 Research Pre-session of the National Council of Teachers of Mathematics Annual Conference, Nashville.

Power, C., & Cotterell, J. (1981). *Changes in students in the transition between primary and secondary school* (ERDC Report No. 27). Canberra: Australian Government Printing Service.

Sullivan, P.A., & Clarke, D.J. (1991a). Catering to all abilities through "Good" questions. *Arithmetic Teacher 39*(2), 14-18.

Sullivan, P.A., & Clarke, D.J. (1991b). *Communication in the classroom: The importance of good questioning.* Geelong, Australia: Deakin University Press.

Yackel, E., Cobb, P., Wood, T., Wheatley, G., & Merkel, G. (1990). The importance of social interactions in children's construction of mathematical knowledge. In T. Cooney (Ed.), *1990 Yearbook of the National Council of Teachers of Mathematics* (pp. 12-21). Reston, VA: National Council of Teachers of Mathematics.

MATHEMATICIANS AND MATHEMATICAL EDUCATION IN ANCIENT MAYA SOCIETY

Michael P. Closs

University of Ottawa, Canada

The Classic Period of the ancient Maya is usually assigned to the centuries from A.D. 300 to A.D. 900. After this period, the Maya civilization continued in existence until the Spanish conquest in the 1540's. Perhaps the most brilliant achievement of the Maya was the development of a system of writing that accurately reflected the sounds of human speech. It consisted of large numbers of intricate logographic and syllabic signs commonly referred to as hieroglyph*s*, or more briefly *glyphs*. The last independent Maya kingdom, still using the ancient writing system, was not reduced until 1696.

Diego de Landa, who had joined the Franciscan Order in Toledo in 1540, first came to Yucatan in 1549. In 1564 he returned to Spain to take part in an inquiry concerning charges about his behavior towards the natives. Around 1566, while in Spain, he wrote an account of the history and traditions of the Maya people (Tozzer, 1941). This work includes practically every phase of the social anthropology of the ancient Maya, much of it supplied by learned native informants. In particular, it contains the first accurate information (in a European language) on the principal Maya calendars and writing system and provides us with some information concerning Maya education. By 1573, Landa, having been exonerated by the inquiry, returned again to the New World where he took office as the second Bishop of Yucatan.

Today we have access to large numbers of pre-Columbian Maya texts. The inventory includes four screen-fold books called codices, thousands of carved stone monuments, and thousands of ceramic vessels. The ability to read such texts was lost within a few hundred years of the conquest. However, through the painstaking labor of a relatively small number of scholars over the last century, we are now able to read, in part, the script. Impressive advances in decipherment have been made in the last few decades. Although many questions remain, there is widespread agreement on the linguistic interpretation of numerous glyphs.

Texts relating to Maya numeration, chronology, calendars, and astronomy were among the first to be understood. These texts show that the ancient Maya employed positional notation and a zero. They also performed sophisticated calendrical and chronological calculations using tables of multiples and a form of residue arithmetic. Their mathematical virtuosity is best indicated by their astronomical achievements. A record of a commensuration of the natural cycle of Venus with their 260- and 365-day calendars has survived in the Dresden Codex in the form of a five-page Venus table. This table maintained its astronomical integrity over several hundreds of years by employing calculation factors embedded within a preface to the table. A second multi-page table in the Dresden Codex commensurates solar and lunar eclipses with the 260-day calendar. This table enabled the Maya to predict potential solar and lunar eclipses, both of which were regarded with an apocalyptic fear. Again, there are mechanisms in the table that allowed it to be serviceable over several hundreds of years.

The common notation for numbers in Maya writing consisted of bars having value 5 and dots having value 1. Combinations of bars and dots were used to represent numbers from 1 to 19. There were also special symbols for zero and twenty. In the surviving Maya texts, these numbers were almost always used for recording chronological counts and calendar dates.

Chronological counts were expressed in two fashions. One method was to attach numerical prefixes to glyphs representing the chronological periods involved: *k'ins* (days), *winals* (periods of twenty days), *tuns* (periods of 360 days), and vigesimal multiples of the *tun*, most commonly the *k'atun* (= 20 *tuns*) and the *baktun* (= 400 *tuns*). The second method employed a system of positional notation in which the lowest position was reserved for the *k'in* count, the next higher position was reserved for the *winal* count, and successively higher positions were used for the place values of the vigesimal *tun* count. The zero signs were used in both types of representations.

THE ANCIENT MAYA CURRICULUM

Landa's manuscript provides some details on the subjects studied by the ancient scribes during the last few centuries before the conquest. The archaeological and epigraphic evidence suggest that this information can be extrapolated back to the Classic Period with considerable consistency. Landa (Tozzer, 1941: 27-28) describes the scribal curriculum in the following words. "The sciences which they taught were the computation of the years, months and days, the festivals and ceremonies, the administration of the sacraments, the fateful days and seasons, their methods of divination and their prophecies, events and the cures for diseases, and their antiquities and how to read and write with the letters and characters, with which they wrote, and drawings which illustrate the meanings of the writings."

The computation of the years, months, and days refers to chronological reckoning, that is to the count of *tuns*, *winals*, and *k'ins*. It is perhaps the most common application of Maya mathematical skills found in the ancient inscriptions. A second reference to this type of computation is made elsewhere, when Landa (Tozzer, 1941: 168) writes that "... this computation of katuns ... was the science to which they gave the most credit, and that which they valued most and not all the priests knew how to describe it." The last comment is of great import since it tells us that not all scribes were competent in areas requiring some degree of mathematical specialization. Moreover, those who had such competence also acquired a higher prestige.

Drawing on our knowledge of the content of the ancient Maya writings and on Landa's remarks, it is possible to offer a summary of the ancient Maya school curriculum. The subjects should be divided into two categories, according as some mathematical specialization is required for the subject matter or is not. I would describe the curriculum as follows.

Arts and Letters: agriculture; disease and medicine; drawing and painting; history; mythology; reading and writing with Maya glyphs; religious ceremonies; tribute and commerce.

Mathematical Sciences: astronomy; chronology and calendrics; divination and prophecy; genealogy.

Evidence that there was a similar division in the curriculum during the Classic Period comes from two sources. One of these relates to the depictions of Maya mathematicians as a distinctive subgroup of scribes, of which more will be said later. The other is a Classic Maya vessel from around A.D. 750 showing back-to-back classroom scenes (Figure 1).

Figure 1. Rollout of a Classic Maya vase depicting back to back classroom scenes (Kerr, 1989: 67).

Both of the scenes illustrate a patron deity of scribes, Pauahtun, instructing two students. Pauahtun can be recognized by his aged face and net headdress. In each case, the first student is the same individual. He is named in a glyphic caption above his neck and back. The second student is clearly different in the two scenes.

In the first case, a speech scroll issues from Pauahtun's mouth and leads to an initial glyph that can be analyzed phonetically as ta-ta-bi, for *tatab* or *tatabil*, inflections of a verb pertaining to written works or sermons. In the second scene, Pauahtun is sitting before a folded codex and holds a paintbrush in his left hand. A speech scroll issues from his mouth leading to a sequence of bar and dot numerals: 11, 13, 12, 9, 8, 7.

The vessel portrays two different aspects of the scribal curriculum in a straightforward manner. The first scene pertains to written works (the literary arts) whereas the second pertains to mathematics. It confirms the notion that mathematics was regarded as a specialization in scribal studies.

THE EDUCATIONAL ESTABLISHMENT

Landa (Tozzer, 1941: 27) also writes of the organization and function of scribe teachers in Maya society.

> ... they had a high priest whom they called Ah Kin Mai and by another name Ahau Can Mai, which means the priest Mai, or the high-priest Mai. He was very much respected by the lords and had no repartimiento of Indians, but besides the offerings, the lords made him presents and all the priests of the towns brought contributions to him, and his sons or his nearest relatives succeeded him in his office. In him was the key of their learning and it was to these matters that they dedicated themselves mostly; and they gave advice to the lords and replies to their questions. He seldom dealt with matters pertaining to the sacrifices except at the time of the principal feasts or in very important matters of business. They provided priests for the towns when they were needed, examining them in the sciences and ceremonies, and committed to them the duties of their office, and the good example to people and provided them with books and sent them forth. And they employed themselves in the duties of the temples and in teaching their sciences as well as in writing books about them.
>
> They taught the sons of the other priests and the second sons of the lords who brought them for this purpose from their infancy, if they saw that they had an inclination for this profession.

Landa begins his account, by mentioning the sage who presided at the top of the educational pyramid. His specific reference is to a priest (*Ah K'in*) or high-priest (*Ahau Can*) with the surname Mai. However, the second title includes the term *ahau* "lord" and informs us that the person in question is a Maya noble. This reality is apparent from his relationship to other lords (who "made him presents" and by whom he was "very much respected") and priests (who "brought contributions to him"). Moreover, it is implied by the hereditary nature of the office he held. I will refer to the person occupying this high office as a *scribe lord*.

The scribe lord, and the master scribes under him (for Landa lapses into the plural), rarely dealt with religious matters. They were primarily educators who "provided priests for the towns when they were needed, examining them in the sciences and ceremonies". They assigned to the priests "the duties of their office" and "provided them with books and sent them forth". Above all, they were engaged "in teaching their sciences as well as in writing books about them".

Figure 2. A Classic Maya polychrome plate in which the central image is a scribe lord seated on a throne (Coe, 1977: Fig. 7, pp. 336-337; drawing by Diane G. Peck).

This late pre-conquest model of scribal organization can also be extended back to the Classic Period. Indeed, I would argue that the central figure on a Classic Maya polychrome plate, previously described by Michael Coe (1977: 336-337), is a frontal portrait of a scribe lord seated on a stone throne (Figure 2). Coe has suggested that this figure is a young god with waterlily headdress and a vertical row of death spots on the cheek. I interpret these spots as personalized scars. In his right hand is a conch-shell ink pot; in his left hand is a feather pen. Placed above his ear is a deer ear with an infixed glyphic element often found on scribal figures. Around the sloping inner wall of the plate are eight figures arranged in four pairs. Dividing two of the pairs from the other two are jaguar-skin bundles (one seems to be a throne) with conch-shell ink pots on top. The pair immediately above the central scene consists of two individuals with deer-like extra ears having the same glyphic infix noted above, and with monkey-like features super-imposed on human forms. Coe refers to these as monkey-men. They gesture towards what may be a codex. Two of the other pairs are engaged in painting masks. One member of each pair is a monkey-man, the other being a Fox God. Both members of each pair wear the extra deer ear with infixed glyphic element and the net headdresses characteristic of Pauahtun, a patron of scribes. The scenes around the edge of the plate represent supernaturals engaged in scribal activities of painting and writing over which the scribe lord has charge.

A second depiction of the same scribe lord appears on another Classic polychrome vessel also described by Coe (1977: 332, 336). I would identify the theme of the vase painting as a classroom scene set in a palace (Figure 3). On one side, the scribe lord is seated upon the same throne as before but now in a profile view. He has the same vertical line of spots on the cheek, the same waterlily headdress, and is likely wearing the same pectoral ornament. An apprentice scribe is seated on a dais in front of him, and is shown painting a mask. Seated on the floor, with his back to the scribe lord, is a Vulture God (?) holding a pen above a closed codex upon which rests a conch-shell ink pot. I suggest that the scene represents an apprentice scribe practising his painting skills under the watchful gaze of a scribe lord. The student may be the son of a ruler since he is shown seated on a dais. The codex with ink pot and pen are in the care of a supernatural servant of the scribe lord, probably until the apprentice is ready to begin another stage of his studies.

Figure 3. Rollout of a Classic Maya vase showing a scribe lord and student (Kerr, 1989: 39).

MATHEMATICS IN MAYA ICONOGRAPHY

Mathematics, as a discipline, had sufficient presence and concreteness in Maya thought that it is incorporated as an element in the iconography of Maya artists and in the paleography of Maya scribes. An excellent example of this has already been seen in the pottery scene of the mathematics lecture (Figure 1). Other examples are found in the Madrid Codex, a pre-Columbian Maya book dating from around A.D. 1325. The three section almanac on pages 22d-23d of this codex is a case in point (Figure 4). In the first section, the Maya god Itsamna, to whom was attributed the invention of writing, is seated and holds a vessel of black paint in one hand and a brush for painting or writing in the other. His name glyph and an augural glyph occur above the scene. The middle section illustrates the death god. His name and an augury of death appears in the associated glyphic text. The last section portrays the seated rain god Chak holding a brush and ink pot. The generic term for "god" and an augural glyph is recorded above the scene.

Figure 4. The almanac on pages 22d-23d of the Madrid Codex.

The brush and ink pot shown in the first and last sections are the tools of scribes and painters. They are intended to indicate the activities of the deities wielding them. Of special interest in the last section is a scroll with bar and dot numerals, coming out of the mouth of Chak. In this instance the iconography tells us that the rain god is not only engaged in writing but is doing some specialized writing involving mathematics.

A related almanac on page 23c of the Madrid Codex is also divided into three sections. The first and the last sections each show a god, Itsamna and a generic deity respectively, seated in front of a temple and, as in the above example, holding a paint brush and an ink pot. The middle section does not have a picture but the glyphic text names the death god as the protagonist. Interestingly, the initial glyph in the passage, the verb of the sentence, describes the action that would be represented if there had been a picture below. Jim Fox (cited in Justeson, 1984: 344) has read this glyph as *u ts'ib*, "his writing, painting." That reading has since been fully substantiated by David Stuart (1987: 1-11). Thus there is linguistic justification for the belief that scenes in which figures are holding a paint brush and ink pot do indicate that the figure is writing or painting.

The almanac on page 73b of the Madrid Codex also depicts the rain god Chak with a number scroll coming out of his mouth (Figure 5). Once again he is holding a paint brush and ink pot, suggesting that he is getting ready to do some mathematical writing or calculation. Such scenes emphasize that Maya scribes distinguished between ordinary and mathematical writing.

Figure 5. The almanac on page 73b of the Madrid Codex.

That the distinction also existed in the Classic Period is shown by a polychrome vessel illustrated and discussed by Coe (1978: 106-110). Among the various deities represented are a pair who are clearly connected with writing (Figure 6). The deity on the right has the facial features of a monkey and carries a codex with effigy head in his right hand. The deity on the left holds one hand to the back of the former figure and carries a conch-shell paint pot in the other. Of special interest is a vegetative scroll, containing bar and dot numerals, which emanates from his armpit. There is also a curl, with single digits, running down from his cheek. Coe describes this pair of seated deities as supernatural patrons of mathematics and writing. The existence of such a pair, one with number scrolls and one with a codex, underlines the distinction which has been made between mathematics and writing in Maya iconography.

Figure 6. Gods of mathematics and writing portrayed on a
Classic Maya vase (Coe, 1978: 109-110).

MATHEMATICIANS

The divine patron of mathematics described above is not the only scribe figure having a number scroll emanating from his armpit. The same feature is also found on a number of human scribes portrayed on Maya ceramics (Stuart, 1987: Fig. 12; Schele & Miller, 1986: Pl. 47; Robicsek & Hales, 1981: Vessel 62). This iconographic convention surely marks these scribes as mathematical specialists.

One Classic Maya vase portrays two seated scribes writing in opened codices bound in jaguar skin (Figure 7). It may be noted that only the second scribe has a number scroll emanating from the armpit. This indicates that while both scribes have been trained in the art of writing, it is only the second who is a mathematician. The differentiation in the portraits of the two scribes supports the notion that the mathematical specialists used the number scroll as a rank symbol to distinguish themselves from other scribes. This is exactly the type of differentiation implied by Landa's comment that not all scribes understood the "computation of the katuns" and that those who did so acquired additional prestige.

Figure 7. Rollout of a Classic Maya vase showing two seated
scribes (Robicsek & Hales, 1981: Vessel 71).

85

Another Classic Maya vase of special interest shows two young scribes, with distinct facial characteristics, writing in opened codices bound in jaguar skin (Figure 8). They have large vegetal scrolls emanating from their armpits with bar and dot numbers upon them. In the first case, the number 13 is clearly rendered, while in the second case, only remnants of the numbers, effaced by erosion, remain. A skyband containing astronomical symbols in rectangular cartouches runs around the upper edge of the vase. The portion of the skyband above the first scribe begins with a cartouche containing the symbol for Venus and the portion above the second scribe begins with a cartouche containing the symbol for Sun. This indicates that the scribes are indeed engaged in an activity for which mathematical specialization is required. They are working on astronomical texts. Since the vase lacks a glyphic inscription, the content of the image must be interpreted through the iconography alone. This underscores the importance of the skyband and affirms the hypothesis that the number scrolls are emblematic of mathematical specialists.

Figure 8. The vase of the Maya astronomers (Robicsek & Hales 1981: Vessel 61; drawing by Michael Closs).

A third Classic Maya vase of unusual importance in the present context exhibits a complex palace scene and lengthy, but for the most part opaque, glyphic text (Figure 9). The central figure is an anthropomorphic supernatural with deer ears and hooves seated on a dais. He is apparently being tickled by a woman standing behind him and is busy vomiting into a bowl held in one hand by an elderly woman who filters the vomit with her other hand. Two other women are seated further back on the dais, one of whom is gazing into a mirror. Facing the central figure is a kneeling scribe mathematician. In this case the scroll emanating from the armpit contains the sequence 13, 1, 2, 3, 4, 5, 6, 7, 8, 9.

In the vignette at the upper right of the illustration is the small picture of a seated scribe. It comes at the end of the glyphic text and appears to be added as a final comment. This strongly suggests that it is a self-portrait of the scribe who painted the scene and text on the vessel. The artifact provides good evidence that some, if not most, of the Maya vessels with scribe scenes portray contemporaneous individuals and not supernatural entities.

Figure 9. A Classic Maya vase showing vomit scene and scribe mathematicians (Clarkson, 1978: Fig. 5).

Persis Clarkson (1978) has described the scribe in the vignette as a woman. She is depicted with a number scroll emanating from her armpit, writing in a codex. The scroll identifies her as a mathematical specialist. The last glyph in the associated text is a title read as *Ah Ts'ib*, "The Scribe" (Stuart, 1987: 2). Given the likely syntax of the text, the name of the scribe should precede the title. If this is the case, then we have both the name and the portrait of a mathematician. It is remarkable that the first mathematician to be identified in this way among the ancient Maya is a woman!

The existence of female scribes among the Maya is attested by yet another ceramic vessel that has been examined by the author (Closs, 1992). The glyphic text on this artifact includes a parentage statement in which the mother is a noble woman called "Lady Scribe Sky, Lady Jaguar Lord, the scribe" (Figure 10). Not only does she carry the scribe title at the end of her name phrase but she incorporates it into one of her proper names, an indication of the importance she herself placed on that reality.

Figure 10. Lady Scribe Sky, Lady Jaguar Lord, the scribe (drawing by Michael Closs).

87

ACKNOWLEDGEMENT

This work has been supported by a research grant (410-89-0451) from the Social Sciences and Humanities Research Council of Canada.

REFERENCES

Clarkson, P.B. (1978). Classic Maya pictorial ceramics: a survey of content and theme. In R. Sidrys (Ed.), *Papers on the Economy and Architecture of the ancient Maya* (pp. 86-141). Institute of Archaeology, Monograph 7. Los Angeles: University of California.

Closs, M.P. (1992). *I Am a kahal; My parents were scribes*. Research Reports on Ancient Maya Writing, 39. Washington: Center for Maya Research.

Coe, M.D. (1977). Supernatural patrons of Maya scribes and artists. In N. Hammond (Ed.), *Social Process in Maya Prehistory* (pp. 327-347). London: Academic Press.

Coe, M.D. (1978). *Lords of the underworld: Masterpieces of classic Maya ceramics*. Princeton: Princeton University Press.

Justeson, J.S. (1984). Appendix B: Interpretation of Mayan hieroglyphs. In J. S. Justeson and L. Campbell (Eds.), *Phoneticism in Mayan hieroglyphic writing* (pp. 315-362). Institute for Mesoamerican Studies, Publication No. 9. Albany, NY: State University of New York at Albany.

Kerr, J. (1989). *The Maya vase book: A corpus of rollout photographs of Maya vases, Volume 1*. New York: Kerr Associates.

Robicsek, F., & Hales, D.M. (1981). *The Maya book of the dead: The ceramic codex*. Charlottesville, VA: The University of Virginia Art Museum; (distributed by the University of Oklahoma Press).

Schele, L., & Miller, M.E. (1986). *The blood of kings*. Fort Worth: Kimbell Art Museum.

Stuart, D. (1987). *Ten phonetic syllables*. Research Reports on Ancient Maya Writing, 14. Washington: Center for Maya Research.

Tozzer, A. M. (1941). *Landa's Relacion de las Cosas de Yucatan*. A translation, edited with notes. Papers of the Peabody Museum, Vol. 18. Cambridge MA: Harvard University.

LES MATHÉMATIQUES
COMME REFLET D'UNE CULTURE

Jean Dhombres

Université de Nantes, France

Culture : quoique peu souvent prononcé, voilà bien un mot qui pourrait servir de bannière sous laquelle rassembler la plupart des questions soulevées à l'occasion du septième Congrès international sur l'enseignement des mathématiques. C'est précisément parce que les mathématiques constituent une composante fondamentale de la culture, dans ses modes d'expression, dans ses représentations comme dans ses ressorts cachés, que leur enseignement soulève tant d'intérêt, tant de passion, mais aussi tant de difficulté. Culture et non technique puisque, tout comme la musique, la mathématique n'est pas réductible à un solfège.

Or elle fait partie du savoir élémentaire de ceux qui ont suivi une scolarité, et même s'il faut sans cesse rappeler que dans le monde d'aujourd'hui encore bien des hommes et des femmes n'ont pas eu cette opportunité, l'installation des mathématiques à la base de toute formation est un fait majeur de civilisation. Par contraste, soulignons que dans les collèges français d'il y a un peu plus de deux siècles, la mathématique se présentait toujours comme optionnelle. Ni Robespierre ni Talleyrand n'en fréquentèrent les bancs. À la même époque, aux *Tripos* de Cambridge, résoudre une équation du second degré relevait de la performance !

Parce que les angles d'attaque sont très nombreux — la vitalité de la didactique des mathématiques en témoigne lors de ce congrès tenu à Québec — mon propos ne saurait être une analyse des conditions de l'intégration culturelle des mathématiques dans la société d'aujourd'hui, quand bien même je me résoudrais à adopter une perspective historique, laquelle m'obligerait tout aussitôt à parler de sociétés au pluriel. C'est dans une direction tout autre que je vous convie à porter le regard, comme un retournement même de la problématique habituelle.

Retournement sur le fond, car au lieu de chercher l'expression des mathématiques dans la culture générale, c'est dans leur cœur même que je vous propose de lire les modes culturels d'une époque.

Retournement dans le temps, car c'est dans le monde baroque des XVIe et XVIIe siècles que je vous invite à un voyage, un monde réduit à l'Europe pour ne pas faire trop long.

Mais deux mots encore avant le départ, en guise de précaution. En associant mathématique et baroque, en visant une époque bien déterminée de l'histoire, un siècle et demi entre le sac de Rome par les lansquenets de Charles Quint en 1527 et la fondation des grandes académies scientifiques vers 1660, je vise aussi et simultanément une science. Et j'associe cette science à l'histoire d'une façon particulière puisque, l'adjectif baroque l'annonçant, je vais évoquer un style. Dans ma ligne de mire, il y donc une forme.

MATHÉMATIQUES ET HISTOIRE : UN COUPLE ANTAGONISTE

C'est grâce à cette forme — ou à ces formes — qu'une époque — l'ère baroque — put exprimer des faits, des résultats, des raisonnements, décrire des objets, faire du nouveau ou refaire de l'ancien dans l'ordre mathématique. Je n'ai alors besoin d'aucune précaution oratoire pour me défier de l'analogie, causalité ou corrélation, des mathématiques à l'art ou de l'art aux mathématiques, puisque j'ai établi mes barrières à l'intérieur d'un seul champ, celui de la mathématique.

Certes, la forme, le regard qu'on lui porte, le discours qui la décrit, c'est ce qui appartient très certainement au critique d'art, au commentateur, j'allais dire plus simplement au consommateur. Et je brûle d'envie de vous rendre consommateur de la mathématique des années 1600 et suivantes. Ma subjectivité se servira d'outils artistiques, de critique artistique dois-je aussitôt corriger, pour viser, pour rendre compte de ces mathématiques, ou plutôt de certaines de ces mathématiques seulement (car vous vous doutez qu'il y a un choix). Je ne requiers donc nulle antériorité de la science sur l'art. On peut tour à tour les valoriser en certaines occasions; *hic et nunc*, je ne soutiens pas l'une par l'autre.

Autre versant, trop classique, forme et contenu. Il est clair, au moins pour moi, que si je traite l'œuvre de science comme une œuvre d'art, comme une construction manifestant un style, une architecture par laquelle s'engage un homme seul — l'auteur — ce n'est nullement pour refouler le contenu. Ma démarche relève d'une quête épistémologique sur les procédures et les imaginations par lesquelles fut, une fois, posé puis approprié ce qui est devenu un patrimoine scientifique, patrimoine nécessairement banalisé et réduit par la pratique scolaire.

De la géométrie algébrique dont il va être question, en un sens bien différent de celui aujourd'hui adopté, j'entends faire une unité stylistique, c'est-à-dire que je me refuse à la réduire à ses deux composantes, géométrie et algèbre, car un ou des hommes incarnés dans l'histoire la pensèrent de cette façon unitaire.

Le « comment » de l'origine de cette géométrie algébrique n'est donc nullement la géométrie algébrique toute prête, telle qu'on l'enseigne et la pratique aujourd'hui. Ce « comment » est l'atteinte d'une conscience initiale qui fut en même temps une intuition d'essence et détermina un horizon. Deux faits irréductibles sont en présence : le projet et l'effectuation de la géométrie algébrique se déroulèrent dans la conscience subjective de ou des inventeurs, dans leur univers spirituel d'une part. D'autre part, la géométrie algébrique n'est pas dans la seule existence psychique : elle n'est pas existence de quelque chose de personnel dans la sphère de la conscience ; elle est désormais existence d'un être-là, objectivement, pour tout le monde.

Voilà deux extrêmes qui doivent encadrer notre voyage, *all the way.*

MARQUES EXTÉRIEURES DU BAROQUE ET DU CLASSICISME EN MATHÉMATIQUES

Style, ai-je annoncé. Qui, se penchant sur les années 1630-1650, ne consentirait à reconnaître au moins l'opposition entre une mathématique « grasse » ou « copieuse » et une mathématique « maigre » ? Comment ne pas soupeser en effet d'un côté les 1225 pages in-folio du *P. Gregorii a Sto Vincentio Opus geometricum quadraturæ circuli et sectionum coni decem libris comprehensum*[1], et de l'autre les quelques feuillets de *La géométrie* de Descartes (ouvrage paru dix ans plus tôt à Leyde[2]) ? D'ailleurs, le jugement du Français sur l'ouvrage de Grégoire de Saint-Vincent s'engage précisément dans le sens d'une condamnation de l'obésité :

> [...] je n'ai encore rien rencontré dans tout ce gros livre, sinon des propositions si simples et si faciles que l'auteur me semble avoir mérité plus de blâme d'avoir employé son temps à les écrire, que de gloire à les avoir inventées[3].

Tous les contemporains soulignent cette opposition : Mersenne, Huygens, Roberval, etc. Baroque contre classicisme ? Nous n'en sommes pas là ; j'ai prévenu d'entrée de jeu que je ne m'arrêterais pas à des formes extérieures, quoiqu'elles aident cependant à classer.

---

[1] Ouvrage paru chez I. et I. Meursios, à Anvers en 1647, et copieusement illustré.

[2] Le *Discours de la méthode* occupe 78 pages. La *Géométrie*, qui est « un des Essais de cette méthode », couvre 117 pages, sous un format réduit.

[3] Lettre du 9 avril 1649 de Descartes à van Schooten, Correspondance, *Œuvres de Descartes*, A. Adam et P. Tannery (éd.), Paris, t. III.

Ne cédons pas non plus à la tentation de réduire la comparaison des deux ouvrages à une différence d'acuité intellectuelle qui serait manifestée aujourd'hui par la différence de renom : si elle est facile à constater, l'épais ouvrage du jésuite flamand n'en contient pas moins la première démonstration du comportement logarithmique des aires sous l'hyperbole (un résultat tout à fait remarquable sur le plan purement technique et de portée théorique notable), ainsi que la résolution du paradoxe de Zénon — celui d'Achille et de la tortue — par sommation de séries géométriques infinies (une première mathématique indéniable, grosse d'une longue tradition philosophique). Le lourd in-folio d'Anvers comporte également un traitement des cubatures au moyen d'un procédé *nouveau*, le *ductus*, procédé propre à préparer — ce qui ne veut pas dire inventer — le calcul intégral, et en tout cas à familiariser les esprits avec la géométrie dans l'espace, deux domaines notablement absents du si petit et si remarquable traité de René Descartes. Tout cela était apprécié des contemporains.

Derechef, entrons dans l'explication de la résolution mémorable du paradoxe de Zénon. Elle débute par une expérience quasiment visuelle de géométrie.

LA GÉOMÉTRIE PREMIÈRE

Le donné que Grégoire de Saint-Vincent donne à voir est un triangle OAB avec choix arbitraire d'un point C entre les points A et B, point déterminant une sécante OC. De C, on mène une parallèle au côté OB coupant le côté OA en A_2, puis une parallèle à AB coupant OC en C_2, puis une parallèle à OB, puis une parallèle à AB, et ainsi de suite. Alternativement sur le côté OA et sur la sécante OC, deux familles de points sont ainsi établies A, A_2, A_3, A_4, A_5, etc. ; C, C_2, C_3, C_4, etc. De même, en prolongeant les parallèles, intervient sur AB une famille A, C, D_2, D_3, D_4, etc., et sur OB une autre famille B, B_2, B_3, B_4, etc.

Tirant parti de la double famille de droites parallèles, une multiple application du théorème, dit de Thalès en France, fournit itérativement la stabilité du rapport[4]

---

4   En repérant l'usage du théorème de Thalès par des triangles, on a en effet :

$$\frac{AC}{A_2C_2} = \frac{OA}{OA_2} \quad \text{(triangles } OAC \text{ et } OA_2C_2)$$

$$= \frac{OC}{OC_2} \quad \text{(triangles } OAC \text{ et } OA_2C_2)$$

$$= \frac{OA_2}{OA_3} \quad \text{(triangles } OA_2C \text{ et } OA_3C_2)$$

$$= \frac{A_2C_2}{A_3C_3} \quad \text{(triangles } OA_2C_2 \text{ et } OA_3C_3).$$

L'itération est acquise puisque $\dfrac{OA_2}{OA_3} = \dfrac{OC_2}{OC_3}$ (triangles OA_2C_2 et OA_3C_3).

$$\frac{AC}{A_2C_2} = \frac{A_2C_2}{A_3C_3} = \frac{A_3C_3}{A_4C_4} = \cdots .$$

Par conséquent, on obtient autant de progressions géométriques[5] sur les droites OA, OB, OC ou AB. Qui plus est, la figure géométrique décompose le continu ou segment AB selon un empilage de segments visuellement distincts AC, A_2C_2 (= CD_2), A_3C_3 (= D_2D_3), etc. Il en est de même pour le continu OB, décomposé en A_2C (= B_2B), A_3C_2 (= B_3B_2), A_4C_3 (= B_4B_3), etc. Cet empilage est une somme — infinie. Dès lors, à partir de ses deux seuls premiers termes, il n'est plus difficile d'évaluer en toute généralité la somme d'une progression géométrique que l'on écrit aujourd'hui avec des points de suspension :

$$AB = AC + CD_2 + D_2D_3 + D_3D_4 + \dots$$
$$= AC + A_2C_2 + A_3C_3 + A_4C_4 + \dots .$$

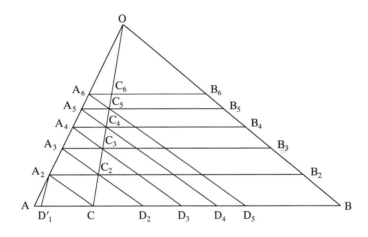

Figure 1

En effet, la stabilité du rapport $\frac{AC}{A_2C_2}$, puis celle du rapport[6] $\frac{AB}{A_2B_2}$, en se transmettant sur la droite AB, fournit l'égalité :

$$\frac{AB}{CB} = \frac{CB}{D_2B}. \tag{1}$$

Le calcul est itératif :

$$\frac{CB}{D_2B} = \frac{D_2B}{D_3B} = \cdots .$$

[5] Proposition 70 du livre 2 de l'*Opus geometricum*. On a bien sûr (en écriture moderne) $A_nC_n = x^{n-1} AC$ pour $n \geq 2$.

[6] Grâce aux triangles OAB et OA_2B_2.

La proportion (1) se transforme en

$$\frac{AB}{CB} = \frac{AB - CB}{CB - D_2B} = \frac{AC}{CD_2},$$ (2)

que l'on modifie à son tour en tenant compte du premier et du dernier rapport en

$$\frac{AB - CB}{AB} = \frac{AC - CD_2}{AC}.$$ (3)

Finalement, la somme AB de tous les termes d'une progression géométrique dont les deux premiers termes sont AC et CD_2 s'obtient à partir d'une moyenne géométrique où ne jouent que ces deux termes :

$$\frac{AC}{AB} = \frac{AC - CD_2}{AC}.$$ (4)

Grégoire de Saint-Vincent énonce à la proposition 80 du livre 2 de son *Opus geometricum* : « la totalité est troisième proportionnelle de la différence entre les deux premiers termes et du premier terme ». Telle est la rhétorique usuelle pour l'énoncé d'un résultat qu'un moderne a plutôt tendance à écrire sous la forme

$$AB = \frac{AC^2}{AC - CD_2}.$$ (5)

En vue d'une lecture géométrique, Grégoire de Saint-Vincent pose $AD'_1 = AC - CD_2$, c'est-à-dire construit le point D'_1 à l'intersection avec la droite AB de la parallèle à OC menée par A_2.

$$AC = \sqrt{AB \cdot AD'_1}.$$

Obnubilés par le seul résultat — la formule de sommation (5) — nous ne mesurons peut-être plus aujourd'hui la force manifestée dans l'expérience visuelle donnée par la seule figure 1, cet empilage itératif de segments, et nous nous laissons prendre par les quelques calculs supplémentaires. Torricelli utilise à son tour le même dessin dans un manuscrit où il traite de la série géométrique[7]. Indéniablement, il y eut en ce début du XVIIe siècle une présence sous forme répétitive de représentations géométriques qui parlèrent à l'imagination du mathématicien.

Ce pourrait donc n'être que banal — un jeu du temps — si Grégoire de Saint-Vincent n'entreprenait pas tout aussitôt une démonstration entièrement analytique de la relation (4), démonstration qui devrait avoir pour but de renier aussi bien le dessin que la géométrie qui le porte. Or, et c'est ce qui est particulièrement significatif, il ne gomme pas le dessin, il ne le présente

---

[7]   *Opera di Evangelista Torricelli*, G. Loria e G. Vassura (ed.), De dimensione parabolæ, vol. 1, Faenza, 1919, pp. 147-148.

ni comme seulement préparatoire, ni comme artifice pédagogique. Une attitude didactique — l'indication d'un cheminement de l'intellect, du sensible figuré à l'abstrait calculé — serait pourtant justifiée puisque Grégoire de Saint-Vincent est un enseignant : toute sa vie se déroule dans le cadre éducatif mis en place par les Jésuites, les collèges ou les maisons de formation de l'Ordre, que ce soit à Rome au Collège romain, à Anvers, à Prague, à Louvain, ou à Gand où il se retira enfin. Si en toute conscience Grégoire donne simultanément et le dessin et la démarche analytique, c'est que cela convient à sa façon scientifique, et son discours explicatif doit se lire comme révélateur d'une attitude culturelle : la profusion — le mélange des genres — est la forme qu'il choisit pour annoncer ce qui sans doute aucun est un résultat original.

Mais il ne s'agit nullement d'un désordre de la pensée chez l'auteur jésuite, pas plus que la cohabitation du droit et du rond, de l'arc et de sa troncature, ne défigure la façade du Gesù de Rome dont l'effet de masse est garanti[8]. Car, à bon escient, le dessin de la figure 1 apparaît presque isolé et créant la surprise dans le livre 2 de l'*Opus geometricum*, un livre qui de fait est dédié à l'algèbre. Non pas certes l'algèbre polynomiale dont Descartes allait faire le pilier de sa méthode, mais une algèbre très particulière, celle que les siècles avaient dégagée à partir du livre V des *Éléments* d'Euclide, c'est-à-dire l'algèbre des proportions[9]. Une des identités les plus familières de cette algèbre, aussi banale qu'aujourd'hui le

$$a^2 - b^2 = (a - b)(a + b)$$

était la séquence

$$\frac{a}{b} = \frac{c}{d} = \frac{a+c}{b+d}. \tag{6}$$

Une séquence qui ne s'écrivait pourtant pas, et se prononçait : « Si a est à b comme c est à d, alors a est à b comme la somme des antécédents à la somme des conséquents. » Nous avons vu les effets de cette façon de procéder avec le passage des relations (1) à (2) et à (3). C'est souvent dans le cadre de cette seule algèbre que d'autres auteurs inscrivent le résultat manifesté par (4). La formulation (5), qui est déjà présente chez Viète[10], est reprise comme chose désormais bien connue par Fermat dans un texte écrit vers 1657 et dont il avait communiqué beaucoup plus tôt les résultats à quelques amis sous la forme :

---

8   Due à Giacomo della Porta en 1575, cette façade termine l'édifice construit par Vignola en 1568.

9   J. Dhombres, *Nombre, mesure et continu, épistémologie et histoire*, Nathan, 1978.

10   F. Viète, *Variorum de rebus mathematicis responsorum libri VIII*, Turino, 1593 ; *Opera mathematica*, Leiden, pp. 347-435.

Étant donnée une progression géométrique dont les termes décroissent à l'infini, la différence de deux termes qui constituent cette progression est au plus petit terme, comme le plus grand des termes de la progression est à la somme de tous les autres à l'infini[11].

En fixant les deux premiers termes — alors que Fermat laisse la liberté de deux termes successifs — cette formulation indique

$$\frac{AC - CD_2}{CD_2} = \frac{AC}{AB - AC},$$

dont il était immédiat de déduire par les règles des proportions la formule (5), du moins :

$$\frac{AC}{AC - CD_2} = \frac{AB}{AC}.$$

C'est pourtant dans ce monde résolument « algébrique », où les seules éventuelles figures sont des segments de droite alignés, qu'en un impromptu d'autant plus visible intervient le dessin itératif de la figure 1 chez Grégoire de Saint-Vincent. L'effet est aussi saisissant que le trompe-l'œil du Bramante à San Satiro de Milan.

L'ONTOLOGIE ANALYTIQUE

L'effet ne vaut pas preuve, mais il la souligne. Porté par un habitus culturel, le mélange opéré par Grégoire de Saint-Vincent a un sens ou, autrement dit, l'effet figuratif ne fait sens que dans la mesure où il est accompagné par la démarche analytique. Cette dernière procure un théorème d'existence, et c'est ce qui est tout à fait exceptionnel dans la mathématique du XVIe et du début XVIIe, une existence dont précisément la géométrie n'a pas à s'encombrer. Par contraste, tel est bien l'effet recherché qui favorise la prise de conscience d'un requis nouveau. La formulation quasiment scolastique du théorème indique suffisamment l'importance philosophique attribuée à la première proposition analytique que nous traduisons :

Si l'on a une grandeur AB qui soit à la grandeur BK comme la grandeur BC à la grandeur CK, je dis que la proportion de AB à BC peut être poursuivie en acte sans terme final à l'intérieur de la grandeur AK, de telle manière qu'elle ne parvienne jamais à K [12].

Figure 2

---

[11]   De æquationum localium transmutatione et emendatione ad multimodam curvilineorum inter se vel cum rectilineis comparationem, cui annectitur proportionis geometricæ in quadrandis infinitis parabolis et hyperbolis usu*s*, *Œuvres de Fermat*, P. Tannery, C. Henry, (éd.), Paris, Gauthier-Villars, t. I, pp. 255-288.

[12]   *Opus geometricum*, livre 2, proposition 75, p. 95.

En somme, si nous revenons à la figure 1, il s'agit de démontrer que, sous la seule régulation itérative, les points A, A_2, A_3,... ou les points C, C_2, C_3,... n'atteignent pas le point K. En l'occurrence, et portée sur une seule ligne, la régulation est devenue

(G_d) $$\frac{AB}{BC} = \frac{BC}{CD} = \frac{CD}{DE} = \cdots.$$

Grégoire de Saint-Vincent, minutieusement, prouve[13] que si les quatre points A, B, C et K sont placés sur une même droite de sorte que

$$\frac{AB}{BK} = \frac{BC}{CK'} \tag{7}$$

les points suivants D, E, F, etc., calculables pas à pas par la formule (G_d), sont tels que

$$CD < CK, DE < DK, EF < EK, \text{ etc.}$$

Naturellement, cette insertion selon (G_d) de points situés avant K ne donne pas le point K lui-même, point qui a d'ailleurs été *a priori* construit par la relation (7). Pourtant, l'objectif de toute la démarche consiste à obtenir K à partir de (G_d) seulement car on « voit » comment les points successifs s'en approchent. De sorte qu'une opération nouvelle doit entrer en jeu, l'attribution d'un « terme » à une série, une opération qui donnera un sens à l'écriture interminée :

$$AK = AB + BC + CD + \cdots. \tag{8}$$

La définition est magistrale : « Le terme de la progression est la fin des séries à laquelle s'il nous est permis de poursuivre à l'infini, aucune progression ne peut aboutir, mais à laquelle il est loisible d'accéder d'aussi près que de n'importe quel intervalle donné »[14]. C'est, en latin, exactement le langage des ε et des δ qu'adoptera Weierstrass au XIXe siècle, et nous à sa suite. Pour que (8) soit justifiée, il suffit avec cette définition de montrer que la suite des longueurs BK, CK, DK, etc., tend vers 0, c'est-à-dire qu'elle peut être rendue inférieure à tout segment donné. Grégoire de Saint-Vincent n'a aucun mal à fournir cette preuve.

LES OPPOSITIONS BAROQUES

Il ne s'en contente pas, ou plutôt jouant comme avec l'opposition précédente entre un dessin et un calcul, il use — procédé véritablement baroque — d'une nouvelle confrontation. Celle-ci prend comme antagonistes (G_d), que

---

[13] Pour une traduction et un commentaire de la preuve, voir J. Dhombres, Les progressions de l'infini : rôles du discret et du continu au XVIIe siècle, *Actes du colloque L'infini en mathématiques*, Brest, mai 1992, 57 p.

[14] Définition 3 du livre 2 de l'*Opus geometricum*.

je peux qualifier de règle discrète d'une part[15] et la règle (7) étendue sous une forme que je veux qualifier de règle continue :

$$(G_c) \qquad \frac{AK}{BK} = \frac{BK}{CK} = \frac{CK}{DK} = \cdots.$$

L'opposition est naturellement dans le fait que, selon (G_d), le point ultime K n'intervient pas : on construit « discrètement », pas à pas, les points successifs qui correspondent à des termes de calcul et en s'ajoutant donnent AB, AB + BC, AB + BC + CD, c'est-à-dire $a, a + ax, a + ax + ax^2$, etc., avec notre notation algébrique contemporaine. Alors que, selon la formulation (G_c), le « terme » K apparaît dès le départ pour successivement définir les points C, D, E, etc. De sorte que dans la définition (G_c) le continu AK est fondateur de la division AK, BK, CK, qui donne ensuite, mais seulement ensuite, AB + BC + CD + $\cdots$.

L'opposition est d'autant plus forte que (G_d) et (G_c) sont des règles *logiquement équivalentes*. La démonstration de cette identité n'est autre qu'une application de la loi opératoire (6) adaptée aussi bien sous forme soustractive. En effet, à partir de (G_c) il est facile de calculer

$$\frac{AK - BK}{BK} = \frac{BK - CK}{CK} = \frac{CK - DK}{DK} = \cdots,$$

soit

$$\frac{AB}{BK} = \frac{BC}{CK} = \frac{CD}{DK} = \cdots.$$

En échangeant les termes moyens dans la première proportion des égalités précédentes, on a $\frac{AB}{BC} = \frac{BK}{CK}$ et la règle (6) à nouveau appliquée fournit

$$\frac{AB}{BC} = \frac{AB + BK}{BC + CK} = \frac{AK}{BK}.$$

Par itération, on déduit aussitôt (G_d), prouvant d'ailleurs que la raison de la progression croissante AB, BC, CD, etc., est la même que celle de la progression décroissante AK, BK, CK, etc. Réciproquement, si l'on part de (G_d), et l'on prend soin de définir K par la relation (7), alors on déduit facilement (G_c). Mais définir K par (7), c'est aussi bien construire le « terme » de la série (8), ou bien appliquer (4). En termes modernes, c'est user de la sommation où n'interviennent que le premier terme et la raison de la progression :

$$(G) \qquad \frac{a}{1 - x} = \sum_{n=0}^{n=\infty} ax^n.$$

---

[15]   C'est ce qui justifie l'indice d dans (G_d).

Une lecture trop rapide de Grégoire de Saint-Vincent, notre lecture modernisante, consiste à réduire[16] tout son discours à la preuve de (G). Or le style même adopté par le professeur jésuite consiste à *juxtaposer* les équivalences (G_c) et (G_d), en profitant de l'opposition entre ce qui est construit et ce qui est donné. Michel-Ange nous surprend de la même façon par ses frêles demi-colonnes encastrées au rez-de-chaussée des arcades du palais des Conservateurs sur le Capitole à Rome : la surprise vient de ce qu'elles ne supportent rien, ce qui magnifie d'autant l'équilibre des masses par rapport au premier étage, et contraint l'œil à l'intelligence du bâtiment. Ici, dans l'*Opus geometricum*, c'est la rencontre de deux horizons qui porte la compréhension. Coexistent l'horizon du discret continué (c'est la relation (G_d)) : « J'appelle progression géométrique la succession d'un nombre quelconque de termes selon la même raison » et l'horizon du continu morcelé (c'est la relation (G_c)) : « J'appelle série géométrique une quantité finie, divisée en succession ininterrompue, selon une raison donnée quelconque ». Nous sommes tellement habitués à la première définition que la seconde nous paraît inutile !

Or, Grégoire ne présente pas un discret qui serait sommé, mais un continu dont seul le découpage est discret ; c'est tout le sens originel de la figure 1. Il fait alors voir le discret continué et, en plus, il prouve un théorème d'existence : le « terme » de la somme. L'emphase est donc nette : une somme infinie ne peut être considérée comme simple extension du cas fini ; il y faut la détermination d'un objet mathématique. Cependant, Grégoire ne fournit pas sa leçon en une glose et c'est la juxtaposition de l'analytique contre la géométrie qui la fait ressortir.

Il ne tranche pas pour autant au profit de l'analytique. Chez Grégoire, continu et discret restent à parité. Doit-on vraiment clore ce qui doit passer pour une mise en perspective ? Dans le *Mariage de la Vierge* qui est présenté à la Pinacothèque de la Brera à Milan, Raphaël n'emprisonne pas le point de fuite du regard : au-delà du long dallage qui rythme l'élévation du regard, au rez-de-chaussée du temple dont les portiques sont inscrits dans un polygone apparaît une porte à la fois ouverte et lumineuse.

Par le jeu de ces contrastes, on perçoit dans l'*Opus geometricum* toute une construction baroque dont les tensions contradictoires ne sont pas résolues ; mais il n'y a pas confusion et ce n'est pas kitsch. Si la règle (G_c) dit évidemment que tendent vers zéro les restes successifs BK, CK, DK, etc., des sommes AB, AB + BC, AB + BC + CD, etc., la régularité même de ces restes n'intervient pas pour la définition d'une limite nulle, pour la définition

---

16 Nous avons vu par exemple que la raison n'est pas intervenue dans les formules fournies par Grégoire de Saint-Vincent.

d'un « terme ». Autrement dit, pour fonder un concept, Grégoire de Saint-Vincent sait éliminer l'anecdotique, que celui-ci relève d'une figure ou d'une formule : en l'occurrence, il néglige à juste titre le fait que les restes d'une série géométrique forment aussi une progression géométrique.

La preuve de cette pensée bien structurée est assénée par la résolution du paradoxe de Zénon, celui que depuis Aristote on décrit avec l'Achille courant désespérément derrière une tortue sans parvenir à la dépasser. Cette résolution fait date.

Qu'on suppose qu'Achille le plus rapide des coureurs, partant du point A veuille rattraper une tortue qui rampe sur le chemin BC en une course très lente. Pendant le temps qu'Achille va de A à B la tortue s'est déplacée d'un certain espace et arrive à F. Donc Achille n'a pas encore rattrapé la tortue. Derechef, pendant le temps qu'Achille court à partir de B pour rattraper la tortue qui était en F, la tortue s'est déplacée jusqu'au point H. Donc Achille parvenu en F n'a pas encore rattrapé la tortue, et cela écherra indéfiniment[17].

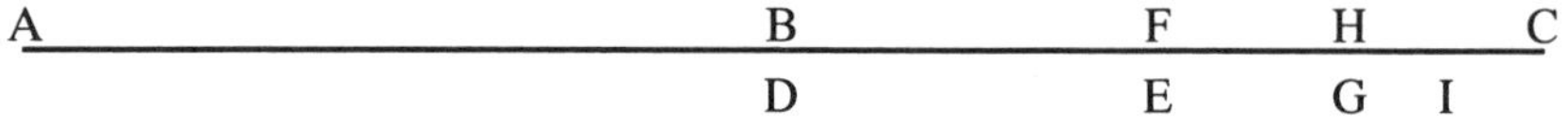

A   B   F   H   C

                         D   E   G   I

Figure 3

En choisissant d'attribuer à Achille une vitesse double de celle de la tortue, la solution proposée fonctionne à partir d'une longueur AC fixée qui sera lue sur deux niveaux, et de son milieu B. La tortue part de D, mais ce point qui coïncide avec B est placé en dessous (figure 3) et Achille quant à lui est placé en arrière au point A et ses positions successives sont indiquées en dessus. Deux progressions géométriques entrent en jeu : le mouvement d'Achille qui, par la pensée, est décomposé en segments successifs AB, BF, FH, etc., F étant le milieu de BC, H celui de FC, etc. ; et le mouvement idoine de la tortue DE, EG, GI, etc., où E est le milieu de DC, G le milieu de EC, etc.[18]. D'après la forme (G), avec $x = \frac{1}{2}$, les deux « termes » de ces progressions sont les mêmes : il s'agit du point C. Ce résultat s'obtient aussi bien avec la formulation (4) du XVIIᵉ siècle :

$$AB + BF + FH + \cdots = AC$$
$$DE + EG + \cdots = DC.$$

---

[17]   *Opus geometricum*, livre 2, p. 101.

[18]   Bien sûr, selon (G_d), $\frac{AB}{BF} = \frac{BF}{FH} = \cdots = 2$ et de même $\frac{DE}{EG} = \frac{EG}{GI} = \cdots = 2$.

    Mais, simultanément, Grégoire pose la forme (G_c)

    puisque $\frac{AC}{BC} = \frac{BC}{FC} = \frac{FC}{HC} = \cdots = 2$ ou $\frac{DC}{EC} = \frac{EC}{GC} = \frac{GC}{IC} = \cdots = 2$.

Par conséquent, Achille rencontre bien la tortue (en C) et ... Zénon n'a été qu'un philosophe « captieux ».

Le terme d'une série tel que défini par Grégoire de Saint-Vincent n'est pas un terminus. Quoique le jésuite ne poursuive pas par ce que nous attendons de lui, à savoir une théorie des séries. Mais c'est que son horizon est le continu, et les propriétés qui lui sont attachées. Le discret sommé est à ses yeux un outil, rien de plus, et il ne le travaillera pas plus. Et pourquoi faudrait-il que sous la forme des séries l'analytique triomphe, quand il s'agit de le mettre au service de la géométrie qui gère le continu ? Ce sont les oppositions et les tensions qui doivent ressortir, non l'anéantissement d'un genre par l'autre. On constate ainsi qu'une façon culturelle ne porte pas nécessairement le futur mathématique.

Tout aussi dramatiquement mises en scène, bien d'autres oppositions scandent le lourd volume de Grégoire de Saint-Vincent. Il n'hésite d'ailleurs pas à jouer de belles vignettes allégoriques — le jour et la nuit par une poule couvant de nuit ses œufs tandis que le coq annonce le jour — ou tout simplement adopte un rythme alterné de gauche à droite, et de droite à gauche pour le placement d'une branche d'hyperbole entre ses asymptotes. Un cas d'opposition savamment construit est particulièrement significatif[19]. D'un côté, Grégoire de Saint-Vincent dispose d'une propriété repérée par les axes de coordonnées (dans la figure 4, si $OB = \sqrt{OA \cdot OC}$, les aires curvilignes sous l'hyperbole ABED et BCFE sont égales) ; dans l'autre cas[20] la propriété paraît tenir aux seuls diamètres naturellement liés à la courbe (dans la figure 5, si C est le milieu de la corde AB et D désigne l'intersection de OC et de l'hyperbole, les triangles ou secteurs hyperboliques DFA et DEB possèdent la même aire). Cependant, les deux propriétés apparemment opposées des

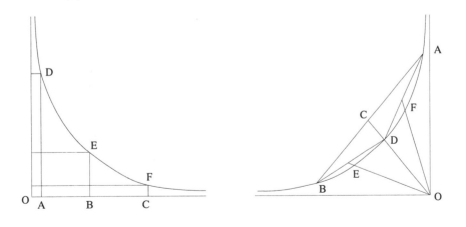

Figure 4   Figure 5

aires curvilignes (trapèzes ou triangles) sont en fait équivalentes comme il n'est pas difficile de le voir par la simple géométrie de l'application des aires[21]. De sorte que, pour l'auteur de l'*Opus geometricum*, l'analytique des coordonnées (figure 4) est placé au même niveau d'intérêt que la géométrie intrinsèque de la courbe (figure 5).

Une fois de plus, le père jésuite ne tranche pas : il juxtapose. Descartes, quant à lui, a tranché pour la seule analytique : c'est un classique !

UNE PAUSE DIDACTIQUE

Dans l'ordre pédagogique, plusieurs réflexions peuvent découler de la description historique à laquelle nous n'avons pourtant accordé qu'un court espace sans suivre l'écriture usuelle de l'histoire des mathématiques, mais, je l'espère, sans dénaturer une démarche inscrite dans le temps[22]. Je donnerai à ces remarques une rédaction succincte, quasi télégraphique. La plus simple de ces réflexions concerne d'abord la démonstration originale et plaisante de la somme d'une progression géométrique qui peut faire l'objet d'une riche séquence didactique orientée sur la géométrie[23] : les mathématiques du passé sont ainsi un grand réservoir de formes, de calculs, de présentation et tout comme le peintre se fait la main en recopiant les maîtres du passé, de même l'élève — et pourquoi pas le professeur — peut s'exercer l'esprit en reprenant les textes d'autrefois.

En adoptant de front plusieurs modes d'expression, Grégoire de Saint-Vincent invite à pratiquer une mathématique « circulaire », c'est-à-dire une mathématique qui ne soit pas une progression toujours tendue vers un plus lointain, mais au contraire où est privilégié le jeu des équivalences, avec des retours en arrière. Nous avons bien vu qu'il ne s'agissait en rien d'une mathématique du cercle vicieux, mais bien plutôt d'une mathématique que

---

[19] *Opus geometricum*, livre 6, proposition 108.

[20] *Opus geometricum*, livre 6, proposition 108.

[21] J. Dhombres, « Is one proof enough ; travels with a baroque mathematician », *Studies in Math. Education*, à paraître, avril 1994.

[22] L'histoire des mathématiques est une discipline, avec ses règles d'écriture, de citation, ses rites qui permettent aussi bien de discriminer les amateurs ; bref c'est un lieu professionnel qui n'a pas besoin de chercher en dehors de son champ propre une justification de ses objectifs ou de ses méthodes. Je n'ai pas respecté toutes ces règles dans les pages qui précèdent : je n'ai, par exemple, pas systématiquement cité le latin de Grégoire de Saint-Vincent, ni respecté ses notations, ni rendu compte linéairement de son *Opus geometricum* (puisque j'ai sélectionné une séquence particulière). Je n'ai pas plus tenté de faire la différence entre des manuscrits (datés à partir de 1617, donc bien longtemps avant la parution de l'*Opus geometricum*) et l'ouvrage publié, ni de fait raconté, même en bref, la vie de Grégoire — sa date de naissance à Bruges en 1584 ne figure pas dans mon

l'on pourrait qualifier de ludique, encore que je préférerais parler d'une mise en scène à la Pirandello : de temps à autre, on redistribue et les rôles et les cartes ! Cette scansion de l'apprentissage mathématique doit pouvoir exciter la curiosité de plus d'un élève en évitant de donner cette impression désespérante d'un espace toujours plus grand entre ce qu'on sait faire, réduit à si peu, et tout ce qu'il va falloir apprendre à faire.

Le jeu même d'une opposition volontairement maintenue entre deux approches — analytique ou géométrique ; discret ou continu — opposition reflétée aussi bien par le dessin que par le calcul et par les raisonnements, présente l'avantage de conserver la liberté de choisir[24]. Alors que, très souvent, au cours des démonstrations scolaires qui ne sont pas de pure routine, on apprend à éliminer ce qui est annexe pour ne dérouler qu'un seul fil. Ici, deux fils au moins sont constamment en cause et disponibles. Le « stress » lié à la psychologie du choix peut donc être amoindri, une situation que certains psychopédagogues reconnaissent comme favorable[25].

Grégoire de Saint-Vincent ne sépare pas l'algèbre — une certaine algèbre — de la géométrie : cette « géométrie algébrique », bien éloignée pratiquement de celle de Descartes (qui fait intervenir quant à lui le degré des courbes algébriques, la décomposition polynomiale, etc.) s'en rapproche cependant sur le plan des principes par la conjonction de deux domaines des mathématiques. Auprès des élèves, ne peut-on mieux faire saisir la force et l'efficacité de la façon cartésienne en examinant à nouveau, et avec un œil critique, la démarche grégorienne ? Chez certains enfants rebelles à l'alphabétisation, des linguopédagogues ont bien expérimenté — en Californie — l'utilisation préalable de caractères chinois pour l'apprentissage de la lecture anglaise !

---

texte jusqu'à cette ligne. Cette façon de présenter est voulue, car l'histoire des sciences entendue au sens strict n'est faite, du moins aujourd'hui, que pour les professionnels. De même que les mathématiques ou la philosophie contemporaine. Or, il doit être possible de donner de l'histoire des mathématiques, non pas une vision vulgarisée, mais en quelque sorte des applications au profit de l'enseignement. Si l'expression peut paraître exaspérante à l'historien — l'un d'entre eux a malgré tout commis en France une *Leçon d'histoire pour une gauche au pouvoir* —, elle est toute naturelle au scientifique. En décrivant un bout de l'œuvre de Grégoire de Saint-Vincent, j'ai pensé didactique. En focalisant sur la forme particulière du style d'expression sur laquelle je me suis déjà exprimé, j'ai donc réalisé une construction bien particulière. Cela ne contredit nullement le choix d'une perspective historique.

23 C'est en tout cas une façon de justifier l'adjectif « géométrique » accolé au mot série. L'habitude des manuels est de sommer une progression géométrique en termes finis, puis de passer à la limite. Grégoire de Saint-Vincent fournit une alternative heureuse. Je dis alternative, et non seule manière « historiquement » convenable !

UN BAROQUE DÉSABUSÉ

Pour évoquer jusqu'à présent le monde baroque, j'ai choisi un auteur — même une démonstration particulière de ce dernier — et tenté à partir de ce découpage de saisir des lignes de force qui me paraissent caractériser une façon historique. Les esprits positifs refuseront sans doute l'utilisation du mot « baroque », quand bien même ils adopteraient mon analyse. Mais à utiliser un autre mot, ne risquent-ils pas surtout de faire sortir du champ de l'histoire une démarche intellectuelle qui s'y inscrit pourtant.

En tout cas, l'observatoire que j'ai adopté doit être replacé dans son contexte. Grégoire de Saint-Vincent est un des nœuds du réseau jésuite des collèges, réseau établi largement dans l'Europe catholique du XVIIᵉ siècle et auquel on doit aussi bien la culture baroque[26]. Créé en 1553 par Ignace de Loyola, le Collège romain, « œil du siège apostolique et du monde chrétien[27] » selon l'ambition du fondateur, est le modèle. Modèle à la façon jésuite, qui pose comme principe la nécessaire adaptation aux circonstances et aux lieux avec, autant que de besoin, la mise en parenthèse des règles. Dans ce Collège, les mathématiques sont instituées comme un rite de passage incontournable et une indispensable formation : la chose est acquise avec Clavius, le mathématicien du Collège jusqu'en 1612, qui dirigea la réforme du calendrier adoptée par Grégoire XIV en 1582. Le Collège devint l'objet de toutes les bienveillances du Saint-Siège, au moins jusque vers 1620. Clavius « engendre » Grégoire de Saint-Vincent et bien d'autres mathématiciens, comme ce Matteo Ricci dépêché en Chine et qui, à partir de la lecture donnée par Clavius, aidé d'un converti, publie vers 1610 la traduction chinoise des six premiers livres d'Euclide. Grégoire à son tour « engendre » de Sarasa, Tacquet, Guldin, de la Faille, etc.

C'est bien avant la « révolution scientifique » que les Jésuites adoptent la mathématique ; avant en tout cas que Galilée et quelques autres ne fassent la preuve de son efficacité dans le décryptage du monde naturel. L'objectif des Jésuites n'est nullement de faire de leurs élèves des ingénieurs et encore moins des physiciens : les mathématiques sont conçues dans les collèges comme un moyen pour apprendre à penser juste. De fait, elles permettent

---

[24] R. Nimier, *Mathématiques et affectivité*, Paris, Le Seuil, 1972.

[25] C'est sans doute dans ce maintien simultané des contradictions que le baroque, tout en marquant une périodisation de l'histoire de l'art, s'inscrit constamment dans la pensée humaine. Eugenio d'Ors a écrit à ce propos quelques très belles pages auxquelles je reconnais volontiers ma dette (*Lo Barroco*; traduction française, *Du baroque*, Gallimard, 1933).

[26] Voir E. Mâle, *L'art religieux du XVIIᵉ siècle*, Paris, A. Colin, nouvelle édition, 1984.

[27] Selon la constitution du Collège.

d'évacuer une autre discipline, considérée désormais comme obsolète, et c'est bien une Europe mathématique qui se constitua ainsi contre la logique aristotélicienne (ce qui n'exclut pas des courants logicistes). Il suffira d'indiquer que la mathématique devenait une matérialisation, une concrétisation de la logique à laquelle un contenu tangible était ainsi trouvé.

L'intervention majeure des mathématiques dans les collèges jésuites ou dans les maisons des profès elles-mêmes n'est que l'un des versants de la culture ainsi propagée. L'autre versant est le peu d'intérêt porté aux résultats auxquels cette science conduit, ou peut conduire. Non seulement la démarche prime sur les objets qu'elle atteint, mais, en outre, le nombre de ces objets est réduit à ceux envisagés par les mathématiques élémentaires, *grosso modo* les mathématiques contenues dans les *Éléments* d'Euclide. Aussi belle soit-elle, la mathématique est seulement scolaire : c'est un exercice volontairement dépouillé de ses applications. De sorte que dans cette culture, l'ambition n'est pas d'ouvrir de nouvelles pistes afin d'adopter de nouvelles théories : elle serait bien plutôt la réalisation du manuel parfait, résumant toute la science euclidienne dans l'ordre le plus nécessaire. Une utopie semblable guette trop souvent les éducateurs qui n'accordent à la science dont ils ont la charge que le statut d'un apprentissage. Voilà bien une tension baroque dans l'ordre intellectuel : l'indéniable prise au sérieux des mathématiques s'oppose à leur réduction à un exercice de formation[28].

Aussi inventif soit-il — les témoignages concordent à ce sujet — Grégoire de Saint-Vincent n'échappe donc pas à la limitation euclidienne, et il inscrit étonnamment son œuvre dans une quête que, presque *a priori*, ses propositions les plus marquantes contredisent. Il veut la quadrature du cercle, c'est-à-dire la construction à la règle et au compas d'un carré d'aire égale à celle d'un cercle donné et partant la quadrature de toutes les coniques. Pourtant, son calcul des aires sous l'hyperbole — le comportement logarithmique indiqué par la proposition 108 du livre 6 (cf. figure 4) — ne pouvait que le convaincre de ce que l'égalité des aires à l'infini ne les ramenait pas à un carré connu, ne permettait en rien la quadrature au sens classique. Elle ouvrait un autre monde, celui de l'intégration.

Qu'importait ! Malgré les quolibets, malgré même plus de vingt ans d'interdiction de publier décrétés par le général des Jésuites dès 1624, Grégoire de Saint-Vincent en 1647 inscrivait crânement « plus ultra quadratura circuli » dans la dédicace de son ouvrage à l'archiduc d'Autriche. Un tel entêtement est fabuleux — mais il ruinera la réputation de Grégoire — puisque dès la parution de l'ouvrage, Descartes et bientôt Huygens en

---

[28] Ce thème est développé dans J. Dhombres, Une mathématique baroque en Europe : réseaux, ambitions et acteurs, *Colloque Mythes et réalités de l'Europe mathématique*, Paris, avril 1992.

signalèrent, non sans dénigrement, la faille algébrique au 10ᵉ et dernier livre. Mais on ne peut lui dénier un courage baroque.

Courage qui n'est nullement synonyme d'optimisme, de poursuite béate d'un rêve. À plus d'une reprise, et sous la rhétorique d'un latin profus, perce le désarroi, causé par le trop grand écart entre une ambition considérée comme naturelle et une réalisation qui au terme de propositions savamment enchaînées, de lemmes calculatoires élégants et originaux, n'atteint pas ses objectifs. Grégoire de Saint-Vincent ne peut que recourir au mode conditionnel : « Ce qui aurait réussi assurément si nous avions pu proposer et résoudre avec un bonheur égal... »[29]. Dès la préface, d'ailleurs, le ton est donné puisque l'auteur oppose en les rassemblant ses tribulations — guerres et maladies — aux ordonnances harmonieuses et divines de la mathématique qui n'en sont pas moins trouvées et prouvées dans la tête d'un homme :

> Et voilà, Lecteur bienveillant, ce qu'à ma manière, c'est-à-dire tout franchement, j'avais en tête de vous communiquer. Dans ces conditions, si dans le cours de mon œuvre se trouve quelque chose de moins parfait, je désirerais que vous le missiez sur le compte d'une trop grande hâte. Car, alors qu'à Prague les forces réprimées de ma maladie reprenaient à nouveau de la violence et semblaient parfois étouffer le vieillard que j'étais en lui enlevant toute énergie, m'étant entouré de toutes parts de collaborateurs sur l'ordre de mes Supérieurs dont je suis les désirs et non seulement les commandements, dirai-je que j'ai tiré de moi cette œuvre que vous voyez ou que je l'ai composée avant qu'une mort subite, toujours menaçante, ne fît avorter cet embryon... Comme, en effet, nous ne nous appartenons pas à nous-mêmes, les produits de notre esprit également ne sont pas à nous et doivent encore moins être revendiqués comme nôtres — nous que notre profession a soumis entièrement à une Règle. Si cependant vous trouvez ici quelque chose digne de louange, mon vœu est que vous le mettiez sur le compte de Dieu, à l'honneur et la gloire de qui j'ai travaillé toute ma vie, non sans une immense admiration pour son art éternel, même dans les petites choses. Car cette ordonnance, cette symétrie, cette proportion que nous avons montrées dans chacune des surfaces et des corps, ce n'est point nous qui, par notre industrie ou notre art les avons créées, mais nous les avons trouvées toutes faites et ainsi disposées par des lois éternelles, grâce à une certaine heureuse disposition d'esprit, ou (ce qui m'est advenu, je le reconnais) grâce à sa faveur qui dispose dans ses parties tout avec tant d'harmonie — et les ayant trouvées, nous les avons démontrées[30].

Les mathématiques d'une époque s'inscrivent jusque dans les aventures d'un homme : certains peuvent regretter cette intrusion du contingent dans la science pure, d'autres s'en nourrir. Il n'en reste pas moins la signature d'une sensibilité baroque.

---

[29] *Opus geometricum*, suite du scholie venant après la proposition 135 du livre 6.

[30] *Opus geometricum*, préface.

IMAGERY AND REASONING IN
MATHEMATICS AND MATHEMATICS EDUCATION

Tommy Dreyfus

Tel Aviv University, Israel

Visual reasoning plays a far more important role in the work of today's mathematicians than is generally known. Increasingly, visual arguments are also becoming acceptable as proofs. Cognitive studies, even though identifying several specific dangers associated with visualization, point to the tremendous potential of visual approaches for meaningful learning. Computerized learning environments open an avenue to realizing this potential. It is therefore argued that the status of visualization in mathematics education can and should be upgraded from that of a helpful learning aid to that of a fully recognized tool for mathematical reasoning and proof.

INTRODUCTION

Visualization is generally considered helpful in supporting intuition and concept formation in mathematics learning. Fischbein (1987), for example, notes that "one of the characteristic properties of intuitive cognitions is immediacy. Visualization ... is very frequently involved ... " Similarly, Bishop (1989), in a recent review of research on visualization in mathematics education, concludes "that there is value in emphasizing visual representations in all aspects of the mathematics classroom". Two qualifications should be added to these generally positive evaluations; one concerns difficulties with visualization, and the other concerns the status accorded to visualization in mathematics education, in other words its epistemological value.

During the past few years, many student difficulties with visualization have been identified. These include students' inability to see a diagram different ways (Yerushalmi & Chazan, 1990), their difficulty in recognizing transformations implied in diagrams (Goldenberg, 1991), their incorrect or unconventional interpretation of variation and co-variation in graphs

(Clement, 1989), their lack of distinction between a geometrical figure and the drawing that represents this figure (Laborde, 1988) and, most importantly, their lack of connections between their visualizations and analytic thought (Presmeg, 1986). These difficulties are all related to what Fischbein called an "intervening conceptual structure". Diagrams and figures contain relevant mathematical information in a form that is determined by certain rules and conventions, which often are specific to a particular type of diagram. They are therefore not accessible to students who have not had the opportunity to get acquainted with these rules and conventions.

The second qualification, and the one that will constitute the central concern of this paper, concerns the low status accorded to visual aspects of mathematics in the classroom. This is typified by the student who, after a detailed and lengthy presentation of a visual argument by the teacher, raises a hand to ask: "Can you also give a *mathematical* proof for this?" The reluctance of students to use visual reasoning has been documented widely in the literature. To cite one typical source: "Despite the calculus teacher's predilection for diagrams, our research indicates that students resist the use of geometric and spatial strategies in actually solving calculus problems." (Balomenos, Ferrini-Mundy, & Dick, 1988). More details on students' avoidance of visual considerations have been reported, for example, by Vinner (1989) and by Eisenberg and Dreyfus (1991).

A significant piece of evidence on the status of visual argumentation is constituted by various classifications of proofs that have been established by mathematics educators. For example, Blum and Kirsch (1991) classify *inhaltlich-anschauliche* (content-visual) proofs as pre-formal. The message is that visualization may be a useful and efficient learning aid for many topics in high school and college mathematics; but nevertheless it is an aid, a crutch, a step, sometimes a necessary and important step, but *only* a step on the way to the real mathematics. Such an attitude on the part of mathematics educators and teachers, whether justified or not, is bound to influence students to avoid the use of visual arguments.

This situation has unfortunate effects: it eliminates a versatile tool of mathematical reasoning for all students, and it may prevent some of the weaker ones from successful problem solving. In fact, Bondesan and Ferrari (1991) report that even poor problem-solvers adapt or invent new strategies in a geometric setting, but not in an algebraic one. And Presmeg (1986) has found that while children have little difficulty in generating visual images their imagery is predominantly concrete pictorial, with far less pattern imagery, and hardly any dynamic imagery. Since pattern and dynamic imagery are more apt to be coupled with rigorous analytical thought processes, this means that students are likely to generate visual images but they are unlikely to use them for analytical reasoning. In this paper, we want to make the argument for precisely such visually-based analytical thought processes or, in short, for visual reasoning.

To make the idea of visual reasoning more concrete, consider an example taken from a unit on geometric loci, designed specifically for developing visual reasoning patterns (Hershkowitz, Friedlander, & Dreyfus, 1991). Suppose you have to deal with the following problem: Given two intersecting lines in the plane, find the geometric locus of all points the sum of whose distances from the two lines equals a given length. One (global) way of starting out is to argue that the locus must be contained in a bounded region of the plane because any point that is very far away must be far from at least one of the lines. A more local way of starting is to ask whether any points of the locus are going to lie on the given lines, and to start searching along these lines. This search may be approached dynamically by starting at the point of intersection and moving out along one of the two lines.

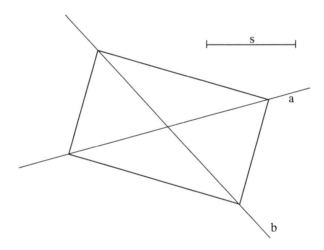

As one does so, the distance from the other line grows from zero without bound, therefore one must at a certain stage pass a point which belongs to the locus. By symmetry reasons, this yields four points. The locus turns out to be the rectangle whose corners are these four points. Establishing this is not trivial but needs a detailed analytical argument, which may be based on appropriate ratios in suitably chosen similar triangles. Every part of the above argument will be considered to be visual reasoning because it makes essential use of visual information. Visual reasoning used in this kind of argument may be global or local, dynamic or static, but it is never purely perceptual. It includes valid analytical argumentation leading from step to step. The thesis of this paper is that such visual reasoning is very frequently used and accorded increasing value in mathematics, and that it would behoove mathematics education to follow suit.

VISUAL REASONING IN MATHEMATICS

Many indicators point to the fact that most mathematicians rely very heavily on visual reasoning in their work. But with few exceptions, mainly in combinatorics and category theory, these same mathematicians do their utmost to hide this fact. Indeed, mathematicians tend to be secretive about their work; they tend to hide very carefully how they obtained their results. They present only the final, finished, formalized product. They do not let the reader see any of the processes. And many mathematicians behave the same way when they lecture about their work.

There are a few instances where mathematicians explicitly describe how they obtained their results. One of these is contained in a publication by Van der Waerden (1954) on the topic of idea and reflection in mathematics research. He used as illustration a discussion with two colleagues during which they found a proof of the following conjecture by Baudet: If the set of natural numbers is split into two disjoint subsets, then at least one of the subsets contains an arithmetic progression of length L (where L is arbitrary). The report on their discussion takes up seven pages and contains eight figures with possible patterns for number sequences to be distributed into two (or more) subsets. The first of these figures is reproduced below. It is accompanied by the sentence *"Wir zeichneten die Zahlen als kleine Querstriche ... auf zwei waagrechten Linien, die die beiden Klassen darstellen sollten."* (We drew the numbers as small crossbars ... on two horizontal lines which were supposed to represent the two subsets.)

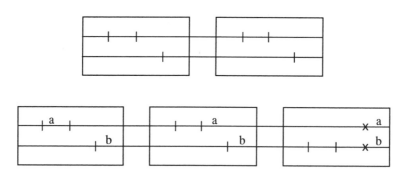

The entire argument rests on the patterns given in these figures. As Van der Waerden states: *"Der Beweis den ich im Nieuw Archief voor Wiskunde 15, 212 (1927) dargestellt habe, ist die genaue Ausführung des hier anschaulich erläuterten Gedankenganges."* (The proof, which I have presented in *Nieuw Archief voor Wiskunde 15,* 212 (1927), is the precise execution of the line of thought presented visually here.) The five-page paper in which he published this proof does not contain a single diagram. I doubt, however, whether many mathematicians are able to understand the proof in that paper without recreating van der Waerden's diagrams (or other, similar ones). Diagrams are essential for mathematical thinking, but their use is hidden by mathematicians as best they can.

Other reports on how mathematicians think also point to the overwhelming importance of visual aspects. A systematic attempt to discuss mathematicians' research thoughts was undertaken and reported by Hadamard (1945). Although he insists on individual differences in the manner in which mathematicians' thoughts rely on mental images, Hadamard concludes that they, very generally, use images and that these images very often are of a geometric nature. He recounts that when thinking, practically all mathematicians avoid not only the use of words but also algebraic or other symbols; they use vague images. In particular, Einstein wrote to Hadamard: "Words and language, written or oral, seem not to play any role in my thinking. The psychological constructs which are the elements of thought are certain signs or pictures, more or less clear, which can be reproduced and combined at liberty." (Hadamard, 1945, p. 82).

Why, then, do mathematicians hide their visualizations and the arguments based on them? Several reasons come to mind. Some, like Einstein's vague images, may never have become sharp enough to be describable in word or picture. Others, like Van der Waerden's diagrams, have probably been judged unacceptable by the standards of mathematical publication common throughout most of the 19th and 20th centuries; these standards were strongly influenced by both logicism and formalism. History shows that the standards have not always been so inimical to visual argumentation (Berra, 1986); and there is some evidence that the situation may be rapidly changing again.

In the past few years, many mathematicians have addressed the importance of visual reasoning not only in discovering but also in describing and in justifying mathematical results. Rival (1987), for example, has written an article with the subtitle "Mathematicians are rediscovering the power of pictorial reasoning". The *Journal of Combinatorial Theory* accepted a paper by Mayer (1972) whose complete text is "$\theta(K_{16}) = 3$"; the remainder of the paper consists of three labelled planar graphs which prove that equation. The fact that these graphs, in and of themselves, constitute a proof of the equations is explicitly confirmed in the abstract of Mayer's paper in *Mathematical Reviews.* The usefulness, even necessity, of visual reasoning patterns in modern mathematical research has also been stressed by Devaney (1989). He recounts how he and three students described certain dynamical processes through sequences of transformations in the complex plane, represented them graphically by means of computer programs, and then filmed these sequences. According to Devaney, the results of these rather time-consuming experiments have always been mathematically stimulating and many new mathematical results have been proved as an outcome.

Davis and Anderson (1979) go beyond stressing the power of visual reasoning for discovering new results in mathematics. They not only describe mathematics "done in actuality—as a series of nonverbal, analog, often kinesthetic or visual insights," but suggest that the "excessive emphasis on the abstract, analytic aspects of thought may have had deleterious effects on the profession." Among their examples is the Jordan Curve Theorem (a simple closed curve in the plane separates the plane into two regions, one bounded and one unbounded), which is visually obvious but whose analytic proof requires notions from algebraic topology and is therefore rarely presented at the undergraduate level. Finally, and most importantly, Davis and Anderson refer to the existence of "purely visual theorems and proofs," and encourage the production of such theorems. Many but not all of these theorems have been found by means of computer-graphical support.

If, following Davis and Anderson, visual arguments are to be admitted as (parts of) mathematical proofs, the question naturally arises how (and even, whether) incorrect visual arguments can be avoided. How often have we seen children rely on particular features of a diagram in a geometry proof, and thus present an invalid or at least incomplete proof? And although one would not expect mathematicians to fall into the same trap as tenth graders learning Euclidean geometry, some mistakes in visual arguments are far more subtle (see e.g. Blum & Kirsch, 1989, for a beautiful example), and it is not known where the limits of such subtlety lie (if there are limits at all). Who is to judge the validity of a visual argument?

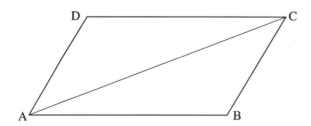

Three replies to this question will be given: first, that in many proofs visual arguments are unavoidable; second, that judgment of the validity of non-visual arguments is not safe either; and, third, that criteria for better judgement of visual arguments should be developed.

In a paper of a philosophical nature, Stenius (1981) analyzes the epistemic function of the figure in a Euclidean geometrical proof. This proof is a modification of Euclid's proof that, in a parallelogram, opposite sides are equal. Given a parallelogram ABCD, in which AB is parallel to CD and BC to AD, prove that AB = CD (and BC = AD). The proof proceeds by drawing the auxiliary line AC (a diagonal of ABCD), and showing that the triangles ABC and CDA are congruent, from which the result follows. Who could understand this proof, even if many more details were spelled out verbally, without imagining a parallelogram in the mind's eye? This already demonstrates that we use the figure in following the proof. But beyond this, Stenius asks, how do we know that BAC and DCA are alternate angles on parallel lines? Could not the point D lie inside the triangle ABC?

Most teachers are well aware that they do use figures in proofs. But many will say, you are only allowed to use those features of the figure which are not particular to the figure; in our case, those which are true for all parallelograms, for which the particular drawn figure serves as a model. And who judges, asks Stenius, whether a figure can or cannot serve as such a model, and which features of the figure are generic? This has not been formalized, and if it had, the formalization would be quite useless to the beginning student of Euclidean geometry. Therefore, the use of diagrams in teaching and learning Euclidean geometry must not be avoided, but quite the contrary, must be analyzed and dealt with explicitly.

Some readers may remain unconvinced and fear that proofs relying on visual reasoning are dangerous, because they depend on a substantial measure of validity judgment by mathematicians and mathematics teachers. These readers should consider that the situation for sentential proofs is not different in essence, only in degree. In a wonderful dialogue between the ideal mathematician and an inquisitive student, in the book by Davis and Hersh (1981), the best definition of a mathematical proof (as opposed to a proof in formal logic) which the ideal mathematician comes up with is "A proof is an argument that convinces someone who knows the subject." In other words: the validity of the argument is judged by the expert—there is no machine algorithm to check a mathematical proof; and there is thus no *a priori* reason why some of the reasoning in a proof should not be diagrammatic or visual. Why, then, do mathematicians often object to visual arguments in proofs and why do they attempt to eliminate the visual reasoning before they publish a proof? This point is eloquently explained by Barwise and Etchemendy (1991). Although they agree that "we are all taught to look askance at proofs that make crucial use of diagrams, graphs, or other non-linguistic forms of representation, and we pass on this disdain to our students," they claim "that diagrams and other forms of visual representation can be essential and legitimate components in valid deductive reasoning." They point out that mathematicians' expertise in judging the validity of linguistic reasoning is based on careful and lasting attention to this form of reasoning and that such a tradition and ensuing expertise for visual reasoning is lacking. Hence, they advocate and have begun a research program to devote similar attention to the judgment of the legitimacy of visual and mixed, heterogeneous reasoning patterns.

We thus conclude that the reasons behind attempts to minimize visual reasoning in proofs are not based on a valid principle. Mathematicians, the experts who are supposed to judge the validity of the proofs, have neglected to develop their ability to carry out this judgment in the case of visual arguments.

To summarize, a clearly identifiable if still unconventional movement is growing in the mathematics community, whose aim is to make visual reasoning an acceptable practice of mathematics, alongside and in combination with algebraic reasoning. According to this movement, visual reasoning is not meant only to support the discovery of new results and of ways of proving them, but should be developed into a fully acceptable and accepted manner of reasoning, including proving mathematical theorems. The availability of powerful graphics computers has played a non-negligible role in the emergence of this movement.

INDICATIONS FROM COGNITIVE SCIENCE

In a review of more than a decade of work on the use of conceptual models for understanding, Mayer (1989) concludes that such "models will improve the ability of students to transfer what they have learned to creatively solve new problems"; the ability to creatively solve new problems is what Mayer terms understanding. There is little doubt that such understanding implies certain forms of reasoning, but this is not spelled out. Obviously, it is crucial for us to know what is meant by conceptual models. They are descriptions of systems from science, technology, programming, and mathematics which spell out the major parts, states, and actions in the system; in each case, the model includes a pictorial representation of the explanatory information, highlighting the key concepts and suggesting relationships between them. Although Mayer specifically includes text in his conceptual models, his findings show that "illustrations help students organize information into meaningful mental models" and these, in turn, are at the root of their successful problem solutions. Thus, Mayer has also avoided explicitly identifying the contribution of the visual component. Therefore the question may be asked, to what extent are the visual features of his conceptual models crucial?

Recently, interest among cognitive scientists in investigations of visual reasoning in general, and in the role of visual reasoning in problem solving in mathematics and science in particular, appears to have grown.

Studies which treat the effect of visual support on making inferences and solving problems show that appropriate visual support has positive effects on students' understanding and problem solving. The following seem particularly relevant here.

Chandrasekaran and Narayanan (1992) argue that there are many commonsense situations in which human reasoning is tightly coupled with perception, in particular with perceptually represented experiential knowledge. They use the term "perceptual reasoning" and explain such reasoning in terms of perceptual inference rules. Koedinger (1992) further points out the advantages of diagrammatic representations for reasoning and learning. However, specifically with science and mathematics problems, the situation is more complex: Larkin and Simon (1987) compare the accessibility of information needed to solve problems when they are presented in diagrammatic versus sentential form. The distinguishing feature is that diagrammatic representations explicitly preserve spatial relationships between components of the problem, whereas sentential representations do not. In diagrams, information is indexed by its location, thus giving the possibility of grouping all information about a single element together, and expressing logical relationships spatially. Thus, diagrams not only describe spatial arrangements: they have inherent interpretations and conventions without which they are unintelligible. Those who know these interpretations and conventions can develop visual reasoning patterns exploiting the advantages of the diagram. Larkin and Simon have thus given precise expression to Fischbein's "intervening conceptual structure" mentioned in the introduction.

A further illustration of the usefulness of diagrams in scientific reasoning is provided by Qin and Simon (1992). They used Einstein's 1905 paper on special relativity, which (like Van der Waerden's paper mentioned earlier) contains no diagrams to guide the reader. Qin and Simon's subjects had to reconstruct the reasoning in the first few paragraphs of Einstein's paper. They concluded that all subjects formed mental images during this process, even those who usually claimed not to be able to do so. The way the subjects derived the equations was closely related to their images. Subjects were able to "watch" these images evolving dynamically, and the images were essential in drawing qualitative conclusions.

Finally, Dörfler (1991) has expanded Lakoff's idea of image schemas as a theoretical basis for generating meaning in mathematics learning. As he states, for very many mathematical concepts, an adequate image schema must include a figural component which has to be complemented by operative, relational, and symbolic ones. The carrier for the figural component will often be a visual representation of the concept. The associated operative components facilitate visual reasoning with and about this concept. Dörfler's theoretical framework is thus not only compatible but fully resonant with

115

Hadamard's description of mathematicians' thinking patterns, and consequently with most of what has been said heretofore about visual reasoning.

IMPLICATIONS FOR MATHEMATICS EDUCATION

Theories and analyses from cognitive science clearly show the potential for an extremely powerful role for visual reasoning in learning many mathematical concepts and processes. A warning should, however, be associated with this promise: Visual reasoning is based on expertise—it will be unhelpful if not impossible for the uninitiated. The promise made by cognitive science appears to be borne out by mathematical research activity: experts make extensive use of visual reasoning during the creative process. In addition, there is an emerging movement to give legitimacy to visual arguments in the presentation of mathematical results.

Mathematics educators seem to have recognized the potential power and promise of visual reasoning; but in spite of this, implementation is lagging: students tend to avoid visual reasoning. The slowness of educational change in general may be one reason for this. But two additional weighty reasons are suggested by the above description. Firstly, while visual reasoning enters curricula and is even presented by teachers in the classroom, it is often given the air of an introductory, accessory, or auxiliary argument, precisely because the experts, be they mathematicians, curriculum developers, or teachers, do not assign full value and status to it. And from this attitude, students soon conclude that they do not really need to know and use visual arguments. Secondly, visual reasoning is difficult; it is achieved by hard reflective work. Unreflective, careless or too rapid introduction of visual representations are likely to result in failure and disappointment.

In order to give our students the chance to profit from and to appreciate the power of visual reasoning we, as a profession, need to upgrade the status of visual reasoning in mathematics. In our own mathematical thinking, we need to generate visual arguments, to learn how to examine their validity and to accord them the same weight which we accord to verbal and formal arguments. In order to overcome students' tendency to avoid visual reasoning we, as teachers, need to use it not only frequently and consistently in searching for problem solutions but also at crucial junctures of our mathematical justifications with the aim of making evident both the full power of visual reasoning and the importance accorded to it. We need to give our students many opportunities not only to visually solve problems but also to discuss valid and invalid visual arguments. Finally, we need to give our students full credit for correct visual solutions. In order to be able to do all this, and to make it permeate teacher education we, as researchers, need to expand our understanding of the cognitive and mathematical processes involved in visual reasoning. Detailed, content specific knowledge about the mathematical and educational validity of visual representations and reasoning patterns needs to be obtained for many different mathematical notions and processes. This includes the investigation of limitations, difficulties, obstacles and possible misinterpretations associated with the proposed visual representations.

Visual reasoning obtains its clearest expression if no alternative is available: that is if some mathematics is presented in purely visual form. Several developments in this direction have been proposed recently, some have been carried out, and a few have been systematically implemented in classrooms. Two which are explicit in their reliance on visual reasoning will be briefly described here as exemplary.

Artigue (1989) has developed and taught a university-level curriculum in which suitable computer software is used to help students develop a qualitative, geometric approach to the properties of solutions of differential equations. This qualitative study of differential equations is based on reasoning with functions which are not given explicitly by a formula, but only by means of information about their derivative(s). One of the explicitly stated aims of the curriculum is to lead students to work with curves without the support of a formula: in other words, to infer graphical information about the curves from graphical information about their derivatives. In order for this aim to become realistic, a complete break with the usual, formula-based treatment of function at the high school level has to be made. Some of the phases in the curriculum are to get acquainted with basic notions such as slope field, isoclines, solution curves, and symmetries, to produce curves in a dialectic interplay between prediction and justification, and to learn about higher level graphical notions such as branching and flows, including the variation of the type of flow in equations depending on parameters. One of the conclusions of the experiment was that, once the break with the habitual, purely algebraic approach had been effected, students accessed the geometric framework with relative ease, due to the fact that the complexity of their tasks was reduced by the possibility of using appropriate software.

Goldenberg (1989) evokes the vision of a radical restructuring of the pre-college mathematics curriculum centered on an introduction of fractal geometry in junior high school. He proposes to "adopt a visual and experimental type of mathematical inquiry and learning" in order to "foster the development and use of qualitative, visually-based reasoning styles"; among these, he specifically includes visual proofs. He illustrates how problem posing may originate at the visual level and shows that questions about trigonometric relationships, about limits, about series, and about iterated processes arise naturally out of the detailed investigation of the geometry of fractal curves, their perimeter, border, enclosed area, etc. The corresponding mathematical notions "are approached in visual, concrete, informal, and intuitive fashions, with formal tools acquired as they are needed." In particular, a concept of function is apt to develop that is not only more general than the one usually developed at high school level, but also more robust and flexible. The entire approach is conditioned by appropriate software tools, that give the students freedom to explore the geometric objects under consideration by changing parameters and variables, including basic shapes and recursion rules.

Other projects based on purely or predominantly visual reasoning have been designed, among others, on feedback systems (Janvier & Garançon, 1989), plane geometry (Yerushalmi & Chazan, 1990), geometric loci (Hershkowitz, Friedlander, & Dreyfus, 1991) and linear programming (Shama & Dreyfus, 1991). It is no accident that in all these projects, computerized learning environments play a major role. We will conclude this paper with some remarks on the potential and the problems arising in the use of computers for visual reasoning.

COMPUTERS AND VISUAL REASONING

Computers make it possible to represent visual mathematics with an amount of structure not offered by any other medium. Graphic computer screen representations of mathematical objects and relationships allow for direct visual action on these objects (rather, their representatives) and observation of the ensuing changes in the relationships. Moreover, the situation can be inverted: it is possible also to investigate which will lead to a given change in the relationships. The result of such actions can often be dynamically implemented. Actions can be repeated at liberty, with or without changing parameters of the action and conclusions can be drawn on the basis of the feedback given by the computer program. The power of the computer for learning visual reasoning in mathematics derives from these possibilities.

Several projects have used the above considerations and exploited them in the development of software to achieve and investigate specific learning goals. To mention but a few examples: Tall (1991) reports using the computer to encourage visually based concept formation in calculus; specifically, local straightness rather than a limiting process is suggested as a basis for developing the notion of derivative. Tall stresses that the goal is not only to provide solid visual intuitive support, but to sow the seeds for understanding the formal subtleties that occur later. This implies that students learn to reason visually with the details of screen representations of concepts such as function, secant, tangent, gradient, gradient function, etc. Kaput (1989) has used concrete visual computer representations to build on natural actions in the students' world with the aim of supporting the learning and application of multiplicative reasoning, ratio, and proportion. In particular, he aims to tie the visually concrete and enactive operations on objects on the screen with more formal and abstract representations of these operations. Thus students' visual operations are directly used in the learning process. Yerushalmy and Chazan (1990) have given students the opportunity to generate empirically visual information about geometrical constructions and to infer conjectures from such information. Again, this cannot be done without visually based action (to generate the geometric information) and visually based cognitive activity to infer a conjecture. Shama and Dreyfus (1991) have used computer-screen presentations of linear programming situations to allow students to develop their own solution strategies. For this purpose also, students need to analyze problems in terms of the visually presented information and thus to give a visual basis for their strategies. All of these projects thus aim for detailed analysis of the relationships contained in the visual screen presentation and for reasoning based on such analysis.

In computerized learning environments it is possible to directly address and overcome some of the problems associated with visualization, mainly those related to lack of flexibility in the students' thinking. It is also possible to transfer a large measure of control over the mathematical actions to the student; but the potential of computers for visual mathematics does not by itself solve the more important problems that were mentioned in the introduction. In every case, visual representations need to be carefully constructed and their cognitive properties for the student need to be investigated in detail. The adaptation and correction of features of these visual representations on the basis of student reaction to them is an integral part of the development, and in some cases has been reported in the literature. Tall's choice of local straightness rather than a limiting process for the derivative is a case in point. Similarly, Kaput describes how he has found dissonances between students' visual experience and the semantic structure of the situation being modelled and has consequently designed a way to avoid such difficulties. These difficulties associated with visual representations can be overcome, but only if they are systematically searched for, analyzed and dealt with. In this endeavor, the design of student activities within the learning environment plays at least as important a part as the design of the computerized environment itself (Dreyfus, in press).

Little has been said in this paper about two important topics: verbalization and multiple-linked representations. Verbal argumentation in mathematics suffers, to a large extent, from similar problems as visual reasoning. My insistence on visual reasoning should by no means be construed as an argument against verbalization—quite the contrary. There are in fact some indications of positive interaction between the visual and the verbal (Bondesan & Ferrari, 1991). Moreover, many of the cited examples do link the visual representations to algebraic ones and thus open the possibility for integrated visual-algebraic reasoning. I have consciously downplayed those aspects because the purpose of this paper was to make the point that visual representations and visual reasoning in mathematics must not be considered as a crutch for those who cannot otherwise make the step to "real mathematics." I have attempted to show that visual reasoning in mathematics is important in its own right and that therefore we need to develop and give full status to purely visual mathematical activities. Although I pressed one point of view, namely the visual one, the final goal is not to be one-sided: not on the algebraic side, not on the verbal side, not on the visual side. One goal is balance, as has been stressed already by Davis and Anderson (1979); and we should aim for more than balance: we should aim for the integration of visual, verbal, and algebraic thinking. Before one can aim for integration, however, one needs balance. And in order to achieve balance, visual reasoning needs to be given equal status to, and as much attention as, algebraic reasoning.

ACKNOWLEDGEMENT

An earlier version of this paper appeared in the *Proceedings of the Fifteenth International Conference of the International Group for the Psychology of Mathematics Education* which was held in Assisi, Italy, in 1991.

REFERENCES

Artigue, M. (1988/89). Une recherche d'ingénierie didactique sur l'enseignement des équations différentielles en premier cycle universitaire. *Cahiers du séminaire de didactique de Grenoble, 107*, 183-209.

Balomenos, R., Ferrini-Mundy, J., & Dick, T. (1988). Geometry for calculus readiness. In M. Lindquist & A. Schulte (Eds.), *Learning and teaching geometry, K-12* (pp. 185-209). Reston, VA: National Council of Teachers of Mathematics.

Barwise, J., & Etchemendy, J. (1991). Visual information and valid reasoning. In W. Zimmermann & S. Cunningham (Eds.), *Visualization in teaching and learning mathematics* (pp. 9-24). Washington: The Mathematical Association of America.

Berra, M. (1986). Knowing how to prove. *Comptes rendus de la IVᵉ école d'été de didactique des mathématiques* (pp. 175-183). Paris: IREM, Université de Paris VII.

Bishop, A.J. (1989). Review of research on visualization in mathematics education. *Focus on Learning Problems in Mathematics, 11*(1), 7-16.

Blum, W., & Kirsch, A. (1991). Warum haben nicht-triviale Lösungen von f' = f keine Nullstellen? Beobachtungen und Bemerkungen zum "inhaltlich-anschaulichen Beweisen". In H. Kautschitsch (Ed.), *Anschauliches Beweisen* (pp. 199-209). Wien: Hölder-Pichler-Tempsky. English translation: *Educational Studies in Mathematics, 22*(2).

Bondesan, M.G., & Ferrari, P.L. (1991). The active comparison of strategies in problem-solving: An exploratory study. In F. Furinghetti (Ed.), *Proceedings of the Fifteenth International Conference of the International Group for the Psychology of Mathematics Education* (Vol. I, pp. 168-175). Assisi, Italy.

Chandrasekaran, B., & Narayanan, N.H. (1992). Perceptual Representation and Reasoning. In N.H. Narayanan (Ed.), *Working Notes of the AAAI Spring Symposium on Reasoning with Diagrammatic Representations* (pp. 24-29). Stanford, CA: Stanford University.

Clement, J. (1989). The concept of variation and misconceptions in Cartesian graphing. *Focus on Learning Problems in Mathematics, 11*(2), 77-87.

Davis, P.J., & Anderson, J.A. (1979). Nonanalytic aspects of mathematics and their implication for research and education. *SIAM Review, 21*(1), 112-127.

Davis, P.J., & Hersh, R. (1981). *The Mathematical Experience*. Boston: Birkhäuser.

Devaney, R.L. (1989). Film and video as a tool in mathematical research. *The Mathematical Intelligencer, 11*(2), 33-38.

Dörfler, W. (1991). Meaning: Image schemas and protocols. In F. Furinghetti (Ed.), *Proceedings of the Fifteenth International Conference of the International Group for the Psychology of Mathematics Education* (Vol. I, pp. 17-31). Assisi, Italy.

Dreyfus, T. (in press). Didactic design of computer-based learning environments. In W. Dörfler, C. Keitel & K. Ruthven (Eds.), *Learning from computers: Mathematics education and technology*. Berlin: Springer.

Eisenberg, T., & Dreyfus, T. (1991). On the reluctance to visualize in mathematics. In W. Zimmermann & S. Cunningham (Eds.), *Visualization in teaching and learning mathematics* (pp. 25-37). Washington: The Mathematical Association of America.

Fischbein, E. (1987). *Intuition in science and mathematics*. Dordrecht, The Netherlands: Reidel.

Goldenberg, E.P. (1989). Seeing beauty in mathematics: Using fractal geometry to build a spirit of mathematical inquiry. *Journal of Mathematical Behavior, 8*, 169-204.

Goldenberg, E.P. (1991). The difference between graphing software and educational graphing software. In W. Zimmermann & S. Cunningham (Eds.), *Visualization in teaching and learning mathematics* (pp. 77-86). Washington: The Mathematical Association of America.

Hadamard, J. (1945). *The psychology of invention in the mathematical field*. Princeton, NJ: Princeton University Press.

Hershkowitz, R., Friedlander A., & Dreyfus, T. (1991). Loci and visual thinking. In F. Furinghetti (Ed.), *Proceedings of the Fifteenth International Conference of the International Group for the Psychology of Mathematics Education* (Vol. II, pp. 181-188). Assisi, Italy.

Janvier, C., & Garançon, M. (1989). Graphical understanding of simple feedback systems. *Focus on Learning*

Problems in Mathematics, 11(2), 127-138.

Kaput, J.J. (1989). Supporting concrete visual thinking in multiplicative reasoning. *Focus on Learning Problems in Mathematics, 11*(1), 35-47.

Koedinger, K.R. (1992). Advantages of diagrammatic representations for reasoning and learning. In N.H. Narayanan (Ed.), *Working Notes of the AAAI Spring Symposium on Reasoning with Diagrammatic Representations* (pp. 154-159). Stanford, CA: Stanford University.

Laborde, C. (1988). L'enseignement de la géométrie en tant que terrain d'exploration de phénomènes didactiques. *Recherches en didactique des mathématiques, 9*(3), 337-364.

Larkin, J.H., & Simon, H.A. (1987). Why a diagram is (sometimes) worth ten thousand words. *Cognitive Science, 11*, 65-99.

Mayer, R.E. (1989). Models for understanding. *Review of Educational Research, 59*(1), 43-64.

Mayer, J. (1972). Décomposition de K_{16} en trois graphes planaires. *Journal of Combinatorial Theory (B), 13*, 71.

Presmeg, N. (1986). Visualization in high school mathematics. *For the Learning of Mathematics, 6*(3), 42-46.

Qin, Y., & Simon, H.A. (1992). Imagery and mental models in problem solving. In N.H. Narayanan (Ed.), *Working Notes of the AAAI Spring Symposium on Reasoning with Diagrammatic Representations* (pp. 18-23). Stanford, CA: Stanford University.

Rival, I. (1987). Picture puzzling: Mathematicians are rediscovering the power of pictorial reasoning. *The Sciences, 27*, 41-46.

Shama, G., & Dreyfus, T. (1991). Spontaneous strategies for visually presented linear programming problems. In F. Furinghetti (Ed.), *Proceedings of the Fifteenth International Conference of the International Group for the Psychology for Mathematics Education* (Vol. III, pp. 262-269). Assisi, Italy.

Stenius, E. (1981). Anschauung und formaler Beweis. *Studia Leibnitiana, 13*(1), 133.

Tall, D.O. (1991). Intuition and rigour: The role of visualization in the calculus. In W. Zimmermann & S. Cunningham (Eds.), *Visualization in teaching and learning mathematics* (pp. 105-119). Washington: The Mathematical Association of America

Van der Waerden, B.L. (1954). *Einfall und Überlegung: Drei kleine Beiträge zur Psychologie des mathematischen Denkens*. Basel, Switzerland: Birkhäuser.

Vinner, S. (1989). The avoidance of visual considerations in calculus students. *Focus on Learning Problems in Mathematics 11*(2), 149-155.

Yerushalmy, M., & Chazan, D. (1990). Overcoming visual obstacles with the aid of the supposer. *Educational Studies in Mathematics, 21*(3), 199-219.

INTERWEAVING NUMBERS, SHAPES, STATISTICS, AND THE REAL WORLD IN PRIMARY SCHOOL AND PRIMARY TEACHER EDUCATION

Andrejs Dunkels

Luleå University, Sweden

Statistics is viewed, by tradition, as an advanced subject whose study is a secondary school matter. Applications like statistics must wait until the basic mathematics has been learnt. However, if one examines the mathematics of primary school, then one finds that much of it is statistics, that is, data handling and describing events, situations, phenomena of the real world with the aid of numbers and geometrical figures.

It is important, I feel, that practicing and future teachers are made aware of this, so that they can explicitly take advantage of situations where one learns something about the real world, while at the same time new insights are gained into numbers and shapes. Most primary teachers I have met have not known how much statistics they have been dealing with all their professional lives.

There is a growing interest in statistics at the primary level (Russel & Corvin, 1990; Rangecroft, 1991; Vere-Jones, 1991; Åberg-Bengtsson, 1991).

This paper contains first a vision, or something that will happen, then an account of something that has happened in some student teacher classrooms and in some primary school classrooms in Sweden.

SUN AND CUSTOMERS

In winter I get up at night
And dress by yellow candle light.
In summer, quite the other way,
I have to go to bed by day.

I have to go to bed and see
The birds still hopping on the tree,
Or hear the grown-up people's feet
Still going past me in the street.

And does it not seem hard to you,
When all the sky is clear and blue,
And I should like so much to play,
To have to go to bed by day?

This poem, "Bed in summer" by R.L. Stevenson, is the real world for everybody, not least primary children, in Luleå on the east coast of northern Sweden. Is there data about this?

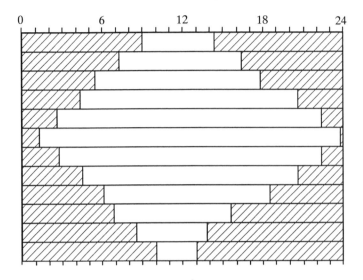

Figure 1. Diagram showing the times of sunrise and sunset on the 22nd of each month in Luleå in northern Sweden, latitude 65° 35′N, less than 1° from the Arctic Circle.

Each day the local newspapers in Luleå publish the times of sunrise and sunset. We could either make a long term project and mark these times each day or once each month, or do the whole year at once by consulting some calendar.

Let us say that we choose the latter alternative, mark the hours along a horizontal scale and depict each day as a long strip (Figure 1). We could, rather than just drawing, choose to cut strips of paper and make the diagram more concrete, and perhaps more spectacular.

After completing the diagram we would spend time describing to each other what the shapes of the various parts of the diagram tell us, relating to our experiences of day-lengths at various times of the year. We would also discuss daylight saving time.

This example would give good practice and might trigger the interest in hours and minutes, telling the time, finding out the duration of events, and so would be useful when treating the concept of time. Working out the duration of the "day" would involve thinking and probably a portion of arithmetic. The sun-data may very well be combined with the study of the time of the day that all the pupils in the class were born (Dunkels, 1992b). It may also be combined with writing or telling a story about long and short days. Or writing a letter to a friend further south—perhaps in Nanyuki in Kenya. What would their sun diagram look like?

Days can also be visualized as in the interesting table in Figure 2. What is its purpose? What does it want to say? To whom is it saying this? Does it do it well? A caption alongside the table, not reproduced here, states that it is easier for the company to give good service at the beginning of the week.

Although there is an indication about absolute numbers of customers in each time slot the intention is most likely not for the receiver actually to work out the numbers. Rather, he or she should get a visual impression— worth more than a thousand numbers. Had the dots been systematically grouped or ordered then some of the visual impact may have been lost.

The table in Figure 2 is an excellent starting point for a discussion with student teachers as well as with children about numbers, shapes, and interpretation of real life situations. Being basically a table, all the time slots are the same width and height, although some represent a shorter time interval, some a longer. Thus we are misled and might get the impression that Thursday 18.00–19.00 is as crowded as Monday 12.00–14.00.

En typisk vecka kan illustreras så här:

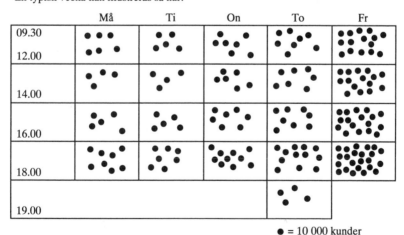

● = 10 000 kunder

Figure 2. A table on the last page of a price list from Systembolaget, the state-owned company that has the monopoly of selling alcohol in Sweden. The text above the table reads, "A typical week may be illustrated thus." The word "kunder" means "customers", and the table heading has abbreviations for the five workdays of the week.

The table can easily be improved to account for such differences by adjusting the heights of the time slots accordingly. Note also that the time slots carry no indication about the number of cashiers on duty.

This also gives rise to quite a few arithmetical questions for the children to pose and, above all, thoughts about the possible arrangement of dots. What would we have chosen if we really wanted to see the numbers of customers in each time-slot without difficulty? This leads to thinking about dice patterns, tallying, and numerals. I would take the opportunity of discussing the tally-by-ten scheme of Figure 3 (Tukey, 1977; Dunkels, 1991) and suggest that the pupils investigate how tallying is done in different countries or cultures (Dunkels, 1992a).

Figure 3. Tallying by tens uses four dots, placed in the corners of a square, then the four sides are filled in, and lastly the diagonals of the square, making the final character for 10, which, by the way, resembles the Roman numeral for 10 which is no disadvantage. The order in which the four dots are placed is unimportant, as is the order of the four sides and the diagonals. However, no side may be filled in before all dots have been entered, and all four sides must be there before a diagonal is drawn. Some counts thus have more than one tally pattern, some have just one. This is in itself worth exploring.

The table for Figure 2 has a connection to real life that might be useful as an introduction to the social joys and problems with alcohol, matters that are extremely hard to address, particularly in primary school. Nevertheless they have to be dealt with sooner or later, and so if mathematics, or statistics, can provide a gateway to this part of the real world then we should seize the opportunity.

HALVING

Some countries use A4-size paper. Sweden is one of them. This particular size offers rich experiences in geometry.

In a student teacher's class we cut out a paper rectangle with dimensions of each one's own choice. We folded it in half with the fold parallel to the shorter side. These three were among the questions that arose:

1) What can be said about the shape of each half rectangle compared to the original rectangle?

2) Are there other ways of folding a rectangle in half?

3) How many?

Question 1 was addressed in class, the rest was left as homework.

Question 1 was not very interesting, the shapes are different, that is all. What if we took a rectangle that really belongs to the real world for all Swedes, the A4-rectangle (Figure 4a)?

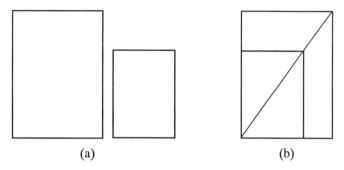

(a)   (b)

Figure 4. a) An A4-rectangle and half of an A4-rectangle side by side.
   b) The A4-rectangle and half of it put on top, both equipped with a diagonal fold.

We compared the original A4-rectangle with half of it by folding both along their diagonals. We put them on top of each other and found that the diagonals then matched exactly (Figure 4b). We tried the same procedure with the rectangles we had used in the previous investigation and found that the diagonals did not match. The conclusion was that the shapes of A4 and half of A4 are the same, or, using the proper technical term, are similar. This is in fact the very idea behind the A-size.

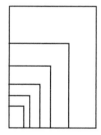

Figure 5. The A4-rectangle is halved 5 times and the successive halves put on top each other. Here is one way of arranging the rectangles, they all have the same relative positions and one common vertex.

Many students knew that on some copying machines one can diminish the size of an A4-document to A5, which is what half of A4 is called. But then the setting of the machine has to be 71%. Why this is so they did not know. Somebody knew that doubling is possible too with the setting 141%. The students said that they had, at times, wondered about these, as it seems, strange settings.

First of all we had to clarify what we mean by "halving" and "doubling". We could clearly see that the shorter side of A5 is not half of that of A4, and so "halving" could not refer to the linear measurements of the figures. We agreed it refers to area.

When the A5-rectangle is put on top of an A4 as in Figure 4b, then the smaller rectangle is of course still half the larger. Yet the students and I felt that the part outside the smaller rectangle seemed bigger. Tangrams are another source of similar experiences (Dunkels, 1990).

Measuring sides and calculating we found the ratio of corresponding sides of A5 to those of A4 to be 0.7, or taking the larger first, 1.4. The students were now motivated to do exact calculations, finding the ratios to be $\frac{1}{\sqrt{2}} \approx 0.71$ and $\sqrt{2} \approx 1.41$, respectively. The mystery of the settings was resolved.

The students agreed that they had heard the phrase "the area ratio is the square of the linear ratio," but it had never had any real meaning to them.

We then continued along two different paths.

One was halving the A5 rectangle successively until we had 6 similar rectangles, using yellow and blue paper. Then we arranged the rectangles as in Figure 5 with rectangles in alternate colors. This in turn led to activities along the lines of Gibbs (1990) and Taylor et al. (1991), related to art and culture.

The other was to see how this is reflected in diagrams of real life, for example, Figure 6. The impression one gets there is that Gorbachev's popularity has decreased more than the numerals indicate, since the visual impression is much stronger than the numbers.

It happens all too often in diagrams in newspapers and journals that linear measurements are doubled vertically as well as horizontally and the resulting figure is thought to be doubled. The visual impression of such a doubling is definitely not just a doubling. What one sees is the magnification of the area by a factor 4. Therefore I find it important that the future primary teachers are made aware of such dangers and given a proper platform for educating the young.

Later we had a methodological follow-up of these two paths of activity. Among other things we discussed the use of geoboards to confront the children with these ideas at an early stage. Starting with the smallest square with just one rubber band one can double the lengths in just one direction and note how this affects the size of the square, then double all sides in both directions and note the result. These are rich geometry activities for primary pupils with relevance to real life.

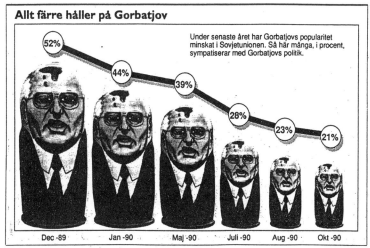

Diagram: Lennart Lindgren

Figure 6. Diagram from *Dagens Nyheter* (Daily News), December 9, 1991. The heading reads, "Fewer and fewer favour Gorbachev". The area of the smallest picture corresponds to only 9% if the biggest corresponds to 52%. Thus the diagram gives the impression that Gorbachev's popularity has decreased much more than it actually has. An additional difficulty in this particular case is that this newspaper, issued in Stockholm, has a narrower paper size in the north, due to the fact that it is electronically sent and printed in a city in the north, where the width of the Stockholm edition could not be handled. So all the linear measurements are decreased horizontally whereas they are maintained vertically.

The discussion also led to a realization that all this has ties to the much celebrated region model, sometimes also called "area model," for multiplication. If one doubles one of the factors, how will the region be affected? If one doubles both factors?

Some 3-dimensional considerations were made. The students played a little with building blocks, predicted and investigated how volume is affected when the linear measurements are doubled in all three directions.

Here a discussion of a generalization of the concept of dimension to fractional dimensions is appropriate for student teachers who specialize in mathematics and natural sciences. This leads to studying something as modern as fractals (Peterson, 1988, in particular pp. 116-120).

STEM-AND-LEAF DISPLAYS

Let me confess at the outset that I am very fond of the stem-and-leaf display—love at first sight (Tukey, 1977)—this ingenious, simple, and versatile mixture of table and diagram. The splitting of numbers into two parts has a particularly strong appeal to me, and my joy was complete when I realized that the splitting can in fact be done physically and used with learners of place value. This was in 1984, late in Grade 1, with 7 and 8 year olds. The purpose was to review and strengthen ideas about place value through data from the real world that the pupils cared for. We worked with parents' ages, and wrote them down on rectangular cardboard cards. Then the cards were cut in two halves, the tens digit on one of the pieces and the units digit on the other. And with these half cards we eventually made a physical stem-and-leaf display of the mothers' ages. (For further details see Dunkels, 1986.)

I wish to point out one important feature of the stem-and-leaf display: The display develops from left to right and from above downwards. This means that it follows the directions of writing and reading of Swedish and many other European languages. This I find most important, and it makes the stem-and-leaf display useful with young children.

An important ingredient in primary education is estimation, for example estimating the duration of a minute, the length of a stick, the weight of a stone. Stem-and-leaf displays enter at the recording phase (Dunkels, 1988; Pereira-Mendoza & Dunkels, 1989; Vännman & Dunkels, 1984).

The steam-and-leaf display also gives good insights into the cardinal and ordinal aspects of counting numbers, and so serves several purposes in primary teacher education (Dunkels, 1991, 1992b).

Since 1984 I have introduced stem-and-leaf displays to different primary classes, as well as in inservice courses, in various ways, often seizing opportunities that have arisen unexpectedly out of pupils' queries or comments (Dunkels, 1987, 1988, 1991).

Here I will describe one such unexpected situation. I visited a Grade 3 class (9-10 year olds) to work with multiplication. On entering the classroom one of the pupils asked about my age. I knew very well that children are interested in ages and that grownups in Sweden often react in strange ways to questions about their age, and often children do not get answers to such questions.

What was I to do? Should I just tell the pupil? Or should I have him guess? Or should I invite the whole class to guess? If so, how should I collect the data? Ask one of the pupils? Or collect everybody's guesses?

I knew that this particular class had not done any stem-and-leaf displays. I decided to change my plans and do some age estimation instead.

I invited everybody to guess my age, to write the guess down without revealing it to their neighbors.

Then on the chalk board I wrote, without explaining, 3, 4, and 5 in a column, the stem, and a vertical line segment immediately to the right (Figure 7a).

I asked the pupils one by one to read, aloud, their guesses, while I recorded on the chalkboard. The first guess was 38, and I entered the 8 in the 3-row.

The next guess was 55, and so a 5 was entered in the 5-row, the next was 52, and so a 2 was entered in that same row. We now had three leaves in our display (Figure 7b). Before we were through I had had to add two rows to the display, so my prediction of the range had not been correct. When all the guesses were recorded the situation was as portrayed in Figure 7c. For a discussion of numerals having a 0 in one of the places see Dunkels (1986, 1992b).

				tens	units	
		2	9	2	9	2	9	(1)

3	3 8	2 9	2 9	2 9	(1)
4	4	3 829	3 289	3 289	(3)
5	5 52	4 498	4 489	4 489	(3)
		5 52480	5 02458	5 02458	(5)
		6 0	6 0	6 0	(1)
					(13)
(a)	(b)	(c)	(d)	(e)	

Figure 7. Successive steps when introducing stem-and-leaf displays to a primary class. The pupils had guessed my age. (a) gives the tens digits of the guesses that I expected the pupils to give. (b) shows the situation when 3 pupils have given their guesses: 38, 55, and 50. (c) contains all the guesses, and I have had to add two more tens digits, 2 and 6. In (d) the units digits have been ordered within each row. In (e) frequencies of all rows and column headings have been entered .

There were immediate suggestions that we should order the units digits, or, using the terminology of Tukey (1977), the leaves, by size leading to Figure 7d.

The time had come for me to tell my age, and I was faced with a problem. My birthday was just 16 days later, and so I considered myself 49, but was in fact 48. I decided to postpone a discussion about accuracy, and claimed that I was 49. The following week I was forced to admit that I had been lying, for of course the inevitable question about my birthday was asked.

This led to a worthwhile discussion about difficulties of deciding what is "a correct answer" in surveys (Dunkels, 1992b).

After having entered the frequency of each row (Figure 7e) we talked about the display, looked at the smallest and the largest guesses, found the middle guess to be the "correct" 49, and reflected about the nice features of the place value system.

I knew that some of the pupils in this class in relation to mental addition and subtraction needed practice and encouragement in splitting numbers into their components, practice and encouragement in viewing the tens' digits as counting multi-units and at the same time seeing them as tens, practice and encouragement in moving units around from one number to the other in mental addition and subtraction with two-digit numbers.

I took this opportunity to enhance the merits of place value, for example the fact that we compute in exactly the same way with the tens digits as we do with the units' digits.

We also played around with our stem-and-leaf displays. We noted that the rows look like bars or strips when viewed from a distance. We emphasized this visual impression by covering the ones' digits (Figure 8), thereby relating the new display to earlier experiences.

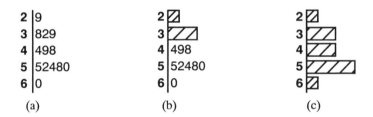

2	9
3	829
4	498
5	52480
6	0
	(a)

Figure 8. Connecting the stem-and-leaf display to earlier experiences of strip graphs. (a) is the display of Figure 7. In (b) two of the rows have been changed into strips with chalk on the board or crayon in the notebook. In (c) all have been changed. What are the advantages of each kind?

"Here we see how the number of people is translated into centimetres," I said. This triggered several pupils' memories, "It is like the spaghetti display," they said referring to something we had done before based on an idea in *Kamratposten,* a journal for school children.

The idea was to measure the size of helpings of spaghetti in centimetres by tying ribbons around 1, 2, 3, 4, etc. helpings which then could be displayed as a strip graph with those same ribbons. A standard helping was estimated to 70 g.

Anything, said one of the pupils, can be a strip, the weight of spaghetti, the time I spend watching TV, the height of people, the measurements around our heads, and the number of people.

All people are interested in their body measurements, for example heights. With Grade 1 pupils, before the whole class has covered numbers greater than 100, one can measure the excess over 1 m of each child's height (Dunkels, 1991).

The heights, expressed as the excess in cm over 1 m, of our

	MOTHERS				FATHERS	
tens	units			**tens**	units	
5	78999	(5)		5		
6	003333334	(9)		6		
6	5678	(4)		6	88	(2)
7	0	(5)		7	00	(4)
7		(1)		7	577889999	(9)
8				8	0024	(4)
8				8	99	(2)
		(19)				(19)

Figure 9. The excess over 1 m of the heights of the parents of a Grade 2 class in northern Sweden. The children themselves initiated the investigation. The rows have been split into two, since they would otherwise have been too long.

YEAR

tens	units	
193	7	(1)
194		
194		
195	3	(1)
195	7	(1)
196		
196	6888999	(7)
197	0002223333344	(13)
197	5555666666667777777788999	(26)
198	000233344	(9)
198	555677	(6)
		(64)

Figure 10. The year of birth of siblings of pupils in a school in a rural area in 1988. The pupils themselves initiated this investigation.

CONCLUDING REMARKS

In order to develop number sense a child needs a rich variety of experiences to build upon. Handling real world data is one source—if it then is called statistics or mathematics is not so important. What matters is that the child gets many opportunities of digging many holes, each hole having its merits, joys, surprises, and limitations. I will end the way I started, with a poem by R.L. Stevenson, "At the seaside".

> When I was down beside the sea
> A wooden spade they gave to me
> To dig the sandy shore.
> My holes were empty like a cup,
> In every hole the sea came up
> Till it could come no more.

REFERENCES

Åberg-Bengtsson, L. (1991). *Children's understanding of graphs.* Gothenburg, Sweden: Department of Education and Educational Research, Gothenburg University.

Dunkels, A. (1986). Exploratory data analysis in the primary school classroom: Graphing and concept formation combined. In R. Morris (Ed.), *Studies in mathematics education: The teaching of statistics, 7,* UNESCO 1989 (reprinted with corrections 1991), pp. 19-26. (Edited version from *Proceedings of ICOTS 2,* pp. 61-66.)

Dunkels, A. (1987). An example from the inservice mathematics classroom. *Zentralblatt für Didaktik der Mathematik, 87*(4), 159-161.

Dunkels, A. (1988). Examples from the inservice classroom (age group 7-12). In A. Hawkins (Ed.), *Training teachers to teach statistics* (pp. 102-109). Proceedings of the International Statistical Institute Round Table Conference, Budapest, Hungary, 23-27 1988.

Dunkels, A. (1990). Making and exploring Tangrams. *Arithmetic Teacher, 37*(6), 38-42.

Dunkels, A. (1991). Interplay of the number concept and statistics using attitudes and techniques of EDA. In Vere-Jones (Ed.) (pp. 129-139).

Dunkels, A. (1992a). Avprickning [Tallying]. *Nämnaren, 19*(2), 26-30.

Dunkels, A. (1992b). *Impact of EDA on primary education.* Paper presented to International Statistical Institute Round Table Conference: Introducing data analysis in the schools: Who should teach it and how?

Gibbs, W. (1990). Paper Patterns 14. *Mathematics in School, 19*(2), 24-28; (3), 24; (4), 28; (5), 16-19.

Pereira-Mendoza, L., & Dunkels, A. (1989). Stem-and-leaf plots in the primary grades. *Teaching Statistics, 11*(2), pp. 34-37.

Peterson, I. (1988). *The mathematical tourist: Snapshots of modern mathematics.* New York: W.H. Freeman Co.

Rangecroft, M. (1991). Graphwork–Developing a progression. Part 1– The early stages. Part 2–A diversity of graphs. *Teaching Statistics, 13*(2), 44-46; (3), 90-92.

Russel, S.J., & Corvin, R.B. (1990). *Used numbers. Real data in the classroom.* Palo Alto: Dale Seymour Publications.

Taylor, L., Stevens, E., Peregoy, J.J., & Bath, B. (1991). American Indians, mathematical attitudes, and the standards. *Arithmetic Teacher, 38*(6), 14-21.

Tukey, J.W. (1977). *Exploratory data analysis.* Reading, MA: Addison Wesley.

Vere-Jones, D. (Ed.) (1991). *Proceedings of the Third International Conference on Teaching Statistics* (ICOTS 3), School and General issues, *1.* Dunedin, New Zealand: ISI Publications in Statistics Education.

Vännman, K., & Dunkels, A. (1984). *Kreativ statistik med EDA.* Gothenburg, Sweden: Gothia.

TEACHING MATHEMATICS AND PROBLEM SOLVING TO DEAF AND HARD-OF-HEARING STUDENTS

Harvey Goodstein[1]

Gallaudet University, United States

I was born deaf to deaf parents, and thus the American Sign Language (ASL) was my first language, and English my second language. After attending residential schools for the deaf in New York, I attended Gallaudet College (later, University), where I now teach, and obtained my bachelor's degree in mathematics. Gallaudet University is the world's only liberal arts college for deaf and hard-of-hearing students, attracting students not only nationally but internationally as well. For my doctoral dissertation I studied the mathematical preparation of pre-college teachers of deaf students and I have subsequently been involved in organizing and conducting summer institutes for pre-college teachers of deaf students.

For the purpose of this paper, deaf and hard-of-hearing students will simply be referred to as deaf students. It should be noted that some deaf students are doing exceptionally well academically in their schools or programs. However, the examples presented in this paper relate to the large majority of deaf students who for the most part have endured restrictive communication environments during their formative years which have adversely affected their language and cognitive development.

There are four parts to this paper. First, I give a few examples of problems in mathematics and problem solving encountered by deaf students based on my observations in schools and "mainstreamed" programs serving deaf students in the United States. Second, I explain some of the difficulties in teaching and learning mathematics and in problem solving, relative to deaf students. Then, after a few brief historical remarks, I outline the desired

---

[1]   Professor Goodstein delivered his paper in American Sign Language (ASL), which was translated into spoken English by an interpreter.

bilingual/bicultural (or multilingual/multicultural) learning environment involving American Sign Language (ASL) and English. Some suggested teaching strategies appropriate for deaf students are highlighted. Such learning environment and teaching strategies have their parallels in bilingual/bicultural programs designed for other learners of English as a second language.

EXAMPLES OF THE MATHEMATICAL DIFFICULTIES OF DEAF STUDENTS

1. Standing in front of a class of 9-11-year-old deaf students, holding a one-foot ruler in my hands for them to see, I asked the class to estimate my height. Impulsively, irrational answers were given, ranging from 10 feet to 50 feet. After the class went through the motions, measuring and learning that my height was between five and six feet tall, I then asked a student (about four feet tall) to stand by me, and challenged the class to estimate her height. Again, quickly (and happily), they answered, 10 feet, 25 feet, etc. (with all of the answers larger than six feet).

2. A class of 10-12-year-old deaf students was assigned to compute the areas of rectangles, given figures with the lengths of the sides shown. The students had no difficulty computing the areas using the formula $A = bh$, yielding answers like 15 for a 3 × 5 rectangle, etc. So, I asked one student, "15 what?" Puzzled, the student replied, "Huh?" I repeated, "15 what? 15 shoes? 15 cows, 15 what?" Bewildered, the student said, "15, that's all."

3. In a class of 7-9-year-old deaf students, given four nickels on the table, one was able to count aloud by fives, and ended up with 20 cents as the result. However, the same student was not able to compute mentally (by fives) the answer to a written "4 × 5 =" problem, nor to understand that "4 × 5" is a symbolic representation of four groups of fives.

4. In most classes, deaf students of practically all ages face particular problems with the concepts of percentages, decimals, and fractions. Incorrect responses are made to questions involving fractions; for example, they will offer statements like "$\frac{1}{2} + \frac{1}{3} = \frac{2}{5}$", "$\frac{1}{3}$ is larger than $\frac{1}{2}$", and others.

5. A group of deaf students, ages 17 through 19, volunteered to participate in a research project (in progress at the time of the lecture). Individually, and one at a time, the students were given a story problem such as:

"Jack has 245 videotapes and wants to put them equally in 4 boxes. How many extra videotapes would there be?"

The students were asked to read the problem, and to sign aloud while reading. Nearly all of them could sign at least 80 percent of the words, fingerspelling the rest (i.e., words they could not comprehend). Then the students were asked to solve the problem, writing everything on paper. Some subtracted 4 from 245; others added or multiplied the two given numbers, or involved some other unrelated, irrational processes or operations. When asked to give a mental picture of the given story problem, as if watching a movie in their heads, nearly all said, "There was none" or, "Blank in head," and some even challenged the question: "What for?" or, "No need for that picture."

At first glance, these examples may not appear different from the sorts of experiences that teachers of hearing students can report, nevertheless a large proportion of deaf students tend to make these errors. Further, although the second and fourth examples can be readily matched among hearing students, the first and fifth examples show a striking failure to coordinate perceptions in the "real" and "mathematical" worlds. The student in the third example makes no connection between a simple counting situation and related symbolic statements.

The examples are just anecdotes, of course, and do not prove anything conclusively about the mathematical difficulties that deaf students are likely to have simply because they are deaf. To get closer to that question we need to take account of the fact that deafness is not solely a physiological condition, which provides difficulty enough, but a constellation of associated factors which affect the upbringing and education of deaf students.

SOME TEACHING AND LEARNING DIFFICULTIES OF DEAF STUDENTS

Considering the home environment first, it is important to note that nearly 90% of deaf students are born to hearing parents, most of whom have had no previous exposure to deafness. Many parents, dismayed and even crushed by their child's condition, are often not able to reconcile themselves to it for a long while. They tend, in the beginning at least, to adopt the pathological view of deafness that they find expressed in the attitudes of doctors, audiologists, speech therapists, etc., who are in most cases the people they first consult for advice and help before they have had the chance to encounter the diametrically opposed viewpoint, held by the Deaf[2] community

---

[2]   The capitalized word "Deaf" is used in the literature whenever the distinctive cultural aspects of deaf people are being emphasized.

and professional staff at schools for the deaf, that Deaf people constitute an authentic linguistic minority. The standard medical view places an overwhelming emphasis on the "hearingization" of a deaf child. In this climate many deaf children grow up with low self-esteem and develop emotional and social problems stemming from their certainty that they can never hope to keep up with their hearing peers.

The majority of deaf students enter school with poor or non-existent skills in ASL and English, not because of their deafness *per se*, but because of the restrictive communication available in their early environment. Not many teachers of the deaf are fluent in ASL, so the communication environment remains impoverished even in schools and programs intended to serve deaf students. Studies show that the average deaf student leaves high school with a fourth grade reading level and an eighth grade mathematics (computational) level.

Most pre-service training programs for teachers of the deaf at the master's level do not make competence in ASL a graduation requirement. ASL competence is not currently required for teacher certification either. Teachers of the deaf who cannot sign fluently are unable to engage in natural and spontaneous communication with the students in their classrooms. Studies show that deaf students of deaf parents perform at significantly higher academic levels than deaf students of hearing parents. Nevertheless, even those students favored with an early exposure to ASL at home are often unable to use that advantage to the fullest when they enter school because their teachers cannot use ASL well enough to work with them.

One of the reasons for the lack of deaf teachers is that many of them, although intelligent and possessing average English skills, are not able to pass the National Teacher Examination (NTE) exam which is mandatory in many states. A few states have waived the NTE requirement for deaf applicants pending further study on the test and the claim that it is culturally biased. There is therefore a small percentage of deaf teachers in schools for the deaf, but virtually none in the "mainstreamed" programs in regular schools. The scarcity of appropriate role models for deaf students in the classroom contributes to their further disadvantaging.

The great majority of teachers of deaf students at elementary through secondary levels have weak backgrounds in mathematics, poor problem solving skills, high anxiety, and poor attitudes towards mathematics. As a group they find it most convenient to teach with an emphasis on rote memory and computation, avoiding story (word) problems as much as possible; they generally do not teach for understanding or concept mastery. Moreover, because of the wide range of backgrounds and cognitive skills in each class and the low level of sign communication between teacher and students, most teachers organize their classrooms for individual drill and do not attempt to encourage group discussion or cooperative learning. Because of the critical shortage of qualified interpreters, deaf students placed in classes of hearing students are for the most part unable to participate in the discussion of mathematical topics or any other interactive situations in the classroom.

I can summarize the situation of mathematics in most schools and programs serving deaf students through the following items of current folklore. (1) The dominant emphasis in the curriculum is on language (English) development, often at the expense of other subject areas such as mathematics, science, and social studies. The "English is intelligence" mentality is all-pervasive. (2) There is a common belief that deaf students "do well" in mathematics, but this is because educators tend to identify mathematics with purposeless computation. Mathematics as problem solving, or as the study of patterns and relationships, is ignored. (3) Story problems are skipped or deferred because teachers have low expectations about the students' capacity to handle the necessary language demands of the tasks. Where they are covered, instruction focuses on looking for cues, not on understanding the nature of the problems.

In the next section I deal briefly with one of the arguments that has dogged deaf education until now. Then in the final section I consider what steps should be taken to improve the generally unsatisfactory state of mathematics in deaf education.

THE GREAT SIGN CONTROVERSY

ASL has its roots in France where, in the 1760s, a methodical sign language system began to be developed by the Abbé de l'Épée from the natural sign language used by Deaf children and Deaf staff members at his school. By 1791 the school had become the Paris Institute for Deaf-Mutes. In 1816 Thomas Gallaudet, accompanied by Laurent Clerc, who was born deaf and had been first a student and later a teacher at the Institute, brought the language of signs to Hartford, Connecticut. Over time, and shaken free of the inflections that had related it to French grammar, this language gradually became the ASL that is now used by a half a million people in the United States of America and Canada.

From the beginning, there has been an ideological struggle between the proponents of oral and sign instruction for the deaf. Behind the well-intentioned concerns of some of those who have argued for oral instruction—that deaf people should be helped to learn the ways of the dominant majority and not forced to become ghettoized, as well as genuine worry about the linguistic shortcomings of sign language—there have often lurked the irrational fears of people faced with behavior they did not understand, and perhaps did not wish to understand. It is not only the simple and uneducated who have associated severe deafness with severe mental limitations. (How significant that being "dumb" is still carelessly and commonly used to mean unintelligent!) Those on the other hand who favored sign instruction, even those who shared doubts about the linguistic adequacy of sign language, knew that signing "unlocked" the intelligence of deaf people and showed them to be as educable as anyone else.

For a hundred years or so the victory went to oralism. The Second World Congress to Improve the Welfare of the Deaf and the Blind, now usually known as the International Congress on Education of the Deaf, in Milan in 1880, pronounced the dangerous inadequacy of signing as an instructional medium and proposed to ban it, and almost all institutions in almost all countries accepted a recommendation from a meeting of exclusively hearing people, few of whom could use a sign language. In the United States of America, for example, ASL was the instructional medium in all 26 institutions for educating deaf children in 1867, but by 1907 ASL was not permitted in a single one of the 139 schools then operating.

As far back as 1827, Jean-Marc-Gaspard Itard (better known perhaps as the would-be teacher of the Wild Boy of Aveyron) had carefully studied two deaf-mute students and showed that the student taught through signs was superior. Comparative tests on matched pairs of congenitally deaf students in the 1970s showed that the signing students were significantly better in reading, writing, psychological adjustment, oral speech, graduation from high school, and college entrance. The future of the exclusively oral approach, though, may be even more affected by post-Chomskian studies which have been able to show that sign language is in fact an adequate instructional language, and by the greatly increased politicization of the issue of deaf education, which must in today's climate be regarded as too important a matter to be left entirely to the determination of hearing people, however well-intentioned.

THE DESIRED TEACHING/LEARNING ENVIRONMENT AND STRATEGIES FOR ACHIEVING IT

Recommendations

1. Bilingual/bicultural programs, involving ASL and English, and the Deaf and American cultures, should be employed as far as possible. Bi/bi programs are currently in operation, officially or otherwise, in only a few schools/programs serving deaf students in the United States of America. Nevertheless, the concept of such a program has gained a strong level of interest among an increasing number of teachers and administrators as evidenced by the large number of workshops and task forces on this topic in recent years. It is anticipated that such heightened interest will ultimately lead to the wider acceptance of bi/bi programs nationally. In these programs

ASL (which includes a variation with some English elements) is used as the language of instruction via visual communication, while English is used primarily for reading and writing.

2. Before most deaf students can begin to communicate and reason mathematically in a precise or formal fashion (in English), they have first to overcome three primary obstacles during the formative years, sequentially if not concurrently: (1) learning how to communicate naturally and visually via ASL; (2) learning and understanding the mathematics concepts and properties involved through visual communication, acting out, use of manipulatives and experimentation; and (3) reading and writing about these concepts and properties while learning English as a second language.

3. Educators of deaf students need to realize that there is more to education than precision in English. Some have even challenged the proposition: What is wrong with telegraphic English as long as one gets the message across? Workshops for elementary school teachers can give them a third grade story problem in Russian, which most of them will not be able to solve until nearly 45 percent of the words are translated into English. They can also be given another problem in simple English, which they can readily understand (say, involving a ball dropped from the top of the Washington Monument), but are not able to solve because they do not have the necessary calculus and science background. The teachers will be quick to agree that students should not be denied opportunities to solve story problems because of their limited English skills. Further, the teachers will quickly acknowledge the importance of having sufficient hands-on experience involving relational thinking, number sense, measurement sense, concept of fractions, etc., in the development of students' cognitive schemas.

4. At the very least, litigation, legislative, and advocacy efforts should be conducted to ensure that teachers of deaf students do not create communication barriers in the classroom. In other words, teachers of deaf students should at least be competent in ASL. Measures should also be taken so that equity in testing of deaf teachers is assured, especially in national and state examinations.

5. Additional in-service courses and workshops in mathematics content and pedagogy are needed to enhance the mathematics background and preparation of teachers. The teachers must also be trained to teach for mathematical understanding, with emphases on problem solving, communication, reasoning, and making connections, as recommended in the National Council of Teachers of Mathematics Curriculum and Evaluation Standards.

6. The sooner the deaf child and the parents of the deaf child accept the deafness, the better. The condition may not be ameliorable, but the stigma associated with it is. The late Frederick C. Schreiber, former National Association of the Deaf Executive Director, liked to say, "It's what is *between* the ears that counts." The Deaf community has existed for many generations, using ASL as its primary language, and transmitting Deaf culture from generation to generation. For that reason, Deaf people as a group often prefer to be viewed as a linguistic minority, like Hispanics and other ethnic groups, than as disabled.

7. Due to communication barriers deaf students have endured at home and school during the formative years, they may have difficulties in understanding story problems in English. It is recommended that in such instances teachers work through a problem with the students using visual communication, acting out, and so on, until the students understand the problem and the required concepts and processes. Cooperative problem solving should be encouraged. Adaptive materials can also be used—like simplified descriptions, smaller numbers—as long as the students ultimately return to the original problem, however wordy or difficult. Other helpful teaching strategies include: posing problems without numbers to force students to focus on the processes involved; asking students to create questions and problems to fit a given statement or set of facts; solving each other's made-up problems, etc.

8. Writing journals or "learning logs" can be helpful in encouraging students to express their mental images of certain mathematical concepts or relations. In the beginning, because of their low level of confidence in their English skills, students will write very little, maybe only a sentence or two. Gradually, with practice, they begin to feel less hesitant about writing, particularly if given positive feedback together with guidance for further refinements. Mistakes in English should not be emphasized, however, or their discouragement will negate the value of the task.

FINAL REMARKS

Teaching deaf students through bilingual/bicultural programs, as is recommended here, draws deaf education into the more general orbit of teaching English as a second language, with the advantage that the more mainstream experience and techniques that have been accumulated in the practice of ASL can be drawn upon. But there are significant differences that should not be forgotten. Hearing students have considerable aural exposure to English words through radio, TV, interaction with first-language

English speakers, and so on, before they enter school; deaf students do not. Hearing students who have acquired a spoken language, even when that language is not English, have experienced the coordination of mouth and ear in the production of utterances and, in particular, know how to monitor what they utter by listening to it; deaf students lack this capability.

Deaf students learn mainly through their eyes. ASL, the language of signs used in the Deaf community in America, through the natural processes of use, disuse, and refinement, has evolved in its own right into a sophisticated language most appropriate for visual communication. On the other hand, the English-based methodical sign systems, commonly classified as Manually Coded English (MCE), which were artificially constructed as "manual codes" for spoken English, have over the past twenty years proved to be ineffective.

I have talked exclusively about ASL because it is the sign system I know and use. In other countries, of course, deaf educators would do well to adopt the language of signs that is current in their own Deaf community in order to comunicate with deaf students about the world, including the world of mathematics, and to teach the spoken and written language of that country as a second language.

REFERENCES

Ashlock, R.B., et al. (1983). *Guiding each child's learning of mathematics: A diagnostic approach to instruction.* Columbus, OH: Charles E. Merrill Publishing Co.

Gannon, J.R. (1981). *Deaf heritage: a narrative history of deaf America.* Silver Spring, MD: National Association of the Deaf.

Garretson, M.D. (Ed.) (1992). Viewpoints on deafness. *A Deaf American Monograph, 42.* Silver Spring, MD: National Association of the Deaf.

Lane, H. (1984). *When the mind hears: A history of the deaf.* New York: Random House.

Lane, H. (1992). *The mask of benevolence: Disabling the deaf community.* New York: Alfred A. Knopf Inc.

Lovett, C.J., & Snyder, T. (Eds.) (1979). *Resources for teaching mathematics in bilingual classrooms.* Columbus, OH: ERIC Clearinghouse for Science, Mathematics, and Environmental Education.

NCTM Commission on Standards for School Mathematics (1989). *Curriculum and Evaluation Standards for School Mathematics.* Reston, VA: NCTM.

Schleper, D.R., & Paradis, S.J. (1990). Learning logs for math: Thinking through writing. *Perspectives, 9*(2), 14-17, 24. Washington: Gallaudet University Press.

Shuard, H., & Rothery, A. (Eds.) (1984). *Children reading mathematics.* London: John Murray.

THE ORIGIN AND EVOLUTION
OF MATHEMATICAL THEORIES

IMPLICATIONS FOR MATHEMATICAL EDUCATION

Miguel de Guzmán

Universidad Complutense, Spain

In this paper I am concerned to consider the right way to introduce young people to mathematics research. How should they be introduced to mathematical content and to mathematical theories? What is the attitude we should try to foster in them? What do those who are most successful in preparing young mathematicians actually do?

The questions need to be answered quite concretely for it must be admitted that the way to prepare researchers is not a matter of general agreement in the profession, it is not always carried out well, and too many details are often left to chance.

Of course there are many ways to involve students personally and actively in their learning of any mathematical topic, especially by motivating them with problems. For example:

- Here is a problem. Don't read anything, just plunge in and try to solve it straight away.

- Read these several passages from these books carefully, then come and get a problem from me.

- Read this recent paper and then work on the problems it leaves open.

- I will be giving you suggestions for problems to solve throughout the course. Choose the ones that you think will be most productive, that most interest you, that you believe you have a chance of solving.

I strongly believe that the crucial insights in research in a particular field tend to come from a deep knowledge of *the origins and evolution of the theory* one is working with, and a familiarity with the *style of thought* in that area. This is acquired by learning its motivations, the circumstances of its origins (historical, social, personal), the right ways of asking questions, and so on.

I shall try to give substance to this claim by looking first of all at what a knowledge of the history of mathematics in general, and of the specific subject in particular, can offer us that is relevant to the context we are exploring here, and by briefly examining afterwards the lessons that can be derived from the knowledge of the evolution of a field in which I was personally involved some years ago.

WHAT KNOWLEDGE ABOUT THE HISTORY OF MATHEMATICS AND ABOUT A PARTICULAR SUBJECT CAN OFFER THE STUDENT

They offer a vision of science and mathematics as human activities.

We see that the truths, methods, and techniques of mathematics do not come out of the blue. They are not impersonal facts and skills without a history, but are the results of the efforts of passionate and deeply motivated people.

We see that, in spite of its many wonders, mathematics is not really a "godlike" or perfect science. Because it is an artefact of human beings it is also incomplete and fallible. Its history gives us many great discoveries and great discoverers to admire, but it also shows us that much of what we now take to be established and obvious truth was only arrived at after many errors and much controversy.

They offer a frame within which to organize the elements of our mathematical knowledge.

We see better how to relate events that took place centuries apart, how to appreciate the temporal contexts in which mathematical discoveries were made.

We see how people invested their efforts in the pursuit of certain questions, how "fashions" arose, and how the fashions of the past can alert us to those of the present.

We get a sense of how the various threads in the fabric of the subject we are working on were woven together over time.

They offer a dynamic vision of the evolution of mathematics.

We understand the driving forces at work developing the basic ideas and methods of mathematics. We get closer to the springs of creativity that generated particular subjects, consequently gaining a sense of their genesis and progress and a better appreciation of their true nature.

We get a flavor of the thrill and adventure of working in mathematics.

We are immersed creatively in the past and better able to understand our own problems.

There is the possiblity of extrapolating towards the future.

We realize the tortuous paths of creativity, the ambiguities, obscurities, and partial illuminations that accompany the first attempts to shape the field.

We see how we can inject some dynamic, some life, into our educational tasks.

They offer an appreciation of the intertwining of mathematical thought and culture in human society: of the importance of mathematics as a part of human culture.

We see the influence of historical trends and developments on mathematics and, conversely, the impacts of mathematics on human culture, its sciences and philosophies, its arts and technologies.

They offer a more profound technical comprehension.

The more simple a theory is in the beginning the easier it is to understand and work with. Technical complications coming along later can begin to obscure the theory unless one grasps their motivations.

The lines of development of a theory point towards the future and provide guidelines for research.

They offer an awareness of the special life of any mathematical theory.

Each theory has its own peculiar character, molded by the special circumstances that gave rise to it. It was born at a particular moment, the result of particular concerns. It was motivated by curiosity about some phenomenon, the wish to apply some known results, to expand some collection of techniques, to complete some existing theory, and so on.

Each theory developed according to its particular style, its expectations and disappointments, its correct intuitions and its false starts.

Each theory inhabits its own "local" atmosphere generated by the personal and social forces that surrounded it.

It seems to me that one can conclude that: *Familiarity with the origin and evolution of a mathematical theory has profound lessons to offer to anyone trying to be inducted into the field.*

A CASE STUDY: THE DIFFERENTIATION OF INTEGRALS

By following the lines of development of a specific theme in mathematical analysis from this century—Lebesgue differentiation and its extensions—I shall now try to show some of the lessons which can be extracted from this study that could be of use to those seeking to do research in this area. If I am fortunate, the example will have some lessons for people working in other fields too.

Some of the ideas and methods stimulated by this theory during this century have proved very useful in other areas of mathematical analysis, particularly in Fourier analysis and in some aspects of geometrical measure theory. I will present a non-technical description of the main highlights of the theory, taking into account that we are not interested in its technicalities here but rather in the educational implications for those wanting to be introduced to the subject. For the sake of brevity I will trace the main points of the theory from its origins in 1904 to the time its progress was interrupted by the Second World War.

The beginning: the Lebesgue differentiation theorem

Towards the completion of an interesting theory.

The Lebesgue differentiation theorem, the equivalent of the fundamental theorem of calculus, was the culminating point of his measure theory. He first proved it for R^1 (1904): If $f \in L(R^1)$ then at almost every point x

$$\lim_{h \to 0} \frac{1}{2h} \int_{-h}^{h} f(x+t)dt = f(x)$$

Essentially this meant that the means of an integrable function over intervals containing a point x converge, at almost every point, to the value of the function at that point when the intervals contract to the point. The idea followed by Lebesgue in the proof was ingenious but not translatable to R^2. Since the order structure of the real line is so crucial for the proof in R^1, what might be the corresponding tool for R^2?

As in so many other cases, the first impulse to develop new techniques came from the need to extend a theory to more general situations.

Vitali's covering theorem

Sharpening tools that have proved to be interesting, deep, and useful; pushing their scope further.

At the end of the 19th century a number of covering theorems were discovered that helped substantially to clear up the structure of Euclidean space from an analytic point of view. The so-called Heine-Borel covering theorem, the Lindelöf theorem, and others, became important tools in this respect. Vitali's covering theorem was an important advance: Let M be a measurable set in the plane with a Vitali cover V for M (i.e. for every point of M a sequence of square intervals centered on the corresponding point and contracting to that point is given). Then one can extract from V a sequence $\{Q_k\}$ of disjoint squares such that

$$\left| M - \cup Q_k \right| = 0$$

Vitali's theorem was not invented for the purpose of obtaining a proof of the Lebesgue differentiation theorem in R^2, but this was the use Lebesgue made of it in 1910, showing that his theorem for the line could be generalized to the plane if one takes the means of an integrable function over squares or circles containing the corresponding point.

The Lebesgue differentiation theorem in R^2

The solution of an interesting problem often leads to deeper questions;
a good problem is never exhausted.

The result Lebesgue obtained was quite satisfactory, but it led immediately to a natural question: Can one replace the *squares* by more general intervals (e.g. by rectangles in the direction of the coordinate axes, or perhaps by rectangles in arbitrary position)? These natural questions turned out to be quite challenging and these problems remained open for a long time, as we shall see.

The value of paradox

A paradoxical situation can be the beginning of a new development.

From 1908 until 1924 there was in the air a belief that Vitali's theorem would also hold if intervals were substituted for *squares*. The theorem of Lebesgue would then admit a nice and direct generalization. The fact, first proved by H. Bohr (1918) and first published by Banach (1924), that intervals in the plane do *not* satisfy Vitali's lemma seemed counterintuitive. This sort of paradox made the study of the covering properties of different systems of sets in the plane more challenging, and at the same time started to throw some new light on the subject.

This is in many cases the effect of perceived paradoxes. It has been reported that in the midst of working on a difficult problem the physicist Niels Bohr was overheard to say: "How wonderful! We have met a paradox. Now we have some hope of making progress."

An impasse concerning the strong density problem (1924-1934)

There are periods of impasse when progress can come from many directions; one must remain open to all possibilities.

Since Vitali's lemma fails for intervals, what will happen to the differentiation theorem of Lebesgue? Even in the case when the function *f* is the characteristic function of a measurable set, the problem of generalizing the theorem to the plane seemed to be quite difficult. This so-called strong density problem (the local density of a measurable set with respect to intervals in the plane) remained open for many years—until 1933, when Saks was able to prove the strong density theorem. In the meantime, many mathematicians were looking in other directions to find some light that could illuminate this challenging question.

The role of a good game

A good mathematical game can be the beginning of a deep theory.

In 1917 S. Kakeya proposed a problem that looked like a puzzle: What is the infimum of the areas of those plane figures within which a needle of length one can be inverted by continuous motions? The problem has a very long and interesting history in which some important mathematicians show up: e.g., Besicovitch, Perron, Rademacher, Schoenberg. Those interested in the ramifications of it are invited to consult the bibliography proposed at the end of the paper. (By the way, the surprising solution, given by Besicovitch in 1928, is that the infimum mentioned in the statement of the problem is zero.) Here it should suffice to mention that the problem has had very profound implications for the subject of differentiation of integrals and for Fourier analysis. By means of the tools developed in order to solve it C. Fefferman in 1971 was able to solve an important problem which had remained open for many years (the multiplier problem for the ball).

Different lines of thought concerning a theory

At the point where different subjects intersect can often be found many deep questions and much light on those subjects.

At the beginning of the century the theory of Lebesgue measure was recognized as an important tool in many connections in mathematical analysis. It generated a strong interest in the geometric structure of measurable sets. Some of the questions proposed at the time later proved to have deep implications for differentiation theory. In 1926 Banach proposed the question: How large in measure can a linearly accessible set in the unit square Q be? ("Linearly accessible" means that each point of the set can be reached by a straight line originating outside Q.) In 1927 Nikodym solved the problem in a long and complicated paper by constructing a set N contained in Q and having measure 1 (a set of full measure in Q) such that through each of its points there is a straight line not intersecting the set N again. N is a strange set that, in spite of "filling" Q, seems to leave many more points of Q in its complement Q − N. At the end of Nikodym's paper appears an observation of Zygmund that shows that the collection of all rectangles in the plane is an unsatisfactory system for proving the Lebesgue differentiation theorem, and, further, that the density theorem with respect to the system of plane rectangles does not hold.

Later on, R.O. Davies, working in this same direction, constructed still more paradoxical and spectacular sets than that of Nikodym.

The versatility of mathematical tools

When you find a good tool, try to make use of it in some connected problems.

The strong density theorem was proved by Saks in 1933. By then F. Riesz was already in possession of a powerful tool concerning continuous functions in R^1, the so-called *rising sun* lemma (also called the water flowing lemma). He was able to apply it to solving several interesting problems of the moment with ease, presenting another simple and easy proof of the strong density theorem in 1934.

In this same year, Jessen, Marcinkiewicz, and Zygmund were able to give the definitive theorem in the direction of differentiation of functions by the system of intervals in R^n: If f is a function in $L(\log^+ L)^{n-1}(R^n)$ then the intervals differentiate the integral of f and this space of functions is in some sense the best one.

After climbing the peak

When the evolution of a theory along a particular path seems to be close to the summit, one may need to start looking for different lines of thought.

After the Jessen-Marcinkiewicz-Zygmund theorem, the attention of the mathematicians concerned with the differentiation of integrals turned in a natural way in other directions. Busemann and Feller took a new path in 1934 and R. de Possel yet another in 1936.

The abstract and the concrete

Examine the concrete and try to discover a general pattern.

Busemann and Feller introduced into the field the consideration of what has been called the *halo* of a measurable set with respect to a differentiation basis (a generalization of the system of all spheres or of all intervals used in the differentiation theorem). From the concrete ideas introduced by Saks and Riesz in their treatment of the strong density theorem, the idea of the halo was a natural development. By means of it Busemann and Feller were able to present the characterizations of systems of sets that would have good differentiation properties. The time had come to try to leap from the concrete cases to some more general formulations which could be used in other cases. They managed it by giving a quantitative characterization— by means of something which was later perceived to be a (1,1) weak-type inequality for the maximal Hardy-Littlewood operator—of the systems of sets used for differentiating the integral.

For his part, R. de Possel proceeded in a similar vein, from the concrete to the abstract. He observed what happens in the plane with respect to the differentiation and covering properties of the different systems:

a) Squares satisfy Vitali's lemma; squares allow the differentiation of $L^1(R^2)$.

b) Rectangles in arbitrary directions do not satisfy Vitali's lemma; rectangles do not have the strong density property.

c) Intervals allow the differentiation of $Llog^+(R^2)$; but not of $L^1(R^2)$.

In a natural way, he decided to try to explore what are the covering properties, if any, of the system of intervals. He was able in this way to initiate an interesting line of research, looking for the quantitative connections between the differentiation properties and the covering properties of a differentiation basis.

So we can see here in action another interesting principle, which should be kept in mind:

When you notice a qualitative connection, try to find the quantitative reasons for it.

The progress of the theory was interrupted by the Second World War. After it came many other interesting developments: in particular, from the work of Besicovitch in connection with Geometric Measure Theory, and from the intervention of many analysts working in Fourier Analysis. Those interested in following up this subject in detail are invited to consult some of the references below.

REFERENCES

Banach, S. (1924). Sur un théorème de M. Vitali. *Fundamenta Mathematicæ, 5,* 130-136.

Bruckner, A.M. (1971). Differentiation of integrals. *American Mathematical Monthly, 78* (Slaught Memorial Paper No. 12).

Busemann H., & Feller, W. (1934). Zur Differentiation der Lebesgueschen Integrale. *Fundamenta Mathematicæ, 22,* 226-256.

Fefferman, C. (1971). The multiplier problem for the ball. *Annals of Mathematics, 94,* 330-336.

Guzmán, M. de (1975). Differentiation of integrals in RR. *Lecture Notes in Mathematics,* 481 pages. Berlin: Springer.

Guzmán, M. de (1981). Real variable methods in Fourier analysis. *North-Holland Mathematical Studies,* 46 pages.

Guzmán, M. de, & Welland, G. (1971). On the differentiation of integrals. *Revista de la Unión Matemática Argentina, 25,* 253-276.

Jessen, B., Marcinkiewicz, J., & Zygmund, A. (1935). Note on the differentiability of multiple integrals. *Fundamenta Mathematicæ, 25,* 217-234.

Kakeya, S. (1917). Some problems on maxima and minima regarding ovals. *Tohoku Science Reports, 6,* 71-88.

Lebesgue, H. (1904). *Leçons sur l'intégration et la recherche des fonctions primitives.* Paris: Gauthier-Villars.

Lebesgue, H. (1910). Sur l'intégration des fonctions discontinues. *Annales scientifiques de l'École normale supérieure, 27,* 361-450.

Nikodym, O. (1927). Sur la mesure des ensembles plans dont tous les points sont rectilinéairement accessibles. *Fundamenta Mathematicæ, 10,* 116-168.

Possel, R. de, (1936). Sur la dérivation abstraite des fonctions d'ensemble. *Journal de mathématiques pures et appliquées, 15,* 391-409.

Riesz, F. (1934). Sur les points de densité au sens fort. *Fundamenta Mathematicæ, 22,* 221-265.

Saks, S. (1933). *Théorie de l'intégrale.* Varsovie.

Vitali, G. (1908). Sui gruppi di punti e sulle funzioni di variabili reali. *Atti Accademia di Scienze di Torino, 43,* 75-92.

Zygmund, A. (1934). On the differentiability of multiple integrals. *Fundamenta Mathematicæ, 23,* 134-149.

LE CALCUL INFINITÉSIMAL

Bernard R. Hodgson

Université Laval, Canada

LES INFINITÉSIMAUX AU FIL DES ÂGES

> It is interesting that a method which had been given up as untenable has
> at last turned out to be workable and that this development [...] was
> brought about by the refined tools made available by modern mathe-
> matical logic. (Robinson, 1973, p. 16)

Le concept d'*infinitésimal*, de quantité « infiniment petite », a connu
un sort variable au fil des âges. Bannis par les uns, utilisés de façon
heuristique mais souvent avec circonspection par les autres, les infinitésimaux, jusqu'à tout récemment, n'avaient pas droit de cité en mathématiques,
surtout après que les analystes du XIXe siècle eurent introduit dans le calcul
différentiel et intégral, par l'approche en ε–δ, un canon de rigueur ayant
cours jusqu'à nos jours. Bien sûr le physicien et l'ingénieur avaient persisté
dans leur utilisation intuitive des infinitésimaux, mais le mathématicien
savait que tout cela pouvait (et devait !) être remplacé par un discours
rigoureux évacuant toute notion d'infiniment petit actuel.

Déjà les Grecs utilisaient les infinitésimaux pour résoudre certains
problèmes de géométrie. Ainsi Archimède (287-212 A.C.) s'autorise à opérer
sur des décompositions infinies des figures. Toutefois, il s'agit là pour lui
strictement d'une méthode de découverte de propriétés, non d'une façon
acceptable de les démontrer rigoureusement. Travaillant dans la tradition
d'Aristote et d'Euclide, Archimède voit les nombres comme satisfaisant à
ce qu'on appelle aujourd'hui la *propriété d'Archimède* : étant donné deux
nombres, le plus petit, additionné à lui-même un certain nombre (fini !) de
fois, en viendra toujours à surpasser l'autre. Un tel contexte interdit donc
l'existence d'infiniment petits. Néanmoins, comme il le révèle dans son traité
La méthode (découvert en 1906 seulement), Archimède n'hésite pas à faire
appel à son intuition des quantités infinitésimales pour identifier certaines
relations (comme le volume d'une sphère). Intervient ensuite une étape de

validation dans laquelle ces relations sont prouvées par une argumentation indirecte (la « méthode d'exhaustion »), débarrassée de toute présence infinitésimale.

Pour illustrer l'apport des infinitésimaux, considérons une preuve de Nicolas de Cuse (1401-1464) établissant le rapport entre l'aire d'un cercle et sa circonférence (Davis et Hersh, 1980, p. 238). Soit un cercle de rayon r que nous envisageons comme un polygone ayant une infinité de côtés infiniment petits et tous égaux entre eux (voir figure 1, où une portion du cercle est observée à l'aide d'un « microscope infinitésimal » à grossissement infini, tel qu'utilisé dans Keisler (1986)). Chacun de ces côtés est la base d'un triangle isocèle dont le sommet est le centre du cercle et dont la hauteur h est le rayon r du cercle, puisque la base du triangle est infiniment courte. L'aire du cercle, étant la somme des aires de ces triangles, est donc égale à la somme des bases (c'est-à-dire la circonférence) multipliée par $\frac{r}{2}$. Une telle argumentation pourrait être remplacée, par exhaustion, par un raisonnement par contradiction n'utilisant que des constructions finies (Davis et Hersh, 1980, p. 240). On obtient ainsi une preuve répondant aux canons classiques de rigueur mais occultant forcément, par son approche indirecte, l'intuition forte suggérée par la vision infinitésimale.

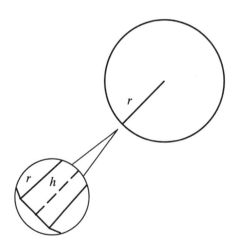

Figure 1

La mise en place d'une théorie générale de la différentiation et de l'intégration fut réalisée simultanément par Newton (1642-1727) et Leibniz (1646-1716). Si Newton utilise à la fois une vision infinitésimale et une vision reposant sur la notion de limite, accordant finalement sa préférence à cette dernière, Leibniz, de son côté, choisit résolument l'approche infinitésimale. Mais pour lui, les infiniment grands ou petits n'ont pas d'existence véritable: ce ne sont que des « façons de parler », des « fictions ». Il oppose l'emploi des infinitésimaux au « style d'Archimède » (entendre les arguments indirects résultant de la méthode d'exhaustion — Leibniz ignorait évidemment les heuristiques infinitésimales d'Archimède dévoilées dans *La méthode*) :

> [...] on n'a pas besoin de prendre l'infini ici à la rigueur [...] Car au lieu de l'infini ou de l'infiniment petit, on prend des quantités aussi grandes et aussi petites qu'il faut pour que l'erreur soit moindre que l'erreur donnée, de sorte qu'on ne diffère du style d'Archimède que dans les expressions, qui sont plus directes dans notre méthode et plus conformes à l'art d'inventer. (Robinson, 1974, pp. 261-262)

Le calcul développé par Newton et Leibniz a vite connu des succès éclatants dans ses applications. Cependant de sérieuses difficultés logiques sont apparues quant à ses fondements, tant selon l'approche de Newton que celle de Leibniz. Ainsi le recours aux infinitésimaux amène une contradiction flagrante, comme l'illustre le calcul de la dérivée de x^2 :

$$\frac{d(x^2)}{dx} = \frac{(x + dx)^2 - x^2}{dx} = 2x + dx = 2x$$

L'accroissement infinitésimal dx, qui se comporte comme zéro à la fin du calcul, ne peut bien sûr être nul au départ. Cette ambivalence n'a pas manqué d'être sévèrement attaquée, en particulier par Berkeley (1685-1753). Dans son célèbre pamphlet *The analyst*, celui-ci condamne avec virulence l'utilisation de ces « incréments évanescents » :

> For when it is said, let the increments vanish, i.e., let the increments be nothing, or let there be no increments, the former supposition that the increments were something, or that there were increments, is destroyed, and yet a consequence of that supposition, i.e., an expression got by virtue thereof, is retained. [...] I have no controversy about your conclusions, but only about your logic and method. (Berkeley, 1734, pp. 25, 30)

Même si la controverse entourant le statut des infinitésimaux n'empêche pas Euler (1707-1783) de les utiliser avec art (voir Robert, 1985, pp. 3-5), de telles attaques eurent néanmoins un effet dévastateur. Et si les infiniment petits se retrouvent encore un siècle plus tard dans les textes de Cauchy (1789-1857), c'est essentiellement dans un rôle heuristique « d'intermédiaires qui doivent [...] conduire à la connaissance des relations qui subsistent entre des quantités finies » (Robinson, 1974, p. 275), comme chez Archimède. Car avec Cauchy, et plus tard avec Weierstrass (1815-1897), se construit la théorie moderne des limites et de la continuité telle que nous la connaissons aujourd'hui, où les considérations infinitésimales cèdent la place à des inégalités en ε–δ. Pour le mathématicien, les infinitésimaux tombent alors en désuétude complète, même s'ils restent un outil commode dont ne se privent pas d'autres scientifiques.

Il y a un peu plus de trente ans, Abraham Robinson (1918-1974) a découvert comment certains outils de la logique mathématique, plus précisément de la théorie des modèles, permettent de construire un corps de nombres *hyperréels* grâce auquel le calcul différentiel et intégral peut être développé de façon rigoureuse dans un contexte infinitésimal : cette légitimation *a posteriori* permet au mathématicien d'aujourd'hui de revenir en toute sérénité aux méthodes si fécondes faisant intervenir explicitement l'infiniment grand et l'infiniment petit (et remet en lumière l'expression traditionnelle *calcul infinitésimal*).

Après un rappel des fondements logiques du calcul infinitésimal moderne, nous en présentons certaines versions qui débouchent sur des approches conçues spécifiquement à des fins pédagogiques en vue du renouvellement de l'enseignement élémentaire de l'analyse.

LE CORPS DES HYPERRÉELS

> Skolem's works on non-standard models of Arithmetic was the greatest single factor in the creation of Non-standard Analysis. (Robinson, 1974, p. 278)

Nous voulons examiner brièvement de quelle façon la logique mathématique intervient dans la construction primitive de Robinson. À cette fin, nous indiquons comment des résultats de Skolem, d'abord perçus comme témoignant d'aspects pathologiques des formalismes, recèlent l'idée maîtresse sous-jacente à une introduction rigoureuse de quantités infiniment grandes et petites.

L'étude des langages formels implique une double vision syntaxique et sémantique, rendant compte à la fois des aspects déductifs (énoncé *formellement démontrable*) et interprétatifs (énoncé *vrai* sous telle interprétation). Plus généralement, on s'intéresse à la notion d'ensemble d'énoncés *cohérent* (n'engendrant pas de contradiction) et possédant un *modèle* (c'est-à-dire une structure d'interprétation rendant vrais ses énoncés). Le *théorème de complétude,* démontré par Gödel en 1930, affirme justement l'équivalence entre la syntaxe et la sémantique, dans le sens qu'un ensemble d'énoncés est cohérent si et seulement s'il a un modèle. Un corollaire immédiat en est le *théorème de compacité,* qui donne l'équivalence entre l'existence d'un modèle pour un ensemble Γ d'énoncés et l'existence, pour chaque sous-ensemble fini de Γ, d'un modèle. C'est cette propriété de finitude qui joue le rôle-clé dans la construction suivante, donnée par Skolem en 1934.

Soit la structure $\mathcal{N}$ de l'arithmétique dans les naturels et le langage formel correspondant $\mathcal{L}$ muni des symboles appropriés (entre autres pour l'addition et la multiplication). Nous désignons par *Théorie* $(\mathcal{N})$ l'ensemble des énoncés de $\mathcal{L}$ vrais dans $\mathcal{N}$. Le « truc » syntaxique permettant d'obtenir un *modèle non standard* de l'arithmétique consiste à enrichir $\mathcal{L}$ par l'ajout

d'un nouveau symbole formel *a* jouant le rôle d'élément infini par l'inter-
médiaire des énoncés *n* < *a* où *n* est un naturel quelconque. Nous obtenons
ainsi, au niveau du langage enrichi $\underline{L}$, l'ensemble d'énoncés $\underline{\Gamma}$ = *Théorie* $(\mathcal{N})$
$\cup$ {*n* < *a* | *n* naturel} qui, par compacité, possède un modèle, disons $\underline{\mathcal{N}}^*$,
dont la restriction au niveau de L donne un modèle $\mathcal{N}^*$ de l'arithmétique
englobant $\mathbb{N}$ et dans lequel vivent des éléments infinis. Par construction
même, les deux structures $\mathcal{N}$ et $\mathcal{N}^*$ sont *élémentairement équivalentes*
($\mathcal{N} \equiv \mathcal{N}^*$), dans le sens qu'elles valident exactement les mêmes énoncés de
L : c'est là le fameux *principe de transfert* qui joue un rôle fondamental
dans l'utilisation des modèles non standard. La figure 2 schématise les étapes
de cette construction, les flèches pleines indiquant les changements de niveau
de langage.

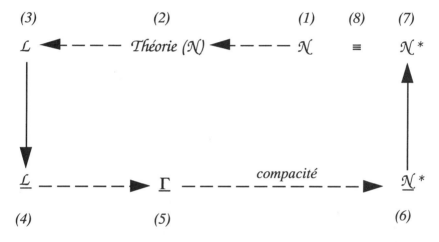

Figure 2

Le constat ayant permis à Robinson de donner des assises rigoureuses
au calcul infinitésimal est que la même démarche, mais cette fois à partir du
corps $\mathcal{R}$ des réels, donne une structure $\mathcal{R}^*$ de nombres *hyperréels* comprenant
des infinis et conséquemment, par inverse multiplicatif, des *infinitésimaux*.
(L'appellation *analyse non standard* utilisée par Robinson pour dénommer
sa théorie indique d'ailleurs clairement son origine dans les modèles non
standard — pour certains (Deledicq, 1992), le sigle anglais « NSA » en est
venu à désigner la Nouvelle et Simple Analyse.) La structure $\mathcal{R}^*$ étant obte-
nue à partir d'un corps, on a donc une « belle » arithmétique des hyperréels.
À noter cependant qu'en tant que corps ordonné contenant proprement $\mathcal{R}$
comme sous-corps ordonné, les hyperréels forment nécessairement un corps
transgressant la propriété d'Archimède (Levitz, 1974) : cela ne contredit
aucunement le principe de transfert si l'on prend garde de traduire « $\forall xy$
réels, $\exists n$ naturel tel que $y < nx$ » par « $\forall xy$ hyperréels, $\exists n$ *hypernaturel* tel

que $y < nx$ », de sorte que le multiple nx peut être vu comme résultant d'une « somme infinie ».

La présence d'infinitésimaux nous permet de définir, outre l'égalité habituelle, une relation d'« égalité à un infinitésimal près » : deux hyperréels a et b sont *infiniment voisins* ($a \approx b$) lorsque leur différence $a - b$ est infinitésimale (et non forcément nulle). C'est cette relation qui fournit la solution à l'aporie révélée par Berkeley, puisque l'on peut maintenant conclure, pour la dérivée de x^2, que $2x + dx \approx 2x$.

S'il a semblé utile de rappeler la construction primitive de Robinson, c'est qu'elle apporte une réponse limpide et éclatante au problème de l'existence d'une structure dans laquelle cohabitent (en harmonie !) des nombres finis, infiniment grands et infiniment petits. Qu'une telle structure puisse exister était fortement contesté par exemple par un Cantor qui prétendait pouvoir en démontrer l'impossibilité à l'aide de sa théorie du transfini (Luxemburg, 1979, p. xxxi) ou un Russell qui concluait ses remarques sur le calcul infinitésimal par les commentaires : « Hence infinitesimals as explaining continuity must be regarded as unnecessary, erroneous, and self-contradictory » (Russell, 1903, p. 345).

De nombreuses approches, donnant lieu à une littérature abondante, ont été proposées en vue de concrétiser la construction précédente, approches qu'il est bien sûr impossible de présenter dans le cadre de ce texte. Qu'il suffise de mentionner l'utilisation des ultrapuissances et élargissements par Robinson lui-même (Robinson, 1974), les approches algébriques de Hatcher (1982) ou Laugwitz (1986), ou encore l'utilisation de séries formelles par Tall (1980). Plusieurs de ces approches sont évocatrices de la construction des réels via les suites de Cauchy, ce qui les rend attrayantes pour quiconque est habitué à ce formalisme (à ce sujet, on consultera avec profit les expositions faites, entre autres, dans Artmann, 1988 ; Ebbinghaus *et al.*, 1991 ; Henle et Kleinberg, 1979 ; Hoskins, 1990 ; ou Hurd et Loeb, 1985). Toutefois, si on a en vue des applications pédagogiques du calcul infinitésimal, il est clair que l'effort consacré à construire rigoureusement les hyperréels vient entraver la démarche d'apprentissage en analyse proprement dite — de même pour les réels d'ailleurs, dans un cadre classique. C'est dans cette optique que des approches axiomatiques ont été élaborées.

AXIOMATISATION DU CALCUL INFINITÉSIMAL

> Once one recovers from the shock of being told that infinitesimals and other idealized elements were there all along in the sets with which we are familiar, [...] one will find our approach very easy to use. (Nelson, 1977)

Une critique fréquente des opposants à un enseignement de l'analyse hyperréelle est qu'un cours de logique est quasiment préalable. La réponse de Keisler a été de produire un manuel d'enseignement élémentaire du calcul (Keisler, 1986) dans lequel les propriétés mathématiques des nombres (réels et) hyperréels sont cristallisées sous forme de quelques axiomes : ceux donnant les propriétés algébriques et d'ordre usuelles des réels ; l'axiome de la complétude des réels ; un axiome d'extension énonçant l'existence d'un sur-ensemble des réels contenant un infinitésimal et auquel toute fonction réelle peut être prolongée ; et enfin un axiome de transfert affirmant qu'une propriété vraie de tous les réels l'est également de tous les hyperréels. On en tire toutes les notions requises pour le calcul infinitésimal, en particulier la fonction st qui associe à tout hyperréel fini le réel constituant sa *partie standard* (de sorte que, par exemple, $st(2x + dx) = 2x$).

Si l'axiomatisation de Keisler présente les hyperréels comme un prolongement des réels, tout comme chez Robinson, il en va autrement de l'approche de Nelson (1977) dans laquelle les « nouveaux » nombres sont en quelque sorte déjà là mais ne peuvent être perçus qu'avec des « lunettes » spéciales. Élaborée dans un contexte ensembliste, l'axiomatique de Nelson repose sur l'adjonction d'un prédicat *standard* à la théorie classique des ensembles (disons ZFC — i.e. Zermelo-Fraenkel avec choix) dont l'utilisation est codifiée par trois axiomes dits d'*idéalisation*, de *standardisation* et de *transfert* (d'où le sigle IST désignant la « Internal Set Theory » de Nelson). La robustesse théorique de cette approche tient dans le fait qu'IST est une *extension conservative* de ZFC (Nelson, 1977), c'est-à-dire que tout ce que IST démontre à propos des objets classiques de la théorie — ceux dont la définition ne fait pas intervenir le nouveau prédicat — est déjà un théorème de ZFC. (Ceci n'est pas sans rappeler l'intuition sous-jacente à l'équivalence élémentaire.) IST est donc *cohérente relativement à* ZFC : si la contradiction $1 = 0$ pouvait y être démontrée, elle serait aussi un théorème de ZFC. Robinson avait clairement envisagé la possibilité d'une approche à la Nelson :

> However, from a formalist point of view we may look at our theory syntactically and may consider that what we have done is to introduce *new deductive procedures* rather than new mathematical entities. (Robinson, 1974, p. 282)

Le cadre restreint de ce travail ne permet pas une étude détaillée de chacun des axiomes d'IST (que le lecteur pourra trouver dans des ouvrages tels Deledicq et Diener (1989), Diener et Reeb (1989) et Robert (1985), ou encore dans l'un des nombreux articles traitant du sujet, entre autres dans Deledicq (1990), Diener et Diener (1989), Gilbert (1992), Robert (1984), et Robert (1989)). Qu'il suffise d'en indiquer certaines conséquences. L'axiome d'*idéalisation* (qui n'est pas sans rappeler un argument de compacité, en ramenant la satisfaction d'une propriété à sa satisfaction dans les parties finies de l'univers) entraîne l'existence d'éléments « idéaux » au sein même des ensembles habituels ; en particulier, il existe dans les naturels des entiers « illimités », c'est-à-dire majorant tout entier *standard* (au sens du prédicat adjoint). C'est ce résultat qui sous-tend l'assertion célèbre de Reeb (1979) :

« Les entiers naïfs ne remplissent pas ℕ. » En d'autres termes, les nombres jouant le rôle d'infiniment grands sont déjà là, parmi les naturels, mais avant Nelson on ne les « voyait » pas (de même se trouvent déjà dans ℝ des « infiniment grands » et des « infiniment petits »). L'axiome de *standardisation* permet d'associer à toute construction un ensemble standard regroupant tous les objets standard résultant de la construction. On en déduit l'existence d'un objet standard « au voisinage » de tout objet : on a ainsi la notion de *partie standard* sur laquelle repose l'étude des limites. Quant au *transfert*, il affirme qu'une propriété classique est universellement vraie dès qu'elle est vraie des objets standard. De façon équivalente, si une propriété classique peut être satisfaite dans l'univers d'interprétation, alors ce fait peut être « observé », en ce sens que la propriété doit être vraie pour certaines valeurs standard. Il résulte de cet axiome que les objets usuels $(0, \pi, \mathbb{R}, \text{sinus}, \ldots)$ sont standard.

Il ne faut pas sous-estimer le « choc culturel » que constitue cette présence d'infiniment grands et petits au sein des ensembles habituels. C'est là un changement majeur de perspective par rapport au point de vue d'un Keisler, pour qui l'univers est modifié par l'*ajout* de ces éléments idéaux. Chez Nelson, les éléments idéaux sont déjà présents dans notre univers numérique (ils sont donc tous finis !), mais on ne les distinguait pas auparavant des nombres standard — un peu, pour reprendre l'image de Deledicq (1992), comme si les nombres avaient été créés en couleur mais que nous ne les percevions qu'en noir et blanc. Un tel cadre permet l'élaboration d'une théorie de différenciation des *ordres de grandeur* qui n'avait pas vraiment trouvé place jusqu'ici en mathématiques. À cet égard, il est préférable de parler de nombre *idéalement grand* (i-grand) ou même simplement *très grand*, plutôt qu'« infiniment grand » (Deledicq, 1992 ; Wallet, 1992). En convenant d'appeler *appréciable* un nombre ni i-grand ni i-petit, on peut mettre en place des règles opératoires (« règles de Leibniz », Deledicq, 1992) pour l'arithmétique des ordres de grandeur — voir figure 3, où l'on désigne par *limité* un nombre qui n'est pas i-grand. (À remarquer que les appréciables sont tous du même ordre de grandeur, mais qu'il n'en est pas de même des i-petits ou des i-grands. Il est utile d'introduire une deuxième généralisation

+	ip	app	ig
ip	ip	app	ig
app	app	lim	ig
ig	ig	ig	?

×	ip	app	ig
ip	ip	ip	?
app	ip	app	ig
ig	?	ig	ig

÷	ip	app	ig
ip	?	ip	ip
app	ig	app	ip
ig	ig	ig	?

Figure 3

de l'égalité où l'on compare a et b en vérifiant si le rapport $\frac{a}{b}$ est i-voisin de 1 : on retrouve ainsi les notions d'égalités arithmétique et géométrique d'Euler — Laugwitz, 1986, p. 91.)

L'intérêt d'un modèle des changements d'ordre de grandeur peut être illustré par certaines analogies, comme l'évolution quotidienne des revenus engendrés par un placement de 1,00 $ à un taux de 8 % : chaque journée correspond à un revenu de 0,00022 $, valeur « petite » à l'échelle de la monnaie courante, de sorte que la valeur de l'avoir, en espèces sonnantes et trébuchantes, reste inchangée jour après jour ; c'est en effectuant le produit par le nombre « grand » 365 que l'on retrouve le revenu annuel (appréciable) de 0,08 $. Ou encore si le passage du singe à Darwin a pu se faire par des étapes correspondant chacune à une évolution « petite », c'est que le nombre de générations intermédiaires est « grand » (mais bien sûr fini). (À noter que comme les réels ne résultent pas pour Nelson d'une extension de corps, il n'est pas étonnant que ceux-ci satisfassent la propriété d'Archimède : l'énoncé « $\forall xy$ réels, $\exists n$ naturel tel que $y < nx$ » est vérifié, pour un x i-petit, en prenant un entier n i-grand approprié.)

APPLICATIONS PÉDAGOGIQUES DU CALCUL INFINITÉSIMAL

> But so great is the average person's fear of infinity that to this day calculus all over the world is being taught as a study of *limit processes* instead of what it really is: *infinitesimal analysis*. (Rucker, 1982, p. 87)

Il n'est pas facile de faire un bilan exact de l'impact pédagogique de la théorie moderne des infinitésimaux sur l'enseignement de base en analyse. Les remarques suivantes pourront néanmoins donner une idée de l'activité en ce domaine. Il convient sans doute de distinguer deux mouvements, le premier étant plus près d'une approche à la Keisler et l'autre, en nette progression, se situant dans la lignée de Nelson.

La réhabilitation des infinitésimaux par Robinson a rapidement suscité des expériences visant à mettre à profit leur potentiel pédagogique, compte tenu tant de l'intuition forte qu'ils véhiculent que de la simplification logique — diminution des quantificateurs — qui résulte habituellement de la formulation dans un contexte non standard de notions telles que limite ou continuité. Le traité de Keisler (1986) a été rédigé dans cette optique et a été utilisé régulièrement dans divers contextes pédagogiques depuis près de vingt ans. L'expérience la plus célèbre à cet égard est sans doute l'étude comparative de Sullivan (1976) établissant clairement que cette approche constitue une solution intéressante et viable — tout en n'étant pas la solution-miracle aux maux de l'enseignement. Un autre document fréquemment utilisé dans l'enseignement est le texte succinct de Henle et Kleinberg (1979). On trouvera dans Artigue *et al.* (1986) le rapport d'un cours fondé sur ce texte ainsi qu'une analyse détaillée des réponses d'un examen qui amène les auteurs à conclure que la majorité des étudiants semblent avoir profité de l'enseignement. Des expériences pédagogiques sont également relatées dans Wattenberg (1983) et Foley (1986), tandis que Fígols (1990) utilise les hyperréels en vue d'un enseignement élémentaire. Tall (1981) compare la vision infinitésimale avec d'autres approches pédagogiques, en particulier avec les méthodes numérique et graphique sur ordinateur. Il convient enfin de souligner le cas assez exceptionnel de l'University of Teesside (Middlesbrough, UK), où l'enseignement de base du calcul, depuis près de dix ans, se fait à la Keisler : l'objectif visé est d'éviter les embûches conceptuelles de l'approche traditionnelle tout en favorisant le développement de l'intuition. L'expérience semble positive et les étudiants paraissent acquérir tout aussi bien, sinon mieux, les habiletés calculatoires habituelles.

L'approche de Nelson a connu un impact considérable, et ce tout particulièrement en France, sans doute sous l'influence de Reeb et de l'équipe alsacienne d'analyse non standard. D'abord utilisée comme outil de développement de l'analyse et des mathématiques appliquées, la théorie IST de Nelson a vite été perçue comme fournissant un cadre conceptuel remarquable à des fins pédagogiques. Parmi la littérature très abondante publiée récemment sur le sujet, soulignons Antoine *et al.* (1992), Deledicq et Diener (1989), Deledicq (1990), Deledicq (1992), Deledicq (non daté), Gilbert (1992a), Lutz (1987) et Wallet (1992). L'article de Gilbert (1992a) cherche à répondre à la question : « L'analyse non standard peut-elle faciliter l'apprentissage de l'analyse ? » en examinant certaines difficultés célèbres de l'analyse classique dans le contexte de Nelson. Antoine *et al.* (1992) vise l'introduction de concepts non standard au lycée, tandis que Deledicq (non daté) est un cours facultatif en DEUG. Ce dernier document présente d'ailleurs une « hypothèse didactique » fort intéressante à propos de la gradation que permet la « Nouvelle et Simple Analyse » par l'introduction successive des trois axiomes d'IST, depuis un *calcul infinitésimal* portant essentiellement sur les ordres de grandeur jusqu'à l'*analyse infinitésimale* des limites et de la continuité.

CONCLUSION

> [...] non-standard analysis, in some version or other, will be the analysis of the future. (Gödel, 1974)

Selon Mac Lane (1986, p. 155), les mathématiques ne sauraient être réduites ni à un formalisme pur ni à une accumulation d'idées empiriques, et consistent plutôt en « idées intuitives ou empiriques formalisables ». Les infinitésimaux constituent un exemple éloquent d'un tel point de vue, leur réhabilitation dans le cadre de l'analyse non standard mettant à la disposition du mathématicien des outils évocateurs et puissants. Leur acceptation se heurte cependant à certaines réticences — tout comme cela fut le cas, jadis, pour les nombres négatifs ou complexes — voire à des oppositions farouches — on se rappellera la polémique provoquée par la critique virulente de Bishop (1977). (On remarquera d'ailleurs la quasi-absence de l'analyse non standard des derniers congrès internationaux des mathématiciens.)

Il est bien connu que les techniques de l'analyse non standard se sont avérées fructueuses dans leurs applications en recherche, en particulier dans l'étude des bifurcations des systèmes dynamiques (Diener, 1984; Diener et Diener, 1989). Même si le nouveau cadre ne permet pas de démontrer « plus » que le cadre classique, car résultant d'une extension conservative, il provoque souvent une importante simplification conceptuelle et factuelle. (On pourrait reprendre ici, *mutatis mutandis*, les mots célèbres de Hadamard : « La voie la plus courte et la meilleure entre deux vérités du domaine réel passe souvent par le domaine imaginaire » (Hadamard, 1959, p. 114)). Une telle simplification se retrouve par exemple dans l'utilisation faite de la « cohabitation » discret/continu dans l'élaboration par Harthong et Reeb d'un modèle du calcul sur ordinateur dans lequel le calcul en virgule fixe, à un ordre de grandeur donné, revient à travailler sur une portion de la droite naturelle, mais « vue de loin » (voir Diener et Diener, 1989).

Les renseignements que nous avons pu recueillir en préparant ce travail font ressortir une certaine utilisation de l'approche infinitésimale dans l'enseignement, mais peut-être dans une moindre mesure que d'aucuns le prévoyaient il y a une quinzaine d'années (il y a lieu de retenir le jugement en ce qui concerne l'impact éventuel du modèle de Nelson, source, mais depuis peu seulement, d'une importante activité pédagogique). Comment expliquer que le calcul infinitésimal n'ait pas été davantage l'occasion d'un renouvellement pédagogique ? L'ordinateur y est peut-être pour quelque chose, lui qui depuis un certain temps déjà monopolise une énergie considérable dans la problématique de l'enseignement quant à l'impact des logiciels graphiques ou symboliques. Sans doute également l'inertie inhérente au système éducatif est-elle si forte que tout espoir d'une répercussion rapide devient illusoire. Mais certains des obstacles sont vraisemblablement d'origine philosophique, de cette philosophie « implicite et quasi-spontanée qui accompagne nos discours et notre enseignement » (Wallet, 1992).

Nous laissons le mot de la fin à Georges Reeb, dont l'influence a été déterminante sur le développement récent de l'analyse non standard :

> [...] notre manière de parler aux élèves évoluera. Je me contenterai d'un exemple : alors que dans un passé récent il était raisonnable d'affirmer : « La méthode ε,δ de Weierstrass est *la* méthode qui permet de fonder l'analyse classique », il est clair que dorénavant on se montrera plus circonspect, on remplacera l'article défini *la* par le plus prudent article indéfini *une*. N'y aurait-il que cette seule implication sur notre enseignement, elle n'en serait pas moins très importante. (Reeb, 1981, p. 259-260)

NOTE

Ce texte est dédié, à l'occasion de son soixante-cinquième anniversaire de naissance, au professeur Shuichi Takahashi, mon mentor, qui très tôt s'est appliqué à faire connaître l'analyse non standard.

RÉFÉRENCES

Antoine, T. *et al.* (1992). *L'analyse au lycée avec le vocabulaire infinitésimal.* IREM de l'Université de Paris 7.

Artigue, M. *et al.* (1986). *Analyse non standard et enseignement.* Cahier de didactique des mathématiques n°. 15, IREM de l'Université de Paris 7.

Artmann, B. (1988). *The concept of number.* Chichester, UK: Ellis Horwood.

Barreau, H., & Harthong, J. (Ed.) (1989). *La mathématique non standard.* Paris: Éditions du CNRS.

Berkeley, G. (1734). The analyst; Or, a discourse addressed to an infidel mathematician. In A.C. Fraser (Ed.), *The works of George Berkeley, III* (pp. 17-60) (1901 ed.). Oxford: Clarendon Press.

Bishop, E. (1977). Review of *Elementary calculus*, by H.J. Keisler. *Bulletin of the American Mathematical Society, 83,* 205-208.

Davis, P.J., & Hersh, R. (1980). *The mathematical experience.* (Nonstandard Analysis, pp. 237-254). Boston: Birkhäuser.

Deledicq, A., & Diener, M. (1989). *Leçons de calcul infinitésimal.* Paris: Armand Colin.

Deledicq, A. (1990). Le (nouveau) calcul infinitésimal. *Bulletin de l'APMEP, 373,* 143-161.

Deledicq, A. (1992). De l'analyse non standard au calcul infinitésimal. In C. Hauchart et N. Rouche (éd.), *L'enseignement de l'analyse aux débutants* (pp. 55-86). Academia-Érasme.

Deledicq, A. (non daté). *Cours d'analyse infinitésimale élémentaire (non-standard).* En préparation. IREM de l'Université de Paris 7.

Diener, F., & Diener, M. (1989). Les applications de l'analyse non standard. *La Recherche, 20,* 68-83.

Diener, F., & Reeb, G. (1989). *Analyse non standard.* Paris: Hermann.

Diener, M. (1984). The canard unchained—Or how fast/slow dynamical systems bifurcate. *Mathematical Intelligencer, 6*(3), 38-49. (Version française in Barreau et Harthong (1989), pp. 401-42.)

Ebbinghaus, H.-D. *et al.* (1991). *Numbers.* New York: Springer-Verlag.

Fígols, R.S. (1990). *Calculo infinitesimal.* Mexico: IPN.

Foley, G.D. (1986). *Using infinitesimals to introduce limits and continuity in a community college calculus course.* Unpublished doctoral dissertation, University of Texas, Austin.

Gilbert, T. (1992). Qu'est-ce que l'analyse non standard? *Mathématique et pédagogie.*

Gilbert, T. (1992a). L'enseignement de la continuité et de la dérivabilité en analyse non standard. *Repères IREM*.

Gödel, K. (1974). Remarks on non-standard analysis. In S. Feferman et al. (Eds.), *Kurt Gödel. Collected works*, (Vol. II, p. 311) (1990 ed.). New York: Oxford University Press.

Hadamard, J. (1959). *Essai sur la psychologie de l'invention dans le domaine mathématique*. Paris: Librairie scientifique Albert Blanchard.

Hatcher, W.S. (1982). Calculus is algebra. *American Mathematical Monthly, 89*, 362-370.

Henle, J.M., & Kleinberg, E.M. (1979). *Infinitesimal calculus*. Cambridge, MA: MIT Press.

Hoskins, R.F. (1990). *Standard and nonstandard analysis: Fundamental theory, techniques and applications*. Chichester, UK: Ellis Horwood.

Hurd, A.E., & Loeb, P.A. (1985). *An introduction to nonstandard real analysis*. New York: Academic Press.

Keisler, H.J. (1986) *Elementary calculus: An infinitesimal approach*. Boston: Prindle, Weber & Schmidt. (First edition, 1976.)

Keisler, H.J. et al. (Eds.) (1979). *Selected papers of Abraham Robinson*. Vol. 2. *Nonstandard analysis and philosophy*. Yale University Press.

Laugwitz, D. (1986). *Zahlen und Kontinuum: Eine Einführung in die Infinitesimalmathematik*. Mannheim: Bibliographisches Institut.

Levitz, H. (1974). Non-standard analysis: an exposition. *L'Enseignement mathématique, 20*, 9-32.

Lutz, R. (1987). Rêveries infinitésimales. *Gazette des mathématiciens, 34*, 79-87.

Luxemburg, W.A.J. (1979). Introduction to papers on nonstandard analysis and analysis (pp. xxxi-xxxix). In Keisler et al.

Mac Lane, S. (1986). *Mathematics: Form and function*. New York: Springer-Verlag.

Nelson, E. (1977). Internal set theory: A new approach to nonstandard analysis. *Bulletin of the American Mathematical Society, 83*, 1165-1198. (Version française in Barreau et Harthong (1989), 355-399.)

Reeb, G. (1979). *La mathématique non standard vieille de soixante ans?* IRMA, Strasbourg: Université Louis-Pasteur.

Reeb, G. (1981). Analyse non standard (Essai de vulgarisation). *Bulletin de l'APMEP 328*, 259-273.

Robert, A. (1984). Une approche naïve de l'analyse non-standard. *Dialectica 38*, 287-296.

Robert, A. (1985). *Analyse non standard*. Lausanne: Presses polytechniques romandes.

Robert, A. (1989). L'analyse non standard. In A. Jacob (éd.), *L'univers philosophique*. (*Encyclopédie philosophique universelle*, vol. 1, pp. 1049-1056). Paris: Presses Universitaires de France.

Robinson, A. (1974). *Non-standard analysis* (2nd. ed.). North-Holland Publ. Co. (First edition, 1966.)

Robinson, A. (1973). Numbers – What are they and what are they good for? *Yale Scientific Magazine, 47*, 14-16.

Rucker, R. (1982). *Infinity and the mind*. Boston: Birkhaüser.

Russell, B. (1903) *The principles of mathematics*. New York: W.W. Norton.

Sullivan, K. (1976). The teaching of elementary calculus using the nonstandard analysis approach. *American Mathematical Monthly, 83*, 370-375.

Tall, D. (1980). Looking at graphs through microscopes, windows and telescopes. *Mathematical Gazette, 64*, 22-49.

Tall, D. (1981). Comments on the difficulty and validity of various approaches to the calculus. *For the Learning of Mathematics, 2*(2), 16-21.

Wallet, G. (1992). Introduction au calcul leibnizien. *Bulletin de l'APMEP, 385,* 431-448.

Wattenberg, F. (1983). Unterricht im Infinitesimalkalkül: Erfahrungen in den USA. *Der Mathematikunterricht, 29*(4), 7-36.

COMPUTER-BASED MICROWORLDS:
A RADICAL VISION OR A TROJAN MOUSE?[1]

Celia Hoyles

University of London, United Kingdom

In this paper I am going to talk about computer-based microworlds; computational worlds where mathematical ideas are expressed and developed. I will address the following questions:

- What is the potential of computer-based microworlds for mathematics learning?

- Why are mathematics educators interested in the design and development of microworlds?

- Is there a mismatch between theory and practice, between aspiration and implementation, and if so why?

From an analysis of these questions, I will attempt to draw out some implications for the future in terms of teacher education, software and curriculum development.

First, I will look back over more than a decade of research and development of computer-based microworlds—mainly in the context of Logo and mathematics since this is work in which I have played a small part. What did we achieve? What were our successes and failures and how can these be understood? What can we learn from these experiences to provide insight that stretches beyond the Logo mathematics community and into mathematics education more generally?

---

[1]   The idea of the computer as a Trojan horse entering the classroom by stealth is taken from Olson (1988).

THE VISION AND THE REALITY

When we started working in Logo mathematics in the early 1980s, we held as our goal the evolution of a mathematical culture—a change in the relationship between teachers, pupils, and mathematics. As Seymour Papert commented in the foreword to the book I have recently edited with Richard Noss, "(We were interested in the) ways in which Logo and Logo research bear on *relocating* the boundary between what is and what is not to be counted as mathematics in the lives of children." (Papert, 1992, p. 13, my emphasis.) What have we achieved in terms of evolution of culture? And, as we develop more powerful and sophisticated softwares for mathematics, do the boundaries shift?

It is useful first to clarify the terms I am using. What *is* a "microworld?" In another paper (Hoyles, in press), I have tracked the subtle (or not so subtle!) changes in the meaning of the word "microworld" from its genesis within universities and research laboratories to its incorporation into school practice. These changes in meaning make it difficult, perhaps impossible, to characterize a microworld in ontological terms; nonetheless I will sketch out what for me at least are its major features.

At the core of a microworld is a *knowledge domain* to be constructed through interaction with software. Papert (1980, p. 125) suggested that a microworld is "a 'province of Mathland' where certain kinds of mathematical thinking could hatch and grow with particular ease." Therefore the *relationship* of the student to the software is central, although the knowledge must also be recognized as *complex*, *interrelated*, and *growing*: three characteristics which are reflected in the software. This rules out software which demands simply a limited set of self-contained and pre-defined allowable actions, although exploration within microworlds is inevitably *constrained.* Feurzeig (1987, p. 51) describes a microworld as "a clearly delimited task domain or problem space whose elements are objects, and operations on objects which create new objects and operations." Yet there is more to microworlds: there must be ease of access simultaneously with deep challenge. As DiSessa (1987, p. 65) has suggested: "(in microworlds) besides a density of observable phenomenon—potential theorems—it seems that salient events ... happen to be correlated with good, investigable and solvable problems."

It perhaps makes sense to view a microworld as a *process* rather than an object. Microworld activity is characterized by active involvement of students within motivated and motivating project work whose goals have been negotiated with the teacher. The literature in Logo mathematics is replete with examples of microworlds. To take just one example, microworld activity was a cornerstone of the Logo mathematics project (Hoyles & Sutherland, 1989). Throughout this research, the students' work was characterized by student autonomy, collaborative effort, and involvement. The feelings of the students are captured in the following interview extract: "What I really like about Logo mathematics is you don't have the teacher telling you all the time. It needs lots of brain power. Our robot took us weeks and weeks!"

Obviously, interaction with the computer is structured by the software tools available, but it is *open,* insofar as the solution paths are not laid down. Students themselves decide upon solution strategies and, as part of their activity, they *use* mathematical ideas *before* the ideas are necessarily fully discriminated or generalized. (See Hoyles, 1987, for a discussion of this approach to learning mathematics.) Let me give an example of this phenomenon by briefly describing some work with a spreadsheet. The goal of the activity was to construct the polygon numbers. (See Figure 1.)

position in seq.	1	2	3	4
triangle numbers	• 1	3	6	10
square numbers	• 1	4	9	16
pentagon numbers	• 1	5	12	22
hexagon numbers	• 1	6	15	28

Generate the triangle numbers on a spreadsheet
Generate the other polygon numbers
Investigate different ways of generating the sequences

Figure 1. Polygon numbers.

Every time we have offered this activity to groups of students, even mathematics educators, we are struck by the flexibility and variety of approaches adopted. Influenced by prior mathematical knowledge, different relationships are constructed by interaction with the software and different goals emerge. Generalizations are made, but first in action, and frequently the *way* they are made and the *language* in which they are communicated appear ambiguous—unless they are interpreted within the micro-culture of the spreadsheet. Gestures—pointing to the computer screen—are crucial and in fact define the processes which have to be replicated. Thus, it is often action and gesture which capture any generalization rather than an articulated language of description. For example, two students described their construction of the triangle numbers by stating, "It's that one, add that one, equals that one, that one add that one equals that one ... and so on"—meaningless to read but completely clear when the words are accompanied by pointing to specific cells.

This is an example of what Richard Noss and I have termed a *situated abstraction* (Hoyles & Noss, 1992), the first step in constructing a mathematical generalization. It is "situated" in that the knowledge is defined by the actions within a context; *but* it is an "abstraction" in that the description is *not* a routinized report of action but, exemplifies the students' reflections on their actions as they strive to communicate with each other and with the computer.

Thus, one way to characterize microworlds is to think of them as environments where students generate situated abstractions of a mathematical nature—a spontaneous process which can be developed later within more structured and formalized settings. In fact, it is easier to describe student activity in microworlds by contrasting it with what it is *not*—not practising routines, not guessing the teacher's agenda, not working competitively. Within microworlds students are "builders" of their own mathematics (See for example, Harel & Papert, 1990; Harel & Papert, 1991)—in collaboration with each other and with the teacher.

So, in summary, interactions in a microworld—guided by "good" activities and "good" teachers[2]—can be characterized as follows:

- They are *playful*. There are rules and constraints guided by mathematical imperatives, but these stimulate activity rather than suppress it.

- They are m*otivated*. Students are interested and develop a sense of ownership over the ideas they construct together.

---

[2] This is a deliberately cryptic way to summarize some crucial ideas; namely that learning environments can only be characterized in relation to activities and teachers. (For a discussion of this see Hoyles & Noss, 1987.)

- There is a continuous dialectic between the *formal* and the *informal*. The computer formalizes the informal and informalizes the formal.

- The mathematics is to some extent *implicit* and an *incidental* part of the activity. It is not necessarily visible as an explicit goal for the pupils.

So our radical vision in the early microworld movement was that students, software, and knowledge would grow together interactively in the pursuit of epistemologically rich goals. There would be change within the practice of school mathematics; change in how the mathematics curriculum was perceived and how it was transacted; change which would democratize mathematics whilst improving mathematical understanding and classroom practice.

But what of the practice? How has the computer revolution affected schools, if at all? It is clear from a review of the available literature (mainly in the United States and the United Kingdom) that the impact of computers on school life does not match the vision. As Becker put it, "There were 'dreams' about computer-using students ... dreams of voice-communicating, intelligent human tutors, dreams of realistic scientific simulations, dreams of young adolescent problem solvers adept at general-purpose programming languages—but alongside these dreams was the truth that computers played a minimal role in real schools." (Becker, 1982, p. 6) In the same vein, Becker later argued, "As we enter the 1990s, it is important to understand how much of that early limited reality still remains and to understand how much of the idea of transforming teaching and learning through computers remains plausible. We need to be aware of the 'old habits' and 'conventional beliefs' that are common among practising educators and the 'institutional constraints' that impede even the best of intentions to improve schooling through technology." (Becker, 1991, p. 6). In the United Kingdom the findings are similar. In a survey conducted by the Department of Education and Science (DES, 1991), computer use in mathematics classrooms was reported to be limited and, where the computer was in evidence, it was simply an alternative medium within a thoroughly conventional framework.

REFLECTIONS

So why is there this apparent mismatch between theory and practice, between dreams and reality? What has happened to the radical dream? Why has the Trojan horse turned into a Trojan mouse? The way to understand this phenomenon is to recognize that most school activity exists in a culture of its own where learning has to co-exist alongside other agendas: management, accountability, selection, and the "curriculum." As any innovation moves into schools, I identify four processes by which the innovation is transformed—pedagogizing, compartmentalizing, incorporating, and neutralizing—each of which stems from requirements of the school culture.

Pedagogizing

In the Logo community, the role of the teacher in the children's mathematical development has increasingly been emphasized. Despite reports to the contrary, Papert himself held that teachers play an important role in the learning enterprise and argued that teachers should be co-explorers with students in their joint pursuit of mathematical goals (Papert, 1980). In the Logo mathematics project mentioned earlier, although we set out to intervene "lightly," in the context of the students' own work—to suggest ideas to explore or to point to "interesting" mathematical extensions—on analysis of our transcripts of student work, we were surprised by the significant structuring role our "subtle" interventions had on student progress and the direction of their work. In the areas we had emphasized, the students made consistent and excellent progress, whilst in others, development was haphazard.

In retrospect, the theories of Vygotsky provide a coherent framework for interpreting these findings within the realm of psychology. Initially, we had taken a Piagetian approach, expecting that students would construct mathematical knowledge through interaction within our micro-worlds. We hypothesized that they would build their ideas through interaction and reflection on the results of their actions: a process facilitated by the feedback provided by the computer. However, we came to appreciate how mathematical knowledge emerged through *social* interaction, with the teacher and other students offering "scaffolding" within a child's zone of proximal development (Vygotsky, 1978). This interpretation brings pedagogic intervention to center stage, as mediating between the child and his or her experience.

Thus as Logo moved into the school context, it came to be recognized that the teacher must bring to attention the "interesting" mathematical issues: to bridge the gap between what the pupils see and what the teachers see; to make links between students' constructive activity on the computer; their expression these links orally and on paper; and to push towards generalization so that the students learn to solve not just the problem in hand but to seek out the general beyond this particularity.

Inevitably, in schools, other social and cultural issues come into play which have to be dealt with by teachers, such as issues of access to and dominance over the machines, particularly in relation to boys and girls. In addition, once the teacher is acknowledged as an important actor in the learning process, the teacher's intentions and beliefs must be considered, as these inevitably shape the nature, intention, and timing of teacher interventions. We have studied how teachers mediate in the context of a course of in-service education concerned with the introduction of computers. We set out to analyze how the course activities and the teacher's goals and beliefs mutually constituted each other: how the teacher structured the computer activities according to his or her aims, and simultaneously how the activities structured the teachers' beliefs and practices.

We constructed *caricatures* of the course participants to provide a synthesis of views, attitudes, and practices of a cluster of teacher case studies. The caricatures attempted to draw attention to teacher characteristics and behaviors which *we* deemed crucial by exaggeration of some facets and omission of others. Thus, they reflected our ideas about categories by which to gauge mathematics teaching and teachers. They mirrored our beliefs as well as reflected the teachers' beliefs in so far as they resonated with any individual viewpoint.

The five caricatures which emerged from our study were: Mary, the frustrated idealist; Rowena, the confident investigator; Denis, the controlling pragmatist; Fiona, the anxious traditionalist; and Bob, the curriculum deliverer (Noss, Sutherland, & Hoyles, 1991; Noss & Hoyles, 1992). Each illustrated very different ways of integrating computers into practice and the different foci upon which they reflected during this process. Thus they represent an attempt to capture the complexities inherent in pedagogizing the computer innovation.

Compartmentalizing

In any review of the local histories of curriculum innovations, a repeating pattern can be discerned. When the innovation first enters the school, it tends to do so as a topic which is added-on to the existing curriculum. For example, in the United Kingdom we have seen "investigative mathematics" transformed into "investigations"—and then timetabled on a Friday afternoon leaving the rest of the mathematics curriculum unchanged and untouched by the new phenomenon! Why does this happen? I suggest two reasons: in order to cope with the change by limiting the disruption caused at its introduction, and to marginalize the innovation by keeping it insulated from mainstream work. These reasons have the same effects despite stemming from very different reactions to the innovation: the first has the ultimate aim of integrating the innovation into practice, the second of excluding it. One effect of the process of compartmentalizing as far as computers are concerned is that computer work frequently becomes separated from mathematics and other knowledge domains, appearing as a new topic in its own right: for example, in courses of computer studies, information awareness, information technology.

The second reason for the process of compartmentalizing can be traced to more psychological considerations. I have already touched upon the notion of situated abstractions: the influence of the medium on mathematical expression and the fragmented and situated nature of students' mathematical understanding. In fact, as you will have noticed, we now talk about "Logo mathematics" which reflects its existence as an entity in itself. I have noted already that it has been consistently reported that pupils tend not to link their computer work with their paper and pencil work—a criticism similar to the oft-lamented absence of connection between science and mathematics, for example. This phenomenon has been described variously as fractured knowledge, knowledge in pieces (Papert, 1980; DiSessa, 1988). Pupils compartmentalize their understandings and "situations co-produce knowledge through activities" (Seely Brown et al., 1989). Thus mathematical abstractions remain inextricably linked to the context in which they are constructed. Thus "psychological" compartmentalizing interwoven with "bureaucratic" compartmentalizing raises real problems of communication and synthesis. How can we bridge the discursive disjuncture between microworlds and other school mathematics, or how can we expand school mathematics to incorporate this new culture and to do this in real classrooms?

Incorporating

Another phase in the move of an innovation into school is a change in the innovation itself in order to meet the requirements of the school culture and the school curriculum: the phenomenon of didactic transposition, as put forward by Chevallard (1985). Chevallard has suggested that any content to be taught must be embedded in the school context to make it teachable; but since the school context consists of lessons, "time" pressure, accountability, and testing, knowledge is forced into linear packages. Management considerations supersede the cognitive and affective goals of mathematical learning and, by this process, the knowledge itself becomes essentially trivialized.

A rather stark exemplification of didactical transposition is evident in the treatment of Logo within the UK mathematics national curriculum. Under the attainment target, Shape and Space, is the statement "recognize different types of movement" illustrated by *Turn to left or right on instruction (PE, games, or Logo)* and at another higher level, under the heading "specify location," is the example *Use Logo commands for distances and direction.* Similarly, within the algebra attainment target, appears *Create shapes by using DRAW and MOVE commands in BASIC in the appropriate graphics mode or by using Logo commands.* In all these examples, Logo is not even specified as a language, let alone a philosophy or culture. It is now a set of commands! In case this is interpreted merely as a Logo phenomenon, let me give you an example of the didactical transposition of spreadsheets as they became incorporated into the same national curriculum. We find the following statement: *Explore number patterns using computer facilities or otherwise* with the example *Use the difference method to explore sequences such as 2 5 10 17 26.* Note how the process of software interaction is clearly laid down: both the goal and the solution path of a well-defined and self-contained mathematical "fragment" is completely specified. There is little (if any) room for pupil decision-making—pupils building their own mathematics. The underlying framework is one of behaviorism and mastery learning, in contrast to the constructivism of the microworld designers.

Neutralizing

A process of transition more associated with computers than with general characteristics of innovation is the shift from seeing the computer as a means of exploration to using the computer simply as a means to a prescribed end: *just a tool.* Often the intention behind this tool designation is to alleviate anxiety among teachers by indicating that there is nothing very special about the computer, that it is after all just like a modern pencil! But is it? What becomes of the radical vision of transforming education through microworlds if we have to pretend that "business is as usual"? More crucially, the designation "just a tool" frequently conveys a veiled attack on the student autonomy made available by programmable software. It focuses attention on the utilitarian function of the computer—to produce an end—and implies that computer tools are somehow value free, and can be "applied" to a curriculum in ways that are insulated from the process and practice of education. Microworlds take on input-output features where process is subsumed under delivery and any revolutionary potential is neutralized and suppressed.

THE FUTURE

So what of the future? What are the implications of this story and what can we learn from this very evident transformation of a radical vision into a Trojan mouse? Many developments in the United States try to "preserve" the innovation from the political misuse of teachers by producing curriculum packages, computer tools with accompanying material which *deliver* the curriculum. The teacher has little or no role in the learning process except to encourage and to manage. The software, described as educational or instructional, is assumed to *produce* learning in ways that are safe. Both curriculum and educational practice remain unchanged. But these metaphors have a clear message, a top-down transmission model of learning that attempts to bypass teachers and keep children on very well-defined tracks.

We know that this inevitably leads to the separation of the bottom-up spontaneous mathematizing of pupils from the top-down specifications of the curriculum. Classrooms will continue to display all their familiar features, such as: students avoiding mathematics wherever possible, using their energies to pick up non-mathematical clues as to how to obtain correct answers, becoming answer-oriented and product-oriented, competing rather than collaborating, and expending the least effort in order to achieve optimal results. Students' performance gives little indication of their mathematical competence, and in fact the most critical questions to address in trying to interpret their productions are, "Whose agenda are the students following?" and "What are the students' goals?"

Thus the production of packages fails to problematize educational practice and presents a picture in which the curriculum, knowledge, and teacher-pupil relationships are givens. Additionally, it deliberately de-professionalizes teachers and in so doing fails to recognize that all packages are *of necessity* mediated by students and teachers. There is no such thing as a teacher-proof curriculum!

So what direction would I like us to take? At the level of software and curriculum design, we still need more expressive computational media tuned for the development of mathematical knowledge, more carefully designed and creative activities with rich avenues to explore with the software available, and more precise analysis of pedagogy and the way the computer structures and is structured by the classroom culture. At the level of the teacher, we need to provide opportunities for teachers to express their own mathematical ideas with the software (to have fun mathematically too!), to support their attendance at substantial courses (half a day is not enough and can be counter-productive) which maintain a mathematical rather than a technical focus, and to make available ample hardware (preferably with no advertising plugs!) and easy access to technical and educational assistance.

An overriding aim should be to resist the pressure to push through change in the short term, to go for technical fixes which have little to do with developing mathematics teaching and learning. As Polin (1991) suggested, "We need to instill a different vision of teacher development in our impatient policy-makers and in our harried teachers, a vision that acknowledges the many years of practice it takes to acquire and integrate a new way of teaching." (Polin, 1991, p. 7). It is important to recognize the tendency of schools to adopt a minimalist approach to change but also to understand that change is a process not an event. Let us not be diverted by the demands of a fragmented curriculum and its associated assessments but rather strive to retain our radical vision of a different culture for learning mathematics.

REFERENCES

Becker, H.J. (1982). *Microcomputers in the classroom: dreams and realities,* International Council for Computers in Education.

Becker, H.J. (1991). When powerful tools meet conventional beliefs and institutional constraints. *The Computing Teacher,* May.

Chevallard, Y. (1985). *La transposition didactique du savoir savant au savoir enseigné.* Grenoble: La Pensée sauvage, France.

DES Survey (1991). *Survey of Information Technology in Schools: Statistical Bulletin 11/91.* London: Department of Education and Science.

DiSessa, A. (1987). Artificial worlds and real experience. In R.W. Lawler & M. Yazdani (Eds.), *Artificial intelligence and education, volume one: Learning environments and tutoring systems* (pp. 55-78). Norwood, NJ: Ablex Publishing Corporation.

DiSessa, A. (1988). Knowledge pieces. In G. Forman & P. Pufall (Eds.), *Constructivism in the computer age* (pp. 49-70). Hillsdale, NJ: Lawrence Erlbaum Assoc.

Feurzeig, W. (1987). Algebra slaves and agents in a Logo-based mathematics curriculum. In R.W. Lawler & M. Yazdani (Eds.), *Artificial intelligence and education, volume one: Learning environments and tutoring systems* (pp. 27-54). Norwood, NJ: Ablex Publishing Corporation.

Harel, I., & Papert, S. (1990). Software design as a learning environment. In I. Howel (Ed.), *Constructionist learning* (pp. 19-50). Cambridge, MA: The Media Laboratory, MIT.

Harel, I., & Papert, S. (Eds.) (1991). *Constructivism.* Norwood, NJ: Ablex Publishing Corporation.

Hoyles, C. (1987). Tools for learning – Insights for the mathematics educator from a Logo programming environment. *For the Learning of Mathematics, 7(2),* pp.32-37.

Hoyles, C., & Noss, R. (Eds.) (1992). *Learning mathematics and Logo.* Cambridge, MA: MIT Press.

Hoyles, C., & Noss, R. (1987). Synthesizing mathematical conceptions and their formalisation through the construction of a Logo-based school mathematics curriculum. *International Journal of Mathematics Education in Science and Technology, 18*(4), 581-595.

Hoyles, C., & Sutherland, R. (1989). *Logo mathematics in the classroom.* London: Routledge.

Hoyles, C. (In press). Microworlds/Schoolworlds: The transposition of an innovation. In W. Dörfler, C. Keitel & K. Ruthven (Eds.), *Learning from computers: mathematics education and technology.* New York: Springer-Verlag.

Noss, R., & Hoyles, C. (1992). Bob – A suitable case for treatment? *Journal of Curriculum Studies.*

Noss, R., Sutherland, R., & Hoyles, C. (1991). *Teacher attitudes and interactions.* (Final Report of the *Microworlds* Project, Volume 2). London: Institute of Education, University of London.

Papert, S. (1980). *Mindstorms: Computers, children and powerful ideas.* New York: Basic Books.

Papert, S. (1992). Foreward. In C. Hoyles & R. Noss (Eds.), *Learning mathematics and Logo.* Cambridge, MA: MIT Press.

Polin, L. (1991). Profiles of accomplished computer-using teachers. *The Computing Teacher,* November, 5-7.

Seely Brown, J.S., Collins, A., & Duguid, P. (1989). Situated cognition and the culture of learning. *Educational Researcher,* Jan.-Feb., 32-42.

Vygotsky, L.S. (1978). *Mind in society: The development of higher Psychological processes.* Cambridge, MA: Harvard University Press.

DIFFERENT WAYS OF KNOWING:
CONTRASTING STYLES OF ARGUMENT
IN INDIA AND THE WEST

George Gheverghese Joseph

University of Manchester, United Kingdom

Many of the commonly available books on history of mathematics declare or imply that Indian mathematics, whatever its other achievements, did not have any notion of proof. To illustrate this viewpoint, with two examples, the first taken from one of the better known texts on the history of mathematics, Kline (1972, p. 190) writes:

> There is much good procedure and technical facility, but no evidence that they (i.e., the Indians) considered proof at all. They had rules, but apparently no logical scruples. Moreover, no general methods or new viewpoints were arrived at in any area of mathematics. It is fairly certain that the Hindus (i.e., the Indians) did not appreciate the significance of their own contributions. The few good ideas they had, such as separate symbols for the numbers, were introduced casually with no realisation that they were valuable innovations. They were not sensitive to mathematical values.

A more recent opinion is that of Lloyd (1990, p. 104) who writes:

> It would appear that before, in, and after the Sulbasutra (the earliest known evidence of mathematics from India), right down to the modern representatives of that tradition, we are dealing with men who tolerate, on occasion, rough and ready techniques. They are in fact interested in practical results and show no direct concern with proof procedures as such at all.

These quotations raise a number of fundamental questions: What is mathematics? how is it created? and how is its quality to be assessed? But a more general question is: How do mathematicians produce information about mathematical objects? Underlying all these questions is the issue of *proof*, often perceived as a litmus test of whether we are "doing" real mathematics or doing it well.

THE CULTURAL CONTEXT OF PROOF:
THE CASE OF THE *SULBASUTRAS*

It is not often sufficiently recognized that, between different mathematical traditions, there are certain basic differences in the cognitive structures of mathematics—differences in their ontological conceptions regarding the existence and nature of mathematical objects and methodological conceptions regarding the nature and ways of establishing mathematical truths. The first quotation above represents a viewpoint that sees ways of establishing mathematical truths (or what are more commonly known as "proofs") as being immutable and infallible. The second quotation is from a text which, while acknowledging the legitimacy of "informal" proof procedures for confirming or checking a result, requires that a formal proof procedure should observe two crucial distinctions: (a) that between the "practice of proof (of whatever kind) and an explicit concept corresponding to the practice, a concept that incorporates the conditions that need to be met for a proof to be given" and (b) that between "exact procedures and approximate ones" (Lloyd, 1990, pp. 74-75). On both these criteria, Lloyd concludes that early Indian mathematics did not have "any explicit notion of what proof is" (Lloyd, 1990, p.75).

Lloyd's argument is interesting. In a comparison of the similarities and differences between Greek and Chinese mathematics, he accepts that both traditions "practised proofs and deploy concepts to describe their procedures that are subject of *explicit* reflection and comment." But he points out three major differences between the two mathematical traditions. First, the Chinese were only concerned with whether a certain formula or algorithm produced a correct solution and showed little interest in the type of self-conscious attempts at abstract justification of the procedure which constituted the Greek notion of proof. Second, the Greek concern with first principles led to "the classification of different types of indemonstrable primary premises, axioms, postulates and definitions, and with making those used explicit at the outset of a sequence of demonstrations." (p. 121) There is no analogue to this concern in ancient China. The final and the most important difference between the two mathematical traditions relates to their two basic preoccupations: the Greek demand for rigorous demonstration compared to the Chinese emphasis on "practical applicability" which led to exploration of analogies and common structures in procedures for solution of groups of problems. Lloyd's argument is not that the ancient Chinese geometry did not have a general procedure for "proof"—this is not in any case a valid claim, given the widespread use of the "out-in complementarity principle" (or what we would call "dissection-and-reassembly principle") in ancient Chinese mathematics—but that the Chinese did not share to the same degree the Greek enthusiasm for foundational questions or the concern with ultimate justification.[1]

Lloyd, as his quotation above implies, denies even this basic accomplishment on the part of the Indians. He bases his case on an examination of the earliest known geometry in India, Vedic geometry, for which the basic sources are the *Sulbasutras*, conservatively dated as recorded between 800 and 500 BC, though they contain knowledge from earlier times. The *Sulbasutras* are instructions for the construction of sacrificial altars (*vedi*) and the location of sacred fires (*agni*) which had to conform to clearly laid-down instructions about their shapes and areas if they were to be effective instruments of sacrifice. There were two main types of ritual, one for worship at home and the other for communal worship. Square and circular altars were sufficient for household rituals, while more elaborate altars whose shapes were combinations of rectangles, triangles, and trapeziums were required for public worship. Some of the most elaborate of the public altars were shaped like a falcon just about to take flight (*Vakrapraksa-syena*), as shown in Figure 1a. It was believed that offering a sacrifice on such an altar would enable the soul of the supplicant to be conveyed by a falcon straight to heaven.

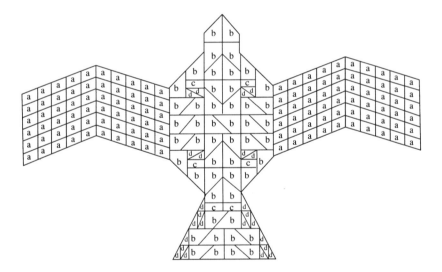

Figure 1a. The first layer of a Vakrapaksa-syena Altar: the wings are each made from 60 bricks of type a, and the body, head and tail from 50 type b, 6 type c, and 24 type d bricks. Each subsequent layer was laid out using different patterns of bricks with the total number of bricks equalling 200.

---

1   For further details of the use of the "out-in complementarity" principle in Chinese mathematics, see Joseph (1992, pp. 180-183).

Most sacrificial altars were constructed with five layers, each of 200 bricks, which reached to the height of the knee. For special occasions ten, fifteen, up to a maximum of ninety-five layers of bricks were prescribed for use in the construction of the falcon-shaped altar. The top layer of the basic altar (Figure 1b) had an area of 7.5 square *purushas*.[2] A "purusha" was defined as the height of a man with his arms stretched above him, say 2.5 metres, which would give the altar an areal measure of approximately 47 square metres.

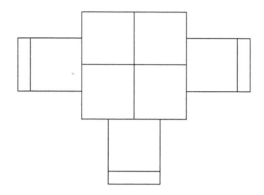

Figure 1b. The basic Altar.

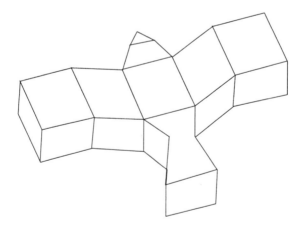

Figure 1c. A Prototype of the Altar.

For the second layer from the top, the prescription was that one square purusha should be added, so that the total area would be 8.5 square purushas. Similarly, each successive layer area should be increased by 1 square purusha, until with the 94th successive increase of 1 square purusha, the area of the base of this huge construction would be 101.5 square purushas

(See Figure 1d). There is the implication that the higher the level at which the sacrifice was performed, the more effective the sacrifice.

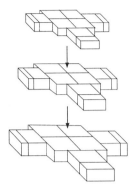

Figure 1d. Constructing the Altar.

It is clear that, in the construction of larger altars, if the same shape as the basic shape is required, there are two "hidden" geometrical problems: (a) that of finding a square equal in area to two given squares and (b) the conversion of a rectangle into a square of equal area or vice versa. These constructions are achieved in the *Sulbasutras* using the Pythagorean theorem.

In the *Katyayana Sulbasutra* (named after one of the authors) appears the following proposition which is more or less replicated in the other two major *Sulbasutras* (those of Apastamba and Baudhayana):

> The rope (stretched along the length) of the diagonal of a rectangle makes an (area) which the vertical and horizontal sides make together. (*Katyayana Sulbasutra*, 2.11)

Using this theorem, the *Sulbasutras* show how to construct both a square equal to the sum of two given squares and a square equal to the difference of two given squares. Further constructions involve the transformation of a rectangle (square) to a square (rectangle) of equal area. A

---

2   Apart from minor variations, the body of the first layer falcon-shaped altar was 4 square purushas square metres, the wings and tail were one square purusha each *plus* the wing increased by $\frac{1}{5}$ of a square purusha each and the tail by $\frac{1}{10}$ of a square purusha so that the image would more closely approximate the shape of a falcon (See Figures 1b and 1c).

Thus the total area of the top layer of *Vakrapaksa-syena* altar is

$4 + (2 \times 1.2) + 1.1 = 7.5$ square purushas.

discussion of these constructions is found in Joseph (1992, pp. 230-232). We will consider only one of these constructions.

A remarkable achievement of Vedic geometry was the discovery of a procedure for evaluating square roots to a high degree of approximation. The problem may have originally arisen from an attempt to construct a square altar twice the area of a given square altar.

The problem is one of constructing a square twice the area of a given square (A) of side 1 unit. It is clear that for the larger square (C) to have twice the area of square A, it should have side $\sqrt{2}$ units. Also, we are given a third square (B) of side 1 which needs to be dissected and reassembled so that by fitting cut-up sections of square (B) around square (A), it is possible to make up a square close to the size of square (C). Figure 2 shows what needs to be done. The instructions given by Apastamba (1.6) and Katyayana (2.13) in their *Sulbasutras* may be translated thus:

> Increase the measure by its third and this third by its own fourth less the thirty-fourth part of that fourth. This is the value with a special quantity in excess.

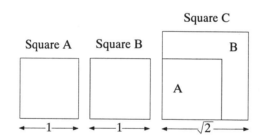

Figure 2a. To draw square C = square A + square B.

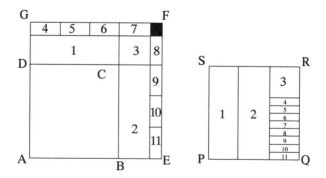

Figure 2b. Application of "Out-In Complementarity Principle."

If we take 1 unit as the dimension of the side of a square, the above formula gives the approximate length of its diagonal as follows:

$$\sqrt{2} = \frac{1}{3} + \frac{1}{3 \times 4} - \frac{1}{3 \times 4 \times 34} = 1.4142156$$

The *Sulbasutras* contain no clue as to the manner in which this accurate approximation was arrived at. A number of theories or possible explanations have been proposed. Of these, the most plausible one is that of Datta (1932), which is discussed in Joseph (1992, pp. 235-236).

THE NATURE OF PROOF: A DIGRESSION

Consider the word "proof" in the sense that Lakatos (1976, p. 9) uses it to mean a "thought experiment which suggests a decomposition *of the original conjecture into subconjectures or lemmas, thus embedding it in a possibly quite distinct body of knowledge.*"

In this broad sense any "proof" has psychological, social and logical features (Resnick, 1992, pp. 15-17). The *psychological* task is to convince the readers of its conclusions. The notation and the way in which the argument is formulated, organized, and presented determines whether the proof succeeds at this task. Yet success in convincing an audience does not necessarily mean that the proof is free of error. Proofs make certain claims about mathematical objects.[3] Understanding such claims requires training and the more "advanced" the mathematics the longer the training required. Nowhere is this training more important than in the comprehension of the *logical* framework in which the proof is embedded. Therefore, it is important to distinguish between the psychological and the logical powers of proof. A logically impeccable proof could appear obscure and unconvincing because the audience has not acquired through training a satisfactory understanding of the mathematical objects of which the claims are being made in the first place.

It is the third feature of a mathematical proof that is often ignored. Proofs are social and cultural artifacts. They evolve in a particular social and cultural context. And this is important since we might tend to forget

---

[3] The nature of mathematical objects determines how we make contact with them. If mathematical objects are based on the Euclidean ideas of atomistic and object-oriented view of space (points, lines, planes and solids) this will be in complete contrast to a Navajo idea of space as neither subdivided nor objectified and where everything is in motion (Bishop, 1990, p. 51). The crucial point is that ideas of proof are culturally created and they must be understood within that culture, resisting the easy temptation to make crude comparisons across cultures and oppositional ways of deciding between ideas which the quotation from Kline at the beginning clearly typifies.

that part of finding out how a proof works includes finding out how well its intended audience (the author included) is prepared to follow it. This is further complicated by the fact that proofs are context-bound—not only in relation to a proof's language and notation but also its reasoning and data (or the uses to which a mathematical result is put).

THE INDIAN PROOF (OR *UPAPATTI*)[4]

For a period going back about two thousand years, a great deal of attention in Indian mathematics was paid to providing what was often referred to as *upapatti* (which may be roughly translated as a "convincing" demonstration) for every mathematical result. In fact some of these *upapattis* were noted by European scholars of Indian mathematics up to the first half of the nineteenth century. For example, in one of the early English translations (1817) of parts of *Brahma Sputa Siddhanta* of Brahmagupta (c. 650 AD) and of *Lilavati* and *Bijaganita* of Bhaskaracharya (c. 1150 AD), Colebrook gives in the form of footnotes a number of *upapattis* from commentators and calls them demonstrations. Similarly, Whish (1835), who brought to the attention of a wider public work in Kerala on infinite series for circular and trigonometric functions, showed sample *upapattis* from a commentary entitled *Yuktibhasa* (1600) which related to the Pythagorean theorem. It would indeed be interesting to find out how the currently popular view, that Indian mathematics lacks the very notion of "proof," has come about during the last one hundred and fifty years.

In this context it is important to realize that the rather scanty discussion of the methodology of Indian mathematics contained in the text on the history of Indian mathematics concentrates on a few original texts, notwithstanding the fact that traditionally the commentaries seem to have played at least as great a role in the exposition of the subject as the original text itself. It is no wonder that mathematicians of the calibre of Bhaskaracharya (c. 1150 AD) and Nilakantha (a 15th century Kerala mathematician/astronomer) wrote not only major original treatises but also erudite commentaries on either their own works or on important works of an earlier period. It is in such commentaries that one finds detailed *upapattis* for results and processes discussed in the original texts as well as more general discussion of the methodological and philosophical issues concerning Indian astronomy and mathematics.

As an illustration let us consider the commentaries of Ganesha Daivajna (c. 1545 AD) on the texts *Lilavati* and *Bijaganita,* both written by Bhaskaracharya.[5] Both texts were highly influential in the development of Indian

---

[4] This section owes a heavy debt to Srinivas (1987) whose work deserves more attention.

mathematics. According to Ganesha, *ganita* (used both as a generic word to describe the subject of mathematics as well as in a specialized sense to describe calculation) is mainly of two types: *vykata ganita* and *avyakta ganita*. *Vyaktaganita* (also called *patiganita* or calculations with the board) is that branch of *ganita* which employs clearly laid out procedures or algorithms well known for general use. This is in contrast to *avyakta ganiti* (also called *bijaganita*) which is distinguished from the first type by including procedures that use indeterminate or unknown quantities in the process of solution. The unknown quantities were referred to by terms such as *yavat tavat* (i.e., "as much as") and different colors (*varna*) denoted by abbreviations such as *ka* (for *kalaka* or black), *ni* (for *nilaka* or blue), etc., just as in modern algebra unknowns are denoted by symbols *x, y, z,* etc.

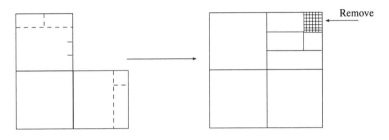

$$1\frac{1}{2} < \sqrt{3} < 1\frac{3}{4}$$

Figure 3a. Evaluation of $\sqrt{3}$ (combining three squares).

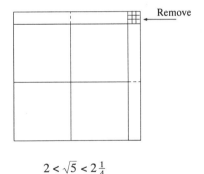

$$2 < \sqrt{5} < 2\frac{1}{4}$$

Figure 3b. Evaluation of $\sqrt{5}$ (combining five squares).

---

5   The two commentaries referred to are Buddhivilasini on Lilavati and Siromani-prakasa on Siddhantasiromani, edited by Apte (1937-41). Ganesha was the son of Keseva Daivajna, a distinguished astronomer. Taught by his father, his commentary on Lilavati is one of the best commentaries on this famous text of Bhaskaracharya.

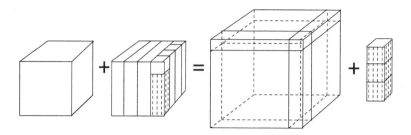

Figure 3c. Combining two cubes.

Many of the *upapattis* relate to the second type of *ganita—bijaganita*. It would be misleading to name the two types—*patiganita* and *bijaganita*— as arithmetic and algebra respectively. *Patiganita* subsumes not only arithmetic and geometry, but also topics included under algebra such as the solution of equations, provided one does not have to make recourse to indeterminate quantities for carrying through the process of solution as in the "method of false position" first used by the Egyptians about four thousand years ago.

A specific illustration of the use of *upapattis* would be useful. In a chapter on solution of quadratic equation from *Bijaganita*, Bhaskaracharya poses the following problem:

> Say what is the hypotenuse of a plane figure, in which the side and upright are equal to fifteen and twenty? And show the upapatti of the received mode of computation.

Later he adds:

> The demonstration follows. It is two fold in each case: one geometric (kshetragata) and the other algebraic (avyaktaritya) ... The algebraic demonstration must be exhibited to those who do not comprehend the geometric one.

Ganesha provides two *upapattis* which are elaborations of the ones outlined by Bhaskaracharya. These are given verbatim below, the only change being that we continue to use the Pythagorean triple (15, 20, 25) given in the original example rather than Ganesha's (3, 4, 5).

The *upapatti* for the *avyakta* method

> Take the hypotenuse as the base and denote it as "ya" in the figure. Let the "bhuja" and "koti" (the two sides) be 15, 20 respectively. Let the perpendicular to the hypotenuse from the opposite vertex be drawn. This divides the triangle into two triangles which are similar to the original. Now use the rule of proportion. When "ya" is the hypotenuse the "bhuja" is 15, then when this "bhuja" 15 is the hypotenuse, the "bhuja" which is now the segment of the hypotenuse to the side of the (original) "bhuja" will be $\frac{15^2}{ya}$. Again when "ya" is the hypotenuse, the "koti" is 20, then when the "koti" 20 is the hypotenuse,

the "koti" which is now the segment of hypotenuse to the side of the (original) "koti" will be $\frac{20^2}{ya}$. Adding the two segments of "ya", the hypotenuse, and equating the sum to (the hypotenuse) "ya" gives "ya" = 25.

Modern notation (See Figure 4a)

Since CDB, CBA, CDA are similar

So $\qquad\qquad \frac{a}{c} = \frac{d}{a} \Rightarrow d = \frac{a^2}{c}$

and $\qquad\qquad \frac{b}{c} = \frac{e}{b} \Rightarrow e = \frac{b^2}{c}$

Therefore, $\qquad c = \frac{a^2 + b^2}{c} \Rightarrow c^2 = a^2 + b^2$

Given $b = 20$, $a = 15$

$$ya = c = \sqrt{20^2 + 15^2} = 25$$

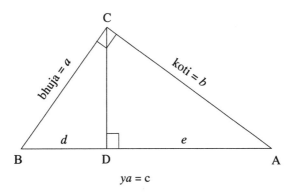

Figure 4a

The *upapatti* for the *kshetragata* method

Take four triangles identical to one another and let different "bhujas" rest on different "kotis" to form the square as shown. The interior square has for its side the difference of "bhuja" and "koti". The area of each triangle is half the product of "bhuja" and "koti" and four times this added to the area of the interior square gives the area of the total figure.

This is nothing but the sum of the squares of "bhuja" and "koti". The square root of that is the side of the (big) square which is nothing but the hypotenuse.

193

Modern notation (See Figure 4b)

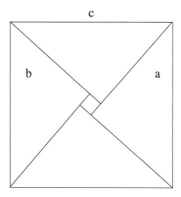

Figure 4b

Let $ya = c, bhuja = a$ and $koti = b$

$$c^2 = (b - a)^2 + 2ab$$
$$= a^2 + b^2$$

(The geometrical representation above bears an uncanny resemblance to that given in the earliest extant Chinese text on astronomy and mathematics, the *Chou Pei Suan Ching,* dated around the early part of the first millennium BC.)

What seems to be all too apparent from this example is that the notion of *upapatti* is significantly different from the notion of proof as understood in the Greek or even in the modern traditions in mathematics.

The *upapattis* of Indian mathematics are presented in a precise language, displaying all the steps of the argument and indicating the general principles which are employed. In this sense they are no different from the "proofs" found in modern mathematics. But what is peculiar to the *upapattis* is that while presenting the argument in an "informal" manner (which is common in mathematical discourse anyway), they make no reference whatsoever to any fixed set of axioms or link the given argument to "formal deductions" performable with the aid of such axioms.

Most mathematical discourse in the Greek as well as in the modern tradition is carried out with clear reference to some formal deductive system, though the discourse itself might be in an "informal" mode, similar to that of Indian mathematics. More importantly, the ideal view of mathematics in both the Greek and modern traditions is that of a formal deductive system. Their view is that "real mathematics" is (and ought to be presented) as formal derivations from formally stated axioms. This ideal view of mathematics is intimately linked with yet another major philosophical presupposition of western tradition: that mathematics constitutes a body of infallible or absolute truths. It is this quest for securing absolute certainty to mathematical knowledge which has motivated most of the foundational and philosophical investigations into mathematics and has also shaped the entire course of mathematics in the western tradition right from the Greeks to contemporary times.

What the *upapattis* of Indian mathematics reveal is that the Indian epistemological position on the nature and validation of mathematical knowledge is very different from that in the Western tradition. This is brought out, for instance, by the general agreement among the Indian mathematicians as to what a *upapatti* is supposed to achieve. Ganesha declares in his preface to the commentary on Bhaskaracharya's *Lilavati* that:

> Whatever is discussed in the vyakta or avyakta branches of mathematics, without upapatti it will not be nirbhranta (i.e., free from misunderstanding). It will not acquire any standing in an assembly of scholar mathematicians. The upappati is directly perceivable, like looking in a hand mirror. It is, therefore, to elevate the intellect (buddhi vriddhi) that I proceed to enunciate the upapattis.

As regards the modes of argument which are allowed in the *upapattis,* one distinctive feature appears to be that Indian mathematics permitted the use of the method of indirect proof (*reductio ad absurdum*) but only to show the *non-existence* of certain entities. The method of indirect proof was called *tarka* by the Indian logicians. Indian mathematicians subscribed to the general methodological dictum of most schools of Indian philosophy: that the *tarka* was not an independent *pramana* and could therefore not be used to prove the existence of an entity whose existence cannot be otherwise proved.

It should be emphasized that this does not mean that Indian mathematics totally abandoned the method of indirect proof. For example, consider the *upapatti* of the result that a negative number has no square root given by another commentator Krishna Daivajna (c. AD 1600) (edited by Dvivede, 1920).

> A negative number is not a square. Hence how can we evaluate its square root? It may be argued that "why cannot a negative number be a square? Surely it is not a royal command" ... Agreed. Let it be stated by you who claim that a negative number is a square as to whose square it is; surely not of a positive number, for the square of a positive number is always positive. Not also a negative number because then also the square will be positive by the same rule. This being the case, we cannot see how the square of a number becomes negative.

In not accepting the method of indirect proof as a valid means for establishing the existence of an entity (whose existence is not even in principle establishable via direct means of proof), the Indian mathematicians took what is referred to today as the constructivist approach to the issue of mathematical existence. But the Indian philosopher-logician did more than merely disallow certain existence proofs. The general Indian philosophical position is in fact one of completely eliminating from logical discourse all reference to unlocatable entities whose existence is not even in principle accessible to direct means of verification. This appears to be the position adopted by Indian mathematicians. And, for this reason, many an "existence theorem" (where all that has been proved is the non-existence of a hypothetical entity incompatible with the accepted set of postulates) of Greek or modern western mathematics would not be considered to have any meaning in Indian mathematics.

REFERENCES

Apte, D. (Ed.) (1937). *Buddhivilasini of Ganesha Daivajna*, 2 Vols. Anandasrama Sanskrit Series, No. 107, Pune.

Apte, D. (1939-41). *Siromaniprakasa of Ganesha Daivajna (Grahagnitadyaya)*, 2 Vols. Anandasrama Sanskrit Series, No. 112, Pune.

Bishop, A.J. (1990). Western mathematics: The secret weapon of cultural imperialism, *Race and Class, 32,* 51-65.

Colebrook, H.T. (1817). *Algebra with arithmetic and mensuration from the Sanskrit of Brahmegupta and Bhascara*. London: John Murray.

Datta, B. (1932). *The science of the Sulba.* Calcutta: University Press.

Dvivede, S. (Ed.). (1920). *Bijaganitan Avyaktaganitan* (with the commentary *Bijanvankura* by Krishna Daivajna). Anandasrama Sanskrit Series, Pune.

Joseph, G.G. (1992). *The crest of the peacock: Non-European roots of mathematics*, London: Penguin.

Khadilkar, S.S. (1974). *Katyayana Sulba Sutra.* Pune.

Kline, M. (1972). *Mathematical thought from ancient to modern times.* New York: Oxford University Press.

Kulkarni, R.P. (1983). *Geometry according to Sulbasutra*. Vedika Samsodhama Mandala, Pune.

Lakatos, I. (1976). *Proofs and refutations: The logic of mathematical discovery*. Cambridge UK: Cambridge, University Press.

Lloyd, G.E.R. (1990). *Demystifying mentalities*, Cambridge UK: Cambridge University Press.

Resnick, M.D. (1992). Proof as a source of truth. In M. Detlefsen (Ed.), *Proof and knowledge in mathematics* (pp. 6-32). London: Routledge.

Saraswati Amma, T.A. (1979). *Geometry in ancient and medieval India.* Molital Banarsidass Varanasi.

Seidenberg, A. (1960-1962). The ritual origins of geometry. *Archives for History of Exact Sciences, 1,* 488-527.

Seidenberg, A. (1974-1975). Did Euclid's elements, book I, develop geometry axiomatically? *Archives for*

History of Exact Sciences, 14, 263-295.

Seidenberg, A. (1977-1978). The origins of mathematics. *Archives for History of Exact Sciences, 18,* 301-342.

Seidenberg, A. (1983). The geometry of the vedic rituals. In F. Staal (Ed.), *Agni, the vedic ritual of the fire altar* (pp. 95-126). Berkeley.

Srinivashchar, D., & Narimhachar, S. (Eds.) (1931). *Apastamba Sulbasutram.* Mysore Oriental Library Publications, No. 31.

Srinivasiengar, C.N. (1967). *The history of ancient Indian mathematics.* Calcutta: World Press.

Srinivas, M.D. (1987). The methodology of Indian mathematics and its contemporary relevance. *PPST Bulletin, 12,* 1–35.

Thibaut, G. (Ed.). (1977). *Baudhyana Sulbasutra, Pandit,* Series 9 and 10, Varnasi.

Thibaut, G. (Ed.). (1982). On the Sulvasutras. In D. Chattopadhyaya (Ed.), *Studies in the history of science in India* (Vol. 2, pp. 415-478). New Delhi: Editoral Enterprises.

Whish, C.M. (1835). On the Hindu quadrature of the circle and the infinitive series of the proportion of the circumference of the diameter exhibited in the four Sastras. *Transactions of the Royal Asiatic Society of Great Britain and Ireland, 3,* 509-523.

MATHEMATICS EDUCATION
IN THE GLOBAL VILLAGE:
THE WEDGE AND THE FILTER

Murad Jurdak

American University of Beirut, Lebanon

Writing from an international perspective is likely to include over-generalizations and biases inadvertently made or held by the author. Inclusive and meaningful statements about international aspects of education run the risk of over-generalizing if they emphasize meaningfulness at the expense of inclusiveness, and the risk of being vacuous if they do the opposite. Moreover, any author's perspective of international affairs is biased by the author's spatial-temporal context including culture, society, and history. As the author of this paper, my perspective is that of a mathematics educator who belongs to a developing country in a very old culture. Having this in mind, I move to describe the contours of the terrain to be covered in this paper.

The 90s promise to be the decade of transition to the information age. Scientists, economists, and educators predict deep changes in society, economy, and education. Countries vary in their response to the challenge of coming to grips with the demands and consequences of the information age. The following four examples taken from the United States of America, India, Jordan, and the world Conference on Education for All are illustrative of the different kinds of responses.

In the United States of America, a number of forward-looking books and reports in the 80s focused on the theme of America 2000 and the transition to the twenty-first century. *Everybody counts (*National Research Council, 1989) was one such report which focused specifically on mathematics education. *Everybody counts* describes vividly the various forces that impinge on mathematics education in the United States and the mobilization of human resources needed to bring about a transition to the twenty-first century. It also outlines national policies, strategies, and support structures for renewal of mathematics education. One underlying theme is to make American mathematics education the best in the world in order to sustain the nation's leadership in a global economy.

Thousands of miles away, the National Institute of Educational Planning and Administration in India prepared a document to spell out the Indian perspective on the subject of Education for All by 2000 (UNESCO, 1990). The report deals with a critical analysis of the present educational system in India, new approaches for securing higher levels of participation and retention in schools, particularly of the main disadvantaged sections of society (women, minorities, excluded castes, ...), curriculum, decentralization, and last but not least increasing financial provisions for education from 4 to 6% of the GNP. Nowhere to be seen is a preoccupation with the information age and its effect on education.

Closer to home, Jordan proposed and implemented a reform plan whose main thrust was to improve the quality of education by up-dating and up-grading the educational system. The reform plan (Ministry of Education and Instruction, 1987) called for a change in the educational ladder by extending compulsory basic education by two years (from 6-14 years to 6-16 years), followed by a two-year secondary school with different tracks. An overhauling of curricula, teacher training programs, school administration and school buildings were key points in the plan. Jordan, a developing country, allocated relatively large resources to this plan. Science and technology, although stressed, do not reflect an apparent sensitization to the demands of the information age.

An international perspective is illustrated by the *World Declaration on Education for All* (Inter-Agency Commission, 1990). In article 1 of that Declaration, the World Conference on Education for All which convened in Jomtien, Thailand, specified the basic learning needs in the emerging global economic, social, and cultural environments of the 1990s. Basically, these learning needs comprise essential learning tools (such as literacy, oral expression, numeracy, and problem solving) for everybody to live and work; to participate fully in development to improve the quality of life; to make informed decisions; and to continue to learn. The satisfaction of these needs is to recognize the collective cultural, linguistic, and spiritual heritage of the community, and to promote the values of cooperation, justice, and tolerance in an interdependent world.

The preceding illustrative examples are too few to warrant any inference but may support the following specific observations:

1. Industrialized countries have set as a priority the development of their capabilities to make the transition to the information age. They are contemplating or implementing educational plans to enable them to educate their citizens for the future. One major driving force for

those countries is to secure a competitive edge in the global economy.

2. Developing countries are primarily concerned with provisions of resources to upgrade their education or to cope with quantitative growth. In both cases, it is not the demands of the information age that guide their policies, but rather the compelling problems of the present and the accumulation of the failures of the past.

3. The international perspective proposes educational goals which aim at the future but are rooted in the cultural heritage of the community concerned. These goals are higher in standard and more forward-looking than those of developing countries, but less than those of industrialized countries. The message is for international cooperation rather than competition.

MATHEMATICAL LITERACY FOR THE INFORMATION AGE

More than any school subject, mathematics is at the forefront of the transition to the information age. In most industrial countries the use of computer technology in all economic sectors and the availability of high-speed communications have dramatically transformed the workplace, the social context, and the home environment. Moreover, continued introduction of innovations in computer and communications technology will continually change learning objectives, making them moving targets. Because mathematical methods, skills, concepts, and attitudes are essential for this technological environment, a new mathematical literacy is called for: a mathematical literacy for the information age. Henceforth, this information age mathematical literacy will be denoted by IA mathematical literacy.

The descriptions of the basic components of IA mathematical literacy in the literature turn out to be essentially the same. It is convenient to sort such components into three categories: abilities, attitudes, and contexts.

Abilities

Three such abilities are often mentioned as essential components of IA mathematical literacy: higher-order reasoning, communication, and problem solving (Romberg, 1988; NCTM, 1989; NRC, 1989). Higher-order reasoning in mathematics consists of non-algorithmic and complex skills which involve multiple criteria, multiple solutions, judgment, interpretation, uncertainty, self-regulation, imposing meaning, and mental effort (Resnick, 1987). Communication refers to the skills of reading, writing, discussing and translating using the language of mathematics. Problem solving encompasses a group of skills for utilizing higher-order reasoning skills and communication skills to understand and resolve non-routine tasks in authentic problem situations.

Attitudes

A number of components of IA mathematical literacy have been identified in the affective domain, including valuing mathematics, confidence in using mathematics, and cooperation while learning and/or utilizing mathematics (NCTM, 1989). Valuing mathematics is seen as a deep-rooted conviction which is indispensable, not only in the school environment but more so at home, at work, in private decisions, and in the social context at large. Confidence in mathematics refers to an attitude of being empowered by mathematics to do things which are not possible without the possession of that power. Cooperation is viewed as the means of imparting the belief that learning and/or using mathematics are not isolated activities, and the attitude that different perspectives enrich the learning of mathematics.

Contexts

IA mathematical literacy requires optimal contexts for its development. The physical context requires the utilization of a high-technology environment for learning, applying, or assessing authentic mathematical tasks. The social context makes it imperative that IA mathematical literacy be achieved by all, irrespective of social or ethnic divisions. IA mathematical literacy for all is assumed to be necessary for economic survival and social harmony. The temporal context refers to a learning environment which provides the student with the power to learn for life. The changing demands of technology and communication require the power to continually learn and adapt to the new conditions.

HISTORICAL PERSPECTIVE

More than at any time before, disparities in the 1990s in mathematics education between industrialized and developing countries are not only of degree but also of kind. In the first half of the twentieth century formal education was almost nonexistent in most of the now-developing countries. In the few countries where formal education existed, the colonial powers and the countries under their patronage did share the same kind of mathematics education—that of the colonial powers. The formal education systems in these countries were modelled after those of the colonial powers and so were the curricula, textbooks, teaching methods, and even the language of instruction. Mathematics curricula could be transplanted across the boundaries of countries, cultures, and traditions because of the deep-rooted belief, at that time, that mathematical concepts and skills are universally meaningful and applicable. The basic difference between the colonial powers and developing countries was a matter of the degree of accessibility of formal education. In colonial countries, a minimum level of formal schooling (including arithmetic as one of the three R's) was almost universally achieved. In the colonies, formal education was limited to the few who were privileged to be admitted to foreign schools in order to prepare them as local counterparts for public service and the professions.

The modern mathematics movement which appeared in Western countries in the 60s triggered similar reforms in the newly independent developing countries. The changes in mathematics education that took place in the developing countries had a number of characteristics. First, the reform was introduced in secondary schools and for college-bound students: i.e., for a very small proportion of the student population. Second, the reform lagged behind similar efforts in Western countries by more than a decade, and most often as the thrust of that reform was going downhill in the West. Third, the new curricular materials were produced by adopting and/or adapting curricular materials developed in Western countries and dominated by Western mathematics educators, or local mathematics educators educated and trained in the West. Fourth, the reform was basically limited to the reorganization, addition, or deletion of mathematical topics. So similar were the reform efforts in developing and industrial countries that Howard Fehr (1965), writing on mathematics education around the world, did not feel the need to refer to any of the developing countries.

In the 70s and 80s , the repeated swings in the Western countries that ranged from " back-to-basics" to emphasizing individual and societal-based objectives, did not resonate in the developing countries. The latter continued to diffuse the excesses of modern mathematics, but always maintaining a content-based orientation.

Perhaps for the first time in this century, the 90s are witnessing a divorce in mathematics education between the industrialized and the developing countries. IA mathematical literacy is radically different from that which is prevalent in most developing countries. The differences encompass targeted abilities and attitudes as well as the physical, social, and temporal contexts of the learning environment. Moreover, IA mathematical literacy is a result of a paradigm shift from the industrial age to the information age. Thus the reform movement of the 90s in mathematics education is expected to be a system-wide transformation, unlike previous reform efforts which focused on one or a few components of a very complex social, economic, and cultural system. The reform movement of the 90s in the industrialized countries promises to be a synchronized movement aimed at transforming mathematics education as a whole while providing for changes in policies, strategies, and support structures in the larger social, economic, and cultural contexts.

Mathematics education is thus poised to act as a wedge sustaining and reinforcing the division among countries along social, economic, and cultural lines. In the global village, the growing gap is developing into some sort of separate development (apartheid) in mathematics education.

CONSTRAINTS AND BARRIERS

Bridging the gap between IA mathematical literacy and traditional math-ematical literacy in the developing countries does not seem to be easily attainable in the near future because of economic, social, and cultural constraints and barriers.

Resource constraints

Within their competing priorities, developing countries are unlikely to be able to afford the material and human resources needed to implement the kind of reform in mathematics education being contemplated or implemented in the industrialized countries. One prominent feature of that reform in the industrialized countries is that it is a system-wide transformation. This entails radical changes in the orientation of the school curriculum and the re-allocation of resources to quality improvement. The development of such authentic skills as higher-order reasoning, communication, and problem solving requires radical changes in the tools, methods, and learning environment of mathematics instruction. Thus resources have to be invested in curriculum development, teacher education and re-education, and the implementation of educational technology. Most developing countries cannot afford to allocate already scarce resources to a system-wide reform on this scale at a time when they have to cope with more basic and urgent needs.

The problems of the developing countries are very different from those of industrialized countries. Table 1 presents macro-level comparative data on some education indicators. Three problems stand out in developing countries but not in the industrialized countries. First, participation in education as expressed in gross enrollment ratios, particularly in the second level of education (12-18 age-group), is a pressing problem in developing countries (a non-participation rate of more than 50% in the second level of education is found in developing countries compared to less than 7% in industrialized countries). Second, the participation of females in education in developing countries is uniformly much lower than males, whereas such differences do not exist in industrialized countries. Third, the adult (15 years or more) literacy rate in developing countries is close to 65%, with a gender difference favoring males. This compares to a literacy level of 97% in industrialized countries with no gender differences. Fourth, to cap such differences, public expenditure on education is almost eight times greater in industrialized countries than in developing countries in billions of dollars and 140% in percentage of GNP.

It is obvious that the gap is bound to increase as industrialized countries increase their investment in education while developing countries struggle with such perennial problems as working to increase participation rates in education, particularly for females, and to increase their human capital by decreasing adult literacy.

Table 1. Education Indicators in Developing and Industrialized Countries.

	Developing countries		Industrialized countries	
	Male	Female	Male	Female
*Gross enrollment ratio**				
First level education	105.5	90.4	102.0	101.1
Second level education	50.3	37.5	93.5	93.8
Third level education	10.1	6.5	37.0	36.5
Adult literacy (percentage)	74.9	55.5	97.4	96.1
Public expenditure on education				
US $ (billion)			125.8[+]	897.9[+]
percentage of GNP			4.1[+]	5.8[+]

Source : UNESCO World Education Report, 1991

+ indicates that the figure is for 1988, other figures are for 1990

* gross enrollment ratio = total enrollment in level regardless of age ÷ population of the age group officially corresponding to that level.

In communications and media, developing countries lag far behind the industrialized countries. Table 2 presents comparative data on communications and media indicators. In all the media, ranging from book production to television, the media indicators for the industrialized countries are more than those in the developing countries. Needless to say this difference is increasing, particularly in respect of the backbone of the information age: the computer.

Table 2. Communications and Media Indicators in Developing and Industrialized Countries.

	Developing countries	Industrialized countries
Book production Titles per million inhabitants	57	507
Daily newspapers Circulation per thousand inhabitants	43	337
Printing and writing paper Consumption (kg) per inhabitant	1.5	41.4
Radio receivers Number per thousand inhabitants	173	1008
Television receivers Number per thousand inhabitants	44	485

Source : UNESCO World Education Report, 1991.

Social barriers

In developing countries, the main social barriers in the way of achieving IA mathematical literacy are the contexts of mathematics instruction and learning. The physical context of the classroom is far from being the high-tech environment that is required for IA mathematical literacy. Even if such an environment could be afforded it would be radically different from the one that applied mathematics in the larger social context, thus reducing the authenticity of classroom instruction.

Mathematics education for all is not easily attainable in developing countries. This is because the priority in such countries is to provide for universal access to and participation in schooling. Moreover, the "human capital" in these communities (with more than 40% adult illiteracy on the average) is lower than the critical threshold needed to graft and sustain a major quality-improvement intervention of this magnitude.

Again, life-long education and the development of the power to learn do not match social beliefs, expectations, and rewards. In developing countries, education is still conceived as a means of upward social mobility.

However, success in education is measured by upward mobility on the educational ladder culminating in official certification. Thus the ultimate goal is not to "develop the power to learn" but to move upward on the educational ladder. Mathematics, because of its perceived hierarchical nature, reinforces the "upward mobility" objective at the expense of developing the power to learn (Jurdak, 1992).

Cultural barriers

The values and beliefs about mathematics and its teaching in developing countries are the main cultural barriers in the way of achieving IA mathematical literacy. The implied conception of mathematics in IA mathematical literacy is that of a mode of thinking, skills, and concepts valued for their power in solving and communicating authentic problems. In developing countries, the prevailing conception of mathematics is that of an external body of knowledge which is valued for its utility in upward mobility on the educational ladder.

IA mathematical literacy conceives of teaching mathematics as a cooperative activity in which students develop new knowledge through active construction and interaction in the social context of the classroom. In developing countries, the teaching of mathematics is conceived as a process of transmitting predetermined concepts and skills to the learner whose ultimate responsibility is to acquire mathematical knowledge and to demonstrate the possession of such knowledge in contrived testing situations.

In addition, the value-systems in different countries may conflict with the values and beliefs embedded in IA mathematical literacy. Values about authority and those who possess it (Hofstede, 1986), social expectations of normative behaviors, and ideological beliefs as cultural carriers (Jurdak, 1989) contribute significantly to the social climate of mathematics instruction. Cultural dissonance is a resilient barrier in the way of achieving IA mathematical literacy.

THE RESPONSES

The challenge of bridging the gap between industrialized and developing countries in the nature and level of mathematical literacy elicited three archetypal modes of responses: the neutral mode, the indigenous mode, and the transfer of technology mode.

The neutral response mode

The response of most developing countries to the challenge has been the neutral mode. This is the case because of an unawareness of the existing gap on the part of developing countries, the unaffordability of the demands of

IA mathematical literacy, or an unwillingness to introduce radical changes. Such countries continue to conceive of mathematics education and any change therein in terms of the assumptions and constraints of the existing framework. No special effort is made to take into consideration the impact of communications and computer technology on the society, economy, and education.

The neutral mode may be judicious in the short term but risky in the long run. It may be wise to wait for the claims and promises of IA mathematical literacy to bear fruit, especially since the field of mathematics education has plenty of unfulfilled promises. However, if the claims of IA mathematical literacy become a reality, then the countries that adopt the neutral response mode will find themselves out of phase with industrialized countries and unprepared to participate effectively in the economy of the global village.

The indigenous response mode

The indigenous response mode advances the premise that mathematics education should look inward in order to achieve authenticity in terms of the meanings of the indigenous cultural and social contexts. Ethnomathematics is perhaps the best-articulated response in this regard (D'Ambrosio, 1985). Although a number of projects involving ethnomathematics have been implemented, their impact is localized.

The indigenous mode has the advantage of optimizing meaningful learning of mathematics in the local context but may run the risk of isolating communities and countries. The emphasis on the indigenous context in mathematics teaching is more likely to produce higher motivation and more authentic learning of mathematics in the local context. However, the de-emphasis on modern demands and modes of thinking, including their interaction with non-indigenous technology, is likely to increase the isolation of mathematics education from the international mainstream. As in nature, the balance between ecology and technology in mathematics is a delicate one.

The technology transfer response mode

Many developing countries have responded to the challenge of bridging the gap by acquiring the educational technology available in the schools of industrialized nations. The majority of these countries have high per capita income because of their natural resources, but otherwise have low level developmental indicators. These countries can afford to buy computers and audio-visual materials, can produce high-quality instructional materials, can build school facilities, and can even import foreign teachers.

The main advantage of the technology transfer approach is that it tends to maintain a technological linkage between developing and industrialized countries. On the other hand, it is often the case that the technology remains at a shallow level of adaptation because of incompatibility with the indigenous ideological and social values inherent in such communities (Jurdak, 1988). The technology transfer is likely to affect the "skill" component of IA mathematical literacy, but is unlikely to change the "value" and "context" components.

The challenge

Until recently, mathematics education has provided a common ground where the international community in mathematics education could meet, talk the same language, ask similar questions, and share different answers. The 1990s seem to be witnessing a growing gap between developing and industrialized countries, thus threatening the common ground, the common language, and the shared concerns of mathematics education.

The three types of responses discussed earlier do not seem to be conducive to the restoration of mathematics education as a common ground of shared concerns with multiple perspectives. I believe that there is a need for a concerted international effort to halt the divergence in mathematics education between developing and industrialized countries, especially the division that is taking place along economic and cultural lines.

Perhaps the need is for a vision similar to the one which motivated the World Conference on Education for All. Three ingredients are essential for such a vision. First, the focus of this vision should be mathematics for all within the framework of basic education for all. Mathematics education for all should cover not only some nations or regions but the international community at large, and not only some advantaged sections of the society but the whole society. Second, the international community in mathematics education should formulate guidelines for sustainable international development in mathematics education in the areas of goals and objectives, curriculum, professional preparation of teachers of mathematics, and assessment. These guidelines should be realistic enough to be attainable by developing countries and ambitious enough to be a basis for industrialized countries to build on. Third, there should be an international support system in mathematics education to enhance the capacity of developing countries to attain these guidelines and also to promote the understanding and utilization of diverse cultural values and practices.

REFERENCES

D'Ambrosio, U. (1985). Environmental influences. In R. Morris (Ed.), *Studies in Mathematics Education, 4,* 29-46. Paris: UNESCO.

Fehr, H. (1965). Reform in mathematics education around the world. *The Mathematics Teacher, 58,* 37-44.

Hofstede, G. (1986). Cultural differences in teaching and learning. *International Journal of Intercultural Relations, 10,* 301-320.

Inter-Agency Commission for the World Conference on Education for All (1990). *World Declaration on Education for All.* New York: Inter-Agency Commission.

Jurdak, M. (1989). Religion and language as cultural carriers and barriers in mathematics education. In C. Keitel (Ed.), *Mathematics, education and society.* Science and Technology Education, Document Series No. 35 (pp. 12-14). Paris: UNESCO.

Jurdak, M. (1992). Assessment in mathematics education in Arab countries. In M. Niss (Ed.), *Assessment in mathematics and its effects.* Dordrecht, The Netherlands: Kluwer Academic Publishers.

Ministry of Education and Instruction (1987). *Recommendations of the National Conference on Educational Development.* Amman, Jordan: Author (in Arabic).

National Council of Teachers of Mathematics (1989). *Curriculum and evaluation standards for school mathematics.* Reston, VA: NCTM.

National Research Council (1989). *Everybody counts.* Washington: National Academy Press.

Resnick, L. (1987). *Education and learning to think.* Washington: National Academy Press.

Romberg, T. (1988). *Curricular interfaces in school mathematics: the "ideal" with the "real".* Madison, WI: National Center for Research in Mathematical Sciences Education.

UNESCO (1990). *Development of education: 1988-1990, National report of India.* Report presented at the 42nd session of the International Conference on Education, Geneva.

UNESCO (1991). *World education report.* Paris: UNESCO.

BONUSES OF UNDERSTANDING
MATHEMATICAL UNDERSTANDING

Thomas E. Kieren

University of Alberta, Canada

A class of 8-year olds has been developing a sense of the nature of fractions (particularly those whose denominators are powers of two) by folding and shading parts of sheets of writing paper taken as units. Now the teacher stands before the class holding a much larger sheet of paper which he has pre-folded and which is shaded as follows.

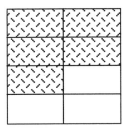

He asks the children what they can say about it. Kara replies immediately and brightly, "It's five fourths." After getting other responses from the class the teacher returns to Kara and asks, "Why did you say five fourths?" Looking thoughtful, Kara replies "Well, a half of a half is a fourth. So, five fourths!"

Would we say that Kara is exhibiting mathematical understanding here? If so, what are the characteristics of the way in which we view understanding which allows us to say this? It is the purpose of this essay to describe one way of understanding mathematical understanding, as well as briefly attending to others, and to illustrate the bonuses of such an understanding when one considers children doing mathematics.

211

It is challenging to try to describe and discuss mathematical understanding. Wittgenstein (1956, p. 298) has put it this way: "Understanding a mathematical proposition—that is a very vague concept." He continues by saying that a person can prove a proposition and justify each step in their reasoning clearly—that is, the person can generate a legitimate sophisticated-looking mathematical product—and yet this is not sufficient evidence that the person is acting with understanding. Acting with understanding, it seems, involves being able to see the significance and consequences of the proposition, to see alternatives to it and alternative approaches in producing it and to be able to situate it or interweave it with one's more informal intuitive knowledge of that area of mathematics (Wittgenstein, 1956; Morascvik, 1979; Bohm & Peat, 1987). If one were to situate such understanding in Ernest's (1991) picture of the social construction of mathematics, it seems that understanding would lie in the realm of subjective knowledge. It would appear that Wittgenstein is alluding to a kind of tension between a clear public mathematical product and the more subjective activity which would have to be considered if one were to judge whether the person who "produced" the mathematics acted with understanding.

If mathematical understanding is an aspect of personal and what appears to be "subjective" mathematics, is it worth studying? Does it not suffice for a teacher or researcher (or fellow mathematician) to simply recognize understanding when it is observed? Bateson (1979, 1987) has associated knowing something, say a piece of mathematics, with the ability to act appropriately or live in a situation which calls for the knowledge. But he says that acting with understanding, the capability to reflect on and organize one's knowing, carries with it a bonus. If one equates knowing with doing or living, then perhaps the bonus of understanding is in raising the quality of that life.

In what follows I will attempt to argue for the bonus of understanding mathematical understanding by presenting one such understanding, a theory for the growth of mathematical understanding which Susan Pirie of Oxford University and I have been developing over the past few years. In addition, a situation drawn from studies of 12-year olds building knowledge of fractions will be analyzed using constructs from our model. The purpose of such analyses will be to highlight the bonuses which accrue from our understanding of mathematical understanding.

In developing our theory we are following (and in part developing) an enactivist view of cognition which holds that a person is autopoietic, bringing forth their world in the sphere of their behavioral possibilities (Maturana & Varela, 1987; Varela, Thompson, & Rosch, 1991). Understanding in such a non-representationist activity is seen when a person, in conjunction with their environment, which often includes other human actors, uses their knowledge structure to organize their own knowledge (von Glasersfeld, 1987). Such understanding is seen as "a series of ongoing meaning (making) events in which a person's world stands forth" (Johnson, 1987, p. 175). In such a view one's understanding is seen to grow out of one's knowing experiences (and to organize them) and complementarily one's understanding configures one's knowing actions.

BONUSES OF UNDERSTANDING IN THE LITERATURE

Of course, it should not be thought that our understanding of mathematical understanding is the only way to gain the bonuses of understanding. Over the past 20 years there has been a continuing dialogue in mathematics education which is attempting to make clearer the "vague concept" of mathematical understanding. Skemp (1976, 1987) distinguished between and elaborated the ideas of instrumental understanding (knowing how without knowing why) and relational understanding (knowing how and being able to elaborate why in terms of one's other mathematical knowledge). Skemp himself felt an immediate bonus of such an understanding of understanding—it enabled him to see that mathematical understanding was not a monolithic entity but to observe that there were possibly many kinds of understanding.

A bonus of Skemp's work for mathematics education has been the continuing generation of ideas on mathematical understanding—including this essay. Herscovics and Bergeron (1983, 1988, 1989, 1992) extended the number of kinds of understanding which a person might have (e.g. concrete, symbolic, logical, formal). But rather than see such types of understanding as isolated acquisitions, they instead organized a two-tiered structure of types of understanding distinguishing understanding of preliminary physical concepts for any fundamental mathematical concept from that of the emerging mathematical concept. Within tiers they distinguished intuition, procedures, abstractions, and formalizations as indicators of a person having acquired particular understandings with respect to a mathematical concept. One of the bonuses which flowed from such an understanding was the capability of making distinctions between different kinds of physical understanding of a concept, say addition of natural numbers or integers. A second bonus was that such a model suggests that teachers can fruitfully engage in epistemological analyses of mathematics concepts in a way that will help them perceive and structurally situate different types of understandings of the concepts which their students might acquire.

Miller, Malone, and Kandl (1992), using ideas from Ryle (1949), understood mathematical understanding as a three-dimensional space with "knowing that" ranging from discrete to integrated knowing, "knowing how" ranging from simple to complex, and "knowing why" ranging from intuitive to rigorous. A person's understanding of a piece of mathematics (such as Kara's at the beginning of this essay) would be situated in this three-dimensional space. (Kara had a somewhat integrated, rather simple and intuitive—and physical procedural, to add a concept from Herscovics and Bergeron—understanding of fractions.) One bonus of such an understanding is that a teacher could think of student understanding of a concept both in terms of current positions and goal positions in such an understanding space. As illustrated in their study with high school teachers and students, Miller, Malone, and Kandl's model provided teachers and students with a language for talking about understanding, thus revealing for teachers and students understanding which occurred in their classrooms.

Rather than viewing understanding in terms of types or acquisitions, Sierpinska (1990) saw understanding in terms of a sequence of action events where understanding changed due to facing epistemological obstacles. She writes, "But the moment we discover something is wrong with (our) knowledge (i.e. we become aware of an "epistemological obstacle") we *understand something* (emphasis added) and we start knowing in a new way." Some bonuses which accrue to such an understanding of mathematical understanding are that the latter is seen as occurring in events rather than as a type of acquisition, that depth of understanding of a topic can be observed in terms of the number of epistemological obstacles faced, and like Herscovics and Bergeron it prompts an epistemological analysis of mathematics on the part of teachers.

A MODEL FOR THE GROWTH OF MATHEMATICAL UNDERSTANDING

In reacting to understandings of mathematical understanding which defined it in terms of types or linear combinations of types of understanding, Pirie (1988) attempted to observe understanding as it occurred in children and found it to be a dynamic non-linear process. She and I combined that thinking with a dynamic model of personal knowledge of mathematics (Kieren, 1988) into stimuli for a five-year continuing project of building and using the model for the growth of mathematical understanding illustrated below (Figure 1).

We observed the growth of a student's understanding of a mathematical topic within an environment of possibilities (provided in part by teachers and other students) as playing itself out within a framework of eight kinds of acts of understanding. It is beyond the scope of this paper to give many details of these levels or modes of understanding, but we have done so in other work (Pirie & Kieren 1989, 1990, 1992; Kieren & Pirie, 1992; Kieren, 1990; Kieren, Mason, & Pirie, 1992). The observer makes assumptions about what a student brings to the current observation task. We call such

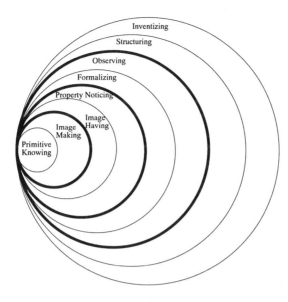

Figure 1. Model for the growth of mathematical understanding.

assumed capabilities *Primitive Knowing* and it forms the core of understanding of a new topic. In the first example studied below it was assumed that Tanya and her 12-year-old classmates could divide various units equally and knew at least some fraction language. The three next inner rings: *Image Making, Image Having, and Property Noticing* are three successively more sophisticated informal, local context dependent ways of understanding. The next three rings—*Formalizing, Observing, and Structuring*—are modes of understanding in which a person knows and understands mathematics in ways which are less context dependent and more abstract. Details of some of these six modes of understanding will arise in the discussion of examples illustrating the bonuses of having and using such a model.

Let me briefly discuss the outer ring: *Inventizing*. We have coined a new word here because we do not wish to say that students or mathematicians are not inventive in the other informal or formal understanding activities. By "inventizing" we mean that a person is capable, once they have a full formal structural command of a mathematical topic, of putting such knowledge "in a box" and developing, without giving up the previously understood knowledge, a completely new way of lookong at and building from phenomena developed in the previous structure. A contemporary example of this is work in fractal or chaos theory where previously structured understandings of pathological functions have given rise in some mathematicians to full and totally new understandings of mathematics.

There are several features and consequences of this model and related theory which allow it to be useful in observing change and growth in a person's mathematical understanding. Notice the asymmetric nested rings. This suggests that the understanding activity (if not disjoint and detached) at an outer more sophisticated level always enfolds and embeds and has access to less sophisticated more context-dependent related inner level understandings.[1] This aspect of the model (and the findings in the example below) is in accord with Varela, Thompson, and Rosch (1991) who suggest,

> If we wish to recover common sense, then we must invert the representationist attitude by treating context dependent know-how not as a residual artifact that can be progressively eliminated by the discovery of more sophisticated rules but as, in fact, the very essence of creative cognition.

Our theory balances *for a person* an emphasis on what Ernest (1991) calls the formal "front" of mathematics with the informal "back", and in fact gives a central position to the latter.

Another critical feature of the model is indicated by the heavy rings which we call "Don't Need Boundaries." When a person has an image, they can talk about and act on the mathematics without doing the explicit activity which brought it forth. Similarly when persons are applying a method or are formalizing they no longer need to reference context-dependent images or local properties. When persons are setting mathematical propositions in a structure, they do not need to think of procedures for doing formal processes (such giving up of processes might be related to Sfard's (1991) notion of reification). So these Don't Need Boundaries illustrate the powerful freeing of mathematical understanding from the constraints of less formal and less logically sophisticated actions. But persons acting beyond such a boundary may act as if they were blind to the history of informal, intuitive, and context-dependent activities which were necessary in generating the outer level mathematical understanding for those persons.

The most critical feature of our model is the notion of "folding back." To illustrate this feature, let's return to the illustration of Kara's work that we started this paper with. Kara had been engaged in folding units, small sheets of paper, into halves, fourths, eighths, sixteenths. From this activity she had generated an image of fractions as amounts coming from folding, or principally related to folding. Now she was faced with a new situation. Here was a fraction which did not come from her action but was simply a very different unit with fractional parts indicated on it. She was, in some sense,

---

[1]　This aspect of our model allows us to reflect on the question of "what is mathematics" and give a language to those, such as Mandelbrot, who are attempting to show the value of "informal" mathematical activity in building a new field, vision, and understanding in mathematics.

stuck. Our evidence suggests that she just applied her image of fractions from folding to justify her answer of five fourths. She knew the five was right from counting the shaded parts; she observed the top part of the display as "half of a half", generating and justifying her sense of "fourths." Although the teacher did not say anything further about Kara's work, that evening Kara went home to fold "giants" of her own and by the next day came back with a knowledge of fractions as amounts, or at least relative amounts, which were independent of the folding activity. They were amounts that you could put together, add up, etc. So here we have a case of a person possessing an image being provoked to fold back to further image making to extend her image.

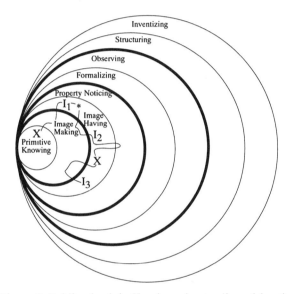

Figure 2. Folding back in Kara's understanding of fractions.

Our theory prompts us to see mathematical understanding, as changing in this way, almost on a continuing basis. That is, a person is more or less continually folding back, building up a larger, if less formal, idea that will support the new situation in which they find themselves. This is, of course, related to Sierpinka's notion of epistemological obstacle and to overcoming one's epistemological obstacles. But for us, folding back provides a mechanism by which a person can weave the path of understanding. Using a weaving metaphor for a moment, one might think of the eight modes of levels as the observational "warp" in which a teacher or a researcher can observe a child's mathematical understanding activity growing through this process of folding back and moving out to more sophisticated understanding. Figure 2 shows Kara's understanding of fractions as it changed over a period of several days (Kieren, Mason, & Pirie, 1992). Other research which we have conducted suggests that analysis of a person's understanding over shorter or longer periods of time would reveal the same kind of dynamically woven pathway.

BONUSES OF THIS UNDERSTANDING
OF MATHEMATICAL UNDERSTANDING

The bonuses of understanding mathematical understanding arise in several ways. Such understanding changes the way in which an observer sees students doing mathematics. Thus one kind of bonus is a change in the actual thinking of the understanding observer. This brings about a second kind of bonus—thinking otherwise about school mathematics. Rather than simply adhering to convention in considering students' mathematics, a person with an understanding of understanding is empowered to move beyond convention. A third kind of bonus is entwined with the two above. A person who understands mathematical understanding, particularly one who uses our model and theory gains a new and different platform and a new language for observing mathematical understanding as it is acted out by students in classrooms.

A VIGNETTE OF PERSONAL UNDERSTANDING

Tanya is a 12 year old, who would agree with her teacher's assessment of her as "OK" in mathematics, in a typical grade seven mathematics class in a large western Canadian city. In her previous schooling she has studied the meaning of fractions but has not seriously considered operations on fractions. This is evidenced by her performance on a pre-test on addition of fractions (Figure 3a). Tanya makes and enunciates the "classic" error with respect to addition and when there are more than two addends she claims not to know what to do.

But in Figure 3b it is clear that Tanya's addition knowledge is radically improved after several days of instruction. This observation was repeated for 20 of 22 of her classmates who, like her, did not know how to add fractions; three classmates showed pre-instruction addition knowledge. A positively changed performance, such as Tanya's, might be considered sufficient knowledge for the observer of Tanya's understanding. It is a bonus of our theory that one can "think otherwise" about Tanya's understanding. As will be seen below, we can explicitly profile Tanya's understanding as it occurred and not reduce such understanding to pre-test/post-test differences.

Tanya's Addition knowledge

a. Prior to instruction:

a) Three other fractions which show the same amount as $\frac{2}{3}$.

$$\frac{6}{9} \quad \frac{4}{6} \quad \frac{8}{12}$$

b) $\frac{1}{2} + \frac{1}{4} = \frac{2}{6}$

c) $\frac{2}{3} + \frac{5}{8} = \frac{7}{11}$ *I'm not sure if it's right but I think it's top + top divided by bottom + bottom.*

d) $\frac{3}{4} + \frac{1}{3} + \frac{3}{24}$ *I don't know how to do this one yet.*

b. Post-Instruction:

a) $\frac{1}{4} + \frac{1}{3} + \frac{1}{2} = \frac{13}{12}$

$$\frac{3}{12} \quad \frac{4}{12} \quad \frac{6}{12}$$

b) $\frac{5}{8} + \frac{2}{3} = \frac{31}{24}$

$$\frac{15}{24} + \frac{16}{24}$$

c) $\frac{1}{8} + \frac{7}{24} + \frac{5}{12} = \frac{20}{24}$

$$\frac{3}{24} \quad \frac{7}{24} \quad \frac{10}{24}$$

d) $\frac{4}{10} + \frac{4}{5} + \frac{19}{20} \quad \frac{6}{10}$ *is about 3 because*

$\frac{4}{10} + \frac{4}{5} = \frac{4}{10} + \frac{8}{12}$ *is about 1 and*

$\frac{19}{20}$ *is about 1 and* $\frac{6}{10}$ *is about 1,*

so approxamately 3.

Figure 3. Tanya's pre- and post-instructional addition of fractions performance.

Tanya's class was one of several involved in a study of the growth of mathematical understanding. To allow an observer to "see" such growth the students worked in a number of settings which provided them space to build their own ideas, working both individually and in groups. While all students were in the same settings, each child responded according to his or her own particular structure of understanding. No instruction on any standard algorithms for operations on fractions was provided. Operational processes, such as those shown in Tanya's work, arose individually in working in the settings in the classroom.

Two central activities used were (Figures 4a and 4b below).

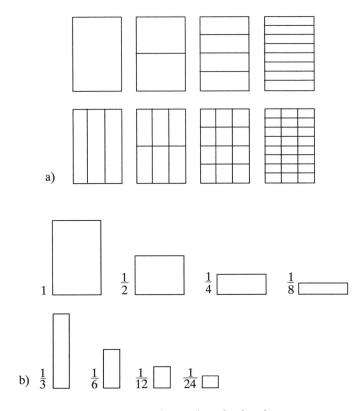

Figure 4. Action settings for fractions.

The first setting, partially illustrated in Figure 4a, engaged the children in folding many different unit fractions and seeing fractions as multiplicative in nature with particular fractions arising out of successive fraction folding actions — one twenty-fourth comes from a half of a twelfth or from a third of an eighth, for example. Such activity was accompanied by significant amounts of drawing, discussion justifying their results, and by complex metaphorical records of such folding behavior as exemplified by

Following the folding, the children worked with what came to be called the "pizza fraction kit" (See Figure 4b above) with fractions shown by pieces cut from $8\frac{1}{2} \times 11$ paper. (One serendipitous consequence of this is that "vertical thirds" and "horizontal fourths" have almost the same width, and twelfths are very nearly square.) It was hoped that students would, in using this kit, come to see fractions as additively combinable quantities.

Let us now pursue the bonus of our understanding using the above theory and model of mathematical understanding by analyzing pieces of Tanya's work taken from several days of instruction and from an interview several weeks later. During the intervening time she had no instruction on addition of fractions. With other students working in groups of three, Tanya attempted to make combinations of fraction pieces which "made" other fractions. Here is a typical example of Tanya's work (Figure 5).

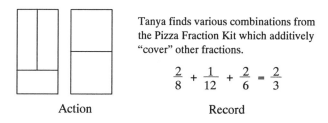

Tanya finds various combinations from the Pizza Fraction Kit which additively "cover" other fractions.

$$\frac{2}{8} + \frac{1}{12} + \frac{2}{6} = \frac{2}{3}$$

Action   Record

Figure 5. Tanya's image making actions.

We call this kind of activity of Tanya's "Image Making" because she is taking elements of her primitive knowing (use of fraction language) and using them toward a new end, physically combining fractions and describing them. Tanya's activity illustrates another feature of our theory. Understanding at any level in our theory consists of two complementary activities, an appropriate mathematical *action* and the *expression* of that action. The latter consists in the recording, reflecting on, describing the nature of, or justifying the action. Here we see Tanya's action (notice the eighths and twelfths exactly fitting on the third) and part of Tanya's expression vis-à-vis the action. She also drew her covering on the board and described how it worked both to her partners and the class at large. Following a day of such activity Tanya was observed as *having an image of addition of fractions*. This was manifested in her writing:

Fractions are equal if they cover the same amount.

She appeared to have an image of addition which could be summarized as follows:

"Adding" means finding known pieces on which the addends can fit.

Of course she did not say this, but it is visible in her response to the following task:

Find combinations of two or three or more fractions which make 1.

Tanya gave the following written response:

$$\frac{1}{3} + \frac{1}{6} + \frac{6}{12} = 1$$

When asked by the teacher to show why this worked, Tanya did an interesting re-write:

$$\frac{1}{3} \qquad \frac{1}{6} \quad \frac{2}{12} \qquad \frac{4}{12}$$

She split the six twelfths into two parts, thus enabling her to show three pieces each of which fits on one third (with three thirds making one).

Tanya's image making activity as characterized and exemplified above seems to be idiosyncratic and very context-bound. But it seems to be a rather clear illustration of student understanding action based on her own cognizing structure, yet co-emerging with her (instructional) environment.

It should not be thought that such context-based images cannot grow. Several days later Tanya was observed noticing a property, based on this peculiar image, as she did the following task:

Here are pizza orders from three tables. How much is needed to fill all three orders?

$$\text{I)} \ \frac{1}{2} + \frac{2}{3} \qquad\qquad \text{II)} \ \frac{2}{3} + \frac{5}{6} \qquad\qquad \text{III)} \ \frac{1}{2} + \frac{1}{6}$$

Tanya responded,

$$3\frac{1}{3} \ \text{because} \ \frac{1}{2}\frac{1}{2} \qquad\qquad \frac{2}{3}\frac{2}{3} \qquad\qquad \frac{5}{6}\frac{1}{6}$$
$$1 \qquad\qquad\qquad 1\frac{1}{3} \qquad\qquad\qquad 1$$

We would infer that Tanya was noticing an image-based property: "Look for fractions you can combine to known fraction pieces." Thus, like DiSessa's (1987) phenomenological primitives (P-Prims) in science, Tanya can build from and generalize her image making here into property noticing.

But her initial image-making actions had their limitations, as seen in Tanya's work in the following:

$$\frac{1}{2} + \frac{1}{4} + \frac{1}{3}$$

Tanya: I don't know how.

Teacher: Why?

Tanya: I can't get them to fit.

This situation and the follow-up activity suggested by the teacher proved to be "invocative in nature" (Kieren & Pirie, 1991, 1992). That is, in the face of this interaction and the suggestion that Tanya, and other students, try making fraction piece combinations and cover them with one kind of fraction (sixths, eighths, sixteenths or twelfths for example), Tanya folded back to renewed image making activity.

After this activity Tanya showed revised image making. Faced with the task

$$\frac{1}{2} + \frac{3}{4} + \frac{1}{8}$$

Tanya responded, "I can make all these fractions using eighths."

Using our model we would infer that her image making is now illustrative of an understanding which could be characterized by the statement:

To add, find pieces (from one's kit or one's imagination) which fit on the fractions you are adding.

Notice, both in the example and the characterization, that Tanya's image making has undergone a subtle but significant transformation based on her new image making.

Her subsequent adding activity can be observed to have new property noticing as well.

$$\left(\begin{array}{cc} \frac{1}{2} & + & \frac{2}{3} \\ \times 12 & & \times 8 \\ \frac{12}{24} & + & \frac{16}{24} \end{array}\right) \begin{array}{l} = \frac{28}{24} \\ = \frac{28}{24} \end{array}$$

Notice two things. Tanya was using her image—finding twenty-fourths— to fit. But she now combines this with her knowledge (in her primitive knowing) of equivalence and notices a new image-based property. As could be seen in Tanya's post-instruction adding, she could use this property to work on a wide variety of fraction piece combinations. But notice that such addition was still based on the analysis of each given fraction piece and hence was seen to be context and image dependent in nature.

Several weeks after the conclusion of instruction on fractions Tanya was interviewed about addition of fractions.

Formalizing:

T: What do you think about adding now?

Tanya: Its easy. You just make fractions that work for them all. Say you had $\frac{2}{3}$, $\frac{4}{7}$ and $\frac{5}{6}$. Well sixths would go for $\frac{2}{3}$ and $\frac{5}{6}$ so you'd have to make forty seconds.

T: Why is that?

Tanya: Well I just know that forty seconds will fit because sixths times sevenths make forty seconds.

T: So.

Tanya:
$$\frac{2}{3} + \frac{4}{7} + \frac{5}{6}$$
$$= \frac{4}{6} + \frac{4}{7} + \frac{5}{6}$$
$$= \frac{28}{42} + \frac{24}{42} + \frac{35}{42} \quad \text{and like that.}$$

Here we see Tanya starting to apply a method or acting in a formalizing way. Notice her choice of fractions to add. She deliberately chooses sevenths. Since she had not worked with sevenths previously and it is not an easy fraction to visually construct, it is suggested that Tanya now thinks of herself as having a method which works for all fractions (even something like sevenths). Further, notice that Tanya is not developing a common denominator on a piece-wise or fraction-by-fraction basis as was the case when she relied on her image of addition as finding pieces which fit (although some of that informal language lingers). Now she has a method which combines denominators of the fractions to be added, Tanya no longer needs her image to additively combine fractions. But, finally, notice that her formalizing method does reflect her previous folding experience: she says that "forty-seconds" comes from "sixths" and "sevenths." Her method reflects and contains elements from the pathway of growth in her understanding.

To this point the model and theory for the growth of mathematical understanding has been used part by part to analyze a number of different mathematical actions of Tanya. But the model can be used to illustrate the pathway of the growth of mathematical understanding for Tanya.

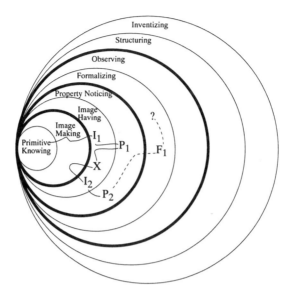

Figure 6. The pathway of Tanya's growth of understanding of addition of fractions.

There is a general outward vector in Tanya's pathway but it is not monotonic. It involves a point, X, where she was provoked to fold back to more image making, leading to changed image having behavior (I_2 signalling that addition now meant find a kind of piece to fit on addends as opposed to pieces(s) on which addends fit). The dashed line joint P_2 to F_1 indicates that we do not know the nature of the pathway joining these indicated actions. We could speculate that the teacher's general question about addition provoked Tanya to think about fractions in a more sophisticated way, independent of her images. The question mark at the end of the pathway indicates that the theory suggests that Tanya could now be invoked to fold back to embedded less formal understanding activities or she could be provoked into observing a general theorem about addition, or she may now simply continue to understand addition of fractions using a formalized general method. But we do know that the pathways of Tanya's understandings will continue to be observed as a back and forth weaving within the modes of the model.

THE BONUSES OF THE UNDERSTANDING
OF MATHEMATICAL UNDERSTANDING

What are the bonuses of thinking using our model for the growth of mathematical understanding? First, it allows us to think about growth in understanding as it is happening and not as simply a pre-test/post-test difference. Although the model can be used to portray the growth of understanding of a concept over time, it is also useful in capturing the "fast dynamics" of understanding in mathematical action as it is happening: the transition following Tanya's image having (I_1) for example. Tanya's case is paradigmatic in showing that the growth of mathematical understanding is non-monotonic, involving movement out to more sophisticated understanding and folding back to less sophisticated understanding activity. This pathway really illustrates that observed understanding is a co-emerging concept: it grows jointly out of the action of the student and the observation and interaction of the teacher or researcher. Similarly, the model and theory provide the bonus of a way of viewing Tanya's constructive processes as she brings forth her mathematical world coupled with her environment. There is no such thing as "the" understanding of mathematics or addition of fractions. But there is Tanya, or any other student, engaging in her understanding of mathematics and the observer's understanding of Tanya through the use of the model and its related constructs.

CONCLUDING REMARKS

If teaching in a way that enhances mathematical understanding in students is valuable, then it is important that mathematical understanding be made less vague. This paper has attempted to show that the bonus of any understanding of mathematical understanding is, in fact, to sharpen the teacher's or researcher's view of the understanding of students. More particularly, it was the purpose of this paper to show how Susan Pirie's and my developing theory for the growth of mathematical understanding provides a rich and active conceptual structure which helps its user to see and talk about mathematical understanding as it is happening.

NOTE

The research upon which this paper is based is supported in part by Social Sciences and Humanities Council Grant number 410 90078.

The author also wishes to acknowledge the intellectual support and collaboration of Dr. Susan Pirie, of Oxford University, in many of the ideas discussed here.

REFERENCES

Bateson, G. (1979). *Mind in nature.* New York: Viking.

Bateson, G. (1987). Men are gras. In W. Thompson (Ed.), *GAIA: A way of knowing* (pp. 37-47). New York: Lindisfarne Press.

Bergeron J., & Herscovics, N. (1989). A model to describe the construction of mathematical concepts from an epistemological perspective. In L. Pereira-Mendoza & M. Quigley (Eds.), *Proceedings of the 1989 Annual Meeting of the Canadian Mathematics Education Study Group* (pp. 99-114). St. John's, Nfld.: Memorial University.

Bohm, D., & Peat, F.D. (1987). *Science, order and creativity.* New York: Bantam Books.

DiSessa, A. (1987). Phenomenology and the evolution of intuition. In C. Janvier (Ed.), *Problems of representation in the teaching and learning of mathematics.* Hillsdale, N.J.: Lawrence Erlbaum Associates.

Ernest, P. (1991). *The philosophy of mathematics.* Basingstoke: Burgess Science Press.

Herscovics, N., & Bergeron, J.C. (1983). Models of understanding. *Zentralblatt für Didaktik der Mathematik, 2,* 75-83.

Herscovics, N., & Bergeron, J.C. (1988). An extended model of understanding. In M.J. Behr, C.B. Lacampagne & M.M. Wheeler (Eds.), *Proceedings of the Tenth Annual Meeting of PME-NA* (pp. 15-22). Chicago: University of Northern Illinois.

Herscovics, N. (1992, August). *The construction of conceptual schemes in mathematics.* Paper presented at the International Congress of Mathematics Education VII. Québec, Canada.

Johnson, M. (1987). *The body in the mind: The bodily basis of imagination, reason, and meaning.* Chicago: University of Chicago Press.

Kieren, T.E. (1988). Personal knowledge of fractional numbers: Its intuitive and formal development. In J. Hiebert & M. Behr (Eds.), *Number concepts and operations in the middle grades* (pp. 162-181). Reston, VA: NCTM/LEA.

Kieren, T.E. (1990). Understanding for teaching and understanding. *The Alberta Journal of Educational Research, 36*(3), 191-201.

Kieren, T.E., & Pirie, S.E.B. (1991). Recursion and the mathematical experience. In L. Steffe (Ed.), *The epistemology of mathematical experience.* New York: Springer-Verlag Psychology Series.

Kieren, T.E., & Pirie, S.E.B. (1992). The answer determines the question: Interventions and the growth of mathematical understanding. *Proceedings of the Sixteenth Psychology of Mathematics Education Conference* (pp. 2-1–2-8). Durham, NH.

Kieren, T., Mason, R., & Pirie, S. (1992, June). *The growth of mathematical understanding in a constructivist environment.* Paper presented at the 1992 Canadian Society for Studies in Education Meeting. Charlottetown, P.E.I.

Maturana, H.R., & Varela, J.F. (1987). *The tree of knowledge.* Boston: The New Sciences Library, Shambhala.

Miller, L. D., Malone J. A., & Kandl, T. (1992, April). *A study of secondary mathematics teacher's perceptions of the meaning of understanding.* Paper presented at the Annual Meeting of AERA, San Francisco.

Morascvik, J. M. (1979). Understanding. *Dialectica, 33,* 201-216.

Pirie, S.E.B. (1988). Understanding–instrumental, relational, formal, intuitive... How can we know. *For the Learning of Mathematics, 8*(3), 2-6.

Pirie, S.E.B., & Kieren, T.E. (1989). Through the recursive eye: Mathematical understanding as a dynamic phenomenon. In G. Vergnaud (Ed.), *Actes de la 13ᵉ Conférence internationale de l'International Group for the Psychology of Mathematics Education* (Vol. 3, pp. 119-126). Paris.

Pirie, S.E.B., & Kieren, T.E. (1990). A recursive theory of mathematical understanding. *For the Learning of Mathematics, 9*(3), 7-11.

Pirie, S.E.B., & Kieren, T.E. (1991). Folding back: A dynamic recursive theory of mathematical understanding. In F. Furinghetti (Ed.), *Proceedings of the Fifteenth International Conference of the International Group for the Psychology of Mathematics Education.* Assisi, Italy.

Ryle G. (1949). *The concept of mind.* London: Hutchinson.

Schroeder, T.L. (1987). Students' understanding of mathematics: a review and synthesis of some recent research. In J. Bergeron, N. Herscovics & C. Kieren (Eds.), *Proceedings of the Eleventh International Conference of the International Group for the Psychology of Mathematics Education Conference* (Vol. 3). Montréal.

Sfard, A. (1991). On the dual nature of mathematical conceptions: Reflections on the processes and objects as different sides of the same coin. *Educational Studies in Mathematics, 22*(1), 1-35.

Sierpinska, A. (1990). Cognitive obstacles and mathematical understanding. In M. Quigley (Ed.), *Proceedings of the Canadian Mathematics Education Study Group Annual Meeting.* St. John's, Nfld.: Memorial University.

Skemp, R.R. (1976). Relational understanding and instrumental understanding. *Mathematics Teaching, 77,* 20-26.

Skemp, R.R. (1987). *The psychology of learning mathematics, expanded American edition.* Hillsdale, NJ.: Lawrence Erlbaum Associates.

Varela, F. (1987). Laying down a path in walking. In W. Thompson (Ed.), *GAIA: A way of knowing.* New York: Lindisfarne Press.

Varela, F., Thompson, E., & Rosch, E. (1991). *The embodied mind: Cognitive science and human experience.* Cambridge, MA: MIT Press.

von Glasersfeld, E. (1987). Learning as a constructive activity. In C. Janvier (Ed.), *Problems of representation in the learning and teaching of mathematics* (pp. 3-17). Hillsdale, NJ: Lawrence Erlbaum Associates.

Wittgenstein, L. (1956). *Remarks on the foundations of mathematics.* Oxford: Basil Blackwell.

CURRICULUM CHANGE:
AN AMERICAN-DUTCH PERSPECTIVE

Jan de Lange

Utrecht University, The Netherlands

To value the changes in curricula, one is often presented with one or two examples to give an impression of the real change at the practitioners level, not from the perspective of the theorist or the researcher. Those same practitioners—the teachers—often object that they cannot value a change in content and philosophy by looking at only one isolated example. It is for this reason that we would like to present a series of student worksheets, intended for 12-13-year-old students, that cover three lessons.

The subject is geometry, but with connections to other strands. The examples are taken from a unit designed for the "Connected Mathematics" project, a cooperative project between the University of Wisconsin and the Freudenthal Institute in the Netherlands.

Example: Worksheets from the Unit "Figuring all the Angles 2." (de Lange et al., 1992)

Ship Ahoy

Photo 1   Photo 2

Photo 3   Photo 4

You are swimming in a canal and a ship is approaching you. It gets closer and closer. In the first picture the captain of the ship cannot see you because you are too far away. In the last picture the captain cannot see you either.

1. Explain why.

Of course it depends on the shape of the ship how close you can get in front of it and still be seen:

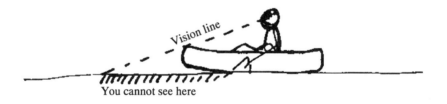

You cannot see here

2. Draw vision lines for the captain for each of the following ships. (the captain is at *)

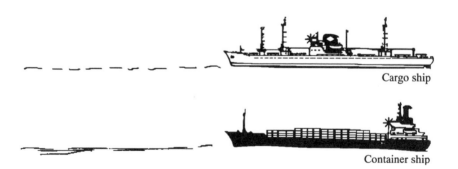

Cargo ship

Container ship

Ferry

3. Measure in each of the cases the angle between the horizon and vision line. What does a small angle mean?

Activity

Bring a small boat to school (plastic or wood).

Compare all the boats. Predict which one will have the biggest and which one the smallest blind spot.

We will use your boat to make visible the blind spot of the captain; that is the part of the water he cannot see. We use:

- a boat;
- a piece of pin-board;
- some pieces of thread;
- pins.

Step 1

Put your boat on the pin-board:

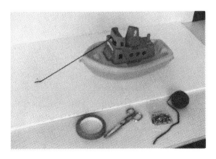

Photo 1

4. Make an estimate of the area that the captain cannot see.

Step 2

Construct a vision line straight forward, as in Photo 2.

Step 3

Construct other vision lines. You may get something similar to Photo 3.

Photo 2   Photo 3

Step 4

Next we compute the ratio between the area of the blind spot and the area of the boat (forward of the bridge). The next pictures show you how this could be done:

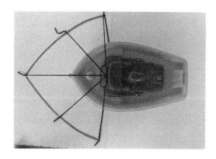

Photo 4

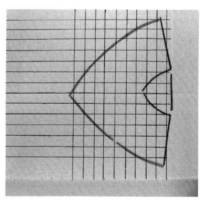

Photo 5

5. Compute these areas and ratios for your boat, and compare them with your estimates in problem 4.

CHANGING GOALS

Mathematics education is changing fast. There were major changes in the eighties in the Netherlands, Denmark, and Australia for example, and right now, in the early nineties, in other countries.

The goals for mathematics education have changed as well. In the Netherlands the goals for the majority of children very much resemble the set of goals stated by the British Committee of Inquiry into the Teaching of Mathematics in Schools in 1982 (Cockroft, 1982). They are as follows:

1. to become an intelligent citizen (mathematical literacy),

2. to prepare for the workplace and for future education,

3. to understand mathematics as a discipline.

Nine goals were prepared by the Commission on Standards for School Mathematics of the National Council of Teachers of Mathematics (NCTM) in its 1989 report, *Curriculum and evaluation standards for school mathematics*. There are four societal goals and five goals for students.

Mathematical literacy is articulated in the NCTM standards by five general goals for students:

1. *Learning to value mathematics.* Understanding its evolution and its role in society and the sciences.

2. *Becoming confident of one's own ability.* Coming to trust one's own mathematical thinking and having the ability to make sense of situations and solve problems.

3. *Becoming a mathematical problem solver.* This is essential to becoming a productive citizen and requires experience in solving a variety of extended and non-routine problems.

4. *Learning to communicate mathematically.* Learning the signs, symbols, and terms of mathematics.

5. *Learning to reason mathematically.* Making conjectures, gathering evidence, and building mathematical arguments.

These goals reflect a shift away from the traditional practice, subsuming traditional skills under more general goals for problem solving, communication, and critical attitude.

NEW THEORIES: REALISTIC MATHEMATICS EDUCATION

At the same time the goals of mathematics education are changing, there is the evolution of new theories for the learning and teaching of mathematics.

233

At the Freudenthal Institute the "theory for realistic mathematics education" evolved after twenty years of developmental research. This theory appears to be related to the constructivist approach. (See Freudenthal, 1983, 1991; Treffers, 1987; de Lange, 1987; Gravemeijer et al, 1990; Streefland, 1991.) However, the realistic mathematics theory is a theory of learning and instruction in mathematics only, while the social constructivist theory is a theory of learning in general.

The characteristics of the realistic mathematics education theory are as follows.

Conceptual mathematization: from concrete to abstract

In Freudenthal's view the learner is entitled to recapitulate the learning process of mankind (Freudenthal, 1973). This means that instruction should not start with the formal system, a final product, nor with embodiments, nor with structural games. The phenomena by which the concepts appear in reality should be the source of concept formation. Others call this process "extracting the appropriate concept from a concrete situation" (Ahlfors et al., 1962) or "conceptual mathematization" (de Lange, 1987).

To put this a little more precisely, the real-world situation or problem is first explored intuitively, for the purpose of mathematizing it. This means organizing and structuring the problem, trying to identify the mathematical aspects of the problem, and discovering regularities and relations. The initial exploration with a strong intuitive component should lead to the development, discovery, or (re)invention of mathematical concepts.

After a formalization and abstraction of the concepts, they are used by applying them to new problems. This leads to a reinforcement of the concepts and to a readjustment of the perceived real world. In this way the learning process has an iterative character. The contexts serve a twofold purpose: as a source for concept development and as an area of application.

Free productions

Students should be asked to "produce" more concrete things. Treffers, (1987) stresses the fact that by making "free productions" the student is forced to reflect on the path taken in the individual learning process and, at the same time, to anticipate its continuation. The form of free productions— to write an essay, to do an experiment, to collect data, to draw conclusions, to design exercises that can be used in a test, or to design a test for other students in the classroom—can be an essential part of assessment.

Interactive learning

Interaction between students and between students and teachers is essential. Balacheff (1985) expresses the point clearly.

Working in pairs is not only a source of explanation but also a source of confrontation with others. This adds greatly to the dynamics of the activity. Contradictions coming from the partner, due to the fact that they are explained, are more likely to be perceived than contradictions confronting the solitary learner, derived only from the facts. They are also harder to refute than in a conflict resulting from the individual and temporary hesitations between two opposing points of view that the solitary learner experiences when confronted with a problem.

Integrated learning strands

Mathematics is integrated with the real world(s). Second, the integration of mathematical strands is essential. One of the reasons is that applying mathematics is very difficult if mathematics is taught "vertically", that is if its various subjects are taught separately, neglecting the cross-connections stated by Klamkin (1968) . In applications one usually needs more than algebra alone or geometry alone. Integration on yet a third level is implied when students compare different models and integrate them.

Authentic assessment

Galbraith (1991) concluded there is a need to confront inherent contradictions that exist when constructivism drives curriculum design and knowledge construction, but positivistic remnants of the conventional paradigm drive the assessment process. In the Netherlands a similar separation is seen in the reaction of many teachers and researchers, such as "I like the way you have embedded your math education in a rich context, but I will wait for the national standardized test to see if it has been successful."

The assessment procedures should do justice to the goals of the curriculum and to the students—context independent generalized testing is unjust when for instruction the context includes the real world of mathematics itself, at least in the realistic mathematics education approach. An essential question is: "Does assessment reflect the theory of instruction and learning?"

LEVELS OF UNDERSTANDING

Most instruction in mathematics education focused on learning to name concepts and objects, and to follow specific procedures. The result, as Bodin (1991) points out, is that a student can solve a given equation without being capable of expressing the steps made or of justifying the results, and without knowing which type of problem it is connected to or without being able to use it as a tool in another situation.

The current emphasis for all students must shift to reasoning skills, communication, and a critical attitude. While these "higher order" thinking skills are difficult to describe, Resnick (1987) listed some of their features that are in stark contrast to current mathematics criteria. De Lange (1987) described experiences with "higher order" thinking mathematics and their assessment, stressing the process versus product character of the new curriculum. During the experiments in the Netherlands (1981-1992) it became clear that the mathematics thinking was non-algorithmic, had multiple solutions, involved uncertainty, and a need for interpretation.

The issue needs to be addressed at the different levels necessary to represent both instruction and assessment. Three arbitrary levels reflect the decade-long experience of experimentation and implementation with the new mathematics curriculum in the Netherlands (de Lange, 1992).

The *lower* level refers to objects, definitions, technical tools, and simple algorithms.

The *middle* level deals with connections (between objects, concepts, strands), the integration of different concepts, and simple problem solving.

The *higher* level deals with higher order thinking skills, developing a critical attitude, reflection, mathematical reasoning—probably including the concept of proof—and generalization.

These three levels of mathematical understanding can help us to see if we really meet our educational goals. The boat example is a concretization of these principles and ideas. The boat example is also a product of an interesting international project, whereby the Dutch Freudenthal Institute develops materials with the perceived American culture in mind. The American collaborators at Madison, Wisconsin then "americanize" the materials which are tried out at pilot schools with both Dutch and American observers. Our conclusions are based on experiences from this project and a smaller project that can be considered as a pilot. (See de Lange et al., 1993.)

To understand and appreciate the project some differences in the educational contexts in the Netherlands and the United States will be described.

DIFFERENCES BETWEEN THE UNITED STATES
AND THE NETHERLANDS

At the school level

One major structural difference between the countries is that the United States has sixteen thousand school districts, with each school district responsible for its own schools. The Netherlands can be regarded as having one school district making many things easier to accomplish.

There is also a difference in the perceived status of the teacher. Complaints about teachers are not uncommon in the Netherlands or the United States, or presumably in many other countries. But close observation in the United States and the Netherlands makes clear that there are considerable differences in the status of the teachers and their mathematical backgrounds.

The Dutch teacher can still be regarded as an expert: the teacher has a lot of freedom, knows mathematics, makes excursions into the unknown, is interested in innovations, and is very willing to criticize them. The American teacher seems to be in a less favorable situation: the impression exists that she is not always considered to be an expert. There are numerous other experts: the superintendent, the school board, the standardized test, and last, but not least, the parents. The pressure of these experts on the teacher seems at times unreasonable and unfair.

Another significant difference is the fact that the Netherlands has a system of tracking students: depending on the choice of the school the students are placed in the lower, middle, or higher track at the age of 12, 13, or 14, though the students still have the opportunity to change tracks during their school career. The decision regarding student placement is taken by the parents and the Head of the school. The United States officially has no tracking, but many schools appear to have some kind of tracking in effect.

The final difference, that in our view has a major effect on the level of (mathematics) education, is the very large role of extra curricular activities at schools in the United States and the almost complete lack of these activities in the Netherlands. For an observer from the Netherlands it is very strange to see that mathematics lessons are cancelled because the high school band or the track-and-field team has to practice, not to mention the cheerleaders.

The teaching and teachers

The background and history of context use is almost non-existent in the United States. When implementing a new "problem oriented context rich" curriculum one is immediately aware of this fact. It is often not clear why a certain context is used, whether or not it is appropriate, what the role of the context is. Discussion is hampered by the fact that there is little history in the use of contexts for many American teachers.

For the Dutch developers it was surprising that even the criteria for the use of contexts differ in the United States and the Netherlands. The cultural differences were larger in reality than anticipated, not that it was ever assumed that the Dutch materials could just be "translated" into English. Both the American and Dutch staff were very well aware that a "cultural adaptation" should be carried out by the Americans. Earlier experiences with "Dutch" materials in other countries had convinced us of this not very surprising fact.

Other differences between the countries are that in Dutch classrooms there seems to be a lot more interaction and group work—interaction between teachers and students, and between students. This does not necessarily mean that Dutch classrooms excel in group work. All kinds of teaching occur in the Netherlands: frontal teaching, group work, whole class discussion and also individual work. The United States classroom tends to be more organized, the lessons have a clear structure, and everybody knows his or her role.

Many American teachers have to be chameleons: part of the year they teach what they want, what they think is useful, in the way they like. At other times they start to teach to the tests: once they know when a standardized test will take place, they teach to the test. In the Dutch system, teaching to the test is also not uncommon, but the tests do reflect the intended curriculum to a degree. And the discussion now focuses on ways to improve the examinations in order to better represent the actual teaching-learning process.

The textbooks used in most American classrooms are very structured and have "closed" questions, with only one correct answer, no need for explanation of strategy, no "real" real-world problems, but "dressed-up" problems where the role of the context is nothing more than cosmetic. On the other hand the Dutch textbooks quite often look less structured, contain a lot of text, have many problems where context plays an essential role, and require students to reflect on the answer.

Parents

A very significant difference involves the role of the parents in Dutch and American schools. In the Netherlands parental involvement in education is very low. Many heads of schools and teachers alike complain about how hard it is to interest parents in their children's progress at school. Even "parents' evenings", where parents may discuss with individual teachers matters relating to their child, are barely surviving. Parents do not seem to be interested in any global issue such as curriculum change, structural changes in the educational system, or authentic assessment. They take for granted being informed by a letter from the principal.

One is tempted to interpret this situation in a positive way by arguing that parents consider the school and the teachers to be the experts. In the United States the impression exists that the real experts are the parents, putting pressure on the teachers and the system. This parental involvement can be frustrating for teachers, especially for those teachers who try to implement certain innovations in their teaching and learning practice.

These differences between the educational cultures in the field of mathematics education seem to be quite large and certainly affect the process of developmental research as implemented in the American Middle School project. But equally interesting is the fact that some very fundamental questions and problems which were confronted in the past decade in the Netherlands turned up in the United States. In implementing our Realistic Mathematics Education materials and philosophy, we had to face a number of problems and for some we have some reasonable answers. Others form a very concrete starting point for future developmental research.

PROBLEMS AND QUESTIONS IN THE UNITED STATES AND THE NETHERLANDS

Some of the problems encountered with the introduction and implementation of new curricula based on the "realistic" philosophy are

- the "loss" of teaching,
- the "loss" of basic skills and routines,
- the "loss" of structure,
- the "loss" of clarity of goals,
- the complexity of "authentic" assessment.

Each of these points will be discussed in some detail.

Teaching

Teaching is often interpreted as an activity mainly carried out by the teacher: he or she introduces the subject, gives one or two examples, may ask a question or two, and invites the students who have been passive listeners to become active by starting to complete exercises from the book. It is not unusual that most of the time this "activity" is carried out in an individual way.

The lesson will be ended in a well organized way, the "closure", and the next lesson will be conducted in a similar scenario.

Realistic-mathematics education makes teaching more complex. The teacher is not supposed to teach anymore. And learning the art of "unteaching" has been proven to be very difficult and very personal.

Referring once more to the boat problems, it will be clear that one cannot "teach" these pages in the traditional way. This does not mean that we have a fixed scenario readily available for the teacher who is eager to learn. The classroom in combination with the teacher will determine in which way an optimal result, consisting of interaction, individual work, group work, classroom discussion, student presentation, teacher presentation, and other activities, can be obtained.

The teacher's role is that of organization and facilitation—a process that cannot be described in detail for "the" teacher. The teacher needs to make personal adaptation. To make things more difficult the teacher faces even more obstacles. Regularly teachers and students will be confronted with problems that have different "correct" answers or one correct answer and different strategies.

Different strategies often involve more than one level of mathematical thinking, forcing the teacher into a discussion about the values of the strategies. To add even more to this already long list of points that need to be addressed one has only to think about assessment. Teachers find it difficult, if not impossible, to design their own tests. This means that the designers should be the persons and institutions responsible for the design of the students and teacher materials. They should not only design a "balanced" package of assessment materials that covers all the content, goals, and levels, but should also provide advice on grading the tasks.

Basic skills

Discussion about the role of basic skills is related to the implementation of realistic mathematics curricula, but it is ongoing in many countries in its own right. For many teachers this discussion has not been part of their daily practice, basic skills are a matter of fact, and form the kernel of mathematics education. Both in the Netherlands and the United States the discussion only slowly entered the ranks of the practitioners, the teachers.

In the Netherlands a group was formed during the seventies to battle against the innovations that are now called Realistic Mathematics Education. For a short period, it had considerable success in pointing out that basic skills were threatened. A report in the Netherlands seems to indicate that at the primary school level the "new" students perform equally well on basic skills as the students in the old curriculum, and that they outperform the old curriculum students on the field of problem solving.

When the new curricula for upper secondary were introduced, many once widely accepted basic skills were minimized. But as the new standardized examinations were trying to operationalize the new programs, one cannot say how poorly prepared the new students are at this moment compared with the students from ten years ago. Both the goals of mathematics education and the examinations have changed.

The attentive teacher notices that in the occasional situation where the students need a basic skill, they often lack it. Of course at one moment in their career they had mastered this skill, but with little need to use it, this outcome was predictable.

We are still in the process of learning, as will forever be the case, and a real solution is not at hand. It seems necessary to analyze the implemented curricula, the "real" world problems that we think are relevant, and the skills that are necessary to solve them. In the United States the *Curriculum and evaluation standards* (NCTM, 1989) make clear that decreased attention should be given to rote practice, rote memorization of rules, written practice, long division, (paper and pencil) fraction computation, developing skills out of context, memorizing rules and algorithms, and manipulating formulas. This is not a cure for the problems and it will take a lot of practice, experiments, developmental research, discussion, and a clear picture and vision of how to integrate technology (graphic calculator) into the teaching and learning process.

Structure

The boat example makes clear that the structure underlying the exercises is not easily recognizable as a traditional mathematical structure. The structure is a didactical one and can have different forms depending on the subject. In general the students will explore a problem in an intuitive way—in some way that relates to their or the real world.

Quite often the context or situation may obscure the mathematical concept. If we want students to understand the concept of vision lines and related subjects (blind area, hidden corners) and use that same idea for introduction of the tangent (much later) we could have chosen the traditional format: just tell the students what a vision line is, give an example, and have them complete many similar exercises. This is definitely easier for the teacher, but the students will be on the loser's side.

Another matter of concern, especially when teachers are confronted with the new curricula for the first time is the fact that the units seem to lack a beginning and an end. The first page does not require the teacher to explain the next topic—the students just have to start working. It is not an introduction for the next subject—"today we are going to a new subject: the linear equations ... etc." Leaving these tasks to the students makes the situation less structured.

The final point we would like to mention here is the fact that mathematics is increasingly taught as a unity, and not as separate strands. In the United States this is a major problem. Algebra 1, Algebra 2, and Geometry, to name a few courses, do not seem very promising in the light of integrating learning strands. But it gives the courses more structure. Just having courses in mathematics indicates clearly the desired integration but the structure, especially the mathematical structure, will be less clear and less visible.

Clarity of goals

In the traditional program the goals were more or less clear. Solving a linear equation was a simple goal that could be reached by working with numerous linear equations. And as many students noticed: "You just do the last ones and then you will know whether or not he or she has reached the goal." But most of the goals of the traditional programs are now classified as "lower" goals—rote skills, simple rules and algorithms, definitions.

However, in the new programs, we have different goals which we classified as "middle" and "higher" goals. At the middle level, connections are made between the different tools of the lower level. Concepts are integrated; although it may not be clear in which strand we are operating, and simple problems have to be solved without unique strategies. This means that, for both the teacher and the students, the intended goals are not always immediately clear.

A final word on the loss of clarity of the goals. Apart from the different levels that tend to obscure the goals, we also have to face the fact that real problems, in the more complex sense, obscure mathematical goals also. It may be even worse. We may not know the goals precisely because the problem is so real and therefore so open ended that the goals can only be reconstructed afterwards.

Assessment

One of the main obstacles in implementing the new curricula will be the availability of appropriate assessment tools. As was mentioned earlier, while teachers in the Netherlands like the context approach, they want evidence of success from national tests before adopting it. Popper (1968) and Phillips (1987) have argued that a theory can only be tested in terms of its own tenets. This means that constructivist or realistic mathematics education teaching and learning can only be evaluated by assessment procedures derived from the same principles.

On the other hand, not only have the new notions about learning influenced the ideas about "authentic" assessment. The new goals will also have their effect. The new goals emphasize reasoning skills, communication, and the development of a critical attitude. Together, these are popularly called "higher order" thinking skills. These thinking skills were seldom or not at all present in traditional assessment and education. The change towards a "thinking" curriculum forces us to focus on "thinking" assessment as well. (Lesh & Lamon, 1992; Romberg, 1992; Kulm, 1990.)

The goals of assessment, or better, the goals and principles of assessment have changed too, which adds to the problem of matching assessment to the teaching and learning process. It is interesting to see that the publication that came out of the National Summit on Mathematics Assessment (*For good measure*, MSEB, 1991) states that their goals and principles are based on commonly held beliefs about assessment. It is not only interesting but somewhat surprising to see that the first principle is "the primary purpose in assessment is to improve learning and teaching".

Surprising because if we compare this statement with the actual school practice there seems to be hardly any relation with this first "commonly held belief". The principle itself is not new at all. Gronlund (1968) stated it clearly and we borrowed his ideas to formulate our principles:

The first and main purpose of testing is to improve learning and teaching.

Methods of assessment should be such that they enable the student to demonstrate what they know rather than what they don't know.

Assessment should operationalize all goals of mathematics education.

The quality of mathematics assessment is not in the first place determined by its accessibility to objective scoring.

The assessment tools should be practical. (de Lange, 1987)

An interesting (teacher designed) item that reflects these principles is the following:

- Here you see a crossroads in Geldrop, The Netherlands, near the Great Church.

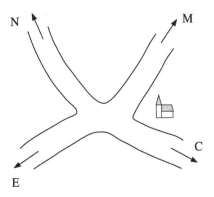

In order to let the traffic flow as smoothly as possible, the traffic lights have been regulated so as to avoid rush-hour traffic jams. A count showed the following number of vehicles had to pass the crossroads during rush hour (per hour):

$$A: \text{from} \begin{matrix} M \\ N \\ E \\ C \end{matrix} \begin{pmatrix} 0 & 40 & 200 & 30 \\ 30 & 0 & 80 & 50 \\ 210 & 60 & 0 & 60 \\ 30 & 40 & 80 & 0 \end{pmatrix}$$
$$\qquad\qquad\qquad M \quad N \quad E \quad C$$

The matrices G_1, G_2, G_3 and G_4 show which directions have a green light and for how long. $\frac{2}{3}$ means that traffic can flow through a green light for a period of $\frac{2}{3}$ minute.

$$G_1: \begin{matrix} & M & N & E & C \\ M & 0 & \frac{2}{3} & \frac{2}{3} & 0 \\ N & 0 & 0 & 0 & 0 \\ E & \frac{2}{3} & 0 & 0 & \frac{2}{3} \\ C & 0 & 0 & 0 & 0 \end{matrix} \qquad G_3: \begin{matrix} & M & N & E & C \\ M & 0 & 0 & 0 & 0 \\ N & 0 & 0 & \frac{1}{2} & \frac{1}{2} \\ E & 0 & 0 & 0 & 0 \\ C & \frac{1}{2} & \frac{1}{2} & 0 & 0 \end{matrix}$$

$$G_2: \begin{matrix} & M & N & E & C \\ M & 0 & 0 & 0 & \frac{1}{3} \\ N & 0 & 0 & 0 & 0 \\ E & 0 & \frac{1}{3} & 0 & 0 \\ C & 0 & 0 & 0 & 0 \end{matrix} \qquad G_4: \begin{matrix} & M & N & E & C \\ M & 0 & 0 & 0 & 0 \\ N & \frac{1}{2} & 0 & 0 & 0 \\ E & 0 & 0 & 0 & 0 \\ C & 0 & 0 & \frac{1}{2} & 0 \end{matrix}$$

- How many cars come from the direction of Eindhoven during that one hour? And how many travel toward the City center?
- How much time is needed to have all lights turn green exactly once?
- Determine $G = G_1 + G_2 + G_3 + G_4$ and thereafter $T = 30G$. What do the elements of T signify?
- Ten cars per minute can pass through the green light. Show in a matrix the maximum number of cars that can pass in each direction in one hour.

- Compare this matrix to matrix A. Are the traffic lights regulated accurately? If not, can you make another matrix G in which traffic can pass more smoothly?

This item is interesting from different points of view:

1. The mathematics is unusual: matrices at grade 9.

2. The format is a restricted, timed, written test; but still very open.

3. Interpretation and the understanding of the question is essential.

4. One could make it suitable for even more open purposes by just asking the last question, and finding out how differently the students will handle the problem.

5. The item can be transformed easily to a "project" like assessment.

The item looks rather straightforward and easy to design. However, practice and research shows clearly that designing problems like this is extremely difficult and time consuming.

The following example shows some other matters of concern:

- Katie bought 40 cents worth of nuts. June bought 8 oz. of nuts. Which girl bought more nuts?

  a. June.

  b. They each bought the same amount of nuts.

  c. Katie bought twice as much.

  d. Katie bought 5 oz. more of nuts.

  e. You cannot tell which girl bought more nuts.

This is interesting from different aspects. In the first place, it is encouraging that an American State Board of Education has the courage to try an item like this one, which is at least unusual. It is a breakthrough to provide insufficient information, certainly for grade 6. But of course there are some questions to be asked too.

In the first place what does the fact that 61% of students have answered (e) correctly tell the teacher? Or, more precisely, What are we measuring here and how certain are we that the proper answer reflects the proper reasoning? The idea behind the item is certainly appealing, but the multiple choice format destroys it—at least in our perception.

Imagine that the item would have been as follows:

- Each of the following four answers is correct under certain assumptions. Describe the necessary assumptions in each of the four cases.

Katie bought 40 cents of nuts. June bought 8 oz. of nuts. Which girl bought more nuts?

a. June

b. They each bought the same amount of nuts.

c. Katie bought twice as much.

d. Katie bought 5 oz. more of nuts.

Now we have a completely different item. The children have to reason, to think, to write down their reasoning. With just a slight alteration, we have created a test item that operationalizes some higher order thinking skills as well as communication.

Another problem still to be faced is the matter of objective scoring. A hypothesis that seems easy to defend is:

> The gains we make by obtaining a more or less complete measure of overall knowledge and capabilities by using a balanced package of assessment will by far outweigh the disadvantage that we have by "losing" a completely objective score. Intersubjective scoring and proper scoring instructions give enough guarantees for a fair measure: fair to the student and fair to the curriculum.

Much more information is needed—pilot studies, and research. But in the first place development of new assessment tools and guidelines for their use and scoring.

CURRICULUM CHANGE

To value the process of curriculum change, its complexity, specifics, and generalities, it is enlightening to compare this process in different countries and contexts. The literature is almost exclusively devoted to local situations, mostly on a small scale, and quite often even on a laboratory scale. Often generalizations based on these studies hardly seem to take the different contexts into account. If mathematics education as a science is to be taken seriously, we should consider these factors more than is done currently, especially at an international forum such as ICME.

REFERENCES

Ahlfors, L.V. et al. (1962). On the mathematics curriculum of the High School. *American Mathematical Monthly, 69* (3).

Balacheff, N. et al. (1985). Social interactions for experimental studies of pupils conceptions: Its relevance for research in didactics of mathematics. In *Proceedings of the second conference on theory of mathematics education* (pp. 1-5). Bielefeld: I.D.M., University of Bielefeld.

Bodin, A. (1991). What does to assess mean? In M. Niss (Ed.), *Investigations into assessment in mathematics education: An ICMI study*. Dordrecht, The Netherlands: Kluwer Academic Publishers.

Cockroft, W.H. (1982). *Mathematics counts: Report of the Commission of Inquiry into the Teaching of Mathematics in Schools*. London: Her Majesty's Stationery Office.

Freudenthal, H. (1973). *Mathematics as an educational task*. Dordrecht, The Netherlands: Reidel.

Freudenthal, H. (1983). *Didactical phenomenology of mathematical structures*. Dordrecht, The Netherlands: Reidel.

Freudenthal, H. (1991). *Revisiting mathematics education*. Dordrecht, The Netherlands: Kluwer Academic Publishers.

Galbraith, P.L. (1991). Paradigms, problems and assessment: Some ideological implications. In M. Niss (Ed.), *Investigations into assessment in mathematics education: An ICMI study*. Dordrecht, The Netherlands: Kluwer Academic Publishers.

Gravemeijer, K., van den Heuvel-Panhuizen, M. & Streefland, L. (1990). *Contexts, free productions, tests and geometry in realistic mathematics education*. Utrecht: OW & OC.

Gronlund, N.E. (1968). *Constructing achievement tests*. Englewood Cliffs, NJ: Prentice Hall.

Klamkin, M.S. (1968). On the teaching of mathematics so as to be useful. *Educational Studies in Mathematics, 1*, 126-159.

Kulm, G. (1990). *Assessing higher order thinking in mathematics*. Washington: American Association for the Advancement of Science.

Lange, J. de. (1987). *Mathematics, insight and meaning*. Utrecht: OW & OC.

Lange J. de (1992). Assessing mathematical skills, understanding, and thinking. In R. Lesh & S.J. Lamon (Eds.), *Assessment of authentic performance in school mathematics*. Washington: American Association for the Advancement of Science.

Lange, J. de, Feijs, E., & van Reeuwijk, M. (1992). *Figuring all the angles 2*. Draft version before americanization. Utrecht: Freudenthal Institute/Madison, Wisconsin: National Centre for Research in Mathematical Sciences Education.

Lange, J. de, van Reeuwijk, M., Burrill, G., & Romberg, T. (1993). *Learning and testing mathematics in context— the case: Data visualization*. Scotts Valley, CA: Wings for Learning.

Lesh, R., & Lamon, S.J. (1992). *Assessment of authentic performance in school mathematics*. Washington: American Association for the Advancement of Science.

Mathematics Sciences Education Board (MSEB) (1991). *For good measure: Principles and goals for mathematics assessment*. Washington: MSEB.

National Council of Teachers of Mathematics (1989). *Curriculum and evaluation standards for school mathematics*. Reston, VA.: NCTM.

Phillips, D.C. (1987). *Philosophy, science, and social inquiry.* New York: Pergamon Press.

Popper, K. (1968). *Conjectures and refutations.* New York: Harper.

Resnick, L.B. (1987). *Education and learning to think.* Washington: National Academy Press.

Romberg, T.A. (1992). *Mathematics assessment and evaluation.* New York: State University of New York Press.

Streefland, L. (1991). *Fractions in realistic mathematics education.* Dordrecht, The Netherlands: Kluwer Academic Publishers.

Treffers, A. (1987). *Three dimensions. A model of goal and theory description in mathematics education.* Dordrecht, The Netherlands: Reidel.

TRAINING TEACHERS OR EDUCATING PROFESSIONALS? WHAT ARE THE ISSUES AND HOW ARE THEY BEING RESOLVED?

Glenda Lappan and Sarah Theule-Lubienski

Michigan State University, United States of America

Current trends in teacher education cannot be separated from current visions of student learning. As Brown, Cooney, and Jones (1990, p. 650) state, "It makes little sense to interpret either students' goals or teachers' goals in isolation one from the other." Hence, we will begin by exploring today's vision for mathematics students and its implications for teaching and teacher education.

VISION OF STUDENT LEARNING OF MATHEMATICS

What society needs from mathematics education for students is changing dramatically. In order to address these changing needs, the National Council of Teachers of Mathematics (1989) created the *Curriculum and evaluation standards for school mathematics* (CESSM*)*. This vision of reform promotes several inter-related components, including: (1) students actively "doing mathematics", (2) mathematics as thinking and sense-making, (3) powerful, but changing, mathematical content, and (4) a belief that *all* students can learn and appreciate mathematics. The implications of this vision of mathematics and mathematics learning for teacher education and professional development are major. We need to begin at ground level and build teacher education programs that can educate and support teachers in changing their minds and their practices to support more powerful mathematics and mathematical thinking for students.

A framework for examining teaching

There are many persistent obstacles to making changes in the teaching and learning of mathematics. In order to examine pre-service teacher education programs and professional development programs for experienced teachers for the likelihood that they can help make teachers change, we need to build a framework of what teachers need to know and be able to do. Teaching is a very complex endeavor, not reducible to recipes or algorithms. Good teaching may look very different in different classrooms. In order to get beyond the surface features, one has to examine aspects of the teachers' decision making, judgments about the classroom, and about the students' learning.

The writers of the Professional Standards for Teaching Mathematics (PSTM) identified four aspects of teaching that were judged to be so central to good teaching that they could be used to craft a framework, in the form of a set of standards, for what teachers need to know and be able to do. These four aspects of decision making are: choosing worthwhile mathematical tasks, orchestrating classroom discourse, creating an environment for learning, and analyzing teaching and learning. (NCTM, 1991).

Worthwhile mathematical tasks

There is no other decision that a teacher makes that has a greater impact on students' opportunity to learn and on their perceptions about what mathematics is than the selection or creation of the tasks with which the teacher engages the students in studying mathematics. Here the teacher is the architect, the designer of the curriculum.

To make selections or craft tasks that give students these deeper, more relevant opportunities, the teacher must be guided by the mathematical content of the task. Problems should not be chosen merely because they are "fun," or because they use a manipulative that is available in the classroom. There must be the potential for students to engage in sound and significant mathematics as a part of accomplishing the task.

A second consideration for a teacher in selecting or crafting tasks is that he or she teaches particular students. What the students already know and can do, what their mathematical needs are, and the level of challenge they seem ready to accept, are all fundamental issues for a teacher. For teachers to be effective at making such judgments they need to know the best results that we have from research and practice about students of the age in question, as well as to have particular insights into their own students' mathematical progress and ways of making sense of mathematics.

We must build responses to the following questions in our teacher education programs:

> What knowledge does a teacher need in order to be able to judge what her students know, to be able to recognize the difficulties that they are experiencing, to anticipate what will be difficult, to anticipate what will be more apt to push students forward in their thinking and their knowledge and skill in doing mathematics?

Classroom discourse

The PSTM describes discourse as " the ways of representing, thinking, talking, agreeing, and disagreeing" (1991, p. 36) as a group of students and a teacher strive to make sense of mathematics. Discourse includes the ways that ideas are represented, exchanged, and modified into more powerful and useful ideas. Teachers have a critical role to play in establishing the norms of discourse in the classroom and orchestrating discourse on a daily basis. It is through the interactions in the classroom that students learn what mathematical activities are acceptable, which ones need to be explained or justified, and which explanations or justifications are acceptable.

The implications of new forms of discourse in the classroom are very great for teacher education. Many teachers and intending teachers have never experienced learning mathematics in situations where what is valued is the quality of the thinking, the quality of the explanation or argument, and the quality of the decisions made based on the evidence. Additionally, many teachers and intending teachers have little experience using tools—intellectual as well as physical tools such as calculators and computers—as ways of modeling, exploring, or representing ideas.

As teacher educators the question we must ask ourselves is, "How do teachers learn to conduct discourse in such powerful ways?"

Classroom environment

What students learn is fundamentally connected to how they learn it. The environment in which students learn affects their view of what mathematics is, how one learns it, and perhaps of more importance, their view of themselves as learners of mathematics. Environment means more than the physical surroundings. It includes the messages that students are given about what is expected of them. What is their work to be? What counts in the classroom? Is it speed? Neatness? Being quiet? Completing tasks? Or is it taking responsibility for listening to and helping others? Asking questions of themselves and of their classmates? Seeking evidence? Being curious? Working independently? Sharing ideas and strategies?

Environment encompasses considerations of tasks and discourse and the emotional climate of the classroom. Is the environment of the classroom conducive to taking intellectual risks? Does every student feel valued? Do all the students feel that their ideas will be respected even if these turn out to be incorrect? Does every student expect to make conjectures or argue points or question others as they build their mathematical understanding? These questions raise further questions about our teacher education programs:

How can teacher education programs and professional development programs help teachers develop learning environments in which students feel empowered to make sense of mathematics and in which they feel confident in themselves as learners of mathematics?

Even if teachers, both pre- and in-service, have experienced such an environment for learning mathematics, it is unlikely that such experience is explicit about the decisions that a teacher makes and the ways that a teacher works to build such an environment. The teacher as analyzer, as researcher, is visible to the students only through tests and other means of evaluation. Perhaps this final aspect of decision making is the most elusive of all since here there is little outward evidence of the teacher's analysis.

Analysis

How well is the system that the teacher has created working? Are the tasks engaging the students? Are they effective in helping students learn mathematics? Do they stimulate the richness of discussion that students need to develop mathematical power? Is the classroom discourse fostering learner independence? Curiosity? Mathematical thinking? Confidence? Disposition to do mathematics? Is the classroom environment encouraging the kind of engagement that reaches every student and supports everyone's mathematical development? These are the kinds of questions that reflective teachers regularly ask themselves. The PSTM refers to these aspects of teacher reflection as "analysis".

Analysis also includes the regular assessment of student progress for the purpose of making instructional decisions. Assessing student performance on skill-level items is not sufficient. The teacher needs to examine all aspects of the mathematical development of students, including how the tasks, discourse, and environment are working to build mathematical power for all students.

In the same way that we argue for an environment for students in which they can explore mathematics we have to consider that preservice teachers do not learn pedagogical reasoning by being told. The environments that we build in which to educate teachers must help preservice teachers construct their own professional knowledge. Teaching is a creative act in much the same way that problem solving is a creative act. It may help to know some heuristics for attacking problems, but a list of heuristics will never make us problem solvers. It may help preservice teachers to have some heuristics with which to consider teaching situations and problems, but such a set of "how to's" will not make anyone into a professional teacher capable of making the kinds of decisions that are envisioned in the PSTM and the CESSM.

How is a teacher to learn how to make such decisions and to engage in such analysis? What experiences in pre-service programs or professional development activities with experienced teachers are effective at developing such professionalism in teachers?

We now turn to an examination of the kinds of knowledge that we must consider in our professional development programs for teachers if we are to develop answers to the questions raised on what teachers need to know and be able to do and where they will learn it.

WHAT DO TEACHERS NEED TO KNOW AND BELIEVE?

Teachers need knowledge of at least three kinds to have a chance to be effective in choosing worthwhile tasks, orchestrating discourse, creating an environment for learning, and analyzing their teaching and student learning: knowledge of mathematics, knowledge of students, and knowledge of the pedagogy of mathematics. These domains of knowledge can be represented in a Venn diagram as shown:

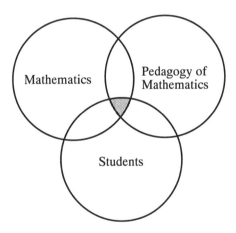

However, the Venn diagram makes clear one of the problems. Teachers work in the intersection of these domains of knowledge. It is the interplay of the various considerations that leads to defensible pedagogical reasoning on the part of teachers. Yet in teacher education programs we typically engage students in each of these domains of knowledge in isolation from each other. The integration of that knowledge in ways that helps teachers reason about their classrooms and their students is often left to the students' teaching experiences. The evidence suggests that this is not an effective means of helping teachers see the connections among the various domains of knowledge that they possess (Feiman-Nemser, 1983).

In the next sections of this paper we examine issues and promising research in areas of teacher learning that reflect the three areas or domains of knowledge diagrammed above.

Knowledge and beliefs about mathematics

The new vision for student learning has great implications for the knowledge of mathematics needed by teachers. Encouraging students to explore mathematics sometimes leads to unexpected mathematical questions and situations, and teachers need mathematical knowledge in order to guide students in their explorations.

McDiarmid, Ball, and Anderson (1989, pp. 13-14) emphasize the importance of teachers' mathematical knowledge. After reviewing current research in this area they conclude:

> Recent research highlights the critical influence of teachers' subject matter understanding on their pedagogical orientations and decisions ... Teachers' capacity to pose questions, select tasks, evaluate their pupils' understanding, and make curricular choices all depend on how they themselves understand the subject matter.

Lampert (1988, pp. 163-164) argues that teachers need to know where the mathematics teaching and learning process is headed, "not in the linear sense of one topic following another, but in the global sense of a network of big ideas and the relationships among those ideas and between ideas, and facts, and procedures." A study by Steinberg, Haymore, and Marks (1985) supports her assertions. They found that well-developed mathematical knowledge correlated with having a more conceptual teaching approach, while a low level of mathematical knowledge correlated with a more rule-based approach. Additionally, Even (1993) found that teachers with limited conceptions of functions taught in a way that emphasized rules without understanding.

McDiarmid et al. (1989, p. 7) also state, "Beyond representing the *substance* of a subject, teachers also represent its *nature*." In order for teachers to help students obtain more authentic and productive notions about mathematics, teachers themselves need to believe that mathematics is more than just memorizing rules. Yet American teachers tend to give inconsistent messages about the goals of mathematics: i.e., neatness, correct answers, rules and procedures (Stigler & Perry, 1988).

Perhaps these mixed messages are indicative of current questions being raised about the goals of mathematics education and the relationship between the discipline of mathematics and mathematics education. Should reasoning, thinking, and problem solving be the primary focus of mathematics education? Or should mathematical concepts, definitions, and theorems be given primary emphasis? To what extent should the classroom community's norms be similar to the norms in the community of mathematicians regarding issues such as evidence and proof?

Despite questions such as these being raised about the relationship between the discipline of mathematics and school mathematics, there does seem to be a great deal of agreement about the importance of teachers' mathematical knowledge. Instead of avoiding these issues with teachers, it might help teachers reconsider their rule-based notions of mathematics to realize that mathematics and mathematics education are both developing fields in which there are unanswered questions and debate.

It seems clear that it is not just the quantity of mathematics that is at issue. Teachers need to learn mathematics in deeper, more connected ways. In order to develop this depth of mathematical understanding and be able to use their mathematical knowledge effectively in classroom, the current way in which mathematics is taught to teachers must be changed. Not only do mathematics teacher educators need to model good teaching, they must also give explicit attention to the relationship between teachers' mathematical knowledge and teachers' knowledge of mathematical pedagogy and students.

Knowledge and beliefs about the pedagogy of mathematics

The PSTM takes the stand that what students learn is fundamentally connected to how they learn it. "Consequently, the goal of developing students' mathematical power requires careful attention to pedagogy as well as curriculum." (NCTM, 1991, p. 21). Couple this stand with Thom's (1972) suggestion that mathematical pedagogy reflects one's philosophy of mathematics, and Hersh's (1986, p. 13) statement, "One's conception of what mathematics is affects one's conception of how it should be presented," and this sends a powerful message about what is important in our teacher education programs. What philosophy of mathematics do our students see in our programs? Is it coherent? Does it pervade all aspects of the education of teachers from the content classes in mathematics to how we work with students in the fields? Do we consciously try to make explicit matters having to do with what mathematics is? Do we engage students in activities that cause them to reflect consciously on their deep-seated beliefs about mathematics and what it means to know and to teach mathematics?

In recent years research on teachers' beliefs and the interaction between beliefs and practice have received increasing attention. Thompson (1984) investigated high school teachers' beliefs and their classroom teaching and found evidence that teachers' beliefs, views, and preferences about mathematics influence what they do in the classroom. Others who have studied teacher beliefs and the impact on teaching and learning are listed in the references for this paper. (Shaw, 1989; Cooney, 1985; Brown, 1985; Dougherty, 1990; Peterson, Fennema, Carpenter, & Loef, 1989; Schram, Wilcox, Lappan, & Lanier, 1989; Nespor, 1987; Ernest, 1988.) We know from research that the deeply held beliefs of preservice teachers about what can and should happen in school, about what is possible and what is desirable, and about the nature of understanding (Stigler & Perry, 1988) are particularly difficult barriers to change. But we cannot improve teaching unless we confront what teachers bring to teaching and, more specifically, to teacher education.

In 1988 a group at Michigan State University began a study of pre-service teachers as a part of the National Center for Research in Teacher Education. The study was based on an intervention designed to help us better understand what it takes to help pre-service teachers confront their beliefs about what mathematics is, what it means to know mathematics, and what it means to teach mathematics. We designed three courses in mathematics, two methods courses, one before and one after student teaching, and seminars during student teaching. We have written about our work in several papers listed among the references (Schram, Wilcox, Lappan, & Lanier, 1988, 1989; Schram & Wilcox, 1988; Wilcox, Schram, Lappan, & Lanier, 1991; Wilcox, Lanier, Schram, & Lappan, 1992; Schram, 1992; Lappan & Even, 1989). Here we summarize what we think we know as a result of this ongoing study.

The 24 pre-service teachers entered the first mathematics course with a traditional view of mathematics as a well-ordered sequence of rules and procedures mostly focusing on number and number operations. They did not expect mathematics to make sense, but they did expect themselves to be able to remember or the teacher to give a rule after which the solution would be swiftly found. They perceived the role of the teacher to be explaining how to do the problems and telling the students when they were correct. We had a year with these students in which to create a new vision of what mathematics learning and teaching—from the perspective of the mathematics classroom—could be. We were able to change in very powerful ways how the students perceived themselves as learners of mathematics. By the end of the intervention, the students valued the kind of environment we had created and the goals of problem solving and deep understanding that had driven our work. However, they valued this as an environment for themselves as learners, but nearly half of the students still held to their more traditional beliefs about what mathematics was important for elementary children and how one should teach that mathematics to children.

We have continued to follow a subset of these students through their first three years of teaching (Wilcox et al., 1992). Our analysis of the data suggests that the choices the teachers make in their teaching of mathematics are influenced by the interaction of their views about knowledge and pedagogy, with the degree to which they perceived the context of the school in which they teach—with its policies and established curriculum—as a constraint. We have observed the complexities that new teachers face in attempting to create environments for learning mathematics in which children engage in personal and group sense-making. We have observed the isolation new teachers feel. We have concluded that disciplinary knowledge and a disposition to engage in mathematical inquiry or sense-making can be developed in an intervention such as ours. However, this is not enough to overcome the deeply-held beliefs about how young children should learn mathematics and what is important for them to know. Additional work must be done to create environments in which these deeply held beliefs are challenged, examined, and reconstructed. This cannot, in our opinion, be done solely in the preservice phase of teacher education. In fact, some professional development programs are based on the tenet that teachers need to change their teaching and see that a new approach "works" in their own classrooms before their beliefs change. (Owen, Johnson, Clarke, Lovitt, & Morony, 1988; Lockwood, 1991) Hence, working models of support systems for novice teachers need to be built.

We turn to the third area of knowledge needed by teachers.

Knowledge and beliefs about students

Most teacher education and professional development programs try to help teachers learn about children. However, it is where this knowledge of children and mathematics meet that is of critical importance to us as mathematics educators. The site for this meeting in many teacher education programs is in the student teaching experience. Yet many of us have experienced the disappointment of students returning from student teaching experiences angry at the university faculty because the world of school was not what their teacher education program espoused. The hard work of moving pre-service teachers to reconsider their beliefs and expectations about mathematics teaching and learning can be undone in a flash by a student teaching or beginning job experience in a school whose culture promotes order in the classroom, teaching as telling, and standardized test results as the measure of teacher success.

A group at Michigan State (Lappan, Fitzgerald, Phillips, Winter, Lanier, Madsen-Nason, Even, Lee, Smith, & Weinberg, 1988) has studied teacher change at the middle grade level in a number of projects. One aspect of teacher change that we have taken very seriously is the challenge of creating environments in which teachers' "knowledge" or beliefs about students as learners of mathematics can be challenged. One effective means of challenging teachers beliefs and expectations—and hence, their knowledge

257

about students—has been intensive summer experiences which have a classroom teaching component and long-term follow-up support.

The teacher participants were observers in classrooms taught by the staff. Each of them picked a particular child to study for two weeks. The teachers were to focus on the cognitive development of their child. What sense were they making of the mathematics? Each day we had a debriefing session at which the teachers talked about their child. It was quite difficult in the beginning for teachers to focus on cognition instead of behavior. They were quick to write students off as not very competent in mathematics. However, as the two weeks passed, all the children provided their "teacher observers" with surprises. Given a chance to listen to children making and defending conjectures about the problem situations being studied, the teachers began to look for more clues as to what the students were thinking.

While this intervention was with experienced teachers, it raises questions about how our teacher education programs, including field experiences, might be constructed. It also underscores the need for the creation of very powerful images of children in the act of making sense of mathematics in order to help teachers learn about students.

SUMMARY

One of our greatest challenges in educating professional teachers is taking seriously the integration of the domains of knowledge on which teachers base their practice. This requires fundamental changes in the ways in which we interact across disciplines within the university and among schools, universities, and the community. Such interactions are difficult. The participants in each of these areas (departments of mathematics, teacher education, educational psychology, schools, communities, business, and industry) do not speak the same language nor value the same activities. However, we are all bound by the same moral imperative—to do the best we can for the children in our communities.

We have a clearer picture of the issues in both pre- and in-service work with teachers. We can be guided by the framework from the PSTM on crucial aspects of teacher decision making:

- selecting worthwhile tasks,
- orchestrating classroom discourse,
- creating environments for learning, and
- analyzing teaching and learning.

We have discussed three domains of knowledge that must be considered in the professional development of teachers: knowledge of content, knowledge of pedagogy, and knowledge of students. We have identified teachers' and pre-service teachers' deeply-held beliefs about each of these domains of knowledge as part of what needs to be addressed. We have identified time and long-term support, as critical aspects of change. Current work is giving us promising direction. The challenge is ours. If we want mathematical power for all students, we must find ways to restructure our university programs and to help restructure schools so that teaching becomes the profession to which we are all dedicated.

REFERENCES

Brown, C. (1985). *A study of the socialization to teaching of a beginning mathematics teacher.* Unpublished doctoral dissertation, University of Georgia, Athens.

Brown, S.I., Cooney, T.J., & Jones, D. (1990). Mathematics teacher education. In W.R. Houston (Ed.), *Handbook of research on teacher education,* (pp. 639-656). New York: Macmillan.

Cooney, T.J. (1985). A beginning teacher's view of problem solving. *Journal for Research in Mathematics Education, 16,* 324-336.

Cooney, T.J. (1991). *Integrating pedagogy and content for preservice mathematics teachers.* (National Science Foundation Project Summary). Athens, GA: University of Georgia.

Dougherty, B.J. (1990). Influences of teacher cognitive/conceptual levels on problem-solving instruction. In G. Cooker et al. (Eds.), *Proceedings of the Fourteenth Annual Meeting of the International Group for the Psychology of Mathematics Education* (pp. 119-126). Oaxtepec, Mexico: International Group for the Psychology of Mathematics Education.

Ernest, P. (1988). *The impact of beliefs on the teaching of mathematics.* Paper prepared for International Congress on Mathematics Education VI, Budapest, Hungary.

Even, R. (1993). Subject-matter knowledge and pedagogical content knowledge: Prospective secondary teachers and the function concept. *Journal for Research in Mathematics Education, 24,* 94–116

Feiman-Nemser, S. (1983). Learning to teach. In L. Shulman & G. Sykes (Eds.), *Handbook of teaching and policy* (pp. 150-170). New York: Longman.

Hersh, R. (1986). Some proposals for revising the philosophy of mathematics. In T. Tymoczko (Ed.), *New directions in the philosophy of mathematics* (pp. 9-28). Boston: Birkhäuser.

Lampert, M. (1988). What can research on teacher education tell us about improving quality in mathematics education? *Teaching & Teacher Education, 4*(2), 157-170.

Lappan, G., & Even, R. (1989). *Learning to teach: Constructing meaningful understanding of mathematical content.* Draft Paper 89-3. East Lansing,

MI: National Center for Research on Teacher Education, Michigan State University.

Lappan, G., Fitzgerald, W., Phillips, E., Winter, M.J., Lanier, P., Madsen-Nason, N., Even, R., Lee, B., Smith, J., & Weinberg, D. (1988). *The middle grades mathematics project: Good mathematics, taught well.* (Final report to the National Science Foundation for Grant #MDR8318218). East Lansing, MI: Michigan State University.

Lockwood, A.T. (1991). Why do I have to change? *Focus on Change, 5,* 12-13.

McDiarmid, G.W., Ball, D.L., & Anderson, C.W. (1989). *Why staying one chapter ahead doesn't really work: Subject-specific pedagogy.* (Issue paper 88-6). East Lansing, MI: National Center for Research on Teacher Education, Michigan State University.

National Council of Teachers of Mathematics (1989). *Curriculum and evaluation standards for school mathematics.* Reston, VA: NCTM.

National Council of Teachers of Mathematics (1991). *Professional standards for teaching mathematics.* Reston, VA: NCTM.

Nespor, J. (1987). The role of beliefs in the practice of teaching. *Journal of Curriculum Studies, 19,* 317-328.

Owen, J., Johnson, N., Clarke, D., Lovitt, C., & Morony, W. (1988). *Guidelines for consultants and curriculum leaders.* Canberra: Mathematics Curriculum and Teaching Program, Curriculum Development Centre.

Peterson, P., Fennema, E., Carpenter, T., & Loef, M. (1989). Teachers' pedagogical content beliefs in mathematics. *Cognition and Instruction, 6*(1), 1-40.

Schram, P. (1992). *Learning mathematics to teach: What students learn about mathematical content and reasoning in a conceptually oriented course.* Unpublished doctoral dissertation, Michigan State University, East Lansing.

Schram, P., & Wilcox, S. (1988). Changing preservice teachers' conceptions of mathematics learning. In M. Behr, C. LaCampagne & M. Montague-Wheeler (Eds.), *Proceedings of the Tenth Annual Meeting of the International Group for the Psychology of Mathematics Education, North American Chapter* (pp. 349-355). DeKalb, IL: Northern University.

Schram, P., Wilcox, S., Lappan, G., & Lanier, P. (1988). *Changing mathematical conceptions of preservice teachers: A content and pedagogical intervention* (Research Rep. No. 88-4). East Lansing: Michigan State University, National Center for Research on Teacher Education.

Schram, P., Wilcox, S., Lappan, G., & Lanier, P. (1989). Changing preservice teachers' beliefs about mathematics education. In C. Maher (Ed.), *Proceedings of the Eleventh International Conference of the International Group for the Psychology of Mathematics Education, North American Chapter* (pp. 349-355). New Brunswick, NJ: Rutgers University.

Shaw, K. (1989). *Contrasts of teacher ideal and actual beliefs about mathematics understanding: Three case studies.* Unpublished doctoral dissertation, University of Georgia, Athens.

Steinberg, R., Haymore, J., & Marks, R. (1985). *Teachers' knowledge and structuring content in mathematics.* Paper presented at the annual meeting of the American Educational Research Association, Chicago.

Stigler, J., & Perry, M. (1988). Cross-cultural studies of mathematics teaching and learning: Recent findings and new directions. In D. Grouws & T. Cooney (Eds.), *Perspectives on research on effective mathematics teaching* (Vol. 1, pp. 194-223). Hillsdale, NJ: Lawrence Erlbaum.

Thom, R. (1972). Modern mathematics: Does it really exist? In A.G. Howson (Ed.), *Developments in mathematical education* (pp. 194-209). Cambridge, England: Cambridge University Press.

Thompson, A.G. (1984). The relationship of teachers' conceptions of mathematics and mathematics teaching to instructional practice. *Educational Studies in Mathematics, 15*(2), 105-127.

Wilcox, S.K., Lanier, P., Schram, P., & Lappan, G. (1992). *Influencing beginning teachers' practice in mathematics education: Confronting constraints of knowledge, beliefs, and context.* (Research Rep. No. 92-1). East Lansing, MI: National Center for Research on Teacher Learning, Michigan State University.

Wilcox, S.K., Schram, P., Lappan, G., & Lanier, P. (1991). *The role of a learning community in changing preservice teachers' knowledge and beliefs about mathematics education.* (Research Rep. No. 91-1). East Lansing, MI: National Center for Research on Teacher Education, Michigan State University.

WHAT IS DISCRETE MATHEMATICS
AND HOW SHOULD WE TEACH IT?

Jacobus H. van Lint

University of Technology, The Netherlands

In the past 25 years the role of discrete mathematics has become increasingly important. The number of fields in which discrete mathematics is applied in some way also keeps increasing. It has been argued that, for some areas, where mathematical knowledge is necessary, one should replace the standard calculus course with a course in discrete mathematics. Although I feel that everybody should know some calculus, it is certainly true that knowledge of techniques from discrete mathematics is often just as useful.

A number of years ago this idea of replacing calculus with parts of mathematics that were more relevant to the rest of the program was pushed strongly by computer science departments in the United States. This led to a stream of books on "Discrete Mathematics for Computer Scientists", most of which gave the impression that discrete mathematics is the union of all subjects in mathematics that are useful for computer scientists but not part of calculus. One finds logic and set theory as part of the hodgepodge of subjects in these books. My opinion is that this is not discrete mathematics at all. Of course logic, set theory, etc., are very useful for students of computer science but a course in these subjects should be given some other name.

What is discrete mathematics? It is that part of mathematics that deals with discrete structures. Usually the objects that are studied are finite; but of course I also include infinite graphs and the integers and other locally finite structures. Essentially the subject includes combinatorial theory, elementary number theory, finite groups, finite geometries, finite fields, and some newer areas such as coding theory.

It is my impression that many courses that deserve the name discrete mathematics are taught in ways that leave students completely baffled. They have the impression that problems in discrete mathematics are solved by ingenious tricks and that any new problem they will encounter requires them to invent the appropriate new trick. Compare this to a calculus course where one teaches methods such as differentiation, integration, solving linear differential equations, etc., and subsequently applies these methods in several different situations. A course in discrete mathematics should be similar! One should treat objects that appear in many places, sometimes disguised; methods of representation should be used in several different situations; ideas that reappear regularly in practice should also reappear regularly in the course; tools that play an important role in discrete mathematics should become part of the students' skills. To give an idea I mention several examples of each of these topics (not a complete list).

1. Objects: graphs, lattices, geometries, designs, codes, coverings, partitions, systems of sets, matroids.

2. Representations: addressing schemes, coding, (0,1)–matrices, (0,1)–sequences, graphs, diagrams, pictures, subsets of lattices.

3. Ideas: counting techniques, probabilistic techniques, (non-) existence methods, construction techniques, unification (association schemes, matroids), optimization methods, max-flow, search techniques, symmetry.

4. Tools: algebra (matrix theory, finite groups, finite fields, group rings), elementary number theory, permutation groups, geometry, analysis (power series, Lagrange inversion).

The course should be structured as a multipartite graph with subsets of (1) to (4) as independent sets and as many edges as possible. Here an edge from say "graph" to "(0,1)–matrices" means that this representation is used to describe graphs but also to derive properties of graphs or to prove theorems about them.

The following situation can and should occur: it has didactic value. One wishes to prove a certain theorem about, say, designs, and decides to use (0,1)–matrices as representation. The rows of the (0,1)–matrix can also be interpreted as words in a code. This leads to a formulation of the theorem that is to be proved, in another terminology. This other theorem may have already occurred in the course or it could be much easier to see how to prove it. One can also prove a "new" theorem about some combinatorial object and in retrospect observe that if this object had been represented in the appropriate way, one would have realized that the theorem had actually occurred earlier in some other form.

If the instructor decides to take the tool "algebra"as a central item in the course, then the ideas used—for example: eigenvalues of matrices—should be applied for many different purposes, such as nonexistence theorems for strongly regular graphs, properties of block designs, theorems in finite geometry. Similarly, the idea of using several small combinatorial objects to construct one large object should reappear (Latin squares, Hadamard matrices, block designs, etc.).

A course taught in Eindhoven for several years started with a chapter on finite fields. A number of objects from combinatorics (Latin squares, Hadamard matrices, finite geometries, block designs, error-correcting codes) in each of which finite fields were heavily used to construct those objects.

A number of ideas that I used will be treated below as examples. First, however, I mention a principle that was suggested by A. Revuz at the meeting on "How to teach mathematics so as to be useful" held in Utrecht in 1967. I have used it ever since with much success. Discrete mathematics is particularly suited for this principle. The idea is to let the students work on problems (usually in groups of two or three), solutions to be handed in as homework, and to teach the standard techniques and theorems necessary to solve the problems a few weeks later. Usually one sees several students in class recognize how useful a theorem is long before the proof is finished: "If I had known that idea two weeks ago, then ..."

THE USE OF REPRESENTATIONS

If possible, use representations of combinatorial objects not only as representations but in such a way that the chosen representation makes it easier to prove the theorem in question.

Example 1

A puzzle known as *Instant Insanity,* involving stacking up multicolored cubes in some way (treated in many books on graphs), is extremely difficult, as the name suggests. It becomes practically trivial when the cubes are represented by graphs that reflect the color-structure.

Example 2

A well known way of representing a partition is a so-called Ferrers diagram. Such a diagram actually is a representation of two partitions. This makes it possible to prove theorems of the type, "The number of partitions of an integer with property I equals the number of partitions with property II", by just looking at the diagrams.

Example 3

Binary rooted trees can be represented by $(0,1)$–sequences with as many 0's as 1's, for which each truncated sequence has more 0's than 1's. These sequences are not difficult to count, whereas counting the trees directly looks very complicated. The problem of counting the number of dissections of an n-gon into triangles looks quite different. Usually one first discovers that this problem leads to the same answer as the previous one before realizing that it can be represented by the same kind of (0,1)–sequences.

Example 4

The reverse situation is also useful as an example. For instance, a problem on (0,1)–matrices can look like a difficult abstract problem. Interpreting the matrix as a representation of some combinatorial object translates the question into other terminology and can make it much easier.

COUNTING TECHNIQUES

This topic includes double counting, the principle of inclusion and exclusion, Möbius inversion, the use of quadratic forms, one-to-one mappings, generating functions, Polyá theory and probabilistic methods. Again a few (favorite) examples.

Example 5

This is one of the problems that students try to solve with no tools. Let the edges of a complete graph on six vertices be colored red and blue in some way. Prove that there is a triangle with all three edges of the same color (a monochromatic triangle). Nearly all students give the same proof. From any vertex there must be three edges with the same color, say red. The three edges between the other endpoints of the red edges are either all blue or one of them is red and in both cases we have a monochromatic triangle. So far, so good. The second question is to show that there are actually at least two monochromatic triangles. This yields three possible solutions: the empty one, complete nonsense, or a several page case analysis that is actually correct. Then comes double counting in class! Every non-monochromatic triangle has two vertices where a red and a blue edge meet; call this a red-blue V. Clearly every vertex yields at most six of these red-blue V's. So, this second way of counting (or estimating) the number of non-monochromatic triangles shows that there are at most 18 of them. As K_6 contains 20 triangles, we are done in a few lines.

Example 6

After the usual examples of inclusion-exclusion it is useful to point out the reverse procedure. Try to prove the formula

$$\sum_{i=0}^{k} (-1)^i \binom{k}{i} (k-i)^n = \begin{cases} n! \text{ if } k = n, \\ 0 \text{ if } k > n. \end{cases}$$

This can be done using analysis but it is not trivial. The term $(-1)^i$ in the sum suggests that maybe something was counted using inclusion and exclusion. What? This takes some thinking. The answer is the number of surjections from an n-set to a k-set and the formula becomes a triviality.

Example 7

The following quadratic form method occurs in very many different situations. Let a_i denote the number of combinatorial objects of a certain kind that have exactly i whatevers. Often one can easily count pairs of whatevers. Since $\sum a_i$ counts the number of objects in question, $\sum i a_i$ counts the number of whatevers, and finally $\sum \binom{i}{2} a_i$ counts pairs of whatevers, one can calculate expressions of the form $\sum (i - m)(i - m - 1)a_i$, where the choice of m is unrestricted. The fact that this quadratic form is non-negative yields an inequality. It is surprising how often this idea is used in combinatorics without it being pointed out that it is a general method.

(NON-)EXISTENCE AND CONSTRUCTIONS

Methods to be treated here include counting (probabilistic methods), the method of descent or minimal counterexample, algorithms and search techniques, induction and recursion, product techniques, substitution, algebraic methods, contraction, introducing extra structure. Here are a few examples.

Example 8

The construction of a Latin square of order mn from one of order m and one of order n is very similar to the construction of a Hadamard matrix of order mn from one of order m and one of order n. Both constructions should occur. Later one can use similar product methods in the construction of block designs. Even the idea of the product of graphs is analogous.

Example 9

A well known proof technique in number theory can be extended to several parts of discrete mathematics, such as graph theory. To prove a theorem on finite configurations one assumes that it is not true, or that a counterexample exists. In that case there exists a minimal counterexample, where minimal refers to the number of components that justify the word "finite." One has to think of a way of reducing this number (delete a vertex or replace the integer n by $n - 1$) in such a way that the reduced object is still a counterexample. This yields a contradiction and thus the theorem is proved. Again, the point of this talk is that if one decides to show an example of the method, one should show several rather different examples.

Example 10

The idea of substitution occurs in many constructions. Examples are replacing a vertex of a graph by some graph, points of a configuration by n-gons (e.g. in Joyal theory), and the following. In a block design with blocks of different sizes (every pair of points is in λ blocks) let there be a block B with seven points. We delete B and replace it by the seven triples (lines) of the Fano-plane (a $(7,3,1)$–design). The $\binom{7}{2} = 21$ pairs that were covered by B are now covered by the seven lines of the plane. This method is used to replace the difficult restriction of constant blocksize by freedom in that respect in the first round of a construction, followed by substitutions of the type mentioned above to achieve a prescribed constant blocksize.

Example 11

Assume that a combinatorial object is defined by combinatorial restrictions only. It may be difficult to construct even one example of such an object. One can freely introduce extra structure, such as symmetry, an automorphism group, and so on, in order to force the construction in a certain direction. If the extra requirements are not already prohibitive, one may have an easy construction of a first example of the theory. Again, this is a principle that should be illustrated by examples.

APPLICATIONS

Discrete mathematics as a course should be full of examples of applications in a wide area of subjects. Students should not only learn a number of applications but should recognize situations where a certain part of discrete mathematics is the natural tool to use. One should move from computer science, to social sciences, to electrical engineering to design of experiments, etc. Examples may be elementary, obvious, everyday, but it is essential to have several others that ensure that the students enjoy the course. They should be surprising, challenging, ingenious (like *Instant Insanity*), recent (such as satellite communication or the compact disc). Again, two of my favorite examples.

Example 12

Suppose one has a standard non-erasable binary memory such as paper tape (or a compact disc). Assume that one wishes to store one of the integers 1 to 7 in this memory on four consecutive occasions. The usual procedure is to reserve twelve bits for this purpose, where the four consecutive triples each take care of one storage of a binary 3-tuple. The world supply shortage has now reached the stage where we cannot afford this and have to achieve the same with a memory of only seven bits! (The reader should try to prove as an exercise that it is not possible to solve the storage problem with a memory of six bits.) The solution is provided by the Fano plane, a finite geometry with seven points and seven lines, three points to a line and three lines through a point, any two points on a unique line. Number the points 1 to 7 and on the first storage let a 1 in position i indicate a storage of the integer i. This is still easy. The next step is not difficult either. If the memory contains a 1 in position i and one wishes to store the integer j as new information, find the unique line through i and j and if k is its third point, put a 1 in position k. The reading device for this binary memory is told that if it sees two 1's, then it should interpret these as "the third point of the corresponding line". Two more usages of this memory to go and we leave it as an exercise to decide how to do it (Hint: a change of memory with two 1's results in four 1's; a subsequent change leads to either five or six 1's).

Example 13

During the treatment of Hadamard matrices one has given the product construction and therefore the trivial Hadamard matrix of order two (rows ++, respectively +−) makes it possible to construct such matrices of order 2^n. As an exercise the students have shown that this leads to a matrix H of order 32 with the property that there are six columns in the array consisting of H and $-H$ such that the corresponding 64 rows in this array are all different in these six columns (Note that $2^6 = 64$). As application one treats the transmission to earth of pictures of Mars by the Mariner satellite. A picture is divided into very little squares (pixels) and for each square the degree of blackness is measured in a scale of 0 to 63 (expressed in binary). In this way the picture results in a long sequence of 0's and 1's to be transmitted to earth. The transmitted sequence is corrupted by noise and the effect is that the receiver sometimes interprets a 0 as a 1 and vice versa. In practice there was so much noise that pictures would have been completely useless. Suppose we are willing to take roughly five times as long to transmit a picture. We could repeat each bit five times; if no more than two out of five are received incorrectly, the receiver makes the right choice. This would be a substantial improvement but what was done in practice in 1969 was very much better. An integer, say 43, in binary 101011 was changed to the corresponding sequence of +'s and −'s (i. e. + − + − ++) and transmitted as the corresponding row of 32 +'s and −'s of the array of H and $-H$. This also takes five times as long (roughly). The reader should convince himself or herself that as many as seven of the transmitted symbols may be received incorrectly and nevertheless the receiver will still have the correct row as the most likely one. The result is known: the pictures were of great quality. A true and recent example!

NOTES

The ideas presented in this talk were used as guiding principle in the book *A course in combinatorics* by J.H. van Lint and R.M. Wilson, Cambridge University Press, 1992.

The talk by A. Revuz in Utrecht appeared as "Les pièges de l'enseignement mathématique", *Educational Studies in Mathematics, 1* (1968), 31-36.

INTUITION AND LOGIC IN MATHEMATICS

Michael Otte

Universität Bielefeld, Germany

PART ONE

I am going to begin with what might appear to be a rather provocative thesis: *Mathematics is the embodiment of intuitive thinking.*

In intuition other than in discursive knowledge something is immediately present. In discursive knowledge it is only represented. A comparison with painting will help to illustrate the difference. In daily life a picture functions as a representation of something. In art it is different. There the pictures, although they might be representations too, do not primarily function as illustrations or guides, but have a value of their own. They constitute, like theories, realities of their own kind.

In his well-known article, *Applied mathematics is bad mathematics,* Paul Halmos (1981) has used the following comparison to describe the difference, as he sees it, between pure and applied mathematics.

> A portrait by Picasso is regarded as beautiful by some, and a police photograph of a wanted criminal can be useful, but the chances are that the Picasso is not a good likeness and the police photograph is not very inspiring to look at. Is it completely unfair to say that the portrait is a bad copy of nature and the photograph is bad art?

This gives a first impression regarding the background of the idea of the difference between intuition and discursive knowledge, which has been of great importance throughout modernity.

The strength of the intuitive is to be seen in its emphasis on acquaintance with an object, since a content has to be given from whence we can advance to knowledge. As Kant said: "In the absence of intuition all our knowledge is without objects, and therefore remains entirely empty." (A 62). The weakness of intuitive insight results from the lack of communicability. In intuition a certain spontaneity and immediacy can be observed in the transition from not understanding to knowledge. Intuitive knowledge is characterized by an unawareness. I do not know how I came to this knowledge. Whenever something is said of an intuition a discursive process of cognition and language must already be occurring. "Intuitions without concepts are blind," as Kant said. For Kant intuitions were given through our sensibility, which is material, and passive, and lacking in internal continuity.

Discursive processes, however, do not provide an object which really exists for us. They are rather metacognitions concerned with our dealing with objects rather than with the objects themselves. So it appears as if cognition has to proceed simultaneously on different levels and that we have to coordinate these levels within our concrete and mental activity.

Up to the middle of the 19th century mathematics was for the most part divided according to whether it was supposed to deal with real meanings and therefore was to be based on axioms, like geometry or mechanics, or whether it was formal knowledge that had accordingly to rely on definitions, like arithmetic. These differences gradually disappeared when it was realized that the application of algebra to geometry may also be based on the algebraization of geometrical constructions rather than on the quantification of objects by means of real-valued functions. The dominant focus of concern shifted away from the "interface problems" between knowledge and the external world and moved towards the problem of the internal dynamics of knowledge and cognition. Mathematics for Kant was synthetic just because it concerned not the analysis of concepts but the fact that they apply to the world. Kant believed that the only role of concepts is that which enables us to get in contact with some objects as a guide for activity on these objects. Operations can be guided by thought, whereas objects can only be described and cannot be influenced in this way. We are not in command of the world, as Wittgenstein used to say. So after it was realized that our conceptualizations are not directed at the world per se, but toward the world as it is present to the system of our activities, people began to stop discussing knowledge altogether. It is (cognitive) activity that matters. The regularities we call mathematical knowledge appear in the relevance of patterns of activities in time. Pure mathematics was turned into an art and applied mathematics became considered "bad mathematics".

Nevertheless: Mathematics is the incarnation of intuitive knowledge. Let me give a first argument for this claim. To understand a mathematical theorem means the same as watching the sun rise. This implies that if I have understood a mathematical theorem I have at the same time understood that it is true. Within intuition, knowledge of a fact and knowledge of its truth coincide. This situation applies to proving as well. With a proof we have simultaneously to present a proof that our proof is correct. If we attempt this we are clearly faced with an infinite regress. The way out is to insist on a purely formal criterion for logical correctness. In one way or another the form of the knowledge becomes subject to intuition. But only the form. If we insist that mathematics has to do with real knowledge, or if we believe, as René Thom has so aptly stated it at the Second International Congress on Mathematical Education, "The real problem of mathematical education is not that of rigor, but the development of meaning, of the existence of mathematical objects" (Thom, 1973, p. 202), then mathematics has to be intuitive knowledge. Existing or being is not a real predicate, as Kant said (B 626).

Intuition, other than plain seeing, is directed at the reality or the essence of something rather than at its mere appearance, and intuition therefore always implies generalization. In intuition I perceive the general as if it were a particular object. By the distinction between essence and appearance, a difference between the actual observation of a thing and its capacities, tendencies, and possible developments is conceptualized. From this it follows that space is essential to intuition and that the processes of experience are transformed into the structures of geometrical vision.

Intuitive knowledge is not discursive knowledge. Our intuitions as such are like a conglomerate of Leibnizian Monads, each of which represents the world from its own particular perspective. Theory as grasped by intuition represents a perspective, a way of seeing that is as such—i.e., in its claim to access reality—incommensurable with other perspectives. And, what is more important, this perspective introduces new ways of interrogating reality, new types of objects and new types of evidence of sentences, and so forth.

Now the essential features of an act of imaginative creation may be summarized by stating that they consist in the seeing of an A as a B : A = B, or "all A are B", or "A represents all B", etc. Important however is the fact that there might be nothing in "A" and "B" per se, no objective suggestion, no similarity in appearance, or whatever it is that establishes the relation, and nothing in the world that will, a priori, guarantee the success of such an act of creative imagination. On such grounds pure mathematics has, since Cantor, been called a free creation of the human mind; but of a mind that has to have the ability to perceive in a mathematical way, to see completely clearly that A is essentially B. The claim to have such an ability constitutes mathematical authority. This authority is based on the assumption of mathematical genius. Nowhere in science is the cult of genius so strong as in pure mathematics.

What distinguishes the genius from the ordinary person is the style of reasoning, a style that becomes a standard of mathematical objectivity. Mathematics is governed by paradigms in Thomas Kuhn's sense. It may even, being intuitive knowledge, become a belief system. Any system, Stolzenberg writes, that is informed by a desire for a world-view that can be maintained and that one will want to maintain will be called a belief system. "A belief system may be like a genuinely scientific system in every other respect, but it has this one distinguishing feature: All acts of observation, judgment, etc., are performed solely from the particular standpoint of the system itself." (Stolzenberg, 1978).

The most dangerous belief of a mathematical system consists in the conviction that every question must have a determinate answer. If a person does not see the answer in a particular case, nor where an answer may be searched for, he or she is in all probability lacking in the ability to perceive the matter in a mathematical way. This may become a drawback when one is confronted with the claim that there exists an absolute and authentic relationship to any mathematical object as well as a determinate answer to any arbitrarily chosen question about it.

Creativity, however, might demand that the whole framework of a problem be questioned. And even creativity is a rather narrow aspect of human life. From the point of view of our social and individual life, it might even be appropriate to question that there exists a definite answer to a very particular problem. Charles Peirce challenged even with respect to theoretical thought what he called the "fundamental axiom of logic": that "Every intelligible question whatever is susceptible in its own nature of receiving a definitive and satisfactory answer, if it be sufficiently investigated by observation and reasoning." (Kloesel, 1986, p. 545f). Unremitting creative technical virtuosity might have to give way to human conditions like dignity, kindness, self-esteem, philosophical reflection, tradition, love, or wonder.

Mathematics is the incarnation of intuitive knowledge. This idea is naturally very attractive. However it is connected with a dilemma. Although the conviction that results from the intuitive character of our mathematical insights may indeed be very strong, it is also very fragile. We are always confronted with the uncertainty whether what seems to be so evident is not based on the error of a false choice of perspective. And when a great authority appears who claims exactly this, then our relationship to the truth in question that was based on intuition is destroyed irrevocably. This can further be illustrated by the following *Gedankenexperiment.*

Suppose I have found a proof for some mathematical theorem, which after having checked out the argument of the proof step-by-step, is now intuitively completely clear to me.

> Suppose that a great authority announces that there is something wrong with the argument. In that case my experience upon checking over the argument may be quite different from what it was before this announcement was made. Just as before, I find that the argument appears to be correct; only this time I do not accept it as being correct. And there we have the difference between

the two situations; in the first there is an act of acceptance as such ,while in the second there is instead an act of questioning something that appears to be correct. (Stolzenberg, 1978)

An act of acceptance as such is present if the perception of the respective reality appears to the perceiver automatically to coincide with reality itself. It is this type of belief that we call an intuition. As mathematical cognitions are essentially intuitive I think, contrary to Stolzenberg, that the kind of "overconfidence" (Fischbein) exhibited in an act of acceptance as such cannot be evaded by mathematical cognition.

This whole argument may appear utterly strange to those who believe that science investigates ideas without regard for their origin. It is however very clear that knowledge demands elements that are transcendental with respect to the particular experience and that in many cases the social context provides these elements. Certain people are to be trusted on certain issues and the newcomer must accept whatever agreements they reach on those issues.

The message of Stolzenberg's thought experiment is somewhat para-doxical because there seems to be a completely clear vision that is all of a sudden destroyed. If nobody could expect from another individual any in-sight into the matter, the statement of the "great authority" would not disturb us at all. What the thought experiment has told us can also be expressed in plain psychological language:

> The need for relying on apparently certain, credible representations and interpretations is, in our opinion, the main factor which explains the general tendency of people to be overconfident in their judgments. The need for certitude leads to this type of apparently very well -structured, self-consistent and apparently self-evident cognitions called intuitions. But overconfidence is an obstacle to self-control and consequently it may block the way to a significant improvement of the quality of reasoning. (Fischbein, 1987)

Everybody has to believe in him or herself beyond the limits of a real-istic evaluation of the situation. Being realistic would cause us very often to give up before we had really tried hard. But on the other hand, as Fischbein shows, the necessity of being overconfident is self-contradictory.

Teachers in practice try to avoid the paradoxical features of the situa-tion by taking refuge in pedagogical formalism. School mathematics becomes an exercise in formal logic and correct phrasing and spelling. If we don't accept intuition as a cognitive basis, all our knowledge disintegrates or de-composes into linguistic or logical formalism on the one side and empirical guesswork on the other. We know from a number of empirical studies that teachers on the one hand endorse the value of geometry and on the other hand tend to dismiss it from their classes when pressed for time.

A historical example of the dilemma that we have described is provided by the philosophy of Descartes. Descartes thought proof irrelevant to truth, basing that instead on the self-evidence of intuitive insight. Leibniz on the contrary thought that truth is constituted by proof. The Cartesian independence of truth from logical proof is illustrated by Descartes' unorthodox views on the necessary truths of algebra and geometry. Even eternal truths are dependent on the will of God, according to Descartes.

> We owe to Leibniz the clear statement that if not-*p* entails a contradiction then *p* is necessary and indeed necessarily necessary. Descartes grants that it is unintelligible how *p* can entail a contradiction and still be true. But this unintelligibility shows the weakness of our minds. (Hacking, 1984)

There can be no doubt that God is the great authority here, and God's intuition is obviously of such a kind that ours must be inferior.

Like Descartes, Kant also believed that mathematics is based on intuitive truths. Nonetheless, Kantian intuition is different from Cartesian intuition. It did not strive to grasp the reality of a thing directly but adjusted itself to the conditions for constructing a mathematical truth. Our insight into mathematics arises, says Kant, because we construct mathematical truths according to conditions that we cannot escape and that are completely manifest to our intuition. The weakness of Cartesianism is to be seen in the lack of any transcendental reference that would transform a particular mental event into true knowledge. Leibniz attempted to make the real substance underlying such an event the criterion of truth by claiming that formal proof will inevitably and objectively lead to the real substance. Proofs that constitute substantial truths become however an infinite task able to be accomplished by God's infinite mind only. With respect to "infinite proofs", Kant's argument that "being is not a predicate" does not apply.

How is it possible to combine transcendentalism with the finite and limited perspective of humans on reality? Such was Kant's problem and he took space and time to be those transcendental forms within which we have to realize mathematical knowledge. Only that which can be developed by means of our own constructions in space and time can lead to new mathematical insight.

PART TWO

Charles Peirce (1839-1914) ascribes to Kant the merit of having been the first in history to give the distinction between intuition and logic its proper weight. Kant saw, according to Peirce, far more clearly than any predecessor had done the whole philosophical import of this distinction.

This was what emancipated him from Leibnizianism and at the same time turned him against sensationalism. It was also what enabled him to see that no general description of existence is possible, which is perhaps the most valuable proposition that the *Critique of pure reason* contains. But he drew too hard a line between the operations of observation and of ratiocination. (Peirce, 1.35).

Not only is a general description of existence impossible because "being is evidently not a real predicate" (Kant *Critique* B 626), but quite a number of predicates cannot be linked to a concept without employing the concept as a rule of construction within the intuition of space and time. For instance the idea of a triangle does not analytically contain the fact that the sum of its angles amounts to two right angles. The philosopher would try, Kant writes, to analyze the concept of triangle, but

> He may analyze the conception of a right line, of an angle, or of the number three as long as he pleases, but he will not discover any properties not contained in these conceptions. But, if this question is proposed to a geometrician, he at once begins by constructing a triangle. He knows that two right angles are equal to the sum of all the contiguous angles which proceed from one point in a straight line; and he goes on to produce one side of his triangle, thus forming two adjacent angles which are together equal to two right angles. He then divides the exterior of these angles, by drawing a line parallel with the opposite side of the triangle, and immediately perceives that he has thus got an exterior adjacent angle which is equal to the interior. Proceeding in this way, through a chain of inferences, and always on the ground of intuition, he arrives at a clear and universally valid solution of the question. (A 716/B 744)

We must intuit an object that we wish to know; hence the unknowability of the thing in itself, which is determined by the fact that we can have no immediate knowledge of it because it does not belong to space and time.

That our mathematical knowledge, although based on intuition, may nonetheless be *a priori* (that is, general), is due to the fact that it is just a concrete instantiation of the general forms that constrain all our activity.

Let us, in order to think of a particular example, reflect on the idea of a "general triangle". The problematic associated with such an idea was expressed by Locke when he remarked that on the one hand the general idea of a triangle is imperfect, "for it must be neither oblique nor rectangle, neither equilateral nor scalene, but all and none of these at once." On the other hand we have need for such general ideas "for the convenience of communication and enlargement of knowledge." (Locke, *Essay concerning human understanding,* book 4, chapter 7).

The general triangle as presented in Figure 1 is not as general as it might be. If we wanted, for example, to derive what is called the cosine law we would have to distinguish two cases as in Figures 2.1 and 2.2.

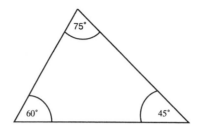

Figure 1

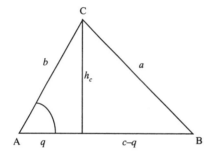

Figure 2.1   Figure 2.2

We get:

$a^2 = b^2 + c^2 - 2cq$ and $a^2 = b^2 + c^2 + 2cq$

respectively, or in more familiar writing:

$a^2 = b^2 + c^2 - 2bc \cos A$

The different values of the cosine function cover the different cases that are distinguished in the more elementary presentation above.

A formula like $A = \frac{1}{2} b \times h$ helps to compare all triangles whatever their form or size might be. The geometrical object as such, the general idea of triangle, disappears. A great deal of geometry has in this manner been replaced by algebra and function theory. The first presentation of the cosine law, although very elementary, nonetheless leads to the introduction of the new idea of a correlative system (Carnot, 1803). A correlative system in the sense of Carnot is a type of equivalence class. It is established completely intuitively, as in the example given.

There could be nothing in common to *all* triangles (or some other point systems), but there is a chain of resemblances representing a law of continuity. This idea led to new thinking about general terms. If two geometrical systems are to be considered as intuitively equivalent then the formulas stating a certain property or law in the two cases differ at most with respect to the signs of certain of their terms. Carnot's ideas stimulated Poncelet to state his famous "law of continuity" that was fundamental in the establishment of projective geometry. A general triangle has now become an equivalence class of particular concrete triangles. The essential differences between all the conceptions of geometry seem to be based on how the equivalence relation in question is selected.

We could start thinking differently about the matter. We could, for example, state that what serves as a "general" idea in geometry should be interpreted in relation to the particular purpose at hand. If, for example, one wants to prove the theorem that the three medians of any triangle intersect at exactly one point (Figure 3), then an equilateral triangle serves perfectly well as an instance of a general triangle because the claim of the theorem mentions only concepts that are independent of distance and angle (one can define the area measure independently of the lengths and the sizes of the angles by means of a determinant function, and the definition of median is also independent of these concepts) or, to put it differently, the conditions of the theorem in question are invariant with respect to affine transformations.

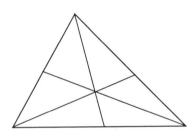 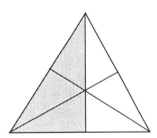

Figure 3.1   Figure 3.2

As early as 1710, Bishop Berkeley aimed what he himself called "the killing blow" at Locke's notion of general idea and asked the readers of Locke's to try to find out whether they could possibly have "an idea that shall correspond with the description here given of the general idea of a triangle—which is neither oblique nor rectangle, neither equilateral nor scalene, but all and none of these at once." (Berkeley 1737, 54). And to this logical impossibility he answered

> that though the idea I have in view whilst I make the demonstration be, for instance, that of an isosceles rectangular triangle whose sides are of a determinate length, I may nevertheless be certain it extends to all other rectilinear triangles, of what sort or bigness soever. And that because neither the right

angle, nor the equality, nor determinate lengths of the sides are at all concerned in the demonstration. It is true the diagram I have in view includes all these particulars, but then there is not the least mention made of them in the proof of the proposition. And for this reason it is that I conclude that to be true of any which I had demonstrated of a particular triangle and not because I demonstrated the proposition of the abstract idea of a triangle. (Berkeley, 1737, 56)

There exist different proofs of the theorem about the medians. One might, for instance, start from the interpretation of the point of intersection as a center of gravity. This interpretation is suggested by the fact that the medians divide the area of the triangle in half. Such a proof, very different from the one using the symmetries of an equilateral triangle, leads to an interesting generalization. By imagining variable weights fixed to the vertices of the triangle we gain as a generalization a proof of the theorem of Ceva (1648-1734). The theorem of Ceva generalizes the situation for arbitrary points of intersection of three line segments joining the vertices of a triangle to points on the opposite sides.

The theorem runs as follows: Given a triangle in the projective plane and a line through each of the vertices of the triangle, then the three lines are either parallel to each other (meet at infinity) or they meet at one regular point of intersection, if and only if the product of the ratios in which they divide the opposite sides of the triangle is unity.

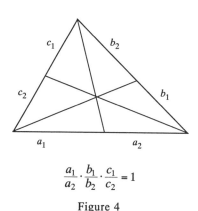

$$\frac{a_1}{a_2} \cdot \frac{b_1}{b_2} \cdot \frac{c_1}{c_2} = 1$$

Figure 4

There exist different proofs of the theorem of Ceva too. It can, for example, be derived from the theorem of Menelaos, or it can be proved very easily by means of a calculation in terms of projective coordinates. This latter proof gives an excellent illustration of Poncelet's law of continuity since the condition of the theorem can be expressed by an algebraic function. This condition in our case just says that a certain determinant is zero.

Carnot gains a generalization of Ceva's theorem from his principle of correlative systems. As the theorem can be stated in terms of an equality of two simple quantities and as a positive quantity cannot be equal to a negative one, the theorem must remain valid for all correlative systems, i.e. even when the point of intersection lies outside the triangle.

From Ceva's theorem the proposition about the intersection of the three altitudes of the triangle can immediately be derived, by verifying that the condition of Ceva is fulfilled in this case also. This is remarkable because the notion of a perpendicular is obviously not a projective invariant.

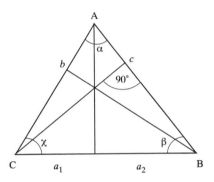

Figure 5

$$a_1 = b \cos \chi \qquad a_2 = c \cos \beta$$
$$b_1 = c \cos \alpha \qquad b_2 = a \cos \chi$$
$$c_1 = a \cos \beta \qquad c_2 = b \cos \alpha$$

Bishop Berkeley wanted to argue that there are no general ideas and no intuitions directed towards them, but only linguistic and formal activities. Kant in contrast stressed that to understand the true character of mathematics one has to observe its axioms (intuitions) and its applications rather than the deductive procedures employed in proving theorems. He accepted however the functional perspective on mathematical knowledge that is so clearly noticeable in Berkeley. "No image", Kant says, "could ever be adequate to the concept of a triangle in general. It would never attain the universality of the concept which renders it valid for all triangles, whether right-angled, obtuse-angled, or acute-angled; it would always be limited to a part only of this sphere." (B 180). The imaginative schema however, although it is in thought and not in the images, is not just a part of conceptual and propositional knowledge. It is necessary to get to the meaning of concepts. The imaginative schema as a "mediating representation must be pure (without empirical content) and yet must on the one side be intellectual, on the other sensuous." (B 178).

The most important aspect of cognition is continuity. For Kant the continuity of experience, or as he sometimes called it, its unity, is the most important hallmark of the objectivity of knowledge. What turns an individual mental event into an idea, what provides a particular image with meaning, is its connection with other such events, is its place within an unending series of the same kind. "Kant understood imagination as a capacity for organizing mental representations (especially images and percepts) into meaningful units that we can comprehend. Imagination generates much of the connecting structure by which we have coherent, significant experience, cognition and language." (Johnson, 1987). Thus Kant seems to aim at a sort of blending or amalgamation of the views of Descartes, Locke, and Berkeley. Berkeley considers mathematics analytically, Locke believes it to be synthetic but *a posteriori*, and for Kant it is synthetic as well as *a priori*.

Kant's work depends on the possibility of being able to operationalize the pure forms of the intuitions of space and time. Space and time were to be transformed into operative categories by means of which we should succeed in constructing our world. This is performed under the constraint of the system of tools and means available to the epistemic subject. Intuition is directed towards the overall context of mathematical activity in as much as the activity objectifies or realizes itself in the external forum of space and time by means of certain tools and artifacts. The complementarity of means and problems is what governs the evolution of our cognitions and of our intuitions in particular. Gregory Bateson has provided us with a very suggestive metaphor for the concept of evolution, presenting it not as a one-sided adjustment:

> Surely the grassy plains themselves were evolved pari passu with the evolution of the teeth and hooves of the horses and other ungulates, Turf was the evolving response to the evolution of the horse. It is the *context* which evolves. (Bateson, 1973)

In our research praxis the context of means or tools seems more powerful than the context of problems or objects. This observation can be reformulated by saying that the theoretical dynamic becomes a largely internally driven process and theories get to be understood as realities of their own kind. At the beginning of the 19th century certain parts of mathematics formed a contextual notion of meaning by claiming, first, that a theory determines the intentions of its terms, and, second, that intentions determine extensions or referents. Even for Kant the comparison between empirical intuitions or perceptions and concepts was a difference in kind, whereas for classical rationalism it had been one of degree. Since mathematics, like science in general, is interested in objective knowledge, mathematicians have to have other means of identifying the referents of its terms than the descriptions provided by the theory as intentions of its terms. The availability of other ways of accessing the referents establishes a practice in which theories are used in a twofold manner, attributively as well as referentially ("A is B" vs. "A represents B").

My last thesis is as follows: The apparent mismatch between empirical observation and mathematical intuition, which is responsible for the neglect of the role of the latter, is due to a misunderstanding about the empirical sciences.

The objects of ordinary perception are constituted or constructed rather than perceived as such, entirely spontaneously and naturally. Visual perception is a highly complex phenomenon which is strongly influenced by socio-cultural factors. Kant's idea of a schema of the imagination expresses these facts, and the philosophy of science speaks of the theory-ladenness of observation in this context. Physicists, as Steven Weinberg observes, are making abstract models of the universe to which they "give a higher degree of reality than they accord the ordinary world of sensations" (Weinberg 1976, 28). The philosophy of mathematics has put forward an even stronger claim, to the effect that all objects are essentially abstract objects, or even mathematical objects (Tymoczko, 1991).

This seems to bring back the time of 17th/18th century "idealism", when thought was a matter of ideas or of mental discourse and when there were no strong boundaries between things and ideas. These times, we recall from Peirce's statement at the beginning of this section, ended with the critical philosophy of Kant. From now on the question of the relationship between the concrete and the operative, or between the intuitive and the discursive, became of fundamental importance for any cognitive or epistemological theory.

The scholar who has most distinctly expressed the constructive position of Kant in current mathematical education is Jean Piaget. A central concept of Piaget's epistemology is the discrimination between *reflective abstraction*, which proceeds from the actions and operations of the subject and is responsible for the construction of mathematical concepts, and *empirical abstraction*, which is directed at the objects of empirical reality.

What is problematic in Piaget's conception is the fact that this differentiation between empirical and reflective abstraction becomes an immediate split as a result of his use of a concept of empirical abstraction that is too primitive. This cuts in two exactly that which Piaget considers the advantage of the operative approach, namely, the unity of subject and object when based on objective activity. If empirical abstraction is considered not to be constructive the tension between the two poles—the constructive and the intuitive aspects of all cognition—is resolved and both aspects stand alongside one another as unrelated characteristics of two different classes of scientific concepts, rather than the two different sides of any concept.

REFERENCES

Bateson, G. (1973). *Steps to an ecology of mind*. St. Albans: Paladin.

Berkeley, G. (1737). *A treatise concerning the principles of human knowledge* (1989 ed.). London: Dent and Sons.

Carnot, L. (1803). *Géométrie de position*. Paris: L'Imprimerie de Crapelet.

Fischbein, E. (1987). *Intuition in science and mathematics*. Dordrecht, The Netherlands: Reidel.

Goodman, N.D. (1983). Reflections on Bishop's philosophy of mathematics. *Math Intelligencer, 5*, 61-68.

Hacking, I. (1984). Leibniz and Descartes: Proof and eternal truths. In T. Honderich (Ed.), *Philosophy through its past* (pp. 207-224). Harmondsworth: Penguin.

Halmos, P.R. (1981). Applied mathematics is bad mathematics. In L. Steen (Ed.), *Mathematics tomorrow* (pp. 9-20). Heidelberg: Springer.

Johnson, M. (1987). *The body in the mind*. Chicago: University of Chicago Press.

Kloesel, Ch. J.W. (Ed.) (1986). *Writings of Charles S. Peirce* (1879-1884) (Vol. 4). Bloomington: Indiana University Press.

Stolzenberg, G. (1978). Can an inquiry into the foundations of mathematics tell us anything interesting about mind? In G. A. Miller & E. Lenneberg (Eds.), *Psychology and biology of language and thought* (pp. 221-270). New York: Academic Press.

Thom, R. (1973). Modern mathematics: Does it exists? In A.G. Howson (Ed.), *Developments in mathematical education* (pp.194-209). Cambridge, UK: Cambridge University Press.

Tymoczko, T. (1991). Mathematics, science and ontology. *Synthèse, 88*, 201-228.

Weinberg, S. (1976). The forces of nature. *Bulletin of the American Academy of Arts and Sciences, 29*.

VERS UNE CONSTRUCTION RÉALISTE DES NOMBRES RATIONNELS

Nicolas Rouche

Université catholique de Louvain, Louvain-la-Neuve, Belgique

Il est rare de nos jours que l'on manie des grandeurs pour effectuer une mesure : on se contente de consulter des cadrans. Par ailleurs les grandeurs, si importantes chez Euclide, ont au XXe siècle disparu des mathématiques et quasiment disparu de l'enseignement. Or c'est la mesure des grandeurs qui, historiquement, a donné naissance aux nombres autres que naturels. Il est donc intéressant de regarder comment, par quelles méthodes diverses, on a enseigné les nombres depuis que les grandeurs se sont estompées.

C'est ce que nous faisons ci-après, d'ailleurs sans prétention d'épuiser le sujet. Ce regard critique débouchera sur la question : sachant comment on a enseigné les nombres dans le passé, comment pourrait-on faire à l'avenir ?

Le présent article explicite et complète certains développements de Rouche (1992a). Il est une version abrégée de Rouche (1992b).

L'ÉVOLUTION HISTORIQUE DES MESURES

Depuis que l'homme existe, il perçoit et cherche à exprimer des quantités. Il n'a pas cessé au cours des siècles de créer des moyens de plus en plus commodes, rapides et précis pour mesurer les grandeurs. Jetons un coup d'œil sur cette évolution millénaire.

Les distances autrefois comptées en heures ou journées de marche sont aujourd'hui fournies automatiquement et directement dans le langage des chiffres par les compteurs kilométriques des automobiles.

L'homme a d'abord mesuré l'écoulement du temps à la hauteur du soleil dans le ciel. Il reconnaissait aussi les saisons au défilé des constellations du zodiaque. Ensuite il a inventé les cadrans solaires : le soleil, source première des divisions du temps, précisait son message sur les heures et les saisons par le truchement de l'ombre d'un bâton. Avec les clepsydres et les sabliers, l'homme a recouru à des mouvements artificiels pour mesurer le temps. Ensuite, il a inventé les horloges mécaniques, bientôt pourvues d'un balancier, puis les horloges à quartz avec encore un cadran à aiguilles et enfin les montres digitales. On perçoit l'évolution globale qui va d'un contact direct avec « la source principale du temps » (les mouvements du soleil), en passant par les cadrans à aiguilles qui, comme les astres, tournent d'un mouvement uniforme, jusqu'aux montres digitales qui exhibent de purs symboles.

Naguère encore la balance à fléau et le peson exhibaient les lois des leviers, tandis que la balance à ressort, tenue à la main, donnait à la fois la sensation du poids et la connaissance de son action sur le ressort. Les balances digitales d'aujourd'hui ne fournissent que des chiffres. Et même, en donnant directement le prix d'une marchandise achetée, elles évitent à l'utilisateur la fatigue d'un problème de proportionnalité.

De même les mesures de capacité se font aujourd'hui sans qu'on ait à se servir des récipients-unités qui en donnaient une perception directe. Et l'essence d'auto se mesure autant sinon davantage en francs qu'en litres.

Ainsi les manipulations de base des grandeurs (comparaisons, sommes, fractionnements, ...) sont progressivement éliminées de la vie quotidienne. Chaque mesure est réduite « à la seule opération de lecture d'un nombre sur un cadran ». En liaison avec les progrès de la technologie, plus les hommes utilisent des mesures et moins ils ont à exécuter des opérations de mesure (voir la préface de Rouche, 1992a).

LES GRANDEURS ONT DISPARU DES MATHÉMATIQUES

Si nous considérons maintenant l'histoire des mathématiques, nous y voyons en quelque sorte les nombres prendre la place des grandeurs. Jetons un regard sur cette évolution, elle aussi millénaire.

La théorie des grandeurs du Ve Livre d'Euclide, un des piliers principaux des mathématiques grecques, a été enseignée jusque tard dans le XXe siècle, dans le cadre de la géométrie d'Euclide. Il n'y était question ni d'unités de mesure, ni de nombres (hormis les naturels) susceptibles d'exprimer la mesure d'une grandeur dans une unité donnée.

À côté de cette théorie des grandeurs s'est élaboré, au cours des siècles, un système de nombres de plus en plus satisfaisant, aboutissant à notre corps des réels. Cette construction des nombres s'est appuyée essentiellement sur la mesure des grandeurs, comme l'histoire en témoigne abondamment.

Mais l'édifice des nombres a été renversé dans la seconde moitié du XXe siècle. À cette époque, pour donner aux réels un fondement logique ferme, on a largué leurs amarres historiques à la mesure des grandeurs pour les rattacher à la seule théorie des nombres naturels (puis plus tard, à travers ceux-ci, à la théorie des ensembles).

Ainsi les nombres réels, nés au cours des siècles de la géométrie et de la physique des grandeurs, ne leur devaient dorénavant plus rien. Et non seulement ils avaient conquis leur autonomie, mais encore, à travers la structure d'espace vectoriel, ils ont plus tard servi à (re)fonder la géométrie. Dans ce cadre nouveau, le corps des nombres est construit avant même qu'on aborde la géométrie. Les premiers objets à mesurer, par exemple les segments sur un axe, sont en quelque sorte mesurés d'avance. Toute la problématique de la mesure, issue des difficultés de manipulation des grandeurs les plus concrètes, a proprement disparu, et les grandeurs se sont évanouies des mathématiques.

Bien entendu, elles n'ont pas en même temps disparu de la physique, dont elles sont le matériau même. Ainsi au cours de la première moitié du XXe siècle, les mathématiques se sont éloignées de la physique dans la mesure sans doute où elles avaient rompu leur très ancien ancrage dans les grandeurs pour en établir un nouveau dans la théorie abstraite des ensembles.

LES GRANDEURS DANS L'ENSEIGNEMENT AUJOURD'HUI

Voyons maintenant comment cette évolution s'est répercutée dans l'enseignement.

Au niveau secondaire tout d'abord, là où les enseignements de mathématiques et de physique sont le plus souvent séparés, la situation est en gros la suivante. Les grandeurs sont traitées en physique. C'est là que l'on affronte l'impossibilité d'un rapport entre deux grandeurs d'espèces différentes, les systèmes d'unités, la possibilité d'un rapport entre les mesures de deux grandeurs d'espèces différentes et la conceptualisation par ce biais de nouvelles grandeurs (vitesse, densité, ...), les formules complexes associant toutes sortes de grandeurs et la théorie des « équations aux dimensions ».

Toutes ces choses sont par contre ignorées dans le cours de mathématiques. Dans celui-ci, un mouvement est une fonction de Â dans Â dont la vitesse est la dérivée. Quelle difficulté y aurait-il à considérer le rapport d'un espace à un temps, puisque de toutes façons espace et temps sont d'avance de même nature : ce sont deux nombres réels ? Il reste à ce stade comme une trace de la difficulté primitive à mettre en rapport une distance et un temps dans la remarque (éventuelle) que le graphe position-temps doit être interprété en géométrie affine et non métrique.

Beaucoup d'enseignants de mathématiques sont embarrassés lorsqu'ils butent sur un symbole de grandeur tel que kg ou m (pour mètre). Ces choses ne sont pas prévues dans la théorie et ils ne savent qu'en faire. Nombre d'entre eux ont d'ailleurs une répugnance pour la physique. Mais ce n'est pas ici le lieu d'analyser plus en détail les raisons du véritable divorce entre les enseignements de mathématiques et physique à l'école secondaire.

La situation est différente à l'école primaire. Là, l'apprentissage des mathématiques est tellement proche de ses sources dans le monde familier qu'un divorce consommé entre physique et mathématiques y est impossible. Ce que l'on constate en gros, mais qui mériterait une confirmation attentive, c'est

- que l'apprentissage des grandeurs à l'écart des nombres donc avant toute idée de mesure est assez peu développé ;

- que beaucoup de phénomènes qui ont pour vocation de conduire à la construction des fractions et des rationnels sont ignorés dans l'enseignement ;

- que les mesures d'aires et de volumes débouchent trop vite sur des formules, au détriment d'une construction des idées de mesure correspondantes ;

- et enfin que sous le titre de grandeurs ne se retrouve dans le programme qu'une nomenclature du système décimal des poids et mesures, accompagnée de nombreux exercices de changement d'unités.

Au total donc, l'enseignement semble bien ne pas accorder beaucoup d'attention à la genèse de l'idée de mesure, liée à l'apprentissage des nombres.

QUELQUES PROPOSITIONS D'ENSEIGNEMENT AU XXᵉ SIÈCLE

La situation que nous venons de décrire au triple niveau de la vie quotidienne, de la science mathématique et de l'enseignement pose au moins deux questions.

1) Comment amener les enfants d'aujourd'hui, qui bien entendu auront accès aux chiffres et aux nombres d'une manière ou d'une autre, à comprendre le sens des résultats de mesure, à savoir les décoder et les utiliser ?

2) Plus généralement, les manipulations de base des grandeurs ayant constitué pour les hommes d'autrefois le contexte intuitif dans lequel les grandes structures numériques prenaient racine, comment faut-il organiser l'apprentissage des mesures et des nombres pour les enfants d'aujourd'hui, compte tenu des évolutions respectives des mathématiques et de la civilisation technologique ?

Examinons certaines des réponses les plus significatives qui ont été données à ces questions depuis quelques dizaines d'années.

Au début du siècle déjà, Weber et Wellstein d'une part, et Burkhardt de l'autre (cités par Klein, 1908) proposaient, chacun à leur façon, de construire les nombres rationnels à partir de la seule connaissance des nombres naturels, et donc sans s'appuyer sur les grandeurs et la mesure des grandeurs, quitte à s'occuper de ces dernières après. Klein s'oppose, dans les termes suivants, à une telle organisation de l'apprentissage (tous les passages soulignés le sont par Klein lui-même) :

[...] *certainement la présentation moderne* [celle des deux auteurs cités] *est plus pure, mais par ailleurs elle est aussi pauvre* [que la présentation habituelle jusqu'alors]. De ce que l'étude traditionnelle offre *comme un tout,* elle ne donne en fait *qu'une moitié : l'introduction abstraite et logiquement complète de certains concepts arithmétiques — nommés « fractions » — et des opérations qu'on leur applique.* Mais alors *une question totalement indépendante et non moins importante demeure pendante : peut-on aussi réellement appliquer la doctrine théorique ainsi déduite aux grandeurs mesurables qui se présentent évidemment à nous ?*

On pourrait de nouveau appeler cela un problème de « mathématiques appliquées », pouvant faire l'objet d'un traitement entièrement séparé; mais il faut évidemment se demander en outre si une telle séparation est aussi *pédagogiquement* opportune.

Chez Weber-Wellstein, cette division du problème en deux parties s'exprime d'ailleurs de façon très caractéristique : après l'introduction abstraite du calcul des fractions, la seule dont nous ayons parlé jusqu'ici, il consacre une section particulière — intitulée « les proportions » — à la question de l'application effective des nombres rationnels au monde extérieur ; et là aussi sa présentation est assurément plus conceptuelle qu'intuitive.

Tout autre est l'enseignement conçu par Papy (1970) dans les années soixante pour les élèves de douze à quatorze ans et dont il a puisé l'inspiration théorique dans la *Geometric algebra* de Artin. Ce dernier avait bâti axiomatiquement la géométrie affine plane sans présupposer l'existence de nombres, mais au contraire en construisant le corps de la géométrie comme un corps d'objets géométriques (les transformations préservant la trace). Bien sûr, ce corps s'avère isomorphe à celui des réels, mais il ne devient corps de nombre qu'a posteriori. À l'usage des classes cette fois, Papy construit lui aussi les réels en même temps qu'une géométrie axiomatique du plan affine. Dans ce cadre, les droites du plan sont graduées et sous-graduées dans le système binaire, et les nombres réels représentés par les nombres binaires illimités à virgule, sont associés bijectivement aux points de la droite. Les nombres décimaux sont introduits ensuite. L'addition des réels est définie à partir de la somme des vecteurs parallèles, et le produit des réels est obtenu comme rapport de la composée de deux homothéties.

Les rationnels comme classes d'équivalence de fractions n'apparaissent pas dans un tel exposé. Mais le choix, de construire les réels dans un cadre géométrique, manifeste le souci de les associer intuitivement aux mesures de longueurs. Tel est aussi le souci de Lebesgue (1975), ouvrage important mais que nous ne mentionnons ici que pour mémoire, car il ne vise pas l'enseignement élémentaire.

Une autre conception intéressante est celle de Steiner (1969), a peu près contemporaine de celle de Papy. Mais alors que le texte de ce dernier s'adresse, comme nous l'avons dit, aux élèves de douze à quatorze ans, celui de Steiner est un texte mathématiquement dense proposant un fondement axiomatique pour soutenir l'apprentissage des nombres à partir du plus jeune âge. Il n'est donc nullement destiné aux élèves, mais aux responsables de l'enseignement élémentaire. Dans la théorie de Steiner, les nombres naturels d'abord et les rationnels positifs ensuite sont engendrés comme opérateurs sur un domaine de grandeurs. L'addition de ces nombres est donc interprétée comme addition d'opérateurs, et le produit des nombres comme composition d'opérateurs. Steiner exprime l'espoir que la connaissance d'un tel système conduira à trouver les moyens adéquats pour enseigner ces matières et ramener l'attention sur un point de vue négligé dans l'enseignement : la relation des nombres aux mesures et leur usage comme opérateurs.

Par-delà les différences relevées jusqu'ici entre les contributions de Weber-Wellstein, Burkhardt, Papy, Steiner et Kirsch, un caractère commun les rassemble, à savoir l'idée de mettre à la base de l'enseignement élémentaire des nombres *une* théorie axiomatique. Et chaque auteur, en proposant la sienne, argumente selon les cas de sa pureté, de sa clarté, de son rapport au vécu quotidien et à l'intuition. Mais dans tous les cas, ce dont il est question, c'est d'une conceptualisation au sens mathématique habituel, débouchant (chez Papy) ou susceptible de déboucher (chez les autres) sur un enseignement effectif.

Tout autre est, un peu plus tard, la démarche de Freudenthal dans sa *Didactical phenomenology of mathematical structures* (1983). L'idée n'est plus ici de construire une structure mathématique déductive qui, représentant le mieux ou le moins mal possible la réalité familière, puisse inspirer un enseignement. Freudenthal cherche d'abord à identifier des *phénomènes*, c'est-à-dire des faits, des relations observés dans le quotidien ou les mathématiques, et qui provoquent la pensée mathématisante. Nous supposons le lecteur familier de cette notion de *phénomène*.

Freudenthal inventorie une quantité extraordinaire de phénomènes divers. Plusieurs fois il s'exclame sur la difficulté d'y mettre de l'ordre :

« J'espère au moins, dit-il, que je ne me noierai pas dans cet océan. » Constatant l'absence de cohérence globale d'un ensemble de phénomènes, par exemple celui qui se rapporte aux grandeurs et aux rationnels, il organise localement cet ensemble à l'aide d'*objets mentaux*. Un objet mental n'est pas un concept construit techniquement comme en mathématiques, avec des quantificateurs et d'autres symboles, et inscrit dans une structure déductive. C'est quelque chose de plus familier, qu'on pourrait aussi appeler *notion*, mais suffisamment élaboré pour en faire précisément un instrument d'organisation d'un champ de phénomènes. Les nombres de tout le monde écrits dans le système décimal, les polygones les plus simples, les graphiques de fonctions sont trois exemples d'objets mentaux, parmi une foule d'autres.

Freudenthal insiste, spécialement à propos des fractions, pour que les phénomènes sous-jacents ayant été organisés localement et donc sans qu'on y reconnaisse une cohérence globale, on appuie l'enseignement sur leur ensemble et non sur une partie d'entre eux. L'insuccès bien connu de l'apprentissage des fractions pourrait, selon lui, être dû à une exploration trop incomplète par les élèves des phénomènes quelque peu hétéroclites qui y conduisent.

L'apprentissage des mathématiques selon Freudenthal doit commencer au niveau des objets mentaux, et non tout de suite à celui des concepts mathématiques formels, mais il a pourtant vocation de rejoindre ces derniers. Le but ultime de l'enseignement demeure bien d'enseigner les mathématiques telles qu'elles sont. Mais force est de reconnaître que beaucoup d'élèves abandonnent l'étude des mathématiques en cours de route. Pour ceux-là, mieux vaut s'en aller avec le bagage sensé des objets mentaux qu'avec le vide des concepts formels mal assimilés et dépourvus de contexte significatif.

Ici s'achève notre examen de quelques propositions faites depuis 100 ans pour l'enseignement des grandeurs et des nombres. Il y en a eu, cela va de soi, beaucoup d'autres. Mais celles que nous avons retenues suffisent, du moins nous l'espérons, à poser le problème assez clairement.

Repartons du constat de Freudenthal : il existe un vaste ensemble de phénomènes divers, impossibles à organiser globalement, mais qui tous conduisent d'une certaine façon aux grandeurs et aux nombres abstraits et en constituent des facettes concrètes. Acceptons en outre l'idée que si dans l'enseignement on néglige une ou plusieurs parties importantes de cet ensemble de phénomènes, on aboutit à une connaissance des nombres à laquelle manquent certains supports intuitifs et qui ne trouve que difficilement certains de ses points d'application dans la réalité.

Si on admet cela, il devient évident que tout enseignement inspiré d'un exposé axiomatique unique tels ceux de Weber-Wellstein, Papy ou Steiner sera *phénoménologiquement trop pauvre*, si on peut s'exprimer ainsi.

Bien entendu, ces exposés sont tous ingénieux et intéressants. Chacun, dans un registre théorique, organise et éclaire d'un jour qui lui est propre une partie des phénomènes en cause. Et à ce titre, ces contributions méritent d'être connues des responsables de l'enseignement d'aujourd'hui. Mais force est de reconnaître que tout tirer d'une source axiomatique unique aboutit à n'éclairer qu'une partie insuffisante de la réalité familière.

Il faut donc bien partir de la réalité multiforme, celle des élèves, et l'organiser en structures locales, ce qui implique qu'on ne rassemble pas d'emblée ces structures en un tout cohérent.

CRITIQUE DE LA PHÉNOMÉNOLOGIE DE FREUDENTHAL

Cela dit, tout reste à faire. Il faudrait que les responsables de l'enseignement mathématique élémentaire abandonnent l'idée d'inculquer les mathématiques comme un produit théorique préparé en dehors d'eux. Il faudrait non seulement qu'ils prennent conscience de la nécessité d'ancrer leur enseignement dans une réalité phénoménologique qui défie tout essai sommaire de structuration *globale*, mais encore qu'ils se familiarisent avec cette réalité, sa richesse et ses incohérences, les obstacles qu'elle oppose à la construction du savoir mathématique ordinaire.

Une réponse d'apparence évidente serait : on n'a qu'à lire et appliquer ce que Freudenthal a écrit, puisqu'il semble avoir vu si juste ! Essayons donc maintenant, en approfondissant sa contribution, de voir ce qui, peut-être, la rend difficile à saisir et à mettre en œuvre.

D'abord, quelle que soit la question qu'il aborde, il identifie les phénomènes pour commencer dans un cadre mathématique et à un niveau susceptible de dissuader la plupart des lecteurs issus de l'enseignement élémentaire. Cela est très clair dans la construction de son texte. Par exemple, au chapitre 1, le premier inventaire des phénomènes liés aux grandeurs est réalisé dans le cadre d'un exposé axiomatique de ceux-ci. Autre exemple : au chapitre 5, une partie importante des phénomènes concernant les rationnels est relevée dans une présentation axiomatique partielle de ces nombres considérés comme opérateurs sur un domaine de grandeurs.

Ayant ainsi d'abord identifié les phénomènes mathématiques, il part à la recherche des phénomènes quotidiens qui ont vocation d'y conduire, de les éclairer, d'en être des contreparties intuitives. Il découvre ainsi quelques ensembles de phénomènes familiers, ayant chacun sa cohérence propre. Mais ces ensembles sont en quelque sorte juxtaposés : le principal lien entre eux est qu'ils préfigurent, chacun partiellement, une même théorie mathématique.

Freudenthal relève que certains de ces ensembles ne se regroupent pas d'eux-mêmes pour constituer la théorie visée. Par exemple, ayant développé les fractions comme « opérateurs de fractionnement », ce qui conduit naturellement à leur multiplication, l'auteur ajoute : « l'addition manque », laissant entendre qu'il faudra aller la chercher ailleurs. Et il dit encore quelques pages plus loin : « dans cette structure [le produit des fractions vu comme composition d'opérateurs de fractionnement] le modèle du rectangle ne s'insère pas facilement. Ceci ne veut pas dire qu'il faille le négliger. » Le « modèle du rectangle » c'est l'ensemble des phénomènes liés aux calculs d'aires de rectangle ayant pour côtés des fractions de l'unité de longueur.

Dans cette optique, la réalité familière est pourvoyeuse de phénomènes *illustrant* les fractions et les rationnels. Elle n'est pas considérée *d'abord*, indépendamment des mathématiques auxquelles elle conduira plus tard, comme organisable localement à l'aide d'objets mentaux. On n'insiste pas sur le fait que les ensembles locaux de phénomènes structurés sont *impossibles*, si on les prend tels quels, à organiser globalement en une théorie cohérente. Certes, ces ensembles locaux coexistent parfaitement dans la réalité et la pensée communes. Mais lorsqu'on insiste pour mettre en correspondance détaillée les grandeurs et les nombres, on se heurte à des difficultés importantes, des contradictions. Nous prenons ici le mot *contradiction* non au sens de la rencontre d'une proposition et de sa négation, mais au sens de difficulté essentielle, d'opposition fondamentale entre deux choses. Les contradictions dont nous parlons ainsi sont à la fois des incitants et des obstacles à l'abstraction, à la construction d'une théorie formelle.

AFFRONTER LES CONTRADICTIONS

Pour pouvoir avancer dans notre réflexion, donnons d'abord l'un ou l'autre exemple de ces structures incompatibles que l'on obtient en organisant localement la masse des phénomènes.

Considérons d'abord l'ensemble des phénomènes liés à la comparaison (plus grand, plus petit) et à l'addition des grandeurs fractionnées. Cet ensemble forme un tout cohérent, bien organisé, où l'on voit commencer à se construire la structure de champ. En particulier l'addition y est une opération binaire interne avec les bonnes propriétés.

La nature des choses veut que cet ensemble ne soit pas muni d'une multiplication, opération binaire interne. Personne n'a jamais obtenu une longueur en multipliant deux longueurs, et jamais non plus une masse en multipliant deux masses. Par conséquent, si on veut construire la structure multiplicative des rationnels, il faut chercher ailleurs.

Mais les fractions (pas les grandeurs fractionnées) peuvent être vues comme opérateurs de fractionnement (de grandeurs). À ce titre, elles forment un tout autre ensemble, regroupant une foule de phénomènes familiers. Cet ensemble admet une structure multiplicative correspondant à la composition des opérations de fractionnement, structure qui préfigure une autre facette du champ des rationnels. En contrepartie, les opérateurs de fractionnement ne se laissent doter d'une addition que moyennnant beaucoup d'artifices.

Les choses rebondissent si on constate que les fractions peuvent aussi servir à mesurer des longueurs, des temps, des masses, etc. Or dans le cas des longueurs (et pas directement dans le cas des autres grandeurs), la multiplication des mesures fractionnaires apparaît bel et bien, mais non sous forme d'une opération interne. Multiplier des mesures de longueur donne des aires, des volumes ou des hypervolumes selon le nombre des facteurs. Cette multiplication s'exécute d'un point de vue formel comme la multiplication des fractions dans la théorie abstraite des rationnels (on multiplie les numérateurs entre eux et les dénominateurs entre eux). Mais pour qu'elle préfigure la structure multiplicative des rationnels, il faut « oublier » qu'elle n'est pas interne. Il faut *abstraire* la forme de l'opération de son contexte concret (les aires et volumes).

Considérons, en guise de deuxième exemple, les rapports entre grandeurs, avec tous les phénomènes associés aux rapports et aux proportions. À l'intérieur de chaque domaine de grandeurs (c'est-à-dire soit les objets allongés, soit les temps, soit les objets pesants...), on trouve un rapport entre deux grandeurs quelconques, et l'on peut former librement des proportions entre grandeurs. Par contre, il n'y a pas de rapport entre deux grandeurs d'espèces différentes, et si l'on veut former une proportion entre quatre grandeurs, il faut que les deux premières soient de la même espèce, et les deux dernières aussi.

Cette circonstance empêche d'échanger les termes moyens dans une proportion où sont engagées des grandeurs de deux espèces distinctes. Corrélativement, car c'est un autre aspect du même phénomène, elle empêche l'existence d'un rapport externe dans une application linéaire d'un domaine de grandeurs dans un autre différent.

Pourtant, les nombres rationnels (et puis les réels) qui vont à terme remplacer les grandeurs, devront bien surmonter ces interdits. Au bout du compte, il faudra par le biais des nombres, donner existence à des rapports de grandeurs d'espèces différentes comme on en voit dans les vitesses, les densités, et bien d'autres. Les incompatibilités de départ ne seront vaincues qu'au prix de difficultés supplémentaires, en l'occurrence celles qui naissent du choix a priori arbitraire des unités de mesure et de la restriction à un système d'unités cohérent.

Ces deux exemples auront sans doute permis au lecteur de comprendre mieux ce que nous avons apppelé structures partielles contradictoires. Ces contradictions sont fondamentales, elles tiennent à la nature des choses, elles font partie de la relation intime de l'homme avec la réalité. À travers les opérations de fractionnement et de mesure, l'homme cherche à mettre en relation les grandeurs et les nombres. Les nombres naturels sont là, au départ, avec leurs propriétés opératoires. Tels quels, ils servent déjà à opérer sur les grandeurs et à les mesurer. Mais viennent ensuite les opérateurs de fractionnement et les mesures fractionnaires. L'homme cherche à étendre à ces objets nouveaux les propriétés opératoires des nombres naturels. Mais cela ne va pas sans peine, sans contradictions, sans quelques ajustements cruciaux. Pour constituer les rationnels en structure abstraite, il faut oublier les connotations concrètes de chaque structure partielle pour n'en retenir que les propriétés formelles, il faut *abstraire*.

Une conclusion s'impose : les rationnels ne sont pas tout formés dans la nature. Il ne suffit pas d'observer celle-ci, fut-ce minutieusement, pour les y découvrir. Les rationnels ne sont pas naturels, il sont artificiels, il sont le résultat d'une construction de l'esprit humain.

Ce n'est d'ailleurs pas par hasard que trois mathématiciens ont affirmé en écho répété à travers le XIXe siècle :

- Le nombre est un pur produit de notre esprit (Gauss) ;

- Dieu fit le nombre entier, le reste est l'œuvre de l'homme (Kronecker) ;

- Les nombres négatifs et fractionnaires ont été créés par l'esprit humain (Dedekind).

Et maintenant que conclure de là sur le plan de l'apprentissage et de l'enseignement ? Il nous semble intéressant d'aborder franchement dans les classes ce que nous avons appelé ci-dessus les contradictions de la pensée commune dans sa première organisation. Ces contradictions vaincues donnent son plein sens à la théorie abstraite et seule leur connaissance peut éclairer les limites d'applicabilité de celles-ci aux situations particulières.

Si l'on accepte cette conclusion, deux de ses conséquences doivent être envisagées.

La première est qu'il faut renoncer à l'ambition généreuse des promoteurs des mathématiques modernes d'enseigner d'emblée aux élèves des connaissances définitives. Papy (1972) écrivait : « il y a moyen d'aller directement de la connaissance commune aux structures et au point de vue moderne ». On peut croire au contraire que sur le chemin qui conduit aux grandes structures mathématiques se trouvent beaucoup d'obstacles significatifs qu'il vaut la peine d'affronter et de ranger dans sa mémoire.

La seconde est que, puisque les rationnels ne sont pas « dans la nature », ne sont préfigurés dans la pensée commune que par morceaux incompatibles, il faut renoncer à une pratique assez fréquente dans l'enseignement : présenter comme ayant une portée générale un modèle particulier d'un concept abstrait.

Par exemple, on pensera avoir montré vraiment ce qu'est $\frac{3}{4}$ en identifiant cette fraction aux trois quarts d'un tout (une tarte, un bâton, ...). On oublie en ce faisant que $\frac{3}{4}$ apparaît aussi lorsqu'on partage 3 tartes entre 4 amis. On oublie (ou peut-être, pour ne pas perturber les enfants, on s'efforce de le camoufler...) le fait qu'on ne peut pas multiplier deux fractions concrètes de ce type : qui a jamais pu multiplier un morceau de tarte par un morceau de tarte ? On pourrait développer cet exemple et en donner beaucoup d'autres. Les contradictions forment obstacle à la construction des rationnels abstraits, mais on peut croire que ces obstacles sont bien plus pernicieux lorsqu'on les ignore. Car alors les élèves passent par des situations embarrassantes, avec en plus le malaise de ne pas comprendre ce qui leur arrive et le risque de conclure que les mathématiques sont une science qui prend les libertés les plus étranges avec la réalité, en somme une science arbitraire.

RÉFÉRENCES

Freudenthal, H. (1983). *Didactical phenomenology of mathematical structures*, Dordrecht, The Netherlands: Reidel.

Klein, F. (1908). *Elementarmathematik vom höheren Standpunkte aus* (vol. 1, 4ᵉ éd., 1933). Berlin: Springer.

Lebesgue, H. (1975). *La mesure des grandeurs* (nouvelle édition). Paris: Blanchard.

Papy, G. (1970). *Mathématique moderne 2*. Bruxelles: Didier.

Papy, G. (1972) *Mathématique moderne 3*, Bruxelles: Didier.

Rouche, N. (1992a). *Le sens de la mesure: des grandeurs aux nombres rationnels*. Bruxelles: Didier-Hatier.

Rouche, N. (1992b). Des grandeurs aux nombres rationnels. In *Actes du Colloque inter-IREM de Géométrie*, IREM de Limoges.

Steiner, H.G. (1969). Magnitudes and rational numbers, a didactical analysis. In *Educational Studies in Mathematics, 2*(2/3), 371-392.

MATHEMATICS IS A LANGUAGE

Fritz Schweiger

Universität Salzburg, Austria

MATHEMATICS AND LANGUAGE

Recent years have seen considerable interest in the relationship between language and mathematics. It is not possible to quote a representative sample of the relevant literature, but some cornerstones to be mentioned are the *Nairobi Report* (1974), the *Seminar-cum-Workshop* (1984), reports presented at previous International Congresses on Mathematical Education (especially ICME-4, 1980), and the recent publication, *Language issues in learning and teaching mathematics* (Davis & Hunting, 1990).

I will mention mathematical linguistics first: the attempt to apply mathematical methods to linguistic problems. Besides being of theoretical interest, this has been an important issue in machine translation, artificial intelligence, and so on. Investigations in syntax and semantics, which use the theory of formal languages and automata theory and programming languages (such as BASIC, PASCAL, LOGO, C, ...), can be seen as another bridge to mathematics. Surprisingly the findings of mathematical linguistics have not had much impact on mathematical education.

Next the language of mathematics, the nowadays elaborated special language in which mathematical ideas, theories, and algorithms are expressed, comes to mind. This language has developed a special written form which has turned out to be more influential than spoken mathematical language.

Another issue is teaching mathematics in a language which for the learner is a first or second (or even third) language, especially in the case of ethnic minorities and indigenous groups. Mathematics in its written form seems to be only partially dependent on the (natural) language in which it is expressed. Plane figures like □, ○, △, ... can be understood worldwide.

297

The classical diagrams illustrating Pythagoras' theorem can be understood in the context of a textbook written in Japanese or German, Arabic or Tamil. This situation is somewhat similar to the almost universality of the pictorial codes used in airports and railway stations.

At an advanced level (when memory has already stored suitable environments) a lot of meaning can be communicated "language-free" (without the need to know the words):

$$\frac{d\sin x}{dx} = \cos x, \quad \int_{\delta A}\omega = \int_{\delta A}d\omega$$

Anyone who has given a lecture in a foreign language knows the uneasy feeling when one is writing down some symbols but is unable to find the proper words. Expressing symbolic statements in oral language has an intrinsic complexity (which is comparable to the complexity experienced when one has to generate such a formula with a text editor on a computer). In the mother tongue one is not aware of this point but in a foreign language one feels it. Therefore it seems reasonable to ask: Is there a connection between learning mathematics and learning a foreign language? One probable difference comes to mind: Learning a second language seems to be closer to the acquisition of a first language and may be influenced by the experience of first language acquisition.

Teaching and learning are parts of the general problem of mathematics and communication. Although language clearly plays a crucial role in all problems related to communication skills, classroom communication and reading mathematical texts, in considering mathematics I have to omit the important areas of research which center on social or psychological aspects. My point of view will be basically that of communicating through mathematics, that is, the use of mathematics as a tool of communication.

MATHEMATICS IS A LANGUAGE

Metaphorical concepts provide us with a partial understanding and hide some other aspects. Therefore "Mathematics is a language" may be seen as a structural metaphor in the sense of Lakoff and Johnson (1980). Their definition states that one concept is metaphorically structured in terms of another. It is easy to find several quotations which express this idea. Mason (1985) says: "Algebra is firstly a language—a way of saying and communicating." Clearly in this quotation "algebra" may be replaced by "mathematics".

Also well known is Galileo Galilei's view:

La filosofia è scritta in questo grandissimo libro che continuamente ci sta aperto innanzi a gli occhi (io dico l'universo), ma non si può intendere se prima non s'impara a intender la lingua, e conoscer i caratteri, ne' quali è scritto. Egli è scritto in lingua matematica, e i caratteri son triangoli, cerchi, ed altre figure geometriche, ... (Galilei, 1623, p. 631). [*Philosophy is written in this grand book–I mean universe–which stands continuously open to our gaze, but it cannot be understood unless one first learns to comprehend the language in which it is written. It is written in the language of mathematics, and its characters are triangles, circles and other geometrical figures, ...*]

To put it in different terms: Galilei considers mathematics to be the way of communicating with nature. Since the days of Galilei the continuing interplay between observations, experiments, and theoretical models which are formulated in mathematical terms has not exhausted its usefulness. One might add: To some extent, mathematics is the language we use in communicating about nature.

What is mathematics?

The statement "Mathematics is a language" invariably provokes two questions: What is mathematics? What is language? Neither question can be answered easily. I can assume that every mathematician, every mathematics educator, and every mathematics teacher has his or her own picture of mathematics. All these individual pictures obviously must have something in common otherwise communication about mathematics would be impossible. It is a challenge for education to provide a common core of mathematical ideas which make it possible to appreciate the role of mathematics in our society and culture.

I will take the broad view of mathematics as emphasized in the recent investigations called "ethnomathematics": Mathematics is a basic competence of mankind. It starts with a whole range of abilities which some educators would call "pre-mathematical": counting and ordering, recognition of patterns and symmetries, generation of patterns and structures, use of recursive procedures (which is closely related to counting) and algorithms (repeated actions to achieve some goals), and the construction of models and their use. As far as we know, in all human cultures, back to the early Stone Age, we find traces of these abilities. There have been some statements that certain tribal communities lack an elaborated system of number words but closer investigation has shown that the matter is in fact more complicated: the skill of recursive procedures is present, as Watson (1990) has emphasized recently in the case of Australian aboriginal cultures. She refers to the *gurrutu* system of classification used in the Yolngu communities. And there is no doubt that geometry has accompanied humanity since its beginnings. Clearly this has something to do with a sense of beauty as well as being rooted in the intrinsic features of arts and crafts, like making weapons, baskets and shelters.

Let's mention logic! Logical thinking seems to be a syntactical abstraction of causal or temporal relations. Any myth tells us something about the origin of certain peculiarities of our life: why there are both men and women, why we must face death, what are the origins of diseases, sin and evil. These narratives may have been told to help mankind to cope with an environment both friendly and hostile. Consider statements involving temporal chaining, such as: If the snow melts, then spring will come and then hunting will be easier, or some fish will show up, or fruit trees will blossom, and so on. The rhythms of sunrise and sunset, shorter and longer days, full and new moon were observed. Calendars were born. Probably the idea of applying the syntax of causal and temporal chaining to arithmetic and geometry was the origin of mathematics as we know it. Logical thinking has been indispensable for the development of mathematics. In return mathematics has been applied to logic, giving birth to a new branch of mathematics: mathematical logic.

Mathematics is present at various levels and in different environments. So is language. Language is a continuum, from baby talk to elaborated speech, and includes novels and poetry as well as scientific articles. A conversation in a cafeteria has something in common with a drama by Shakespeare.

What is language?

If I were writing this paper in French I would have a problem in translating its title.

"Les mathématiques sont-elles un langage ou une langue?" In French "langue" means the idiom of a group of people like English, French, or Inuktitut. One also says "langue maternelle" for "mother tongue" (which is not so strange because "langue" originally means "tongue", an important part of our speech organ). Clearly mathematics is not a language like English, French, or Inuktitut. One can convey and express mathematical ideas in these languages. The same mathematical content can be encoded in different languages with the helpful addition of diagrams and symbols.

One may replace the symbols as long as the decoder knows or can guess the encoding rules: The statement

$$\frac{d\sin x}{dx} = \cos x$$

may also written as

$$\sin' y = \cos y$$

The conventionality of signs is quite clear, but there are practical and educational limits to their proliferation. Communication needs memory capacity. The need to change symbols is a burden. "Good" symbolism may even reveal striking similarities. Some of these similarities can nowadays only be recovered by historical or linguistic considerations. Capital Greek ∑ (sigma) is related to *sum*, capital Greek Π (pi) is reminiscent of *product*. The integral sign ∫ is a fossilized form of an S for *sum*, the operator ∂ is an old hand-written *d*, standing for *derivation*. This is similar to the use of letters in handling the menu of a computer. Very often C stands for "copy", F for "format", and so on. There has always been a claim that mathematical symbols are the last stage of a triad: rhetorical (expression in vernacular)—syncopated (use of abbreviations)—symbolistic (use of symbols). The evolution of mathematical symbolism is a fascinating topic of its own.

In French "langue" also means a particular mode of expression, as one speaks of the "language of poets" ("la langue des poètes"). In the same sense, mathematics is obviously the language of mathematicians, and at least part of the language of physicists, engineers, and others.

The other French word, "langage", also expresses a variety of meanings. Basically "langage" can be described as the ability of mankind to express ideas and to communicate. Bolinger and Sears (1981) stress the importance of language this way: "Whatever success a culture has is largely due to the understanding and cooperation that language makes possible." Langacker (1967) says, "Most human knowledge and culture is stored and transmitted in language."

One may ask about the relationship between "langue" and "langage". Following Martinet (1970) one can say: Any language, in the sense of "langue", is an expression of language, in the sense of "langage". Any (natural) language like English, French, or Inuktitut is a tool of communication, a special encoding of the human competence for expressing ideas, feelings, and thoughts. Therefore, basically, any (natural) language serves the same purpose. To some extent, switching from one code to another code, namely translation, is always possible.

Natural languages can be very different and have changed dramatically throughout history. Language as a basic human competence has not changed so much. Mathematics can be seen as a powerful extension and refinement of this competence.

SOUNDS, WORDS, SENTENCES, AND MEANINGS

Sounds, letters, and symbols

Linguistics traditionally distinguishes different levels of language activity: phonology, lexicon (words), syntax, and semantics.

Obviously, in its oral form, mathematics has not added new sounds to languages generally. In linguistics it is generally accepted that sounds are the basic units of any natural language. This priority does not change if one uses spoken language to express mathematical ideas, but the phonetic system of any language will not give insight into the specific role of mathematics.

It is entirely different if we look at mathematics in its written form. Here, one basic property of the surface structure of natural languages can be questioned, namely their linearity. Speech sounds and words follow in a linear order due to their sequential realization in time. This principle is well observed in the more elaborated writing systems: alphabetic, syllabic or ideographic. Clearly there are some exceptions: in some Indian scripts like Devanagari (which runs from left to right) the sequence *ki* is written *i* + *ka*, but this can be seen as a special cluster. Mathematical texts normally follow the linearity of their contextual environment, but sometimes the order of reading or writing is just conventional and basically *not* linear, as in complex formulas and diagrams:

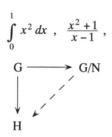

$$\int_0^1 x^2\, dx \ , \ \ \frac{x^2+1}{x-1} \ ,$$

The order of operators is conventional: compare x^2 and sin x! If one uses a pocket calculator, in both cases one normally has to enter x first and then to press the appropriate function key. A top-down strategy would start with the functions "square" or "sine" first and then enter the argument x.

The most obvious fact is that mathematics has introduced a symbolic notation (mostly on the basis of a Western heritage). It uses the letters of the Roman alphabet $a,b,c, \ldots , x,y,z$, in such a way that for the layman the use of letters has become almost synonymous with mathematics. Clearly other fonts (gothic, script, and so on) are often used freely (but are pronounced differently). Mathematics also uses Greek letters α, β, γ, ... and at least one Hebrew letter $\aleph$ (aleph) (for the cardinality of countable sets) and one Cyrillic letter Ш (for the Shafareviz group in algebraic number theory). But there are also subscripts, superscripts, and diacritics like ~, ', ⁻, and *. Furthermore think of $\partial, \int, \cup, \cap, \sqrt{\ }, \ldots$! The knowledge of a certain number of these symbols and their correct contextual interpretation is necessary to appreciate the communicative power of mathematics. The use of symbols is nowadays a characteristic of mathematical texts. The statement of Pythagoras' theorem in classical Greek contains fewer symbols than the statement of the same theorem in a modern textbook:

Εν τοις ορθογωνιοις τριγωνοις το απο της την ορθην γωνιαν υποτεινουσης πλευρας τετραγωνον ισον εστι τοις απο των την ορθην γωνιαν περιεχουσων πλευρων τετραγωνοις. Εστω τριγωνον ορυογωνιον το ΑΒΓ ορθην εχον την υπο ΒΑΓ γωνιαν λεγω οτι το απο της ΒΓ τετραγωνον ισον εστι τοις απο των ΒΑ, ΑΓ τετραγωνοις. [Liber I, 47. Quotation from *Euclidis Elementa* (Eukleides, 1969)].

It is especially interesting that the familiar form $a^2 + b^2 = c^2$ is not given. But in this more compact version one has to know the meaning of the letters a, b, and c in this context as well as the fact that a^2 stands for $a \cdot a$ Definitions are condensed to a single letter or to a small string of letters and their combinations are used to create new meanings, which has serious implications for the use of short term and long term memory.

A comparison with musical notation comes to mind. Musical notes can be read and understood (linearity also breaks down here), but to get the full picture—active decoding by playing a passage on the piano, for example—is very often necessary. Understanding derived from the pictorial representation very often needs active reinvention in both music and mathematics. Mathematics may be seen to be easier in this respect. One may proceed "allegro" or "andante" according to ability. Teachers should give students more freedom in this respect.

Words

There is no doubt that mathematics has developed a special vocabulary of its own. One can distinguish the following basic processes:

- The use of words with a specialized meaning, different from their meaning in everyday language : vector, angle, set, function ...

- The use of words in a metaphoric sense: space, collection, normal, regular ...

- Words arrived at by translating words from other languages: "field" (French "champ").

Word building processes:

- Compounds:

type A: Abelian group (An Abelian group is a special type of group.), complete metric space (A complete metric space is a special type of metric space.)

type B: complex number (There is no received definition of number such that complex number is a special type of number. Complex number obviously is a structural metaphor in the sense of Lakoff and Johnson (1980). Historically complex numbers were seen as new numbers. The notion of number provides a partial understanding only.), metric space, vector space.

- Derivations: to rectify, to zornify (i.e., to apply Zorn's lemma).

- Neologisms: homomorphism, homeomorphism, morphism (!).

There are also prefixes and suffixes like co- and contra- or hyper-. The word "million" is derived from Italian "miglione", a great thousand by the use of the magnifying suffix "one". A reanalysis then led to billion, trillion, etc. A recent formation is fractal, derived from fractional: "broken"!

Clearly my comments here are restricted mainly to English. Similar observations could be made for French, Italian, Spanish, or other languages. One wonders how languages of quite different types, such as Arabic, Japanese, or Hindi, deal with the growing amount of mathematical vocabulary (See e.g., Seminar-cum-Workshop, 1984). Outsiders may think that all mathematical terms are coined as descriptive terms like injective, or coproduct (from product). But very often, at least at the time when these words were coined, emotions or affects or humor played a role: the classification of finite simple groups includes a group called a "monster" and another one is called "baby monster". Transcendental numbers had at least some metaphysical flavor. The term "square root" is a metaphor from botany. The words "square" and "cube" for a^2 and a^3 reflect the use of geometric intuition in ancient mathematics. Clearly this belongs more to semantics than to (formal) derivational processes.

Syntax

At first glance it seems there should be no special syntax of mathematics since a mathematics book written in Japanese belongs to the corpus of Japanese texts. A speech delivered in French clearly uses the devices of French syntax, and so on. A second look reveals that mathematical texts (more than oral utterances dealing with mathematics) employ a restricted syntax. Certain sentence types prevail in mathematical texts: equational statements or conditional chains. It has been observed that nominalizations and the passive voice are used much more than in everyday language (See e.g., Laborde, 1990). At least in the Western European languages the subjunctive mood is employed frequently: "Let us assume ... ℝ denote the field of rational numbers ... G be an Abelian group ... ". Mathematical texts are the literature of mathematics. English texts belong to English language in so far as they say something about the structure of the English language! A third look shows that mathematics has already developed some syntactical structures of its own. The syntagma $a + b = c$ is well formed but $ab + c =$ is not well formed (as a complete sentence in every day arithmetic). The formula

$$\sum_{k=1}^{\infty} \frac{1}{k^2} = \frac{\pi^2}{6}$$

is well formed (and correct).

The formula

$$\sum_{k=1}^{\infty} \frac{1}{j^2} = \frac{\pi^2}{6}$$

is less well formed. A basic rule of mathematical syntax is violated, namely the anaphoric use of the same letter, although as in ordinary language some errors do not impede the communicative power.

Finally, mathematical language has not developed word classes (such as nouns, verbs, adjectives ...) of its own with the notable exception of number words and quantifiers that are fundamental to mathematics. It is worth mentioning that these word classes display remarkable syntactical diversity in the languages of the world. Number words sometimes behave like adjectives, but also like nouns. In a number of languages, mainly found in Asia, the choice of number words depends on the noun to be quantified. There are no grammatical categories (like person, gender, number, tense, mood, or aspect) which are specific to mathematics. Again mathematical texts use the devices given by the "matrix language". It is well known that the different organization of natural languages causes considerable problems in understanding mathematical texts which may also be of importance for teaching and learning (e.g., devices for quantification or negation).

Semantics

The semantics of mathematics is what makes mathematics a powerful language. The dialogue with nature, as Galilei metaphorically says, is only possible if mathematical language transports meaning. The symbols and words may be exchangeable and may vary considerably from language to language (according to the language in which a mathematical text is written or spoken).

The communicative power lies in the semantics. An expression like $z = xy$ can communicate an infinite set of meanings. Basically it can be interpreted as follows: The quantity z depends linearly on both the quantities x and y. It is the prototype of a bilinear map. Very often substitution of special symbols, depending on the context, is used:

$$U = iR, \quad s = ct, \quad T = pV, \quad \ldots$$

The exponential function $t \mapsto e^{-\lambda t}$ is the vehicle of communication about various problems of decay (radioactivity, atmospheric pressure, dampening ...). For measurements mathematics provides prototypes: $\mathbb{Z}$, discrete and linear; $\mathbb{Z}$ mod m (equivalently: any cyclic group of order m), discrete and cyclic; $\mathbb{R}$, continuous and linear; S^1 (the unit circle), continuous and cyclic. The real line $\mathbb{R}$ is used as the mathematical model for time which flows from $-\infty$ to $+\infty$. Everyday language structures time as an object which moves in the opposite direction: the coming weeks, the preceding years, time has passed ... .

Shapes are classified roughly as triangles, squares, rectangles ... in the plane, as parallelepipeds, pyramids, cylinders, cones, spheres ... in space.

Recently the dialect of fractals was added to the mathematical toolkit. I am not sure if it is Nature's preferred dialect, as Voss (1988) claims since coming generations may recognize other dialects which are still unknown to us.

Bolinger and Sears (1981) characterize the linguistic aspects of mathematics as follows:

> Another specialized language is mathematics ... Its specialty is making precise the way we deal with things in space—amorphous space, where we group things together by addition and multiplication, separate them by subtraction and division, and compare them for equality and inequality, and structured space, where we locate them in geometrical ways. Mathematics is less language-dependent than logic is; in fact, it is an alternate route to a special part of the real world.

Centuries of research have enriched the meaning of mathematical concepts. The classification of crystallographic groups reveals facts about the possible arrangements of molecules; the existence and uniqueness theorems for functional equations and differential equations govern the outcome of models. More or less any application of mathematics is based on the meaningfulness of mathematical concepts. There has been some argument that not only mathematical language, but mathematics itself, has been strongly influenced by the structure of Indo-European languages. Especially with a side view on logic and foundations it was said "If Aristotle had spoken Chinese or Dakota, his logic and his categories would have been different." (Quoted in Bolinger & Sears, 1981, p. 139). Clearly there is some truth in such a statement; but, on the other hand, mathematics seems to be built on a bundle of human abilities which are universal. Every culture has contributed, to some extent, to the variety of mathematically-based arts and crafts. This has been documented by the recent emphasis on ethnomathematics and ethnogeometry. Furthermore linguistic research has hinted at the existence of language universals, which is not just an empirical fact but seems to point at deeper rooted structures of linguistic competence.

306

ACQUISITION OF MATHEMATICS AND LANGUAGE

When I say, "Mathematics is a language", I am considering language as an instrument of communication. Mathematics is an extension of the communicative power of any natural language like English, French, Cree or Tamil. The acquisition of writing, the knowledge of literature, and learning a foreign language are important extensions too.

The capacity for acquiring a language as a first language is in fact remarkable. It has often been observed that adults are not capable of learning a language in the natural, spontaneous way that children do. If one keeps in mind the complexity of the grammars of natural languages this is really astonishing. It seems clear that mathematics is not learned in the way children acquire their mother tongue. But wait! This is not entirely true. The basic competencies, like counting, ordering, recognizing patterns and structures, the use of recursive processes, are acquired in a similar way. We know from language acquisition that linguistic input is necessary for children to build up their own competence. Such an input is clearly also crucial for counting, ordering, designing, recognition of patterns, and so on. Writing and reading are normally taught in a controlled way and are seen nowadays as an obvious extension of linguistic capacity. The interesting question about the extent to which "natural" mathematical learning is possible is discussed in Robinson (1990).

Foreign languages can be learned in two ways: in a "natural" way or by controlled instruction. In both cases, age is very often claimed to be a crucial factor: learning from simple exposure seems to be more successful for young children only. For the other age groups controlled instruction works much better. A critical account of the evidence supporting or questioning an age factor in language acquisition is given in Singleton (1989). Obviously the situation for learning mathematics can be compared with learning how to read and write, with learning a musical instrument, or with learning a foreign language. It is much easier to build up mathematical competence at an early age.

Current linguistic theories claim that language acquisition can be described as setting parameters in a language module (Roeper, 1988). So, learning a second language essentially means resetting the parameters (Flynn, 1988). I would hypothesize the existence of a mathematics module which interacts with the language module. Metaphorically speaking, it is a device which enables the growing learner to decode and encode mathematical messages. I do not know of any empirical investigations into a fact which I have observed in university studies: anyone who is interested to begin studying arts or humanities in his or her older years can successfully do so. The only senior citizens I have met who were students of mathematics were former engineers or mathematics teachers, which means they were already exposed to mathematical subject matter in their youth. People who have successfully mastered a second language normally do quite well learning a third or even a fourth language. (In the framework of the linguistic theories mentioned before, resetting parameters is easier.) People who play a musical instrument very easily adapt to an additional instrument. I have the feeling that there are devices that are better installed at early ages: an interpreter for foreign languages, a driver for musical performance, and last, but not least, an interpreter for mathematics. (I do not claim that human thinking is closely related to the way a computer works, but the metalanguage I use uses ideas from computers as metaphors.) Clearly it should be possible for highly motivated students to master mathematics at older ages too.

This hypothesis has an immediate consequence for mathematical education. Mathematics is a basic educational component, not only due to its importance for understanding and controlling our culture, but because a lack of mathematical education could be a serious hindrance to continuing tertiary education in natural sciences, or to entering a profession which needs mathematics.

REFERENCES

Bolinger, D., & Sears, D.A. (1981). *Aspects of language*. New York.

Davis, G., & Hunting, R.P. (Eds.) (1990). *Language issues in learning and teaching mathematics*. La Trobe University: Institute of Mathematics Education.

Eukleides (1969). *Euclidis Elementa. Vol. I, Libri I-IV cum appendicibus Post I.L.* Heiberg edidit E.S. Stamatis. Leipzig: B.G. Teubner Verlagsgesellschaft.

Flynn, S. (1988). Second language acquisition and grammatical theory. In F. J. Newmeyer (Ed.), *Linguistics: The Cambridge Survey* (Vol. 2, pp. 53-73). Linguistic theory: Extensions and implications. Cambridge, UK: Cambridge University Press.

Galilei, G. (1623). Il saggiatore. In *Opere di Galileo Galilei a cura di Franz Brunetti*, Volume Primo. Torino: Unione Tipografico-Editrice Torinese 1964.

Laborde, C. (1990). The role of language in the teaching and learning of mathematics. *Proceedings of the Second Bratislava International Symposium on Mathematics Education* (pp. 22-36). Bratislava.

Lakoff, G., & Johnson, M. (1980). *Metaphors we live by*. Chicago: The University of Chicago Press.

Langacker, R.W. (1967). *Language and its structure*. New York: Harcourt Brace Jovanovich, Inc.

Martinet, A. (1970). *Éléments de linguistique générale*. Paris: Armand Colin.

Mason, J.H. (1985). *Routes to/Roots of algebra*. Milton Keynes: Open University Press.

Nairobi Report (1974). *Interactions between linguistics and mathematical education.* (Final Report) Symposium sponsored by UNESCO, CEDO, and ICMI Nairobi, Kenya, September 1-11, UNESCO: ED-74/CONF, 808.

Robinson, I. (1990). Mathematics and language: The experiences of EMIC and key group. In I. Robinson (Ed.), *Language issues in learning and teaching mathematics* (pp. 84-99). La Trobe University: Institute of Mathematics Education.

Roeper, T. (1988). Grammatical principles of first language acquisition: Theory and evidence. In F.J. Newmeyer (Ed.), *Linguistics: The Cambridge survey* (Vol. 2, pp. 35-52). Linguistic theory: Extensions and implications. Cambridge, UK: Cambridge University Press.

Seminar-cum-Workshop. (1984). *Proceedings of Seminar-cum-Workshop on mathematical linguistics, mathematical language, and interaction with mathematical education* (pp. 16-21). Calcutta. Paris: UNESCO.

Singleton, D. (1989). *Language acquisition: The age factor.* Clevedon-Philadelphia: Multilingual Matters Ltd.

Voss, R.F. (1988). Fractals in nature: From characterization to simulation. In H.-O. Peitgen & D. Saupe (Eds.), *The science of fractal image.* New York: Springer-Verlag.

Watson, H. (1990). The Ganma Project: Research in mathematics education by the Yolngu community in the schools of Laynhapuy (N.E. Arnhemland). In *Language issues in learning and teaching mathematics* (pp. 33-50). La Trobe University: Institute of Mathematics Education.

Zweng, M. (Ed.) (1980). *Proceedings of the Fourth International Congress on Mathematical Education*, ICME. Boston: Birkäuser.

MATHEMATICAL THINKING AND REASONING FOR ALL STUDENTS: MOVING FROM RHETORIC TO REALITY

Edward A. Silver

University of Pittsburgh, United States of America

The theme of "mathematics for all students" is not a new one. It has its roots in compulsory education movements in many countries over 100 years ago, and the writings of Dewey in the early part of the twentieth century were influential internationally in focusing attention on universal access to quality education (Ernest, 1991). Despite indications of historical interest in the teaching of mathematics to all students, and despite the fact that mathematics is often viewed favorably by a large portion of society in the recreational contexts of games and puzzles (de Guzmán, 1990; Howson & Kahane, 1990), even a cursory review of the history of mathematics education reveals that most students have definitely not found mathematics to be a safe haven in their educational world. Throughout the world, mathematics is the school subject most likely to be taught and learned poorly. Although mathematics is taught for extensive periods of time in formal schooling, it is often taught as if the primary instructional goal were to teach students to dislike it and to fail rather than to grow in affection and continue to pursue it.

Conventional instructional practices in mathematics have been so effective in "weeding out" those who are not exceptionally mathematically talented that too few students reach the end of the "pipeline" and enter mathematical or scientific careers in many countries. In the United States, this trend—which is dysfunctional for the growth of the academic discipline of mathematics—has led in recent years to a serious re-examination of mathematics education (National Research Council, 1989). As a result, there is currently a great deal of reform rhetoric built around the possibility that new forms of instruction can be invented to transform the current situation, in which we have "mathematics for the few", into a new one in which we have "mathematics for all."

In general, previous attempts to provide universal access to mathematics have resulted in the creation of two forms of mathematics education: one for social and economic élites, emphasizing thinking, reasoning, and higher forms of mathematical content, and another for the rest of society, emphasizing basic computation (Resnick, 1987). More recent discussions of mathematics for all students (Boero, 1989; Freudenthal, 1991) have tended to stress the need for all students to experience the more thoughtful aspects of mathematics (e.g., reflective thinking, reasoning, problem solving), and it is this version that is at the heart of this paper. The major goal of this paper is to begin the process of connecting the rhetoric of "mathematics for all" to unifying themes, to samples of promising practice, and to theoretical formulations that may help advance our thinking as we continue school reform efforts. The paper begins with a fairly brief review of the current situation in the United States with respect to mathematical performance and participation. Next a vision is sketched of some forms of instructional practice that hold promise as purveyors of the new goals for mathematical thinking and reasoning for all students. Finally, the implications for teacher development are considered. The themes of communication, culture, and community are stressed throughout as an argument is made for the building of communities of collaborative, reflective practice both for students and for teachers.

MATHEMATICAL THINKING AND REASONING FOR ALL STUDENTS: THE CURRENT RHETORIC AND REALITY IN THE UNITED STATES

Mathematics education in the United States finds itself in a state of crisis related both to a low rate of student participation and to inadequate student performance in mathematics. With respect to participation, data available from recent national mathematics assessments (Dossey, Mullis, Lindquist, & Chambers, 1988; Mullis, Dossey, Owen, & Phillips, 1991) indicate that only nine of every one hundred graduating high school students completes four years of college preparatory mathematics. With respect to mathematics performance, results of national and international assessments (e.g., NAEP, SIMS, IAEP) provide sobering statistics regarding the impoverished state of American students' mathematical proficiency, especially with respect to complex tasks and problem solving.

For those the educational system now serves least well, especially females, the poor, and members of ethnic and language minority groups, the situation is considerably worse.[1] For example, in urban schools serving

---

[1]   For a more complete discussion of mathematics education reform in the United States as it relates to equity issues see Secada (1991) and Silver, Smith, and Nelson (1993).

economically disadvantaged communities, four of five students take no mathematics beyond the minimum required for graduation. Further, NAEP data indicate that less than half the students in urban schools take any mathematics beyond one year of algebra, and one in five do not study algebra at all. As far as performance is concerned, white males and some white females from affluent families are the most likely to perform at high levels in mathematics, while the vast majority of students are achieving at levels substantially below international standards. Although mathematics achievement differences between majority and minority students have decreased during the past two decades (Mullis, Owen, & Phillips, 1990), substantial gaps still remain.

Many worry that the gaps in participation and achievement between majority and minority segments of society pose a serious threat to the economic and social well-being of the United States. This warning was sounded by the National Research Council in *Everybody counts*, a report to the nation on the state of mathematics education:

> Because mathematics holds the key to leadership in our information-based society, the widening gap between those who are mathematically literate and those who are not coincides, to a frightening degree, with racial and economic categories. We are at risk of becoming a divided nation in which knowledge of mathematics supports a productive, technologically powerful élite while a dependent, semiliterate majority, disproportionately Hispanic and Black, find economic and political power beyond reach. Unless corrected, innumeracy and illiteracy will drive America apart. (1989, p. 14)

There is a compelling need to improve mathematics course enrollment and mathematics achievement for all American students, with special attention to students in poor communities, and at all grade levels, since the trajectory for high school participation and performance in mathematics is set well before ninth grade (Oakes, 1990).

Although recently promulgated in the United States as a national education goal, increasing mathematics participation and improving the quality of performance of all American students is a formidable challenge. Adding to the challenge is the need to address the matters of participation and performance in a manner consistent with the spirit of the more general mathematics education reform efforts, which have been stimulated by NCTM's publication of the *Curriculum and evaluation standards for school mathematics* (1989) and the *Professional standards for teaching mathematics* (1991). These reform-oriented reports paint a portrait of school mathematics with textures and hues that emphasize thinking, reasoning, problem solving, and communication rather than memorization and repetition. The complex challenge before us is to move forward with an agenda simultaneously aimed at achieving equity and access to good mathematics instruction, and reconceptualizing such instruction around mathematical thinking and reasoning rather than memory and imitation.

Some have argued that what is needed is a new form of education emphasizing higher forms of literacy for all students (e.g., Brown, 1991; Resnick, 1987). Such an education would ensure that students would not only be able to read, write, and perform basic arithmetic procedures, but also would know when and why to apply those procedures, would be able to make sense out of complicated situations, and would be able to develop strategies for formulating and then solving complex problems.

The complexity of providing high-literacy education for all students can be appreciated by considering some of the pernicious legacies of conventional school mathematics instruction. Consider, for example, reports by researchers (e.g., Resnick, 1988; Baranes, Perry, & Stigler, 1989; Schoenfeld, 1991) that many children come to see school mathematics as a domain which is disconnected from sense making and the world of everyday experience. One specific example of this dissociation comes from a series of studies that my colleagues and I have conducted over several years (Silver & Shapiro, 1993), in which we have examined children's difficulties in solving story problems involving division with remainders, such as the following problem that appeared on a national assessment and was successfully answered by only 24% of 13-year-old students: "An army bus holds 36 soldiers. If 1,128 soldiers are being bused to their training site, how many buses are needed?" (National Assessment of Educational Progress, 1983).

In one recent investigation (Silver, Shapiro, & Deutsch, in press), we asked students to answer a problem similar to the one asked by NAEP, and to provide an explanation for or an interpretation of their answer. We found that students' interpretations of their answers dealt more with technical mathematical concerns than with sense making. Thus, for example, many students were content to propose answers that involved a fraction of a bus, even though they knew that buses do not have fractional parts, because the technical process of computation produced such a fractional answer. The observation that most children divorced sense making from mathematical activity was clear not only from the answers they gave but also from the explanations they did not give. Reports from their teachers, who discussed the problem with children after they handed in their papers, suggested that some children appeared to be capable of more sense making than was evident in their written responses to questions, but that they did not see their "sensible" answers (e.g., arguments based on assuming that some travellers would be absent, or that people could be arranged to accommodate larger numbers on a bus, or that a mini-bus or van could be used as the "fractional part" of a full bus) as having any validity in the context of responding to a mathematical problem.

Student performance was clearly adversely affected by the dissociation of sense-making from school mathematics, which points to the need for more instructional attention to sense-making as a part of instruction, but the results of our investigation identified another issue that must also be addressed in order to improve student performance. Specifically, students had great difficulty in providing written explanations of their reasoning or justifications for their answers. Although some students may have been somewhat more capable of explaining their thinking and reasoning orally, the finding suggests the need for explanations, especially written explanations, to become a more prevalent feature of school mathematics instruction. Unless and until solution explanations and interpretations become a regular item on the menu of instructional activities in mathematics classrooms, it is unlikely that many students will spontaneously engage in such activity when it is appropriate to do so. And if students continue to dissociate thoughtfulness from the solution of problems, there can be little hope of substantially improving the poor mathematics performance of American students.

Another challenge to providing a high-level mathematics education to all students relates to the forms of instructional practice that currently dominate school mathematics. As many studies have suggested (e.g., Stodolsky, 1988), conventional mathematics instruction emphasizes students learning alone, producing stylized responses to narrowly prescribed questions for which there is a single answer, which is already known by the teacher and which can and will be validated only by teacher approval. At all educational levels, *drill-to-kill* or *assembly-line* instruction, consisting of repetitive drill and practice on basic computation and other routine procedures, has characterized school mathematics, especially in impoverished urban and rural schools. Although minority students have made achievement gains over the past two decades, the gains have generally come from improved performance on those portions of tests related to factual knowledge and basic calculation skills. Despite the positive trend in reducing intergroup performance differences, data regarding instructional practices suggests that students assigned to the lower tracks of many high schools (predominantly ethnic minority and poor students) tend to receive less actual mathematics instruction, less homework, and more drill and practice of low-level factual knowledge and computational skill than students assigned to middle and higher tracks (Oakes, 1985). Although these instructional practices may be sufficient to support the narrowing of performance differences on tasks requiring only basic factual knowledge or on routine computational skills, they are unlikely to lead to improved performance on more complex tasks requiring mathematical reasoning and problem solving.

An effective response to this current situation will require solid commitment to a revolutionary invention and implementation of new forms of educational practice—classrooms as communities of collaborative, reflective practice—in which students are challenged to think deeply about and to participate actively in engaging the mathematics they are learning. In such communities, students not only listen but also speak mathematics themselves—discussing observations, explanations, verifications, reasons, and generalizations. In such classrooms, students have opportunities to see, hear, debate, and evaluate mathematical explanations and justifications. The classroom becomes a place in which the emphasis is less on memorizing procedures and producing answers and more on analyzing, reasoning and becoming convinced. Surely, some exceptional examples of such classrooms exist today in the United States and in many other countries, but our challenge is to make these kinds of classrooms the norm rather than the exception.[2]

CLASSROOMS AS COMMUNITIES OF COLLABORATIVE, REFLECTIVE MATHEMATICAL PRACTICE

In the book, *Thinking through mathematics* (1990), Jeremy Kilpatrick, Beth Schlesinger, and I sketched a picture of mathematical classrooms as places rich in communication of and about mathematical ideas, places in which justification and verification were emphasized, and places in which teachers and students engaged in authentic forms of mathematical practice. In short, we attempted to portray a vision of mathematics classrooms as communities in which students were engaged in collaborative, mathematical practice—sometimes working collaboratively with each other in overt ways, and always working collaboratively with peers and with the teacher in a sense of shared community and shared norms for the practice of mathematical thinking and reasoning.

Agreeing with Bishop (1988), we took classrooms to be arenas in which students develop their own interpretation of mathematical culture and values, and we argued that if school mathematics is to become more authentic in its

---

[2] It is not assumed that the entire solution is contained in the educational proposals advanced in this paper. For example, there are closely related issues of knowledge ownership and cultural identification that are not addressed herein. Moreover, there are important, interrelated social and economic issues that must also be addressed in order to attain a truly equitable solution. For example, urban and poor schools are more likely to serve populations whose needs are not being met in the areas of health care, housing, transportation, and economic and personal security. As a consequence, poor urban students are less likely than their more affluent suburban counterparts to attend school regularly, to have available energy and attentiveness to focus squarely on an academic agenda, and to be sufficiently free of family and other responsibilities to study well at home. Although it is not possible to deal with these issues in this paper, their absence should not be construed as being due to ignorance of their importance.

relationship to the culture of mathematical practice, then mathematics education will need to pay more attention to the social nature of mathematical knowing, and that classrooms will need to be viewed as communities of mathematical thinkers. Rather than giving a myopic, naively romantic portrait of classrooms as places inhabited by little mathematicians, however, we tried to depict these classrooms simply as places where mathematics was connected in fundamental ways to important cognitive activities that have validity from a disciplinary perspective. As the title of the book implies, the central message was that mathematics classrooms should become places in which students regularly engaged in thinking. Since more than half of American students assert the belief that learning mathematics is mostly memorization (Mullis, Dossey, Owen, & Phillips, 1991), a shift in pedagogical emphasis more fundamentally toward thinking rather than memorizing would be quite revolutionary.

The view of mathematical knowing as a practice (not in the sense of drill-and-practice but rather in the sense of professional practice) is supported by recent trends in the philosophy of mathematics. In particular, Lakatos (1976) has portrayed a social process of debate to illustrate the nuances of mathematical discourse and culture, and Kitcher (1984) has developed an epistemology of mathematics based on the importance of shared meanings and not simply shared results. This work suggests the view, that to understand what mathematics is, one needs to understand the activities or practices of persons who are makers or users of mathematics. This deviates from the more conventional view that understanding mathematics is equivalent to understanding the structure of concepts and principles in the domain.

For many purposes, it has been and will continue to be valuable to think of mathematical knowing in terms of the acquisition of cognitive structures and procedures, but this view provides an incomplete account of mathematical experience, and it fails to provide an adequate theoretical base for new forms of pedagogy. The complementary view, emphasizing mathematical practice, clearly links to current calls for changes in pedagogy, which emphasize reasoning, problem solving, and communication, since it suggests that one should focus on the activities in which students engage in mathematics classrooms as well as the relationship between those activities and the characteristic practices within communities that make or use mathematics. Combining these views, the goal of school mathematics would be the development of a richly textured knowledge base, in which knowing is connected to important intellectual tasks and activities, rather than the communication of decontextualized and abstract skills and concepts.

Viewing mathematics as a practice as well as a knowledge domain challenges us to examine and accept social and cultural aspects of mathematics and mathematics education that have been largely ignored in the United

States.[3] The popular image of a mathematician is someone isolated in a paper-strewn study, but sociocultural perspectives suggest that mathematical knowledge is as much socially constructed as it is individually constructed, and that the practice of mathematics is fundamentally a social practice. In brief, the argument is that mathematics is created using socially appropriated tools and conventions and that ideas attain validity only when they are accepted within the mathematical community (Tymoczko, 1986). The controversy and disagreement over the acceptability of the computer-based solution for the famous, and long-unsolved "Four Color Problem" (Appel & Haken, 1977) provides a contemporary illustration of this process (Peterson, 1988). The history of mathematics teaches us that communication and social interaction have played fundamental roles in the development of mathematical ideas.

Although conventional mathematical pedagogy has generally ignored the role of communication in learning mathematics, except in the sense of providing technical vocabulary and symbolism as components of a language of mathematics, there is an increasing awareness of the centrality of communication and discourse in mathematics education (Barnes, 1976; The Mathematical Association (UK), 1987; NCTM, 1991). As was noted above, students need opportunities not simply to give answers, but also to explain their thinking—to discuss what they have observed, why procedures appear to work, or why they think their solutions are correct. Within mathematical communities, communication in the form of verification and justification is natural. When students are challenged to think and reason about mathematics and to communicate the results of their thinking to others orally or in writing, they are faced with the need to state their ideas clearly and convincingly. Thus, communication lies at the heart of activities that have mutual benefits for the individual student and for the community to which the student belongs. Moreover, the act of communicating one's ideas within the cultural norms of mathematical practice provides both need and value for mathematical reasoning, as classrooms are transformed into arenas in which convincing and justifying become for students a central focus of attention rather than a peripheral matter. In such classrooms one would expect to see communication fostered through the use of open-ended problems, which lead to discussions of multiple interpretations and multiple solution methods;

---

[3]   Mathematics educators outside the United States have been much more alert to a broad range of sociocultural aspects of mathematics education. For example, Bishop (1988) has provided an extensive account of a culturally-based view of mathematics education; D'Ambrosio (1985) has written eloquently about the need to consider mathematics from the perspective of the culture of the people who make it, use it or are asked to learn it; and Mellin-Olsen (1987) deals with issues of cultural transmission in his consideration of power relationships and ownership of mathematical knowledge.

the use of journals, which allow students to communicate their reflections on their mathematical activity; and work in pairs or small groups, which provide contexts that promote communication and collaboration.

Other authors (e.g., Lampert, 1987; Greeno, 1988; Lave, Smith, & Butler, 1988; Cobb, Wood, & Yackel, 1993) have also provided interesting visions of what a more social view of mathematics classrooms might look like. One general, unifying feature of these accounts is the view of mathematics classrooms as places where students, under the careful tutelage of their mathematics teacher, engage in doing mathematics rather than having it done to them. As Schoenfeld (1991) has argued, school mathematics has suffered from its inability to provide students with experience in and an appetite for collaborative mathematical thinking.

There are important consequences for teachers in the emerging view of mathematics classrooms as environments for collaborative mathematical thinking. Not only will teachers need to be skillful in orchestrating the dynamics of such classrooms but they will also need to be deeply knowledgeable about the mathematics they are helping children learn and capable of modeling reasonably good mathematical thinking and reasoning. These increased requirements for teachers represent a major challenge for reform efforts in mathematics education.

In order to realize a vision of mathematics classrooms as communities of collaborative, reflective practice for students, teachers will need to become more confident and competent in their own ways of knowing and doing mathematics. To orchestrate a group engaged in mathematical discourse, or to help individuals or groups formulate and revise learning goals or problem-solving approaches, a teacher must possess broad, deep, flexible knowledge of content and pedagogical alternatives. Without such knowledge of content and pedagogy, teachers will be unable to quickly reformulate goals and relate students' conceptions to the characteristic intellectual activities, knowledge structures, and cultural norms shared within the larger mathematical community. Unfortunately, teachers in the elementary and middle grades, though often quite flexible and child-centered in their pedagogy, usually possess quite limited knowledge of mathematics; and secondary school mathematics teachers, although generally more knowledgeable about mathematics, often possess only a limited array of conventional pedagogical practices and tend to resist change.

Among the many distinctive features of professional practice identified in the *Professional standards for teaching mathematics* (NCTM, 1991, p. 168), are "experimenting thoughtfully with alternative approaches and strategies in the classroom"; "reflecting on learning and teaching individually and with colleagues"; and "participating actively in the professional community of mathematics educators." The current situation is typically quite different—teachers working in isolation and with little or no motivation to change. For example, a recent survey of mathematics teachers found that only about half of the teachers at all grade levels saw their colleagues as a source of information on new teaching ideas and even fewer saw professional meetings as a source of such ideas (NCTM, 1992).

What mechanisms might be needed to assist teachers as they assume more complex roles and responsibilities? As was the case when we analyzed the situation for students, the answer is likely to be found in a form of education that is different from what currently exists. In the conventional practice of teacher education and teacher development, the three major resources and activity structures are (a) preservice teacher preparation in content (which is typically quite meager for elementary and middle school teachers and which is often disconnected and decontextualized for secondary school teachers) and pedagogy (which is usually quite limited for teachers at all levels); (b) inservice staff development sessions, which are typically single-session encounters with little or no support for implementation; and (c) university-based, graduate degree programs, which often have an academic rather than an applied focus, or which are quite general. These resources provide some support for teachers, but they are unlikely to be sufficient in these times of shifting pedagogical emphases and increasing intellectual demands in teaching. Helping teachers move beyond a pedagogy of isolation and recitation is likely to require new forms of assistance.

BUILDING COMMUNITIES OF COLLABORATIVE, REFLECTIVE PRACTICE FOR TEACHERS

What is needed is a new way to think about teacher education and teacher development as the building of communities of collaborative, reflective practice. In this view, teachers would come to see themselves as being joined with colleagues within their school in an effort to provide quality mathematical experiences for their students. Teachers would plan together, discuss each other's teaching practice, develop consensus on ways to evaluate their students' thinking, and support each other through difficult points in the change process. A simple version was provided in *Thinking through mathematics* (Silver, Kilpatrick, & Schlesinger, 1990) in the story of Mrs. Holmes, whose entry into new forms of pedagogical practice was closely associated with the formation of community, first with a single colleague, Mr. Jarvis, and then with a larger group of teachers at her school. Within this community, Mrs. Holmes was able to discuss and reflect on her pedagogical practices in ways that both enhanced and supported her efforts to improve her teaching.

Moving beyond the school, teachers would also see themselves as members of collaborative, reflective communities involving teachers outside their building—such as other teachers within the same school district or even at the state or national level—and they would see themselves as members of a larger, more extended community of educators trying to create new forms of practice in mathematics education. This latter community would include university teacher educators or researchers, curriculum supervisors, and others who might not have classroom teaching responsibilities but who could be available as intellectual partners and collaborators. In these larger communities, teachers would actively reflect on issues and contribute their individual and collective experiences.

The kinds of communities to which I refer do not simply involve membership in professional organizations, although such organizations can provide a support base for the formation of real communities of practice, especially since their communication mechanisms, such as meetings, journals and other publications, and newsletters, establish opportunities for discourse among members. Beyond group membership, however, I am suggesting a view of collegiality that is both reflective and supportive, in which the activity of central concern is the social construction of new forms of pedagogical knowledge and practice. In these communities, teachers would be challenged to think deeply about and to participate actively in engaging the mathematics they are teaching. In such communities teachers would not only teach within their individual classrooms but also participate in larger forums of discussion about pedagogical practice and student performance. As with student communities of practice, the discourse in these teacher communities would be filled with observations, explanations, verifications, reasons, and generalizations. Moreover, in such communities, teachers would have opportunities to see, hear, debate, and evaluate mathematical explanations and justifications as well as mathematical pedagogical practice.

Although it is not possible to give many details in this paper, it is important to stress that this vision of reflective communities of practice for teachers is not some romantic fantasy with little connection to reality. In fact, there is emerging both a theoretical foundation and an empirical evidence base to support our thinking about the construction of communities of collaborative, reflective practice for mathematics teachers. As far as empirical evidence is concerned, the experiences of teachers working within school districts associated with the Urban Mathematics Collaboratives (Webb, Pittelman, Romberg, Pitman, Middleton, Fadell, & Sapienza, 1990) illustrates, the power of teachers joining as collaborators to induce some forms of institutional change. In the QUASAR project (Silver, 1991), many examples can be found of teachers and resource partners (usually university teacher educators) creating communities of reflective collaboration as they develop new forms of instructional practice in middle schools serving economically disadvantaged neighborhoods. At QUASAR schools, teachers and resource partners have used common meeting time to plan instruction, to visit each other's classes or to watch videotapes of each other's teaching, to reflect on their individual and collective pedagogical practices, and to discuss the work of their students. Moreover, they have made time to explore and examine foundational mathematical concepts and principles, thereby enhancing individually and collectively their mathematical content knowledge and identifying areas in which further assistance is needed. As a result of these interactions, they have begun to challenge conventional, externally mandated testing and to build alternative assessment systems; to design ways of integrating and supporting the entry of new teachers into the culture of the program; and they have begun to shape the use of staff development time to suit the needs of their own mathematical development and those of their instructional program (Smith, Stein, & Seeley, 1992). In general, teachers and resource partners in these settings have come to see mathematics instruction as a collaborative practice, which is improved through communication and discourse with colleagues, and by capitalizing on the distributed network of expertise within the community, in which the resource partners are seen as playing a vital role rather than being viewed as "outsiders" in the school community.

As far as theory is concerned, theories of distributed cognition (Salomon, 1993) appear to hold promise for describing the ways in which expertise and knowledge are held and accessed in these communities. Individual students in the classrooms and teachers in the schools come to be seen as sources of particular forms of expertise that they share within the community.

New theories about the nature of pedagogy, such as the notion of teaching as "assisted performance" provided by Tharp and Gallimore (1988) may help us to think about the activities needed to build communities of collaborative, reflective practice both for students and for teachers. According to Tharp and Gallimore, who have extended and applied Vygotskian theory to innovative educational practice, assisted performance refers to what a person can do with the help of a supportive environment. The gap between the person's individual capacity and the capacity to perform with assistance is taken to be their version of the Zone of Proximal Development (ZPD), originally defined by Vygotsky (1978) as "the distance between the actual developmental level as determined by individual problem solving and the level of potential development as determined through problem solving under adult guidance or in collaboration with more capable peers" (p. 86). The first of several stages of passage through the ZPD, according to Tharp and Gallimore, involves performance assisted by capable others. This form of assisted performance, which is sometimes called scaffolding, is precisely the kind of assistance that a skilled teacher may provide to individuals or groups of students as they struggle to understand complex mathematical ideas, and it is also descriptive of the forms of support provided by members of a community of teachers who model lessons for each other, explain mathematical ideas to one another, or provide other forms of advice and support.

As far as membership in the larger communities of educational practice—those that spread beyond the boundaries of school and local community—and in thinking of how newcomers enter the communities of practice established at a particular school, Lave and Wenger's (1991) notion of "legitimate peripheral participation" seems helpful. They use the term to refer to their observation, drawn from ethnographic work on apprenticeship and other work on the sociocultural basis of learning, that learners participate in communities of practice and that mastery of knowledge and skill requires that newcomers move toward fuller participation in the practices of that community. Applied to the issues discussed in this paper, we can think of individual teachers, like those in the QUASAR project, as moving themselves and their students toward fuller participation in the community of mathematics education reform and in the culture of mathematical practice. In fact, Forman (1992) has analyzed aspects of classroom activity in one QUASAR teacher's classroom and used the notion of legitimate peripheral participation to describe that teacher's functioning within a larger community of mathematics education reform. Furthermore, she suggested the applicability of this concept in describing how students in this teacher's classroom gradually became integrated into the cultural norms and practices (shared with the larger community of mathematics education reform) that the teacher was attempting to establish. Thus, the theoretical notions of distributed cognition, of teaching as assisted performance and of legitimate peripheral participation appear to be applicable at all levels of the process of building communities of reflective practice in classrooms, in schools, and in more extended communities.

It should be emphasized that attaining the goal of mathematical thinking and reasoning for all students promises to be difficult work. It would be naive to assume that schools can be easily transformed into learning communities for students and for teachers. Yet, this paper has not only argued the urgent need to do so but also hinted at some forms in which the goal might be accomplished. What is abundantly clear is that attainment of this goal requires that the themes of communication, culture, and community must become more common topics of both conversation and action within the community of collaborative, reflective practice that we call mathematics education.

NOTE

Preparation of this paper has been supported in part by a grant from the Ford Foundation for the QUASAR project. The opinions expressed herein are those of the author and do not necessarily reflect those of the Foundation. I wish to acknowledge the positive influence and productive impact of interactions with many colleagues on the QUASAR project, especially Catherine Brown, Ellice Forman, Peg Smith, and Mary Kay Stein, and by discussions with Jeremy Kilpatrick and Beth Schlesinger in writing the book, *Thinking Through Mathematics*. They should not, however, be held responsible for any deficiencies in this paper that are due to my failure to comprehend what they were trying to help me understand.

REFERENCES

Appel, K., & Haken, W. (1977). The solution of the four-color-map problem. *Scientific American, 237*, 108-121.

Baranes, R., Perry, M., & Stigler, J.W. (1989). Activation of real-world knowledge in the solution of word problems. *Cognition and Instruction, 6*, 287-318.

Barnes, D. (1976). *From communication to curriculum.* London: Penguin.

Bishop, A.J. (1988). *Mathematical enculturation: A cultural perspective on mathematics education.* Dordrecht, The Netherlands: Kluwer.

Boero, P. (1989). Mathematical literacy for all: Experiences and problems. In G. Vergnaud, J. Rogalski & M. Artigue (Eds.), *Proceedings of the 13th Conference of the International Group for the Psychology of Mathematics Education* (pp. 62-76). Paris: CNRS

Brown, R.G. (1991). *Schools of thought: How the politics of literacy shape thinking in the classroom.* San Francisco: Jossey-Bass.

Cobb, P., Wood, T., & Yackel, E. (1993). Discourse, mathematical thinking, and classroom practice. In E.A. Forman, N. Minnick & C. A. Stone (Eds.), *Contexts for learning: Sociocultural dynamics in children's development.* New York: Oxford University Press.

D'Ambrosio, U. (1985). Ethnomathematics and its place in the history and pedagogy of mathematics. *For the Learning of Mathematics, 5*, 44-48.

Dossey, J.A., Mullis, I.V.S., Lindquist, M.M., & Chambers, D.L. (1988). *The mathematics report card.* Princeton, NJ: National Assessment of Educational Progress.

Ernest, P. (1991). *The philosophy of mathematics education.* London: Falmer Press.

Forman, E.A. (1992, August). *Forms of participation in classroom practice: Implications for learning mathematics.* Paper presented at the Seventh International Congress on Mathematical Education, Québec, Canada.

Freudenthal, H. (1991). *Revisiting mathematics education.* Dordrecht, The Netherlands: Kluwer Academic Publishers.

Greeno, J.H. (1988). For the study of mathematics epistemology. In R.I. Charles & E.A. Silver (Eds.), *Research agenda for mathematics education: The teaching and assessing of mathematical problem solving* (pp. 23-31). Reston, VA: National Council of Teachers of Mathematics (Co-published with Lawrence Erlbaum Associates, Hillsdale, NJ).

Guzmán, M. de (1990). Games and mathematics. In A.G. Howson & J.-P. Kahane (Eds.), *The popularization of mathematics* (pp. 79-88). Cambridge, UK: Cambridge University Press.

Howson, A.G., & Kahane, J.-P. (1990). A study overview. In A.G. Howson & J.-P. Kahane (Eds.), *The popularization of mathematics* (pp. 1-37). Cambridge, UK: Cambridge University Press.

Kitcher, P. (1984). *The nature of mathematical knowledge.* New York: Oxford University Press.

Lakatos, I. (1976). *Proofs and refutations: The logic of mathematical discovery.* New York: Cambridge University Press.

Lampert, M. (1987). Knowing, doing, and teaching multiplication. *Cognition and Instruction, 3*(4), 305-342.

Lave, J., Smith S., & Butler, M. (1988). Problem solving as everyday practice. In R.I. Charles & E.A. Silver (Eds.), *Research agenda for mathematics education: The teaching and assessing of mathematical problem solving* (pp. 61-81). Reston, VA: National Council of Teachers of Mathematics (co-published with Lawrence Erlbaum Associates, Hillsdale, NJ).

Lave, J., & Wenger, E. (1991). *Situated learning: Legitimate peripheral participation.* New York: Cambridge University Press.

Mathematical Association (UK). (1987). *Math talk.* Portsmouth, NH: Heinemann.

Mellin-Olsen, S. (1987). *The politics of mathematics education.* Dordrecht, The Netherlands: D. Reidel.

Mullis, I.V.S., Dossey, J.A., Owen, E.H., & Phillips, G.W. (1991). *The state of mathematics achievement: NAEP's 1990 assessment of the nation and the trial assessment of the states.* Washington: National Center for Educational Statistics.

Mullis, I.V.S., Owen, E.H., & Phillips, G.W. (1990). *Accelerating academic achievement: A summary of findings from 20 years of NAEP.* Princeton, NJ: Educational Testing Service.

National Assessment of Educational Progress (1983). *The third national mathematics assessment: Results, trends and issues* (13-MA-01). Denver, CO: Educational Commission of the States.

National Council of Teachers of Mathematics (1989). *Curriculum and evaluation standards for school mathematics.* Reston, VA: NCTM.

National Council of Teachers of Mathematics (1991). *Professional standards for the teaching of mathematics.* Reston, VA: NCTM.

National Council of Teachers of Mathematics (1992). *The road to reform in mathematics education: How far have we traveled?* Reston, VA: NCTM.

National Research Council (1989). *Everybody counts: A report to the nation on the future of mathematics education.* Washington: National Academy Press.

Oakes, J. (1985). *Keeping track: How schools structure inequality.* New Haven, CT: Yale University Press.

Oakes, J. (1990). Opportunities, achievement, and choice: Women and minority students in science and mathematics. In C. B. Cazden (Ed.), *Review of research in education* (Vol. 16, pp. 153-222). Washington: American Educational Research Association.

Peterson, I. (1988). *The mathematical tourist.* New York: W.H. Freeman and Co.

Resnick, L.B. (1987). *Education and learning to think.* Washington: National Academy Press.

Resnick, L.B. (1988). Treating mathematics as an ill-structured discipline. In R.I. Charles & E.A. Silver (Eds.), *Research agenda for mathematics education: The teaching and assessing of mathematical problem solving* (pp. 31-60). Reston, VA: National Council of Teachers of Mathematics (co-published with Lawrence Erlbaum Associates, Hillsdale, NJ).

Salomon, G. (Ed.). (1993). *Distributed cognitions.* New York: Cambridge University Press.

Schoenfeld, A.H. (1991). On mathematics as sense-making: An informal attack on the unfortunate divorce of formal and informal mathematics. In J.F. Voss, D.N. Perkins & J.W. Segal (Eds.), *Informal reasoning and education* (pp. 311-343). Hillsdale, NJ: Lawrence Erlbaum Associates.

Secada, W.G. (1991). Agenda setting, enlightened self-interest, and equity in mathematics education. *Peabody Journal of Education, 66*(2), 22-56.

Silver, E.A. (1991). *QUASAR.* Unpublished manuscript, Learning Research and Development Center, University of Pittsburgh.

Silver, E.A., Kilpatrick, J., & Schlesinger, B. (1990). *Thinking through mathematics.* New York: College Entrance Examination Board.

Silver, E.A., & Shapiro, L.J. (1993). In J.P. Mendes da Ponte (Ed.), *Advances in mathematical problem solving.* New York: Springer-Verlag.

Silver, E.A., Shapiro, L.J., & Deutsch, A. (In press). Sense-making and the solution of division problems involving remainders: An examination of students' solution processes and their interpretations of solutions. *Journal for Research in Mathematics Education.*

Silver, E.A., Smith, M.S., & Nelson, B.S. (1993). The QUASAR project: Equity concerns meet mathematics education reform in the middle school. In E. Fennema & W. Secada (Eds.), *New directions in equity in mathematics education.* Madison, WI: University of Wisconsin Center for Educational Research.

Smith, M.S., Stein, M.K., & Seeley, M. (1992). *Vision: A framework for teachers' professional development.* Unpublished manuscript, Learning Research and Development Center, University of Pittsburgh.

Stodolsky, S. (1988). *The subject matters: Classroom activity in mathematics and social studies.* Chicago: University of Chicago Press.

Tharp, R.G., & Gallimore, R. (1988). *Rousing minds to life: Teaching, learning, and schooling in social context.* Cambridge, England: Cambridge University Press.

Tymoczko, T. (Ed.) (1986). *New directions in the philosophy of mathematics.* Boston: Birkhäuser.

Vygotsky, L.S. (1978). *Mind in society: The development of higher psychological processes* (M. Cole, V. John-Steiner & E. Souberman, Eds. & Trans.). Cambridge, MA: Harvard University Press.

Webb, N.L., Pittelman, S.D., Romberg, T.A., Pitman, A.J., Middleton, J.A., Fadell, E.M., & Sapienza, M. (1990). *The urban mathematics collaborative project: Report to the Ford Foundation on the 1988-89 school year.* Madison, WI: Wisconsin Center for Education Research.

HUMANISTIC AND UTILITARIAN
ASPECTS OF MATHEMATICS

Thomas Tymoczko

Smith College, United States of America

Philosophers of mathematics and mathematics educators did not always have much to say to one another. Philosophers dealt with the more abstract aspects of mathematics, attempting to provide foundations for mathematics and to place it in a general context of human activity. Educators dealt with the more concrete aspects of mathematics, attempting to convey the details and to instill the techniques in students who might range from elementary school to college. In recent times the philosopher (and educator) Ludwig Wittgenstein decried this separation. He emphasized the interplay between philosophy analysis and pedagogy.[1] The questions, "But how do we teach this concept? How do we convey it to a pupil?" mark a constant theme of his philosophy.

After Wittgenstein, there were many others who developed the previously ignored connection between philosophy and pedagogy in mathematics.[2] In this essay, I join the attempt to further dialogue between philosophers and educators by suggesting that we can learn from each other. In particular, I suggest we can correct a reciprocal misreading of mathematics. My twin claims are that philosophers cause themselves problems by focusing their attention on pure mathematics while ignoring applied mathematics, and that educators cause themselves problems by focusing their attention on applied mathematics while ignoring pure mathematics.

---

[1] See Wittgenstein (1953, 1967). For an account of Wittgenstein's mixed career as an educator, see Monk.

[2] From the mathematical side, George Polya deserves special mention as an early pioneer. For references to his and other more recent work, see the anthology Tymoczko (1985).

My essay is theoretical. Sadly, I must ignore the social and political influences on educators that leave them so little room for educated experimentation in the classroom.[3]

This essay is divided into three main parts. The first addresses the current state of philosophy of mathematics. I suggest that philosophers have created a pseudo-problem for themselves by refusing to recognize the real world basis for mathematics. Traditional problems of mathematical existence can be answered by recognizing mathematics as an integral part of common sense and science.

The second part of the essay asks whether the preceding pragmatic account can answer all philosophical questions about mathematics. It answers that an essential ingredient—"human interest"—has been left out of account.

Finally, the third part of the essay tries to show how the ingredient of human interest must influence mathematical pedagogy. It is not always the utility of mathematics that should matter in the classroom, it is often the mathematical beauty that is at stake.

A year ago, when predicting the contents of this essay, I said that a crucial topic would be the role of the community in mathematics. Only by regarding mathematics as the practice of a community of mathematicians, and not as the product of an isolated mathematical geniuses, can we arrive at an educationally sound philosophy of mathematics, or so I believe. The community still figures in the present essay, but in a somewhat disguised form. What I call "humanistic mathematics" or "the discipline of pure mathematics" is essentially tied to a community of practitioners. Ultimately, humanistic mathematics is no more and no less than the general practices of a mathematical community.

UTILITARIAN ASPECTS OF MATHEMATICS

By and large Western philosophy has regarded pure mathematics as the essence of mathematics. That is, pure mathematics is regarded as a discipline that could exist in and of itself; pure mathematics is thought to be logically, metaphysically and epistemologically prior to any applications of it.[4] Moreover, it is pure mathematics that is assumed to manifest the philosophically interesting traits of mathematics—knowledge of it is a priori, certain, absolute, eternal.

---

[3] This point was stressed to me by commentators at ICME-7 in Québec.

[4] The empiricist, John Stuart Mill was an exception to the general tradition. For more recent exceptions, see Tymoczko (1985) where the contemporary school of quasi-empiricism is discussed.

I believe that this focus on pure mathematics has distorted philosophical perspectives on mathematics. That there is a distortion is immediately felt by both mathematicians and mathematical educators. Typical philosophical questions about mathematics seem very remote from the business of creating new mathematics and of teaching old mathematics. Nowhere is this distance between those who do and teach mathematics and those who philosphize about it more pronounced than it is over the question of mathematical existence. Philosophers seem obsessed with the question of whether we should assert or deny that mathematical objects exist. A large portion of current research papers in the philosophy of mathematics is devoted to this question.

Ordinarily the existence of a given subject matter is of critical importance. It matters that there is no phlogiston, no ether and no ghosts. We should discourage any student who wished to study how ghosts moved by pointing out that there are no ghosts and never were any ghosts. Alternatively, we should encourage anyone who wanted to study inherited traits by observing the demonstrated existence of an inherited trait carrier, namely DNA.

But it is obvious that the debate about mathematical existence shares few features with serious debates about existence. The discipline of mathematics is well established and will continue to flourish—or not—quite independently of the final philosophical word on mathematical existence.

The philosophers' mistake, or so I claim, is their focus on pure mathematics, in isolation from practical applications. This focus mystifies mathematics. Indeed, I'm not content to simply reverse the polarity and to elevate applied mathematics above pure mathematics because the very notion of applied mathematics, the application of some mathematical theory to some independent non-mathematical area, should be challenged. At the very least, what we call applied mathematics is better called "utilitarian mathematics" or even "extracted mathematics", the result of extracting a mathematical component from an already existing fundamental human activity of which it is an essential ingredient. Among fundamental human activities I would count business, trade, farming, warfare, navigation and science, to name a few.

My view is that these activities or institutions are possible only because they have an essential mathematical component from the beginning. In just the same way these activities are possible only because they have a linguistic component. If human beings could not speak then they could not conduct business or wars, and if they could not "do mathematics", then they could not conduct business or wars. Look more closely at the example of warfare. To be sure, animals and insects can kill and fight each other, occasionally even in groups. So I do not deny that inarticulate, unmathematical human groups could throw stones at one another. But without some mathematics, they could come no nearer to warfare than they could without speech. Warfare requires planning, for example, and planning would be impossible without speech and without mathematics.

Let me make the same point with respect to economic activity or business. Business does not just apply various already existing mathematical theories to facilitate an activity that is, in principle, independent from such mathematical applications (although it can do that). Business could not exist in anything like its historical form without some mathematics. Certainly we cannot imagine a modern economy struggling along without mathematics then suddenly becoming more efficient because of the introduction of mathematics! No mathematics, no economy: even primitive business needs some form of accounting.

So mathematics is not just applied to human activities: sometimes it makes those activities possible in the first place, just as language does. Indeed, we do not speak of applied language, as if there could be some original pure language independent of any use to which humans put it. It is for this reason that I speak of extracting mathematics from forms of life that we humans engage in; the practice is not there before the mathematics. After the fact, by an effort of abstraction, we extract "the mathematical component" from the human practice. But we are misled if we think we can imagine that practice without its mathematical component. There is no version of the institution without mathematics. That's why I hesitate to call this mathematics "applied mathematics", a term which suggests we got the mathematics from somewhere else and applied it to ongoing human concerns. No, what I call utilitarian mathematics is part of our heritage as human beings, much as speech is.

If we turn to science we find the same phenomenon writ large. The truism that mathematics is the language of science applies to classical physics and the calculus and even more to quantum physics and its various mathematical theories. (Can we even describe the subject matter of quantum physics without mathematics?) The view I challenge is the view that there are, in principle, two independent areas. According to this view, physics makes a major advance when physicists realize that they can apply mathematics to their subject matter. In my view, it makes no sense to try to imagine classical physics without mathematics, specifically the calculus. Indeed, I claim, we actually have to work to extract something specifically mathematical from classical physics. Both Newton and Kant regarded fundamental mathematical concepts as simultaneously fundamental physical concepts: mathematical quantities were generated by temporal processes or continual motions. Time, space and motion were the common province of mathematics and physics. Kant subsumed the calculus under his general discussion of physics as the a priori study of motion.[5]

So far, then, I have advanced two variations on a theme. The theme is that mathematics springs from human institutions, ancient ones like trade and warfare, and more modern ones like science. Utilitarian mathematics is a constituent of these institutions and practices. Pure mathematics, of which we shall speak more shortly, is parasitic on the utilitarian aspects. Pure mathematics is not merely historically dependent on utilitarian mathematics, it is logically dependent. Moreover, this shift in perspectives has philosophical consequences. The hitherto vexing question of mathematical existence now can get the same kinds of answer that the less vexing question of scientific existence and the hardly vexing question of common sense existence get. Things like numbers, atoms and dogs exist because the very best theories describing and predicting our experience in the world assert the existence of (or quantify over) numbers, atoms and dogs. I've defended this answer in considerable detail elsewhere (Tymoczko, 1991) but here I should acknowledge that the basic idea is due to Willard Quine. It was his idea that we ought to admit that x's exist whenever our best theory of the world and of our experience in it quantifies over x's. (Intuitively, Quine's is a "no-double-talk" theory—if one insists on saying that there are x's, then one ought to admit that x's exist. See Quine (1961) for his account of ontological commitment.) Thus Quine would say that we are as deeply committed to functions and derivatives as we are to velocities and accelations, to numbers as we are to regiments and francs.

Thus from our new radical point of view, we can answer the oldest problem of the philosophy of mathematics: Do mathematical objects exist? Our answer is a simple yes, mathematical objects exist in the same way that scientific objects (atoms) do and ordinary objects (dogs and dollars) do. We can answer thusly because we regard mathematics as an essential part of human activities which we cannot give up. Note that this answer is not available to those who begin by considering a pure mathematics that is essentially independent of human activities in the real world.

---

5 See Friedman for a detailed discussion. To be sure Newton did not mention the calculus in his *Principia* (although he may have used calculus to discover his principles). But that hardly effects the point that mathematics and physics are essentially intertwined. At worst, the mathematical concept of functions supplemented by the classical method of exhaustion would be the basis of physics. More seriously, physics as we teach it today, is impossible without the special features of calculus (try to imagine physics without differential equations!).

IS UTILITARIAN MATHEMATICS ENOUGH?

Have we found, then, a happy home for mathematics as a part of science, perhaps as experimentation lives as a part of science? Not for mathematics as we know it; so far we have left pure mathematics totally out of account. Just how this pure mathematics arises out of its utilitarian underpinnings is the question to which we now turn (note the inversion—philosophy traditionally asked how pure mathematics could be applied!).

Let us begin by trying to imagine what a culture would be like with just utilitarian mathematics. In a sense, this is not difficult, possibly the ancient Babylonian and Egyptian cultures had only utilitarian mathematics. I conjecture that even a very advanced modern culture could exist with only utilitarian mathematics. But it would differ from ours not merely by lacking pure mathematics, but perhaps by lacking the very idea of mathematics. My reason is that although we can imagine a culture with lots of mathematical techniques and sophistication, but there seems no reason to imagine these as forming a unity, we do not have to imagine these techniques as forming a unity for the culture. Instead, there might be just analogous parts of various human endeavors—science, business, industry, etc. In analogous fashion, the experimental aspect of science, the totality of experiments including trial and error, seems to lack any intrinsic unity.

There is an interesting quote by C.H. Edwards, Jr., in his account of the history of the calculus that bears on this:

> It is arguable that, had all succeeding generations [after the Greeks] also refused to use real numbers and limits until they fully understood them, the calculus might never have been developed, and mathematics might now be a dead and forgotten science. (Edwards, 1979, p. 79)

What a provocative idea—"mathematics might now be a dead and forgotten science"! Surely what Edwards means is not that, without calculus, people would forget how to count, measure plots of land, etc. What would die and be forgotten is a separate discipline of mathematics, a subject that is internally coherent and worth pursuing for its own sake. What would die is what is traditionally called pure mathematics, and what I call humanistic mathematics, though Edwards himself calls it a science.

Utilitarian mathematics, or applied mathematics, is unified by its connections to pure mathematics. In pure mathematics, the distinctively mathematical concepts, objects and techniques are recognized—recognized by their very inclusion in pure mathematics. (In short, what belongs to mathematics is what mathematicians say belongs to mathematics! In ways such as this the mathematical community makes its presence known.)

But what is pure mathematics? This is the question that challenged traditional philosophy. We, on the other hand, ask it in a different context.

We ask it after we have made a place for utilitarian mathematics; we ask it after we have established the existence of mathematical objects. Indeed, perhaps we have already answered the question: pure mathematics is just the dispassionate study of mathematical objects, pure mathematics is just the science of mathematical objects as physics is the science of mass and energy, space and time. However, there is a decisive objection to this answer. The problem is that there are too many mathematical objects and they are too varied.

For the sake of argument, let us restrict ourselves to the domain of natural numbers and their accessories, such as functions on the natural numbers and sets of natural numbers. It is rather tempting to think that number theory is just the study of numbers and their properties and functions. The trouble is that from an objective point of view, there are far too many properties and functions. Besides the primes, for example, there are such properties as the odd primes, the primes greater than 3, the primes greater than 5, etc., not to mention the primes but including 4, the primes but also 4 and 6, etc. In other words, there are a whole lot of number theoretical concepts out there for mathematicians to study—why focus on some concepts instead of others? A similar question could be raised with regard to arithmetic functions like successor, plus and times. The problem is that the objective mathematical universe (as well as the formalists' or the constructivists' universes) is filled with many variants of what we take to be the basic concepts of mathematics and many other plain monstrosities. My worry is that the study of variant concepts and functions is not mathematics, but it is part of the study of mathematical objects. Studying arbitrary mathematical objects permits too much (see Tymoczko, 1986, for more on this argument).

Exactly the same point can be made with respect to formal theories of mathematics. While it might be tempting to define pure arithmetic as the set of theorems of formal Peano arithmetic, my objection is that if this definition were correct, then random computations would count as doing arithmetic, as would the proof of arbitrary formulas. But we—mathematicians, educators, and philosophers—would not count such things as doing mathematics. If someone insisted on filling notebooks with pointless calculations we would call him a crank if not just crazy. The point is that proving theorems is not mathematics—at best, proving relevant theorems is. Our earlier point was that studying mathematical objects is not mathematics, at best, studying interesting objects is.

So we must abandon the trivial answer to the question: What is pure mathematics? It's not just the study of arbitrary mathematical objects or the production of arbitrary proofs and computations. I suggest we can understand what pure mathematics is only if we abandon the claim that mathematics is simply the study of the mathematical universe and embrace the thesis that mathematics is interest relative—that is, what counts in mathematics is only what counts to mathematicians (eg., humans) at a given time in mathematical history. Mathematics is not just a universe of mathematical objects or formalisms or constructions; at the very least it includes a point of view on that universe. This is the essence of humanistic mathematics—mathematics requires a perspective and a human perspective is the only perspective we can get![6]

Several years ago, Alvin White of Harvey Mudd College in the United States began a campaign for what he called "humanistic mathematics".[7] While I admired the pedagogical reforms that issued from White's campaign—he wanted mathematics taught in a humane way—I failed to appreciate the significance of humanistic mathematics. To be sure, it was interesting to consider teaching mathematics as if it were one of the humanities, but what made mathematics one of the humanities? Certainly not the mere fact that humans did it; humans do science too. In writing this essay, I have rediscovered White's point. Pure mathematics is ultimately humanistic mathematics, one of the humanities, because it is an intellectual discipline with a human perspective and a history that matters. There is no answer to the question: What is important in mathematics, once and for all? We can only ask what is important in mathematics to human beings, with given abilities and limitations at a given point in their mathematical development. The discipline of pure mathematics is much more like geography than it is like physics. That is why I want to rename it "humanistic mathematics".

If, for the sake of argument, you grant my conclusions so far, then we can turn to the topic of how mathematics might be taught in a way that reveals its humanistic side.

HUMANISTIC MATHEMATICS

Earlier, I accused philosophers and mathematicians of making reciprocal mistakes. Philosophers have ignored utilitarian mathematics and thereby created for themselves the problem of mathematical existence. But educators, I claim, are prone to make the opposite mistake. In teaching

---

[6] A case in point might be the rise of complexity theory and the resurgence of interest in discrete mathematics. My intuition is that in recursion theory, all finite sets are trivially recursive and so uninteresting. But the development of computer technology has enabled us to raise interesting questions about distinctions in the finite realm, eg., the P = NP problem.

[7] Further information on White's project is available in the *Newsletter on Humanistic Mathematics,* published by White at Harvey Mudd College, Claremont, CA.

mathematics, they insist on stressing its utility, even when it has none. As a result, they often hide from their students the excitement and intrinsic interest of mathematics: they hide it behind a facade of supposed utility. It's rather like trying to awaken someone to the joys of mountain climbing by trying to convince her that someday she might need to climb a mountain (as if cars and buses would not be able to satify any practical need).

Let me try to explain my view of humanistic mathematics in two ways. The first is by means of a concrete example concerning the teaching of quadratic equations in secondary schools in the United States. The second is with a more global metaphor for humanistic mathematics.

In my experience there is a "standard" way of teaching quadratic equations. It is organized according to utilitarian mathematics. The motivation is supplied, supposedly, by practical needs expressed in word problems. For example, suppose you have a rectangular plot of land and you want to build a sidewalk one metre wide around it, etc., etc. The student is led through hundreds of execises involving various techniques of factorization. Finally the quadratic formula is derived (thus rendering otiose the effort that the student put into earlier attempts to factor or to complete the square). This project easily consumes half of a school year.

Now, if the educators' aim is to teach applied or utilitarian mathematics, perhaps this approach is all right—although it's unethical, from a utiliarian point of view, to delay the quadratic formula for so long. But, before committing yourself to the utilitarian viewpoint, you might try to remember the last time that you needed to solve a quadratic outside of a classroom, and you might try to explain why a computer program (or calculator) is not a better way to solve such problems. Be that as it may, the standard approach is not introducing students to the discipline of mathematics or to humanistic mathematics as I conceive it.

To introduce students to humanistic mathematics is to introduce them to a human adventure, an adventure that humans have actually partaken of in history. The story of quadratics is part of a more general story of investigating equations: linear, quadratic, cubic, biquadratic, etc. These form "a natural class" of problems to us humans and the quadratic equations are a piece of this richer puzzle. This puzzle is challenging to human mathematicians for the same reason that mountains are challenging to human mountain climbers: because the puzzles and the mountains are there for us.

By the time that they approach quadratics, students will find linear equations easy. But do students realize what a significant thing it is to find linear equations easy? The Greeks did not recognize negative solutions to linear equations, and even 16th century mathematicians classified quadratics into various subclasses because of their suspicion of negative numbers. It

335

took human beings thousands of years to progress to the mathematical level of today's high school students, and perhaps teachers should mention this to students.

I was saying that humanistic mathematics tells the human story of mathematics. It puts the discussion of quadratics into the human-mathematical context that gives the mathematical topic its sense and its beauty. The general story of quadratics provides an opportunity to discuss Arabian mathematics and the mathematician al-Khowârizmî who preserved and developed the partial Greek solutions to the quadratic (of course the words "algebra" and "algorithm" are derived from him and his work). Moreover, and this is the surprise, the investigation of quadratics could be put into perspective by spending just a week or two on cubic equations.

For starters, one could use the story of the cubic to expose students to the very different mathematical culture of Renaisannce Italy, where mathematicians challenged each other like gun fighters in modern spaghetti Westerns. According to William Dunham's book *Journey through genius,* from which I get my story, one Antonio Fior was bequeathed the solution to so-called "depressed cubics" by his teacher.[8] Fior immediately challenged Niccolo Fontana, known as Tartaglia (the Stammerer), to a mathematical contest. Fontana proposed 30 problems, each asking for the solution to a depressed cubic equation! Tartaglia knew what was going on, and by working night and day found the general solution in time to thoroughly humiliate Fontana, who did not know much besides the formula for the depressed cubic. In the next twist of fate, that most bizarre, if not lunatic mathematician, Cardano extracted from Tartaglia his solution of a particular form of cubic equation. The price he paid was a solemn oath to Tartaglia "by the Sacred Gospel, and on my faith as a gentleman, not only never to publish your discoveries if you tell them to me ..." Cardano went on to use Tartaglia's discovery to solve the general cubic and his student Ferrari, exploited it to solve the biquadratic.[9]

My idea is that Cardano's analysis is well within the reach of secondary students; essentially, it applies the quadratic formula to cleverly contrived cases of the cubic. And my suggestion is that the teaching of quadratic equations could be far more exciting if teachers used the quadratic solution to derive the solution of the cubic—as opposed to those endless and boring word problems. By highlighting the similarities and differences

---

[8] Depressed cubics are cubic equations lacking a term involving the square of the unkown.

[9] For an interesting interpretation of the dispute between Cardano and Tartaglia, and of the practical difficulties that beset Albe and Galois, see Collins and Restivo.

between the quadratic solution and the cubic solution, the comparison can give the student a deeper appreciation and understanding of mathematics for its own sake. Moreover, even less than bright students would rather listen to the story of Cardano, no doubt, than do a hundred so-called practical problems about quadratics.

Thus I suggest that some discussion of the cubic should be an essential part of the teaching of quadratic equations: not because it is useful, but because it makes sense. It puts the quadratic in its proper mathematical perspective. By comparing and contrasting the quadratic and the cubic, a student can begin to see the overall shape of the forest instead of just hundreds of trees.[10]

Moreover, if I were inculcating the discipline of mathematics—humanistic mathematics—I would not finish quadratics without mention of the work of the Norwegian Abel who showed that quintic equations were not solvable by radicals. This should generate an interesting class discussion. How can a mathematician show that a mathematical problem is unsolvable as opposed to merely failing to solve it? And of course, it would be sinful not to mention the Frenchman Galois who explained why equations to the 4th degree were solvable and why none higher were. This might even provide an opportunity to mention the concept of "group"—as well as ending the story where it began, with a "dueling mathematician"!

Let me briefly summarize. Standard approaches to the quadratic formula embed the quadratic formula in purely utilitarian mathematics. They suppress the aesthetical, the historical, and the purely mathematical aspects of this mathematical problem in favor of touting the practical significance of answering various canned word problems. Students spend half a year mastering a variety of techniques leading up to a general solution which eliminates the need for their mastery of those techniques. But they are never told why anyone would think a general solution was intrinsically interesting for its own sake.

Humanistic mathematics can give quadratic equations their rightful mathematical significance by placing them in a context of pure mathematics, more particularly, by placing them in the context of historical progress toward answering a natural mathematical question. This is a history of approaches and conquests that stretches millennia from the halting efforts of the Greeks to the final summation of Galois. The general solution to quadratic equations

---

10   By the way, a natural human interest story arises here: how could Cardano and Ferrari reconcile the oath to Tartaglia with their desire to publish perhaps the most important mathematical discovery of the 16th century? Since we are interested in pure mathematics, I won't distract you by discussing their solution, but Dunham explains it in his lovely book.

is but one piece of this history. Humanistic mathematics is not just "friendly" mathematics or "touchy feely" mathematics . It is mathematics with a human face because there is no mathematical discipline without a human face. Stories of mathematicians are "color". It is interesting that Tartaglia was a stammerer who extracted a promise from Cardano. But stories about what historical individuals saw when they looked on the mathematical universe at historical points in time are not color. They are mathematics. No one can learn mathematics, without being inculcated into this tradition.

CONCLUSION

In conclusion, I want to sketch an analogy between humanistic mathematics and another human endeavor, the practice of mountain climbing.

Neither humanistic mathematics nor mountain climbing are practical human concerns; but both of them are rooted in practical concerns, for example, both have a foot in business and trade.

Neither humanistic mathematics nor mountain climbing are sciences; but both are bounded by objective constraints, mathematical facts and geological facts.

Both humanistic mathematics and mountain climbing fail as sciences for the same reason—each depends on the contingencies of the human condition. Mountain climbing is what it is because human beings are what we are; we have such and such size, such and such natural abilities, can do this easily and that with practice. Exactly the same applies to humanistic mathematics. It is shaped by human abilities and limitations, because we can do some things easily, others only with difficulty. God's mathematics would be very different from ours—as would a beetle's conception of "mountain climbing" differ from ours.

Moreover, as with other humanistic disciplines, mountain climbing and humanistic mathematics both have a history. What is difficult at one period, becomes easy at another. The historical context of a given period sets the goals of that period. If no one has solved the general cubic or climbed that particular mountain, then those are the goals of the day. Later, such goals might become exercises for apprentices. Furthermore, technology is especially important. It alters what can be done and our evaluations of various achievements. (Solving particular quadratic equations is not too impressive to one who has seen the formula for general solutions.)

In the end, humanistic mathematics and mountain climbing are both driven by a fundamental human characteristic: the ability to take joy in complex endeavors. In both cases we find activities or processes driven by goals or achievements. Without the results, the theorems or the mountains climbed, we would not have the activity, but it is the journey to the results—

the actual doing of mathematics and the actual climbing of mathematics—that provides the day-to-day gratification that keeps these practices alive.

Perhaps I could press the analogy between mathematics and mountain climbing even further, but rather than press my luck, I will spend a final minute in recapitulation.

The point of the analogy between mathematics and mountain climbing is to exhibit a critical human, or subjective, component of mathematics. This human component is not a frill that might make teaching mathematics more enjoyable to the mathematically handicapped. This human component is a *sine qua non* of a separate discipline of pure mathematics. In a nutshell, the human component imposes sense or intelligibility on mathematics. It imposes a human perspective on the arbitrary complexities of the mathematical universe, exactly as our human perspective shapes a coherent practice of mountain climbing on otherwise unwieldy mountains.

Educators ignore humanistic mathematics to their peril. Without it, educators may teach students to compute and to solve, just as they can teach students to read and to write. But without it, educators can't teach students to love, to appreciate, or even to understand mathematics.

REFERENCES

Collins, R., & Restivo, S. (1983). Robber barons and politicians in mathematics: A conflict model of science. *The Canadian Journal of Sociology, 8*, 199-227.

Dunham, W. (1990). *Journey through genius.* New York: John Wiley & Sons, Inc.

Edwards, C.H. Jr. (1979). *The historical development of the calculus.* New York: Springer-Verlag.

Friedman, M. (1985). Kant's theory of geometry. *Philosophical Review, 94*, 455-506.

Kant, I. (1985). *Metaphysical foundations of natural science.* Indianapolis: Hackett.

Monk, R. (1990). *Ludwig Wittgenstein: the duty of genius.* New York: Free Press.

Quine, W.V.O. (1961). *From a logical point of view.* Cambridge, MA: Havard University Press.

Tymoczko, T. (1991). Mathematics, science and ontology. *Synthese, 88*, 201-228.

Tymoczko, T. (1986). Making room for mathematicians in the philosophy of mathematics. *Mathematical Intelligencer, 8*, 44-50.

Tymoczko, T. (1985). *New directions in the philosophy of mathematics.* Boston: Birkhäuser.

Wittgenstein, L. (1953). *Philosophical investigations.* Oxford: Blackwell.

Wittgenstein, L. (1967). *Remarks on the foundations of mathematics.* Oxford: Blackwell.

FROM "MATHEMATICS FOR SOME" TO "MATHEMATICS FOR ALL" [1]

Zalman Usiskin

University of Chicago, United States of America

There have been in this century two major developments in mathematics education. The first of these, a movement that is several centuries old, is the teaching of more and more mathematics to more and more people. For instance, the study of algebra and geometry, which even a century ago was reserved for a small percentage of the population even in the most technological of our societies, is now a part of the core curriculum for all students in many countries. The second development, only within the past 30 years or so, has been the emergence of computer technology, which enables much mathematics to be done more easily than ever before, and enables some mathematics to be done that could not be done at all previously. As a result, more and more people are encountering and doing far more mathematics than ever before, and there is great pressure nowadays to teach a great deal of mathematics to all people. This is the origin of the title "From 'Mathematics for Some' to 'Mathematics for All'".

In this paper, I wish to place these developments in an even longer historical framework than this century, and use that framework as well as some recent work to suggest directions in which mathematics in school and society may be moving and should be moving.

DEFINITIONS OF TERMS

The word "all" in the title of this paper refers to all of the population except the mentally disabled, which means at least 95% of any age cohort.

---

[1] The talk as given was almost twice the length of this paper and contained many examples not presented here. The longer version may be obtained from the author at the University of Chicago School Mathematics Project, 5835 S. Kimbark Avenue, Chicago, IL 60637 USA.

In the United States, it is reported that about 75% of 18-year-olds graduate from high school with their age cohort, and about 10% more earn their high school diplomas later. So for the United States, my "all" constitutes a population larger than those who finish high school. In contrast, in Japan, 95% is almost the percentage of students who graduate from high school.

On the other hand, here the phrase "mathematics" for all refers to *school* mathematics for all, and so these remarks are not meant to apply in those places where children do not attend school, or cannot attend school, or choose not to attend. Mathematics *for* all refers at different times in this paper to the mathematics that *has been* learned by all, that *is* being learned by all, that *could* be learned by all, that *should be* learned by all, or that *will be* learned by all.

The content of school mathematics is broad, and includes: skills and algorithms; properties and proofs; uses and mathematical models; and representations of many kinds. In the UCSMP secondary materials these are termed the SPUR (S = skills, P = properties, U = uses, R = representations) dimensions of mathematics[2].

THE CURRENT STATE OF MATHEMATICS FOR ALL

In most of the world, all students are expected to learn a considerable amount of arithmetic. Until recently, because one needed to know paper-and-pencil skills in order to use arithmetic, the Skills dimension was the most emphasized everywhere. Because of the emergence of calculators, at the present time in some countries there is a decrease in the attention given to the Skill dimension, and a corresponding increase in attention to both the Uses and Representation dimensions. Yet I think it is fair to say that in most classrooms in the world, the teaching of paper-and-pencil skills still dominates class time.

Some elementary school teachers are fearful of the calculator for they know that it can do all of the arithmetic they have been teaching. They understand that arithmetic is important for every child to know, but when the calculator comes in these teachers do not know what to teach and they may stop teaching arithmetic entirely. This is not just a view of ignorant teachers; there have been recommendations by some science educators in the United States that much of the time spent on mathematics in the elementary school can now be spent on science because the content that has been

---

[2]   A general description of UCSMP may be found in the annual project brochures, obtainable from the project. The SPUR characterization of mathematics is described in the Teacher's Edition of any of the six UCSMP textbooks published by ScottForesman, 1900 E. Lake Avenue, Glenview IL 60025 USA.

taught is no longer needed. So we must be careful to explain the breadth of arithmetic to those outside of mathematics or we will lose the time that is devoted to mathematics in the elementary school. Thus though it would seem that "arithmetic for all" is so ingrained in schooling that it will not leave, I believe we should not be complacent.

Obviously, as zealots for mathematics education, there are many of us who might wish as much mathematics as possible to be learned by everyone. But there are zealots in all fields, who wish the same for their fields. Furthermore, children these days need also to know more about other subjects than they have hitherto been expected to know. Thus we cannot simply dictate that more and more mathematics be learned by all; we must have the strength to take out old content as well as put in new content.

It is already the case that, in some countries, some of the more complicated arithmetic algorithms, such as long division, are not being taught to all students and are not being tested. It is a case of "arithmetic for all" becoming "arithmetic for some".

Despite the fact that some mathematics is becoming obsolete, more and more mathematics is entering the curriculum. As an example, in the United States only a generation ago, most students encountered not one day of probability and the only statistics taught was how to calculate the average of a set of numbers. A national report in 1959 recommended merely that an optional course in probability and statistics be available to 12th grade students.[3] By 1975, only 16 years later, there was quite a change: a report recommended that statistics be taught at all levels of the curriculum, a recommendation that has been repeated many times.[4]

Similar increases in the mathematics all students are expected to learn has happened in all countries. For example, students in almost all countries today are expected to know a great deal more about measurement than they used to know. In some countries, all students are expected to know some algebra and some geometry, and this algebra is quickly becoming quite graphical with an earlier study of functions. There are trends that indicate the geometry is becoming quite a bit more visually sophisticated, with the increasing use of coordinates, isometries and other transformations, and continuous deformations.

---

[3]   College Entrance Examination Board Commission on Mathematics. *Program for College Preparatory Mathematics.* New York: CEEB, 1959.

[4]   National Advisory Committee on Mathematical Education (NACOME). *Overview and analysis of school mathematics: Grades K-12.* Reston, VA: National Council of Teachers of Mathematics, 1975.

FROM ARITHMETIC FOR SOME TO ARITHMETIC FOR ALL

To obtain guidance regarding what may happen or, what should be our policies towards these changes, it is useful to ask if there has ever previously been a time like ours, when there was such a revolution in the amount of mathematics which the average citizen was expected to know. From a Western perspective, a corresponding revolution began in the 15th century.

Compared with the situation today, in the 15th century very little mathematics—only counting and the simplest of addition—was known to all people even in the most advanced of countries. Nowhere near 95% of children went to school, and arithmetic was one of the liberal arts, taught in colleges which few attended. We might say that in the 15th century all mathematics was for some. Tobias Dantzig tells a story that supposedly took place in the first half of the 15th century of a trader in Germany who wanted his son to get the best mathematics education he could. He consulted a professor at a German university who advised him that his son could learn to add and subtract at his university, but if he wanted to learn to multiply and divide, then he should go to Italy, where they were more advanced in such matters.[5] Yet 500 years later, by the end of the last century, whenever there was compulsory schooling arithmetic was present, and the expectations for arithmetic were quite formidable, the complexity of the problems being enough to challenge any of us today.

Three fundamental developments changed the situation. The first was the increased amount and sophistication of trade between peoples. These increased the need for accurate records that were understandable to traders and to those who benefited from the trade: manufacturers of goods, owners of land from whom farmstuffs and minerals were obtained, and all others in the marketplace. Great numbers of people were engaged in these activities and so the increasing need for mathematical knowhow in the marketplace was no small influence on the amount of mathematics known to the average citizen.

The second development was mathematical: the invention of algorithms that made it easier to do arithmetic than had previously been the case. Roman numerals were not well suited to computation beyond addition and subtraction, and algorithms for multiplication and division were in their infancy in the 15th century. At the end of the 16th century when Simon Stevin first considered decimal places to the right of the unit's place, one of the main

---

[5]   Tobias Dantzig. *Number: The language of science.* (New York: Macmillan, 1954.) Cited in Frank Swetz, *Capitalism and school arithmetic: The new math of the 15th Century.* LaSalle, IL: Open Court Publishing Co., 1987.

arguments he put forth for using them was that there existed algorithms for multiplication and division that could be applied to what he called "decimal fractions", and thus computation would be simplified. Within 30 years of Stevin's invention of decimals, logarithms had been invented and decimals were established as the preeminent way to represent numbers.

The third development that enabled the expectation for competence in arithmetic to become universal was the invention of printing. Arithmetic skills are not easily learned; certainly they are not usually learned merely from one or two books that might be community property. Thus in order for competence in arithmetic to become universal there had to be enough books to enable all students to have their own books. Printing made it possible to have enough books. Printing also helped to standardize the language of arithmetic throughout the western world. Today's differences in notation throughout the world are minor: numerals and other symbols are the same, enabling traders world-wide to use the same arithmetic language.

Thus between 1400 and 1900, "arithmetic for some" became "arithmetic for all", and necessary for this were three developments: a societal need for the competence, the mathematical language and tools that made this competence a reasonable expectation, and technology that made it possible for this competence to be realized. At the same time that arithmetic changed from being for some to for all, so did reading, and for the same reasons. An enlightened citizenry and an intelligent work force came to require both the ability to read and the ability to compute and apply arithmetic.

FROM ARITHMETIC FOR ALL TO ARITHMETIC AS A PART OF LITERACY

One need only examine a daily newspaper to get an idea of the extent to which arithmetic is ingrained in our cultures and has become a necessary part of communication, indeed, a part of literacy. In various countries I have invariably found the *median* number of numbers on a newspaper page is somewhere between 120 and 150. The *mean* number of numbers is far higher—the last time I calculated it for a Chicago newspaper, the mean number of numbers on a page was over 500, due to sports pages, want ads, the weather page, and the business pages.

These numbers are used in many ways: as counts, often large, and, with a wide variety of counting units as measures; in scales of various kinds; as ratios; both interval and single number estimates and exact values. There are various kinds of graphs, sometimes daily analyses of lotteries, results of polls, many stock averages, and sports statistics, all of which could be simplified at times if algebraic formulas were used. There are advertisements with discounts given as percents, annual percentage rates for investments, dimensions of the articles being offered, computer specifications, powers of zoom lenses, and other technical information.

An exhaustive listing of numbers in the newspaper is not needed to make the point that to read a newspaper today requires that the reader be able to process mathematical information to an extent far beyond that required even one generation ago. It is often said that we are in an information age; it is the case that much of that information is numerical or pictorial, and thus is mathematical.

Concomitant with the evolution of arithmetic as a part of literacy is a major change in the views of society toward who can be competent in these things. No longer is arithmetic seen as the province of a few. In places where arithmetic is a part of literacy, no longer is it seen as a subject that is so abstract that only a few can learn it. In most places, no longer is a special degree of competence in arithmetic skills viewed as an indicator of intelligence.

THE CURRENT STATE OF ALGEBRA AS A PART OF LITERACY

Could we replace "arithmetic" in this summary by any mathematics other than arithmetic? A reasonable first candidate is algebra since in some countries algebra is already taught to all. But algebra does not have anything near the stature that arithmetic has in society. Many well educated people ask why algebra was taught to them in school; they would never ask that about arithmetic. Many people have been taught algebraic skills and, perhaps, algebraic properties; and they may have even been taught some graphical representations. But they never were taught the uses, and they do not see the societal need for all to learn algebra. Algebra is viewed by many people as so abstract that it really does not have uses of its own.

If we view the newspaper as signalling what mathematics is needed by society, then we see how far we have to go before algebra becomes viewed as a part of literacy. There may be thousands of numbers, tables, graphs, and charts in newspapers; but it is seldom that one finds any algebra. It is unusual to find one overt example of algebra in a newspaper despite the fact that there are simple formulas underlying many of the sports statistics, discounts, and business data. So if algebra becomes a part of literacy, I do not think it will be the algebra that is now being taught.

Indeed, whereas the level of political analysis one finds in newspapers is often quite deep and requires a thorough knowledge of a nation's governmental system, even the simplest algebra—even though it may be studied by the vast majority of people in a nation—is taboo. When such mathematics is presented it is often preceded by cautionary statements, such as "For those who understand such things ..." Unlike arithmetic, algebra is still viewed as a sign of intelligence by those who do not use it.

WILL ALGEBRA FOR SOME BECOME ALGEBRA FOR ALL?

It is appropriate to ask whether we can ever expect algebra to become as much a part of literacy for future generations as arithmetic is now. Will algebra ever be as universal as arithmetic?

Following the clue provided by the history of arithmetic, the first component in the question of algebra for all would have to be a perceived need by society for that algebra. I believe the general view of the nonmathematical public is that algebra is certainly required if you wish to be an engineer or scientist of any sort; or if you wish to work with computers, statistics, economics, or any field that seems dependent on numbers; or if you are in a field that uses science, such as medicine. The general public might also realize that the building trades, such as carpentry or plumbing, use algebraic formulas. It may well be that this is enough to insure that algebra should be and will be taught to all.

In the policy arenas of the advanced industrialized countries, the arguments for major attention to algebra and higher mathematics for the entire populace go somewhat as follows. The economic well-being of a country must be based on having jobs for its people. The new jobs in the 21st century will be based on achievements in sectors such as biotechnology, telecommunications, computers and software, robotics and machine tools, and microelectronics. Better products in these areas require statistical quality control. To have statistical quality control workers need to understand it, which requires that they have studied statistics and operations research, and for these a person needs a considerable amount of mathematics.

For a couple of hundred years there have existed the mathematical language and tools that make competence in algebra a reasonable expectation. World-wide we use the Latin alphabet in elementary algebra; we use coordinate graphs to picture functions. The big change—within the past five years—is that there now exists technology that makes the graphing of functions and data, and even curve-fitting and data analysis, accessible to all, that can be taken anywhere one has a pocket, and which is user-friendly enough so that one does not need to know huge amounts of mathematics in order to use it. Not only is algebra more accessible, but so is elementary analysis.

The widely available technology does not yet cover all of algebra. I am waiting for the symbolic algebra calculator that is easy to use and cheap. I want it to be able to solve literal equations as well as numerical ones. I want a simpler form of *Derive* or *Mathematica* or *Maple* on my calculator for under $100. This technology seems certain to come.

For this reason, I believe that algebra will become a subject for all, though not the same algebra that we now teach, and with it will come many of the concepts of elementary analysis and calculus.

WILL ALGEBRA FOR ALL
BECOME ALGEBRA FOR SOME?

As with arithmetic the technology does not necessarily suggest an increased emphasis on algebra in schools. Because the purpose of technology is to avoid work, to make it possible for us to direct machines to do tasks even when we do not understand how the machines work, the same technological advances that have made it possible to do great amounts of algebra easily may also make it less necessary for people to learn certain parts of algebra.

For example, suppose we wished to predict future population from recent data and an exponential model. The data can be plotted without knowing algebra. Transforming the variable p to log p can be done simply by writing a formula if one is using a spreadsheet, or by pressing a button if one is using a calculator, and then the points on the second graph can be found. The line of best fit can be found without any algebra: simply press another few buttons. This line can be used for predicting the population from the graph. Thus an activity that in the past might have required a considerable amount of algebraic skill can now be done with none of the traditional skills. Instead, what are needed are the facility of graphing functions using an automatic grapher and knowledge of the inverse relationship between the exponential and logarithmic functions.

On the most recent graphing calculators there is a key that solves any type of a large number of equations arithmetically by successive approximation methods hidden from the user. A student who has this calculator does not need to know the quadratic formula in order to obtain the solutions to a quadratic equation to the nearest thousandth, nor does the student need to know the inverse trigonometric functions in order to solve a trigonometric equation.

We make the assumption, because we are in mathematics, use mathematics, and love mathematics, that an increasingly technological world requires more and more mathematics for all. However, what may be the case is that such a technological world requires more and more mathematics for *some* but less for *all* due to the advances that those few make. Just as we use algebra to solve problems which the ancient Greeks solved or attempted to solve geometrically, and many of us in mathematics have never learned exactly how they did that, it is possible that future generations will learn how to use the latest technology to solve our algebra problems and never learn how we solved them using algebra.

The situation is made more interesting by spreadsheets, which have their own algebra. Possibly in the near future the language of spreadsheets will become the most commonly used algebraic language. So we may think we have the mathematical language and tools for algebra for everyone, but when everyone comes to learn an algebraic language it may be a different one than the one we have been teaching. The difference between algebra in school and algebra in the real world is akin to the difference between arithmetic in school and arithmetic in the newspaper. In school the tendency in almost all countries is to concentrate on the Skills and Properties of algebra, while in the world at large the Uses predominate, with Representations also being quite important.

The same technology that enables algebra questions to be treated without algebra also enables calculus questions to be treated without calculus. The very same software programs and calculator technology that enable one to avoid symbolic algebra also make it possible to avoid the symbolic manipulations of calculus and statistics. It is possible today to answer max-min problems without having to resort to derivatives; to obtain areas under curves without integrals. In many places we have justified algebra not on its own merits but on its importance in the more advanced mathematics of calculus and differential equations. But with technology these subjects, too, are not so advanced. We must be careful that, despite its importance, we do not lose algebra in school because of the other means we now have for tackling problems that used to require algebra.

CAN ALGEBRA AND CALCULUS CONCEPTS BE LEARNED BY ALL?

There are many countries in which the national curriculum includes a study of algebra for everyone. Within the United States there is a trend to attempt to teach algebra to all. Yet I know of few algebra teachers in any country who believe algebra can be learned by all; and as for calculus, that is out of the question: the subject matter itself is beyond the students, or so the teachers think.

If these subjects remain unchanged both in the classroom and in the society at large, I agree with this point of view. But all of the current developments suggest that "algebra for all" will be quite different from the traditional algebra that we have been teaching, and I believe that it will include calculus.

The reason for my optimism can be found in any country where our language is not the mother tongue. In the United States we tend to teach foreign languages in senior high school, so the students study that language at about the same time that they take algebra through calculus. Many American students have a great deal of trouble learning languages. Their accents are atrocious, it seems as if the language is beyond them, and only a small percentage seem to do well in their language study. Yet in the countries where the language is spoken, even small children know it. Are these children all brilliant?

Of course their proficiency in their mother tongue is not due to any special brilliance, but because they are immersed in it and so become fluent in it. With instruction virtually all of them learn to decode the incredibly complex combinations of letters and other symbols that constitute their own written language. It is difficult to believe that any person who can learn to read and write and comprehend his or her native language does not possess the ability to read and write and comprehend algebraic symbolism, part of the language of mathematics.

What makes it possible for children in foreign countries is an environment in which these languages appear in context. Thus, in the United States, the effective teacher of French tries to make the classroom into a bit of Montréal or Paris or Grenoble. The movements within mathematics education to put context into the mathematics, to utilize applications of mathematics in everyday teaching, and to engage students in classroom discussions can be seen as an attempt to speak the language of mathematics in the classroom. Because mathematics beyond arithmetic is not yet commonplace outside the classroom, this is a necessary move within the classroom if we are to achieve higher levels of mathematics for all.

Because mathematics is so much a language, there are many aspects of it that are better learned when the child is younger than when the child is older. Part of the reason for the difficulty of calculus is certainly that ideas are often first encountered at the ages of 17-20, quite late for one to learn a language.

FROM ALGEBRA/CALCULUS FOR SOME
TO ALGEBRA/CALCULUS FOR ALL

In the future the algebra-calculus sequence will give less attention to algebraic techniques for solving problems, because these will be solved by preprogrammed software. But the sequence will need to place increased emphasis on two aspects of algebra: the uses to which algebra, functions, and calculus can be put; and the importance of algebra as a language for communicating generalizations and functional relationships. Both of these aspects increase in importance because of computers. In the parlance of the SPUR characterization, algebra of the future will undoubtedly contain less of the Skills dimension and more of the Uses and Representations dimensions. As for the Properties dimension, due to the importance of the language of algebra, it ought to maintain its role in the curriculum. In particular, the broad properties of functions, of matrices, and of vectors will probably enter the domain of mathematics for all.

Critical in all this is that we encourage the use of algebra as a language of communication. In addition to our current emphasis on variables in formulas and variables as unknowns, we must place greater emphasis on the uses of variables to generalize patterns, the use of variables as indicating places in spreadsheets or computer storage, the use of variables as arguments in functions. Here are some ways in which this could be done: (1) emphasize how much easier it is in many circumstances to apply a formula rather than read a table; (2) demonstrate how the language of algebra, functions, matrices and vectors makes it easier to handle certain problems; (3) show how some patterns and trends can be described algebraically more compactly than with graphs; (4) show the power of functions to predict, and how picking the wrong function can lead to errors.

GEOMETRY

The world is geometric. Although in school geometry students are taught as if the only planar shapes are polygonal or circular, and the only 3-dimensional shapes are spherical, cylindrical, or conical, every object in the world, from the chair you are sitting on to the leaves of a tree considered individually or as a set, has a shape and a size. Computer graphics have greatly increased our ability to draw pictures to represent this world and to examine those pictures. They have made the Skills and Uses of geometry more accessible; and, as mentioned earlier, they have increased the importance of geometrical Representations of functions. So I believe that sets of points will play an ever increasing role in the curriculum, but these may not be the traditional sets of points, but more ordered pairs and triples, graphs of functions and relations, representations of graphs and networks. The importance of coordinates and transformations will certainly increase, and the traditional work with polygons and circles is likely to decrease or be encountered by students earlier in their mathematics experience. It is likely that experiences with all these topics will be encountered by all students.

MATHEMATICAL SYSTEMS

The traditional role of geometry as a vehicle for displaying a mathematical system is already gone from many countries, and I do not see much call for its return where it has left. Moreover, it does not seem that other parts of mathematics have picked up this loss. Less and less formal deduction is being taught in schools.

Here computers present particular problems. Because of their ability to display example after example they encourage induction as a valid method of argument. Picture a triangle with its medians drawn. A student who is able to deform this triangle continuously on a screen, and who sees that the medians are still concurrent, will surely be less likely to think that a proof of the concurrency is needed. Similarly, a student who can zoom in on the graph of a function to determine its maximum value to virtually any desired accuracy is not likely to see calculus as powerful as previous generations saw it. For this reason, the current condition, in which deduction is taught only to some, is not likely to change. Formal deduction may even be taught to fewer students in the future, but I hope I am wrong. The requirement that results be deduced in order to be valid is one of the fundamental characteristics of mathematical thought; it is too important not to be taught to all.

SUMMARY

We are in an extraordinary time for mathematics, a time unlike any that has been seen for perhaps 400–500 years. The accessibility of mathematics for the population at large has increased dramatically due to advances in technology. These advances make it likely that more mathematics than ever before will become part of the fabric of everyone's education and everyday literacy. But the mathematics will not be a superset of what is taught today for those things that can be done quickly and easily by computers are very likely to disappear from the curriculum. What will remain is a more conceptual, more applied, and more visual mathematics. The result—if history repeats—will be a field of mathematics which will be even more exciting than our wonderful field is today.[6]

---

[6]   I would like to thank my wife Karen for her help in organizing this talk, Ed Zegray and the son of Bernard Hodgson for helping translate many of my transparencies into French, and Ed Jacobsen of UNESCO for his introduction.

ON THE APPRECIATION OF THEOREMS
BY STUDENTS AND TEACHERS

Hans-Joachim Vollrath

University of Würzburg, Germany

When a theorem has been taught, students are expected to understand it and to know a proof. They should be able to reproduce the theorem and its proof, and to apply the theorem correctly. But for a real understanding they need to know something about the historical background of the theorem, about its place within the theory, and its relevance for applications. Therefore students should learn not only theorems but also the importance of these theorems. This can only be accomplished by teachers who have learned to appreciate theorems adequately. Therefore, an important part of teacher education must be concerned with the interpretation, discussion, and evaluation of theorems.

DISCUSSING THE PYTHAGOREAN THEOREM

At the beginning of my geometry lecture for future teachers I usually ask them which theorems they remember from their school geometry. Most years, the best-remembered theorem is the Pythagorean theorem. After I tell them that this is almost always the one selected by students, we try to find out why this theorem is so prominent. Typical comments by the students include the following:

This theorem is interesting (important, beautiful, highly regarded, surprising, central).

It has a simple (beautiful, impressive, suggestive, meaningful) formula.

The theorem concerns an important geometric figure, the right triangle.

These are very general judgments. In further discussion, more specific answers are given:

The Pythagorean theorem

- reveals a relationship between the sides of a right triangle.

- helps to express one side of a right triangle in terms of the other two sides.

- is a special case of the law of cosines.

- is an inference from the theorem: $a^2 = p \cdot c$; $b^2 = q \cdot c$.

- shows how to transform two squares into one square.

This theorem

- is named for Pythagoras, the Greek philosopher and mathematician.

- was known to the ancient Egyptians.

- has been discovered in most cultures.

There are more than 200 proofs of the theorem, including one by Garfield, who became president of the United States.

To summarize, there are four general types of response:

- affective: beautiful, interesting, surprising;

- cognitive: special case, inference, reveals a relationship;

- instrumental: useful, applicable, helpful;

- cultural: known by Pythagoras, and the ancient Egyptians.

What are the origins of the students' appreciation for this theorem? We can presume that the most important source for their views is personal experience, gained by studying the theorem, its proofs and its applications. However, it seems likely that judgments by teachers have some influence as well.

But how can teachers teach adequate views of theorems? How effective are their methods?

APPRECIATION OF THEOREMS IN MATHEMATICS INSTRUCTION

It is helpful to understand how teachers can express their appreciation of a theorem to their students, either explicitly or implicitly.

Explicitly expressed appreciation of a theorem

It is traditional in mathematics to give hints about the importance of a proposition by identifying it as a lemma, corollary, theorem, or fundamental theorem. These assessments are handed down from generation to generation. They often have their origin in papers or books of the mathematicians who discovered the propositions. Well known examples include Gauss' *Theorema Egregium* or Sperner's Lemma. In the latter case, the lemma has become more famous than a normal theorem.

The teacher can give explicit expression to the appreciation of a theorem by comments such as:

- This is an important theorem.

(which is a bland statement!) or by a more specific comment:

- This theorem is very useful for calculations concerning triangles.

In the second comment, assessment is directed to the use of the theorem, whereas the following example expresses an appreciation for the knowledge gained by the theorem:

- The theorem expresses a relationship among the three sides of a right triangle.

An assessment about a theorem can also include a kind of reasoning about its importance:

- There are more than 200 proofs for the Pythagorean theorem. It is therefore one of the most prominent theorems in mathematics.

Sometimes the estimation of the importance of a theorem changes. A well known example is the "fundamental theorem of algebra" which is currently referred to as the "so-called fundamental theorem of algebra" in modern books on algebra. This makes clear that one should not overestimate these qualifications. But in both cases they express estimations explicitly.

In my personal experience, an explicitly expressed appreciation of a theorem is only impressive if it is specific, and based on reasons, knowledge, and experience.

Implicitly expressed appreciation of a theorem

In the name "Pythagorean theorem" special prominence is given to this theorem. The reference to a famous mathematician suggests that he discovered the theorem, though it is well known that this is often not true, as indeed it is not true for the Pythagorean theorem. Perhaps more importantly, the names of theorems can differ from country to country with a national identification. The name of a theorem can also refer to its contents, for example "mean value theorem", or "prime number theorem". In all these cases teachers can implicitly express their appreciation of the theorem.

But the way in which teachers deal with a theorem also reveals their appreciation of it. By starting with an interesting problem, discussing assumptions, giving different proofs, studying applications, or making remarks about its history, the teacher can bring the students to think: "This must be an important theorem because there is so much ado about it."

There is a strong conviction among mathematicians that the importance of a theorem is evident when it is really understood. Many mathematicians therefore avoid speaking or writing about their estimation of a theorem. For experts, their "hidden appreciation of a theorem" is recognizable in several ways. The position of a theorem within the theory, the numbers of references to a theorem, and the consequences drawn from a theorem all indicate appreciation.

Unfortunately many students feel lost when they are asked to express their estimation of a theorem because they have not received clear hints that are relevant for judging it. Implicitly expressed appreciation of a theorem allows students a free hand to make their own judgments, but they must learn to interpret the teacher's behavior correctly.

Comparing explicit and implicit judgments can be summarized as follows. Explicit judgments of theorems are recognizable by the students. They reveal the personal preferences of teachers and ask for agreement, but can also invoke opposition. Above all, explicit judgments demand reasons. Implicit judgments allow students more freedom for their own assessment, but the students can also be misled by or misinterpret their teacher's behavior.

THE PROBLEM OF JUSTIFICATION

A proposition is called a theorem if it is true relative to a system of axioms. The statement that a proposition is a theorem belongs to metalanguage, and can also be true or false. But what about the statement:

The theorem is important with respect to mathematical knowledge.

One may agree or disagree either on a rational or an emotional basis.

Some typical situations in which mathematicians are asked to evaluate theorems include theorems in a doctoral dissertation, theorems in a paper presented to a journal, theorems in a paper under review, comparing the "value" of a theorem in an award, or deciding which theorems shall be selected for a report in an encyclopedia.

There are not many statements by mathematicians about their standards. Let me give one example: Behnke (1966) wrote about the procedure for judging a research paper for a journal. Novelty and correctness of the results are necessary but not sufficient merits for publication. Criteria for the significance of a paper include:

- elegance of the presentation,

- ingenuity of the proofs,

- fertility of the considerations,

- adequacy of the resources,

- suitability of the reasoning.

But obviously each criterion is as vague as the quality which it is expected to judge. When Behnke characterized the qualified mathematician by the ability to apply these criteria correctly, the result was a circle between the judgment and qualification of a mathematician. After all, the community of mathematicians sets the values, and it is also responsible for the justification of the decisions. But the community pretends a harmony which is not always present.

Recent discussion about the status of the mean value theorem of calculus will illustrate the discord. Van der Waerden (1980) and Laugwitz (1990) judged the mean value theorem as:

- historically unimportant,

- clear by intuition,

- rather useful because of the conventions used in its proof,

- only interesting in its systematic aspects.

They concluded that the mean value theorem is rather unimportant.

Schweiger (1987) and Winter (1988), reviewing the same theorem, emphasized:

- it expresses practical intuitions from physics and economy,

- it opens a field of discoveries,

- it expresses the fundamental completeness of the real number system,

- it is important for approximations,

- it is a bridge from local to global changes,

- it is a paradox that the mean value theorem is equivalent to both a more special theorem (Rolle) and a more general theorem (Taylor),

- it is an example for a non-constructive theorem.

On this basis, they decided that the mean value theorem is very important.

Perhaps you will think that it is not so important whether the theorem is confirmed to be important as to know it. But from a didactic point of view this was a rather important discussion. The background was the question of the role the mean value theorem should play in a calculus course. The experts were mathematicians and didacticians who were influenced by their knowledge and experience, but also by their personal preference and taste. Their argumentation was impressive, though their emotions were rather irritating.

In my opinion there was not just one winner of this discussion. We all profited from it because we learned a lot about this theorem which we would not have found in textbooks. Perhaps teachers feel lost. What should they tell their students about the value of this theorem when the experts do not agree? But is it not an advantage to take part in an open discussion? It protects us from handling judgments of theorems dogmatically. The reasons given in arriving at the judgment help teachers in curriculum decisions, but they also reveal aspects for their own estimation of the theorem's importance.

DEVELOPING ADEQUATE ESTIMATIONS
IN STUDENT TEACHERS

Mathematics books which are used at the university for the mathematics education of future teachers rarely comment on the assessment of theorems. While lectures are used to give more comments, in my experience students tend to relax during such commentaries. My remarks are often not seen as relevant for the examination, even though an important task of courses in the didactics of mathematics is to discuss theorems which the students already know from their mathematics lectures, under the aspect of evaluation. Again, I demand that the students get the chance to reflect on their experiences, to listen to other students' judgments, and to consider them carefully. Usually it is very surprising for the students to realize that people can have different opinions about mathematical facts!

I would like to invite mathematicians, when they are writing books for future teachers, to comment more about theorems from different points of view, and on specific ways of reasoning. My request of the didacticians is that they discuss questions of evaluation in an open way without being dogmatic.

As we have seen, the appreciation of a theorem refers to four aspects: knowledge, usage, culture, and beauty. It is rather easy for the students to judge the efficiency of a theorem because they have only to remember their own use of the theorem. Therefore it is not surprising that the assessments of student teachers are mainly directed to usage.

Students are able to discover the knowledge provided by a theorem by reflecting on it for a while. It is well known that consideration of the problem context which led to the discovery of a theorem enables student teachers to appreciate the theorem in the context of a culture. But the realization often seems to be not worth the effort for the students.

Questions about the beauty of a theorem are sometimes irritating to student teachers, though my students were very interested in David Wells' (1988, 1990) investigation about the evaluation of theorems by the readers of *The Mathematical Intelligencer.* Each of 24 prominent theorems had to be given a score for beauty. The winner was Euler's identity. Teachers should be aware that there are many books and papers about the beauty of mathematics which can stimulate students and teachers.

In summary, student teachers need explicit comments and discussions about the aspects of knowledge, usage, beauty, and culture to develop adequate estimations of theorems.

APPRECIATION OF THEOREMS BY STUDENTS

When theorems are taught at the *gymnasium,* teachers are used to discussing them. We were interested in the student assessments of theorems that resulted from this. We interviewed students from Grade 8 and Grade 10 about their estimations of geometry theorems, and students from Grade 13 about calculus theorems. For the 8th graders Thales' theorem—The angle in a semicircle is a right angle—and the congruence theorems for triangles were the most prominent. Thales' theorem was interesting to them because of its use in constructions. The congruence theorems were seen as important for proofs, and as a basis for the construction of triangles.

The 10th graders appreciated the Pythagorean theorem and Thales' theorem most. They reasoned that they are logical, easy to understand, often used in tests, and used in constructions. The appreciation of the Pythagorean theorem resulted from tests, the great numbers of problems solved in connection with this theorem, the great variety of examples, and the impressive formula.

In our interviews with the 13th graders we asked them and their teacher about their appreciation of the calculus theorems. The most important theorems for these students were the theorems about minima and maxima, L'Hôpital's rule, and the theorems of limits.

The most important theorem for the teacher was the fundamental theorem of calculus. The differences of the assessments between students and teacher resulted from their different viewpoints. The students' interest was more directed to usage while the teacher's interest was more directed to knowledge.

Such differences can appear quite dramatically. I remember a classroom situation from my own teaching in Grade 7. When I became very enthusiastic about a theorem, a girl jumped up and cried: "This is all rubbish!" This was an evaluation too!

Our appreciation of theorems may provoke our students to protest. And their rejection can be a provocation for the teacher. How should we react adequately? I think we can agree that it is useless trying to convince the students about the importance of a theorem. Why not let the students know that they are allowed to have different views? Perhaps they will discover the importance of the theorem by themselves. On the other hand, it is also true that many students like mathematics because of its objectivity. They get the chance to appreciate mathematics based on their own criteria and decisions.

In summary, in working with an important theorem, teachers should try to balance the different aspects of knowledge, usage, beauty, culture. They should become aware of the students' appreciations and should accept them as expressions of their personality. But they also should give their students a chance to make adequate estimations of theorems by reasoning without being dogmatic or autocratic.

BALANCED TEACHING

When I recently asked my students about their appreciation of theorems from their school mathematics, one student said (and many agreed): "Mathematics instruction was not theorems. It had more to do with techniques." They therefore felt rather lost at my question about their appreciation of theorems. It seems to be more important for students, and perhaps for their teachers too, that a method works, rather than to know why the method works. It is more comfortable, and with respect to tests and examinations more effective. But the result is unbalanced teaching.

We emphasized different aspects of significance. Obviously these aspects have to be balanced in mathematics education. There must be a balance between knowledge and usage, theory and practice, beauty and rigor, culture and technique. One-sided assessments can reveal unbalanced teaching. But it is also true that balanced estimations of theorems can help to balance different aspects of teaching. They can help the students to gain a valid impression of mathematics. Thus, balanced assessments play a key role in teaching.

But is it not a question of the subject matter? In a geometry course, there are many theorems which express knowledge and a few concerning techniques. But in an algebra course in secondary schools there are usually "laws", and "formulas" and, above all, techniques for transforming expressions and solving equations; but only a very few "theorems" , such as the binomial theorem, or Vieta's theorem (about the relationship between the roots and the coefficients of a quadratic equation).

There are different traditions of teaching geometry and teaching algebra with respect to theory. This is also true for the history of mathematics. Axiomatic presentations of arithmetic and algebra appeared rather late. Hilbert's *Foundations of geometry* and Landau's *Foundations of calculus* can be seen as the culmination of this development, offering equivalent presentations in geometry and arithmetic. From Landau's book one learns that a large number of propositions in arithmetic can be treated as theorems, which is not common in mathematics instruction. To better balance geometry and algebra teaching I suggest writing, for example, the law of commutativity of multiplication, or the rule for adding fractions, or the formula for the solution of a quadratic equation as theorems.

Above all, properties which are fundamental for the understanding of arithmetic and algebra should be pointed out as theorems. As illustrations, consider:

- Natural numbers can be presented as sums of units.
- Real numbers can be presented as the limits of sequences of rational numbers.
- The square of a real number cannot be negative.

Students can only develop a valid impression of mathematics if they receive a balanced teaching in which they can appreciate theorems as a distillate of knowledge and potential.

ACCENTUATED TEACHING

We started with an outstanding theorem. But every theorem can be appreciated with respect to cognition, usage, culture, and appearance. To some extent each theorem is important. If a certain theorem were omitted in an axiomatic theory it could be critical for the whole theory. However, if teachers call every proposition an important theorem, this is not credible. It would have the same effect as underlining every word in a book (as some readers appear to do). "If everything is important, then nothing is important." (Shenitzer, 1986).

Nevertheless, to illustrate properties by appropriate theorems helps students in several ways. They become aware of what is noteworthy, find out what they are expected to know, and develop a basis to which they can refer when they are trying to prove a statement. However, it is also necessary to differentiate between theorems so that students can recognize the structure of a subject area, become aware of the key properties, and develop standards.

To give special prominence to a theorem, say by referencing it to a mathematician, helps students appreciate the achievement of mathematicians and understand their contributions to culture. Emphasizing the importance of theorems may help students to appreciate that mathematics is something important for culture and for themselves.

As a consequence, students need a kind of teaching in which they get a chance to distinguish between important and less important facts. They can only develop standards when they become acquainted with the really outstanding results of mathematics.

STEPS TOWARDS ADEQUATE ESTIMATIONS OF THEOREMS

We understand the appreciation of a theorem as a part of the meta-knowledge that we want students to develop in mathematics education. Students learn to reflect upon theorems by asking questions such as:

- What does the theorem represent?

- What is the essential point of the theorem?

- What consequences does this theorem have?

- What problems can be solved with this theorem?

Students can initiate their assessments of a theorem by tasks such as:

- Trying to formulate the theorem in your own words.

- Giving a descriptive title for the theorem.

- Trying to find a suitable name for the theorem.

Mathematical knowledge is often tested through problem solving. For testing students' meta-knowledge it seems to be more convenient to let the students write an essay about the theorem. This is not very common in mathematics instruction. Writing mathematical essays was recommended in Germany by M. Wagenschein, but students are rarely asked to do so. Problem solving is still predominant in German schools.

Finally, I think it is very important that students have a chance to discuss their assessments of theorems with other students and with their teacher. They should be willing to listen to other students' reasons, to give reasons for their appreciation of a theorem, and be prepared perhaps to change a personal assessment during discussion.

Discussing assessments of theorems is a training method and a test for scientific culture. It can be seen as a contribution to "mathematical enculturation" (Bishop, 1988).

ACKNOWLEDGMENTS

I wish to acknowledge with gratitude the influence of Alexander Israel Wittenberg on my philosophy of education. He was professor at Laval University in Québec, and later on at York University in Toronto. His book, *Bildung und Mathematik* (1963), is a program for mathematics education through a genuine experience of mathematics. I fear most didacticians do not know what they are missing by not having an edition in English. I wish to close with a statement that accords with Wittenberg's philosophy:

> Students and student teachers have the right to learn in what respect the theorems they are expected to learn are important.

REFERENCES

Behnke, H. (1966). Die Auswirkung der Forschung auf den Unterricht. *Mathematisch-Physikalische Semesterberichte, 13*, 1-12.

Bishop, A.J. (1988). *Mathematical Enculturation.* Dordrecht, The Netherlands: Kluwer Academic Publishers.

Laugwitz, D. (1990). Zur Rechtfertigung mathematischer Unterrichtsinhalte: Das Beispiel "Mittelwertsatz der Differentialrechnung. *Journal für Mathematik-Didaktik, 11*, 111-128.

Shenitzer, A. (1986). Some thoughts on the teaching of mathematics. *The Mathematical Intelligencer, 8*, 21-24.

Schweiger, F. (1987). Was spricht für den Mittelwertsatz der Differentialrechnung? *Mathematische Semesterberichte, 34*, 220-230.

Van der Waerden, B.L. (1980). Die "genetische Methode" und der Mittelwertsatz der Differentialrechnung. *Praxis der Mathematik, 22*, 52-54.

Wagenschein, M. (1970). Zum mathematischen Aufsatz. In M. Wagenschein (Ed.), *Ursprüngliches Verstehen und exaktes Denken* (Vol. 1, pp. 170-172). Stuttgart: Klett.

Wells, D. (1988). Which is the most beautiful? *The Mathematical Intelligencer, 10*, 30-31.

Wells, D. (1990). Are these the most beautiful? *The Mathematical Intelligencer, 12*, 37-41.

Winter, H. (1988). Intuition und Deduktion – zur Heuristik der Differentialrechnung. *Zentralblatt für Didaktik der Mathematik, 20*, 229-235.

Wittenberg, A.I. (1963). *Bildung und Mathematik.* Stuttgart: Klett.

GEOMETRY AS AN ELEMENT OF CULTURE[1]

Alexandr D. Alexandrov

St. Petersburg Department of the Steklov Mathematical Institute, Russia

Geometry (elementary Euclidean geometry) occupies a specific position among other branches of mathematics and among all other disciplines because of its unique character, consisting of the union of logic, imagination and practice. Geometry in its essence *is* this union.

Practice is the origin and the purpose of every science; one may say that, in its beginning, geometry is one of the natural, technical sciences. Every one of its concepts must be demonstrated and understood in material form as a reflection of reality not merely drawn on paper or a blackboard, but rather seen somewhere in the surrounding world. This will broaden the mental horizons of all students.

In fact Euclid's initial constructions and proofs are nothing but descriptions, mental images of practically possible operations. For instance, the proof of the congruence of triangles by means of superposition is a mental experiment: an image of a real, possible operation. The clearest proof of Pythagoras' theorem by means of shifting figures is another such experiment. The construction of regular systems of figures, of ornaments, where geometry unites with art, is another example of practical operations in geometry.

Geometric intuition grows in this fertile soil. The essence of geometry is the organic union of intuition—a vivid visual imagination—on the one hand, and strict logic on the other; they interrelate, interpenetrate, and guide each other.

Therein lies the importance of a geometry course being taught in all secondary schools.

---

[1]   Professor Alexandrov was unable to travel to Québec City to deliver his lecture. A short version of it is given here.

Geometry can, of course, be reduced to the application of algebraic methods, but this entails the liquidation of the specific importance of geometry as a subject and as a component of culture.

Strict logic is a characteristic of mathematics while vivid imagination belongs rather to the realm of art, which obviously appears to be the exact antithesis of logic. Nevertheless, their union and interaction produce the essence of geometry.

One of the greatest architects of our century, Le Corbusier, wrote, "Geometry provides a means whereby we perceive the environment and express ourselves. Geometry is a basis. Moreover it is a material realization of symbols which express everything that is perfect and sublime. It gives us great satisfaction through its mathematical precision."

Visual imagination provides a direct perception of geometric facts and suggests to logic how to express and prove them, while logic provides imagination with precision and guides it in building images which reveal essential logical connections.

Imagination is a very important facility for man; and geometry, especially solid geometry, develops it, lends it precision and subtlety. The objects of solid geometry cannot be depicted as simply as the objects of plane geometry and they demand the use of visual imagination.

Geometrical method deals with images. In teaching geometry one must ensure that students perceive every concept and every theorem in its intuitive visual content, which is more important than its formal expression. The latter has no geometric meaning without the former. The true geometrical method demands that the proof of a theorem be made as intuitively evident as possible. One is allowed to sacrifice some strictness for the sake of an evident, graphic clarity. Thus geometric reasoning develops not only the visual perception of geometric facts but also spatial intuitive thinking.

Along with the development of spatial imagination, geometry sharpens our perception of the world surrounding us and brings structure into our perception of its forms.

There is a saying that the general culture of a person is whatever remains when all that was ever learned has been forgotten. Someone may forget geometry as such, but its traces in spatial perception and imagination will remain.

Geometric intuition plays an important role beyond geometry itself: we mention only its fundamental role in mathematics. Starting with the concept of continuity, which is based on the intuition of the continuity of a line, one recalls the presentation of functions by means of curves, the complex plane, etc. Although functional analysis lies far beyond the domain of school mathematics, it is worthwhile to observe the fundamental role played by geometric intuition in the spaces that have been developed out of the three-dimensional intuition of ordinary geometry. Beyond pure mathematics we can mention relativity theory, of which we now have a deeper and, I dare say, a truer understanding through the geometric presentation given to it by Minkowski.

The other component of the spirit of geometry, its logic, is represented in particular by its characteristic construction, springing from Euclid: a sequence of theorems with their proofs. It tells us first of all that whatever is stated has to be proved. Here geometry militates against the immorality implicit in the comparatively common habit of making statements without any proof.

In teaching geometry it must be forbidden to affirm and accept anything except axioms without proof. It is not, of course, forbidden to communicate interesting geometric facts without proofs, but these cannot enter into the chain of deductions and proofs.

Geometry is a chain where every link is formed by a theorem and its proof. The sequence of these links represents a brilliant product of the human spirit: we watch a theory as it unfolds. When all the theorems and proofs have been forgotten, the idea of a proof, the idea that proof is essential, as well as the image of a consistent theory, will persist.

The logical component of geometry has its strongest realization in the axiomatic method. The construction of Euclid's *Elements* has served as a pattern of strict exposition for ages (remember, for instance, Spinoza's *Ethics*). Moreover, the analysis of geometric axioms plays an important part in the elaboration of the modern axiomatic method.

The general idea of establishing an axiomatic basis for any sphere of intellectual activity, such as ethics, is popular in our culture and has one of its sources in geometry.

The task of axiomatics in geometry consists in absorbing intuition by logic, to get rid of its embrace, as in the problem of the fifth postulate. The problem consisted in the impossibility of imagining the consequences of the denial of the postulate.

Lobachevski (as well as Bolyai) had the courage to accept these consequences as the facts of a logically possible geometry. But neither Lobachevski nor Bolyai could see the possible real or intuitive meaning of their geometry. This was discovered much later (40 years after the first publication by Lobachevski); and, strangely enough, the intuitive presentation of Lobachevski's geometry proved to be simpler than the Cayley-Klein and Poincaré models, each of which has its own advantages.

Thus the union of intuition and logic—broken by Lobachevski's course of action—was restored on a higher level.

Lobachevskian geometry can hardly be included in secondary school curricula, but it seems essential to give pupils an idea of it and to show them the greatness of the human spirit, capable of creating unimaginable concepts and theories which, in the course of time, proved to be comprehensible and fruitful.

ADDRESSES OF AUTHORS

ADRESSES DES AUTEURS

Alexandr D. Alexandrov
Steklov Mathematical Institute
27 Fontanka
St. Petersburg 191011, Russia

Gérard Audibert
14, rue Verdier Allut
30700 Uzès, France

Alan W. Bell
Shell Centre for Mathematical Education
University Park
Nottingham NG7 2RD, United Kingdom

Raffaella Borasi
University of Rochester
2135 Westfall Road
Rochester, NY 14627, USA

John L. Clark
94 Sutherland Drive
Toronto, ON Canada M4G 1H7

David John Clarke
Australian Catholic University
Christ Campus
17 Castlebar Road
Oakleigh, VIC 3166, Australia

Michael P. Closs
Department of Mathematics
University of Ottawa
Ottawa, ON Canada K1N 6N5

Jean Dhombres
CNRS – Laboratoire d'histoire
des sciences, UPR 21
49, rue Mirabeau
75016 Paris, France

Tommy Dreyfus
Center for Technological Education
Tel Aviv University
P.O. Box 305
Holon 58102, Israel

Andrejs Dunkels
Department of Mathematics
Luleå University
95187 Luleå, Sweden

Harvey Goodstein
Gallaudet University
800 Florida Avenue N.E.
Washington, DC 20002, USA

Miguel de Guzmán
Facultad de Matemáticas
Universidad Complutense
28040 Madrid, Spain

Bernard R. Hodgson
Département de mathématiques
et de statistique
Université Laval
Québec, QC Canada G1K 7P4

Celia Hoyles
Department of Mathematics
University of London
20 Bedford Way
London WC1H 0AL, United Kingdom

George G. Joseph
University of Manchester
Oxford Road
Manchester MI3 9PL, United Kingdom

Murad Jurdak
Division of Education Programs
American University of Beirut
P.O. Box 11-0236
Beirut, Lebanon

Thomas E. Kieren
Department of Secondary Education
University of Alberta
Edmonton, AB Canada T6G 2G5

Glenda Lappan
Department of Mathematics
Michigan State University
East Lansing, MI 48824, USA

Jan de Lange
Freudenthal Institute
Herensteg 10
2311 SJ Leiden, The Netherlands

Jacobus H. van Lint
Department of Mathematics and
Computer Science
Technische Hogeshool Eindhoven
P.O. Box 513
5600 MB Eindhoven, The Netherlands

Michael Otte
Institut für Didaktik der Mathematik
Universität Bielefeld
Postfach 8640
4800 Bielefeld 1, Germany

Nicolas Rouche
12, Place de la Neuville
B-1348 Louvain-la-Neuve, Belgique

Fritz Schweiger
Institut für Didaktik der
Naturwissenschaften
Universität Salzburg
Hellbrunnerstrasse 34
5020 Salzburg, Austria

Edward A. Silver
729 Learning Research &
Development Center
University of Pittsburgh
3939 O'Hara Street
Pittsburgh, PA 15260, USA

Thomas Tymoczko
Philosophy Department
Smith College
Northampton, MA 01063, USA

Zalman Usiskin
Department of Education
University of Chicago
5835 S. Kimbark Avenue
Chicago, IL 60637, USA

Hans-Joachim Vollrath
Mathematisches Institut der
Universität Am Hubland
D-8700 Würzburg, Germany